Big Ten Basketball,
1943–1972

ALSO BY MURRY R. NELSON

*Abe Saperstein and the American
Basketball League, 1960–1963: The Upstarts Who Shot
for Three and Lost to the NBA* (McFarland, 2013)

*The National Basketball League:
A History, 1935–1949* (McFarland, 2009)

# Big Ten Basketball, 1943–1972

MURRY R. NELSON

McFarland & Company, Inc., Publishers
*Jefferson, North Carolina*

LIBRARY OF CONGRESS CATALOGUING-IN-PUBLICATION DATA

Names: Nelson, Murry R., editor.
Title: Big Ten basketball, 1943–1972 / Murry R. Nelson.
Description: Jefferson, North Carolina : McFarland & Company, Inc., Publishers, 2017. | Includes bibliographical references and index.
Identifiers: LCCN 2016049644 | ISBN 9781476664712 (softcover : acid free paper) ∞
Subjects: LCSH: Big Ten Conference (U.S.)—Juvenile literature. | Basketball—Middle West—Juvenile literature.
Classification: LCC GV885.415.B547 N45 2017 | DDC 796.323/630973—dc23
LC record available at https://lccn.loc.gov/2016049644

BRITISH LIBRARY CATALOGUING DATA ARE AVAILABLE

**ISBN (print) 978-1-4766-6471-2**
**ISBN (ebook) 978-1-4766-2561-4**

© 2017 Murry R. Nelson. All rights reserved

*No part of this book may be reproduced or transmitted in any form or by any means, electronic or mechanical, including photocopying or recording, or by any information storage and retrieval system, without permission in writing from the publisher.*

On the cover *from top* All-American Jerry Lucas rebounds and looks to pass to John Havlicek of the OSU Buckeyes (Ohio State University Archives); Archie Clark, one of the first African Americans to play for Minnesota, was an All-American and played in the NBA for 10 seasons (University of Minnesota Athletics); Dave Schellhase drives to the bucket in a game against Wake Forest in December of 1964 (Purdue Athletics Communications); *background* basketball © 2017 Pali Rao/iStock

Printed in the United States of America

*McFarland & Company, Inc., Publishers*
*Box 611, Jefferson, North Carolina 28640*
*www.mcfarlandpub.com*

# Table of Contents

*Acknowledgments* vi

*Preface* 1

I. Big Ten Basketball Beginnings 3
II. The Old Guard Fights the New Pretenders 13
III. Into the '50s 25
IV. The Big Ten in the New Age of Ike 44
V. Sticking with Ike and the Traditional Powers 62
VI. Into the '60s in the Big Ten 82
VII. The Coaches 106
VIII. The Big Ten Up for Grabs 116
IX. Michigan Muscles the League 139
X. The 1967 Season: A Year to Forget for the Big Ten 158
XI. InsurMOUNTable? 172
XII. The "Run and Gun" '70s 190

*Afterword* 215

*Appendix 1: The First African American Players at Each Big Ten University* 217

*Appendix 2: Big Ten Coaches, 1947–1972* 218

*Appendix 3: Big Ten Champions, 1943–1972* 219

*Chapter Notes* 221

*Bibliography* 243

*Index* 245

# *Acknowledgments*

Over the past three years many people have helped me to put this book together in a form that I hope is readable and enjoyable. Former players and coaches who provided interviews to me were gracious and insightful, and often humorous. Thanks are due to the late Ab Nicholas, Dan Fife, Dave Schellhase, Nolden Gentry, Rudy Tomjanovich, Ron Smith, Bill Butterfield, Bill Ridley, Dave Merchant, Phil Judson, Butch Joyner, Larry Glass, Mark Wagar, and Carl Cain. At the various Big Ten institutions, a number of people provided photos or helped with tracking down former players. These folks include Bob Lopez, Nick Brilowski, Kevin Leonard, Dan Reisig, Patrick Herb, Nathan Wiechers, Bradley Cook, Tom Wywrot, David McCartney, Greg Kinney, Michelle Drobik, Steve Roe, Marcia Iles and Steve Herb.

This book was written using the materials and facilities of Pattee/Paterno Library of the Pennsylvania State University. For that I thank my friends in the library, but most specifically the librarians in the Microfilms Department and those in the Archives Department. It is odd to thank a book, but the late Bill Mokray's *Ronald Encyclopedia of Basketball* has the best collection of college basketball data in one spot through the 1961–62 season, and it was a great asset.

Jennifer Glasgow provided copying and other extraordinary staff assistance. Russ Rose negotiated an interview for me. My three amigos and traveling companions, Jack Selzer, Andy Stephenson and Steve Wartick, provided manuscript commentary, interviewee contacts and overall encouragement.

No one, however, could have been more supportive over the years than my wife of 42 years, who has had to hear my daily reports of progress or lack of it on this book and the previous ones. Thank you, Elizabeth, for all you've put up with.

# *Preface*

I have been a Big Ten basketball fan since I first learned to play basketball. Growing up in Chicago, I somehow managed to miss seeing or being aware of basketball until attending a YMCA camp when I was ten years old. After winning some age group ribbons I was hooked, and soon afterwards began playing regularly. Starting in junior high, I became aware of Big Ten basketball broadcasts every Saturday afternoon on WGN-TV, and through high school, I rarely missed a contest. Once we were of driving age, my teammates and I also attended a few Northwestern games at McGaw Hall each season. We would arrive when the doors opened and sit directly behind the basket in the first row of the raised court. Tickets were cheap, attendance was small and there was open seating. The Wildcat players of 1963–65 were our guys, players like Richie Falk, Rick Lopossa, Jim Pitts and Marty Riessen. Through my college years in the Midwest, Big Ten basketball was exciting for me and nationally, as the Big Ten turned out championship-caliber teams in the 1960s at Ohio State, Michigan, Indiana, Illinois and Purdue.

In 1971 I began a master's degree program at Northwestern and attended Wildcat games frequently, despite their poor showing in the Big Ten (3–11). I left the Midwest and moved to the West Coast to pursue a doctoral degree, and was forced to follow the Big Ten from afar. Then, in 1975, I accepted a position at Penn State University and was a bit closer to the Big Ten action, but it was not until 1992 that Penn State began play as a full Big Ten member. No longer did I have to travel far to see Big Ten action in person. Since that time, three colleagues and I have attended at least one away game a year and have been to all Big Ten venues for Penn State games. Seeing each of the campus arenas, as well as many of the athletic halls of fame for each university, made a book like this almost a natural pursuit. I wanted to know more Big Ten history as well as to relive my memories of Big Ten action. Interviewing former players, reading accounts of each league contest, and making other observations of teams and play during the postwar period to 1972 was a pleasure for me, and I became eager to share that through this volume.

My research relied heavily on newspaper accounts of games, most notably the *Chicago Tribune*, which has been viewed by some as the "mouthpiece" of the Big Ten because of its proximity to the Big Ten offices. This manuscript has been viewed by one reviewer as "just annals" and, that is somewhat true. The year-by-year description of each Big Ten race drives each chapter, as I try to capture the excitement of those pursuits and place them in a historical context of national and world events.

I begin with World War II. Basketball generally, and Big Ten basketball specifically, flew "under the radar" to a great degree during the period from 1906 to 1938, as summarized in Chapter I. With the advent of the NIT and NCAA tournaments, college basketball had somewhat of a national presence, but the war put a damper on much of that. Players were not immediately drafted, so there were some excellent teams that were altered as the war began and reshaped as many players returned after the war to play once again in the conference.

A perceptive reader will note that there are no photographs from University of Illinois or Michigan State players. This was no affront, but rather a function of the security that their archives and libraries have regarding access to potential users not of the specific university. Another "shortcoming" is the lack of discussion regarding early Big Ten television contracts. Despite the existence of a quasi-network in the 1960s, neither the Big Ten nor contacted television stations that were part of that network have archival material relating to the network.

An obvious question is, "Why stop at 1972?" I could say because that was when I left the Midwest, but that was simply coincidental. The 1971–72 Big Ten season ended with controversy and disappointment for the league as a result of a brawl in Minnesota that involved fans coming out of the stands to join in the melee. It was a sad watershed moment for the conference and seemed to provide a coda for this volume. The NCAA also changed the nature of the game at that time, allowing freshmen eligibility for football and basketball, beginning with the 1972–73 season. Then, in January of 1973, the NCAA altered scholarships from four-year to one-year, giving coaches greater control over athletes.

In addition, Bob Knight began his first season of recruiting in 1972, after being hired to replace Lou Watson at the end of the 1971 season. As Dan Fife noted to me in his interview, before Knight, every team pretty much played man-to-man defense, but Indiana under Knight emphasized team defense, with constant help on open players and double-teams low on the ball. This would pay off swiftly for the Hoosiers with an undefeated national title team in 1975–76.

Nevertheless, my hope is that there will be a Volume Two to continue the exciting Big Ten basketball saga.

One small aside: this book is titled *Big Ten Basketball*, not men's basketball, because the Big Ten supported no women's basketball until 1982. But that's another story.

# I

# *Big Ten Basketball Beginnings*

The Big Ten was originally formed as the Interconference of Faculty Representatives in 1895 at a meeting held at the Palmer House in Chicago. The organization was formed by seven university presidents (representing Purdue, Illinois, Northwestern, Wisconsin, Michigan, Chicago and Minnesota) as an academic enterprise, and the jointure for athletic purposes seemed useful and natural at the time. Almost immediately the athletic league was referred to as the Western Conference (one must keep in mind that there were only forty-four states at the time and anywhere west of Pennsylvania was "out west" to many folks in the east), but the more popular name was the Big Nine, then the Big Ten, after three other schools (Indiana and Iowa, both in 1899, and Ohio State) joined between 1896 and 1905. The formation meeting was initially seven universities, but within three years the conference was composed of nine, eight of which retain their membership.[1] The only "defector" was the University of Chicago, which left the league after the 1945–46 season, immediately making the league the Big 9 once again. That appellation remained until the 1950–51 season when Michigan State accepted an invitation to join the league and it became once again the Big Ten.

Basketball was invented in 1891 and it spread quickly throughout the country, mostly through the YMCA network, and by the time the Big Ten conference was formed, every school had some sort of basketball team. The first intercollegiate basketball game was played on January 18, 1896, when the University of Chicago squad traveled to Iowa City to play the Hawkeyes. The Maroons emerged with a 13 to 12 victory before approximately 400 spectators at the Iowa Armory.[2] Other games would follow slowly over the next five years. In 1905 a so-called national championship game was played that pitted Wisconsin against Columbia, with the Lions emerging victorious.

The next season, 1905–06 a conference schedule was played, and the Minnesota Golden Gophers were the first Western Conference basketball champions with a conference record of 6–1 (13–2 overall). The Gophers would repeat as champions in 1907, 1911, 1917 and 1919. Rivaling Minnesota for dominance was the University of Wisconsin under their coach Walter Meanwell. From 1912 to 1918, the Badgers won or tied for five Big Ten championships, then won titles again in 1921, 1923 and 1924.

In that same decade, the Boilermakers of Purdue, coached by Ward "Piggy" Lambert, became one of the top teams in the country. They won or tied for Big Ten titles in 1921, 1922, 1926, and 1928 before becoming the acknowledged bully of the league in the 1930s by taking championships in 1932, 1934, 1935, 1936, 1938 and 1940. The league was moving towards having "bigger" men play more, as evidenced by this observation in the *Spalding Basketball Guide 1927–28*: "Another feature of the season's play was the large, heavy type of player engaged. Few small men played regularly and on the other extreme many of the tallest men in conference history participated. This was especially true as to centers. Practically every team was represented at tip-off by men over six-feet-one in height and they ranged to six-feet-four."[3]

In 1930 Purdue was undefeated and declared national champion by a vote of sportswriters. They were led by John Wooden later in the decade, and were acclaimed national champions once again in 1935. Wooden then went on to star in the Midwest Basketball Conference, the forerunner of the National Basketball League that operated from 1937 until merging to form the National Basketball Association in 1949.[4]

Also in the 1930s, there was at least an effort at one Big Ten university to integrate the basketball team. Franklin Lett tried, personally and through intermediaries, to join Coach Frank Cappon's roster at the University of Michigan, but he "had no intention of introducing blacks to Big Ten basketball." In the late 1940s, Len Ford, an All-America football player at Michigan, was interested in also playing basketball, but no tryout was allowed.[5]

In 1939 the National Association of Basketball Coaches (NABC) decided to hold a national tournament with eight invited schools, four from the east and four from the west. The tourney followed the success of the National Invitational Tournament (NIT), which had begun in 1938, and was held in Madison Square Garden before capacity crowds of 18,000. That tourney consisted of six teams, three from the east (Temple, New York University and Long Island University) and three from the west (Colorado, Bradley and Oklahoma A&M, now Oklahoma State). Up until this time, "national champions" had been crowned by sportswriters, but the NIT, and now the NABC tournament, would offer a better manner of asserting national recognition.

The NABC tournament in 1939 consisted of eight teams from eight regions of the country. For its first formative years the tournament would consist of one team from each of eight districts, four in the east and four in the west. Generally they would play for a championship in each region, then meet for a national championship at another site. The initial tournament was hastily planned and poorly executed. Some schools did not accept invitations for these reasons or feeling that their student athletes should not miss class for such a venture, despite the stated idea that the tournament "was that the number of games should be kept at a minimum so as to avoid as much as possible the charge that competing in the N.C.A.A. tournament involved a lot of 'post season' play."[6] The Big Ten champions from Ohio State played and defeated Wake Forest, then Villanova in the Palestra in Philadelphia for the right to meet the University of Oregon Ducks, who had defeated both the University of Texas and Utah State in the California Coliseum in San Francisco. The eastern (Ohio State) and western (Oregon) champions met in Evanston, Illinois, on the Northwestern campus, at Patten Gym before 5,500 spectators, most of whom were admitted for free because of the poor planning and publicity done by the NABC.[7] Peter Bjarkman asserts that the tournament was played at Patten as a compromise when Harold Olsen, the Ohio State coach and most energetic backer of the tournament, "decided that his Buckeyes couldn't afford the financial strain of travel to east- or west-coast venues, despite the prospects of higher gate revenues."[8] Oregon and their "Tall Trees" defeated the Buckeyes, 46–33, although Jimmy Hull of

**Patten Gym at Northwestern University, the site of the first NCAA basketball championship contest in 1939. Note the wooden backboards and bench seating (Northwestern University Archives).**

OSU, who had led the Big Ten in scoring, was also the new tournament's scoring champion, despite playing the championship game with a heavily taped ankle as a result of a severe sprain in the prior game. Said Hull, "I had more tape on my leg than most drugstores have."[9]

Not long after that, the NCAA purchased the tournament from the NABC, i.e., agreed to be responsible for the finances of the tournament in return for paying off the debt of the initial tournament (just over $2500) and agreeing to provide free tickets to NABC coaches at future championship games.[10]

In 1940, Purdue was conference champion with a record of 10–2 (16–4 overall), but both of those losses were to Indiana, who finished at 9–3 (20–3 overall). Indiana was selected as the district representative, after Ward (Piggy) Lambert, the Purdue coach, refused the invitation because of the plethora of gamblers at Madison Square Garden, which seemed very dangerous for his players, or so one story goes.[11] Tony Hinkle tells another and he was on the committee. He said that the two losses to Indiana made the Hoosiers the clearer choice to the committee.[12] The Hoosiers were coached by a young Branch McCracken and led by Marv Huffman and Bill Menke. Aided by playing the eastern regional in Indianapolis, the Hoosiers defeated Springfield and Duquesne for the opportunity to play for the title against Kansas, which had beaten Rice and edged USC in games at Kansas City's Municipal Auditorium, where the NCAA

**Patten Gym at Northwestern was emblematic of the classical architecture of the turn of the century period when it was built. It was demolished in 1940 (Northwestern University Archives).**

championship game was also to be held. The proximity of the Kansas campus notwithstanding, Indiana pounded the Jayhawks by a score of 60–42, and Huffman was named Most Valuable Player.

The 1940–41 season found the Wisconsin Badgers as the power of the Big Ten, with a record of 11–1, which was quite surprising, given their ninth-place finish the year before. "Largely responsible for the Badger surge were Captain Gene Englund, an All-America center; sparkling sophomore John Kotz, and steady Teddy Strain."[13] Englund went on to star in the National Basketball League for the Oshkosh All-Stars.[14] Wisconsin was selected as the district representative to the NCAA Tournament. They defeated Dartmouth, "in a furious second half rally,"[15] 51–50, and Pitt, 36–30, in the eastern regionals, held in Madison, to advance to the championship game in Kansas City. Their opponent was Washington State, who had knocked off Creighton and Arkansas in earlier rounds. In a nip and tuck contest, the Badgers claimed the second NCAA title in a row for the Big Ten with a 39–35 victory. Englund scored 13 and Kotz 12, but Kotz was selected the MVP for the tournament.

On December 7, 1941, the United State entered World War II, following the bombing of Pearl Harbor by the Japanese. Although the war had been going on for more than two years, the U.S. had avoided entering, but now had to scramble to put together the massive armed forces needed to challenge the Axis powers. Initially, college students were not drafted, but many, including Big Ten athletes, enlisted; and over the next five years, there would be significant alterations in the manner in which college athletics were conducted. Athletes, both college and professional, were drafted or enlisted, and were sent to various training locations, most of which had athletic teams, which played against college squads. Some of the top teams were at Great Lakes Naval Training Station near North Chicago, Illinois; Camp Grant, outside of Rockford, Illinois; and Norfolk Naval Air Station in Norfolk, Virginia. All of these military teams played against Big Ten teams, and the Big Ten (and NCAA) allowed this, despite the presence of former professional players on most of the military fives.[16] Other adjustments that would be made for the war regarding Big Ten play were that freshmen would be eligible for varsity play; players no longer had to complete their eligibility within four years (because of war absences); and transfer rules were relaxed for returning veterans. Another unusual aspect was the older age of players through the late 1940s because of the returning veterans.

The 1942 Big Ten season was still relatively unaffected by the war call-ups, but there were concerns about excessive travel and the conservation of fuel. The surprise winners of the conference title were the so-called Whiz Kids of Illinois, a group of sophomores led by Andy Phillip. The other young starters were Gene Vance, Ed ("Jack") Smiley[17] and Ken Menke, who were joined by junior Art Mathisen. The Illini went 13–2 in the Big Ten, 18–3 overall, winning the conference title by three games. John Kotz of Wisconsin led the league in scoring, setting a new conference record of 16.1 points per game. That record would be broken on a regular basis over the next twenty years. The second leading scorer in the league was a Northwestern sophomore from Waukegan, Illinois, who also played a little football, named Otto Graham. Illinois was selected as the district representative to the NCAA tourney and lost to Kentucky in the first round of the eastern regionals, held in Tulane Gym in New Orleans. It was a disappointing end, but the youth of the team seemed to bode well for the future.

As Tug Wilson noted, 1943 was the year of the 17- and 18-year-olds, as older players entered the service. Veteran players who were 4-F, who had not been called up yet, or who attended colleges with special naval training programs populated the rosters of Big Ten teams. (The army would not allow its trainees on college campuses to participate in varsity programs.)[18]

Indeed, 1943 was the future for the Illinois Whiz Kids. By the time the Big Ten season started on January 9, the Illini had only one loss and that was to Camp Grant, one of the top two service teams. The other, Great Lakes, was beaten by Northwestern on January 3, with Otto Graham and Russ Wendland each scoring 13 points in the 59–47 victory. Great Lakes was led by Forrest Anderson, former Stanford star, who had 13. Judging by the box score, and not the game account, Great Lakes was less concerned with winning at that time of the year and more concerned with playing lots of players and building cohesiveness. Bob Davies, former Seton Hall All-America and Rochester Royals star, had 3 points, and George Glamack, former North Carolina star who would also star in the NBL, had 4 points.[19] On that same day, the Illini had topped Stanford, the 1942 NCAA champion, by a score of 38–26.[20]

As the Big Ten season began, Illinois, on the basis of being defending champions with their starting five back, was favored. Wisconsin and Northwestern were highly rated, as was Indiana. On opening weekend, Wisconsin and Northwestern met in Chicago Stadium, as part of a college double-header. Northwestern played about half its home games in the conference at the Stadium as part of college double-headers involving DePaul or Loyola. In a tight battle, the Badgers emerged as victors by a 67 to

65 score, led by 19 from Patterson and 14 from Kotz. Northwestern countered with 19 from Robert Jake and 17 each from Russ Wendland and Otto Graham.[21]

The other favorites played lesser opponents; Indiana topped Ohio State in Bloomington, and Illinois won handily over Michigan. Two days later, as part of the regular Saturday/Monday Big Ten schedule of games, Illinois easily beat Wisconsin, while Northwestern did the same to Michigan. Indiana had no trouble with Ohio State.[22]

By mid-season, the Illini were still undefeated, as was Indiana, and Northwestern had two losses. The Northwestern-Illinois game in Champaign on February 1 was seen as crucial to the Wildcat hopes, but Illinois dashed them by winning 68–51 before a packed house in Huff Gym (6766 fans squeezed in). Illinois had its balanced and deadly attack, with Mathisen scoring 18, Phillip 15, Menke and Vance 12 each. Otto Graham led Northwestern with 19.[23]

Two weeks later, as the season drew to a close, the Hoosiers lost on the same night as the Illini won, and Illinois opened a one-game lead on Indiana. Illinois, with 25 points from Big Ten scoring leader Andy Phillip, and Art Mathisen's 15, pummeled Minnesota, 67–43. Illinois had won two nights earlier over the Gophers in Champaign, 56–35, and this game was no closer. The Hoosiers lost to Wisconsin in Madison, 57–53, as John Kotz and Bob Sullivan each had 19 for the Badgers. The loss left Indiana at 9–1 with two games remaining, while Illinois, at 9–0, had three.[24]

Five days later, the Big Ten representatives met and lifted the ban on freshmen playing varsity basketball for the next season, because of the enlistment of so many upperclassmen. Michigan State, not yet a member of the conference, had already done so, effective March of 1944. The Big Ten waiver would go into effect for all sports at the conclusion of the winter season of 1943. In addition, the conference welcomed all servicemen on campus to play varsity sports (even professionals) and waived the one-year transfer rule that the league had imposed, allowing players to be immediately eligible (unless they were delinquent in their academic records).[25]

Two days earlier, in the Illini's 50–26 win over Wisconsin, two landmarks were reached. The first saw Andy Phillip, with 22 points, break the Big Ten scoring record for a season in only ten games. The second was John Kotz's failure to score in a game, the first and only time that occurred in his three-year career at Wisconsin. Indiana kept the pressure on Illinois by defeating Minnesota, 51 to 30.[26]

Indiana ended its home season on February 22 with an easy victory over Minnesota in Bloomington, 40–28. The Hoosiers were 11–1. Illinois would end its conference play with a game against Northwestern in Chicago Stadium, and then a home contest against the University of Chicago, which was in the midst of another winless Big Ten season. The Stadium double-header on February 27 also featured DePaul against Bradley; the Blue Demons had only four losses, two to Camp Grant, who had beaten Illinois for its only loss.

A Big Ten conference attendance record was set at the double-header as 19,000 fans crowded into the arena to see DePaul and George Mikan overwhelm Bradley, 68–38, and Illinois pound the Wildcats, 86 to 44. Phillip extended his scoring record with another 16 points, but the top scorer was Ken Menke, with 22 points. Two nights later, Illinois won by a score of 92 to 25 over the Maroons of Chicago. Andy Phillip had 40 points as the Illini ended the conference season undefeated. To make it even more definite as to who was the top team, Indiana, in a thirteenth league game, lost to Purdue in West Lafayette, 41 to 38.[27]

On March 4, the *Chicago Tribune* published the all-conference team, and four of the five players on the first team were from Illinois. Only Otto Graham of Northwestern, the second leading scorer in the league, spoiled the Illini "sweep." Andy Phillip, who would be named later in the month as the Big Ten's Most Valuable Player, led the Illinois honors, and he was joined by Gene Vance, "Jack" (Ed) Smiley and Art Mathisen. Tug Wilson notes, "Ken Menke made the second team. It was the only time in conference history this had happened,"[28] i.e., that an entire starting five was all-conference. But according to the *Chicago Tribune*, it did *not* happen, as Ralph Hamilton and Ward Williams of Indiana, Leo Ehlers of Purdue, John Kotz of Wisconsin, and Russ Wendland of Northwestern comprised the second team.

It would seem obvious that Illinois, with a record of 17–1 and the acknowledged best team in college basketball,[29] would be the District 4 representative to the NCAA tournament, but instead, DePaul, with a record of 18–4 and their sophomore star George Mikan, got the bid. Tug Wilson says in his history of the Big Ten, "Strangely enough, Illinois was by-passed as a district representative to the NCAA tourney in favor of DePaul. Later in 1951 under a revised set-up, Big Ten champs automatically went to the tourney."[30] Peter Bjarkman claims that the team was "broken up when all five starters went on active military duty on March 1, 1943,"[31] but that, too, seems to be in error. In another place in his book, Bjarkman says again that "on the very day of the season-ending rout of Chicago, the team disbanded and the five starters who had played together so well as a unit departed campus for military duty."[32] According to the *Chicago Tribune* of March 9, both Illinois and Notre Dame refused invitations to compete in the tournament. Dale Ratermann professed that the refusal was due to wartime travel restrictions.[33] The likelihood is that Illinois administrators and the players involved knew that call-up was imminent and, indeed, Menke, Smiley and Mathisen were all called up on March 13, so the University of Illinois refused the invitation. What is most odd about this story of different memories and conflicting facts is that the chair of the District 4 Selection Committee was the athletic director of Northwestern (and future Big Ten Commissioner), Tug Wilson![34]

"By the 1944 basketball season, wartime manpower regulations had limited Conference schools to 18-year-olds; upperclassmen excused on physical grounds, and on-campus naval trainees."[35] Ohio State, led by Don (the Great) Grate and Arnie Risen, rolled to a 10–2 conference mark and represented the conference and the district in the NCAA meet. The Buckeyes topped Temple in the opening round in Madison Square Garden, then lost 60–53 to Dartmouth, who were edged in the title game, also in the Garden, by Utah and their star, Arnie Ferrin, by a score of 42–40.

In 1945, more effects of the war altered the results in the Big Ten. Iowa, led by Dick Ives, Murray Weir and Herb Wilkinson, went 17–1, 11–1 in conference, with only a one-point loss to Illinois staining their record. They were a team of "iron men," usually only playing six players in their games. But the Hawks had service members on their team, which made them ineligible for the NCAA tourney, and so second-place Ohio State, 10–2 in the conference and 15–5 overall, was selected to represent the Big Ten. The Buckeyes defeated Kentucky in Madison Square Garden, 45 to 37, but lost to NYU, 70–65, in the national semifinals.

Iowa also had on their roster the first African American to appear in a Big Ten contest, Dick Culberson. Culberson, a back-up center, was a transfer from Virginia Union and was likely one of the service people playing on the team. He made his first appearance in a Big Ten conference game on January 14, 1945, in a 61–34 Iowa victory over Purdue in Iowa City. He did not score, but on February 4, he had two points in a 50–37 win over Michigan. Thus, he scored the first points by an African American in a Big Ten contest.

The next season, 1946, with the war over, servicemen were returning to campuses, now older and more experienced, although not necessarily in basketball. Iowa and Ohio State were the preseason favorites, and they, along with Indiana, led the conference at midpoint. Despite the end of the war, the reduction in force took more than a year and the service teams continued to play at a high level, often meeting top teams in Chicago Stadium double-headers. In early February, Northwestern topped Purdue in the Stadium, 63–54, to run its conference mark to 4–3, while Purdue sank to 4–5. In the other game, DePaul lost to Great Lakes, 69–67, despite 30 points from George Mikan. Mel Riebe, a star in the National Basketball League, led the Sailors with 19 points.[36] The Big Ten was a tough league, as evidenced by the Wildcats' returning to the Stadium the next night to defeat Notre Dame, handing the Irish their first loss in 14 games, before a record crowd of 19,624. Max Morris, who would lead the Big Ten in scoring, had 24 points, while Vince Boryla, All-America and future pro star, had 17. Also on the Notre Dame squad were George Ratterman, All-America quarterback and future AAFC and NFL player, and Johnny Dee, who would be the Irish basketball coach from 1964 to 1971.[37]

There were times that did not indicate the conference's big-time status. Northwestern played some of their home games at Evanston High School, about a mile off campus, with a seating capacity of 3,000. They topped Minnesota in such a game on February 8, winning by a 72–49 score. Morris got 30 in that contest, while Tony Jaros, future Minneapolis Laker, led the Gophers with 13.[38]

The University of Chicago was riding a five-year Big Ten losing streak that would continue the rest of 1946, after which the Maroons would withdraw from the conference. The return of servicemen to the conference also brought the return of big crowds to almost all venues. Schools without a large venue were planning on building one, although it would not be until the 1960s that all campus arenas had a capacity of at least 7500. Still, there were no venues like Chicago Stadium, where 20,442 saw Northwestern top Illinois and DePaul defeat Long Island University one cold Saturday night in mid-February. Max Morris had 20 for the 'Cats in their 48 to 43 victory. In Illinois's lineup was Ed Smiley, of the 1943 champions, who had 10 points.[39]

The next weekend, the Stadium attendance record was broken once again as 21,000 saw Ohio State top Northwestern and DePaul defeat Notre Dame. The Buckeyes were led by Robert Bowen with 17 and Jack Underman with 12, while Max Morris was held to eight points by the tenacious OSU defense. In the second game, Mikan had 30 for the Blue Demons.[40]

A loss to Iowa in late February eliminated Indiana, and the conference title was won by Ohio State, who had finished the league season with ten wins in twelve games. The Hoosiers' loss left them at nine and three. The end of the season began the awards period, and Max Morris was quickly named the MVP of the Northwestern Wildcats, after leading the Big Ten in scoring (198 points, 16.5 pg) and helping Northwestern to an 8–4 mark, which tied Iowa for third in the conference. Not surprisingly, Morris was first team All–Big Ten, along with Jaros of Minnesota, Underman of Ohio State, Herb Wilkinson of Iowa and Fred Hoffman of Purdue. The second team had two Hoosiers, Wallace and Schwartz; two Buckeyes, Amling and Doster; and one Illini, Jack Burmaster, a future pro in the NBL, BAA and NBA. Burmaster would gain more fame as the coach of Evanston High School from 1952 to 1975, where he won 362 games, including a state title in 1968.[41]

As an aside, lest one think that servicemen were being flooded with thanks as they arrived home, the *Chicago Tribune* noted that Stan Musial, the National League's MVP in 1943 and star of a three-time World Series team, had been discharged after serving in the Navy in 1945. He immediately hitchhiked back to Donora, Pennsylvania, to see his family.[42]

Max Morris was an All-American in both football and basketball for Northwestern in the 1940s (**Northwestern University Archives**).

At the end of the season, three coaching positions were vacant. At Ohio State, longtime coach Harold Olsen resigned and was replaced by Tippy Dye. At Michigan, Bennie Oosterbaan resigned to concentrate on football coaching exclusively, and was replaced by Ozzie Cowles, the head coach at Dartmouth. At Purdue, Piggy Lambert had fallen ill at the end of the season, then resigned and became commissioner of the National Basketball League. He was replaced during the season on an interim basis by Assistant Coach Mel Taube. According to former Purdue player Bill Butterfield, the president of the university, Frederick Hovde, went to the players and asked them to vote on the top two applicants for the Purdue job for 1946–47. They were former Purdue All-American John Wooden, returning from military service after the war and a high school coach for 11 years; and Mel Taube, whom the players knew. Taube was their choice and became the university's also. Wooden was hired by Indiana State.[43]

The end of the season also brought other league news: the University of Chicago withdrew and there was speculation as to potential contenders for a tenth berth in the league. The leading candidate seemed to be Michigan State, but both Notre Dame and

Nebraska were seen as possibilities. Max Morris was named the winner of the first Silver Basketball awarded to the Most Valuable Player in the Big Ten by the *Chicago Tribune*. The electors for this honor were the 10 league coaches, eight league officials, the league commissioner, the sports editor of the *Tribune*, Arch Ward, and the *Tribune*'s Big Ten correspondent, Wilfrid Smith. It might seem as if the newspaper was a part of the Big Ten itself, but not quite, although the relationship was obviously close.[44]

Ohio State was the District 4 representative to the NCAA Tourney, and they would open play in Madison Square Garden on March 22 against Harvard. In the west, Oklahoma A&M and Kansas were to meet on March 18 in Kansas City's Municipal Auditorium in a playoff to become the District 5 representative. Led by Bob Kurland's 28 points, the Aggies won by a score of 49 to 38 to secure the last spot in the field of eight. They would play Baylor, while Cal played Colorado on March 22.

In the east, North Carolina defeated NYU, 57 to 49, and Ohio State defeated the Crimson of Harvard, 46 to 38. Jack Underman had 14 for the Bucks. The next night Cal defeated Colorado, 50 to 44, and Oklahoma A&M topped Baylor easily, 44 to 29, with Kurland getting 20 points. The Aggies went on to defeat the Golden Bears, 52 to 35, with Kurland again dominant with 29 points. They would meet the Eastern winner for the title on March 26 in Madison Square Garden.[45]

Meanwhile, the Buckeyes played a tight game with North Carolina. The Bucks led by a bucket when North Carolina tied the score at 54 with 10 seconds left. The game went into overtime and both teams played deliberately, but the Tar Heels won by a score of 60 to 57. Underman had 23 for Ohio State to lead all scorers. Despite the loss, the Buckeyes also went to the finals, as there was a third-place game, which they won by 63 to 45 over Cal. Underman had 19 for Ohio State. In the championship game, Bob Kurland had 23 of his team's 43 points in a narrow 43–40 victory over North Carolina.[46] Mike Douchant speculated that Ohio State might have been able to top Oklahoma A&M "had their top two scorers from Final Four teams the previous two years been around. But Don Grate ... signed a pro baseball contract with the Philadelphia Phillies prior to his senior year, and Arnie Risen played just six games in the first semester before becoming academically ineligible and ending the season with the a pro franchise in Indianapolis."[47]

The end of the season was the end of an era for the Buckeyes, as most of their top players graduated and their coach, Harold Olsen, resigned to become the coach of the Chicago Stags in the Basketball Association of America. After three seasons, he returned to the Big Ten as the coach of Northwestern for two seasons (1950–52). He was inducted into the Naismith Memorial Basketball Hall of Fame in 1959, six years after his death in 1953.

Ohio State's loss left the conference with a wide-open race for 1947. Most of the servicemen would be back by then, and the league would have a number of older players as a result. It would be the beginning of the great prosperity that followed World War II in many aspects of American society.

# II

# *The Old Guard Fights the New Pretenders*

The outlook for the 1947 Big Ten season was optimistic. Almost everyone still eligible who had gone off to serve in World War II was now back on campus. This included the Illini Whiz Kids of 1943, and they would surely be a force to reckon with. In American society, wartime restrictions on wages and price controls were gradually lifted. The film that best exemplified 1946 may have been *It's a Wonderful Life* with Jimmy Stewart recognizing, even amidst disappointments, how great things really were, thanks to his guardian angel, Clarence. That was the American attitude: although times had been so tough for so long, things could have been a lot worse, and Americans became enamored of the new prosperity. Despite the fears of Communists "sneaking" into the nation, times were good.

Internationally, the United Nations had been established, and war crimes trials in Nuremburg and Tokyo were seen by many as proper punishment for those Axis leaders who still were alive. President Truman grew in stature, although not in popularity, as the year went on, despite difficult labor strikes.

The Big Ten had become the Big 9 after the departure of the University of Chicago from the conference, and basketball had become so popular that a second professional league, the Basketball Association of America, began, mostly in the eastern U.S. The long-established National Basketball League, which had begun in 1937, continued to operate, predominantly in the Midwest, with teams also in the east and extending as far west as Denver. Any notions of a 10th team joining the Big 9 were deferred, and a new schedule was devised with 12 league games still in place. Iowa had the best non-conference record and was established as the pre-season favorite as the league opened play on January 11, 1947. Illinois, Wisconsin and Indiana were also seen as threats to win the league championship.

The conference season started with the favorites winning as expected. For Wisconsin, Bob Cook emerged as their leading scorer; so, too, did Dick Ives, a 1945 All-American, at Iowa; as well as Ralph Hamilton, who had returned to Indiana after three years in the U.S. Army. The Illini had the Whiz Kids, Andy Phillip, Gene Vance, Ken Menke and Ed Smiley back, but Phillip was seen as the scoring key. The years away might have a negative effect on their play. Ives had help from big Noble Jorgensen, as well as little Murray Weir, and Michigan looked to be tougher than expected with freshman Mac Suprunowicz their key scorer.

In early games of import, Wisconsin pummeled Indiana in Madison, 70–49, with Cook getting 24 points and Hamilton leading Indiana with 14, while Iowa flexed its muscles against the weak Buckeyes of Ohio State. In a balanced attack, Wier had 14, while Jorgensen and Williams had 13 each, in a 61 to 35 Hawkeye victory.[1]

A week later, the Hawkeyes faced Indiana in Bloomington and the Hoosiers upset Iowa, 50 to 48, before 9,330 hysterical Hoosier fans. Hamilton had 21 for Indiana with Lou Watson, a 22-year-old freshman who had also served in World War II, chipping in 13. Iowa shot poorly, with Spencer leading with 14. Ives had 10, but Weir failed to crack double figures. Two nights later, it got much worse for Iowa as they lost to Purdue in West Lafayette. Ed Ehlers had 19 for the Boilers, while Jorgensen led the Hawks with 15.[2]

Purdue was basically a two-man team, according to Bill Butterfield, a freshman on the team at the time. Freshmen were eligible, since the wartime expansion of eligibility was still in place and would be for another couple of years, as servicemen returned to the universities. Ed Ehlers and Paul Hoffman were the top Purdue players, and they were both outstanding players, but they did not play well together. The result was a lot of individual play by each of them as the team stood around. The offense was very slow and deliberate anyway, but the lack of real team play hurt the Boilermakers.[3]

The Big 9 scoring leaders at the end of January were Wisconsin's Bobby Cook with an average of 17.2 in conference games, Ralph Hamilton at 16.4, followed by a steep drop to Weir with 11.7, Jorgensen at 11.5 and Suprunowicz, also at 11.5. The mid-season standings had some surprises, with Iowa being the biggest. They were at 2–5, only ahead of Northwestern's 1–6. The leader was Wisconsin at 5–1, with Indiana (4–2), Michigan (3–2) and Purdue (3–2), nipping at the heels of the Badgers.

Illinois topped Ohio State in Columbus on February 1, but the close game (59–58) did not bode well for the Illini. Vance (16), Smiley (13) and Phillip (12) led the scoring. For Ohio State, Jack Underman with 20 and Warren Amling with 17 were the scoring leaders. That same night, a new force in the league appeared as 6'8" sophomore center Jim McIntyre of Minnesota dropped 30 points on Northwestern in a 63–61 overtime win for the Gophers.[4] Iowa suffered an unexpected blow when Noble Jorgensen was declared academically ineligible for the remainder of the season.

Indiana and Wisconsin continued to win; the Badgers beat Iowa, 60–53, despite Murray Weir's 26 points, and the Hoosiers beat Michigan. Purdue pulled into a tie for third by upsetting the Illini, but then promptly lost to Northwestern, giving the Wildcats their first victory in the conference. Then, the Badgers won three in a row, beating Minnesota, Michigan at the buzzer, and Northwestern in a Chicago Stadium double-header before 19,165.[5] Illinois tried to stay in the race by bumping off second-place Indiana to edge them for second. Menke and Smiley led in scoring with 17 and 15, respectively, while Indiana got 16 from Hamilton.[6] Iowa topped Michigan with Wilkinson of Iowa and Suprunowicz of Michigan matching each other for game-scoring honors with 13. Jim McIntyre had 31 and Bud Grant (future Minnesota Viking coach) had 15 to lead the Gophers in an easy 81–69 win over Purdue.[7] That same duo (McIntyre 19, Grant 12) led the Gophers two nights later in a close contest before over 16,000 in Minneapolis, as Minnesota won over Iowa, 59–55. Weir had 30 points, more than half his team's total.

The next weekend, Illinois picked up ground on the leaders, Wisconsin and Indiana, as they both lost in upsets and the Illini defeated Northwestern in a big Chicago Stadium double-header that attracted 22,543. Game Two saw Kansas drub DePaul, 58 to 41. In Game One, Illinois edged the cellar-dwelling Wildcats, 52 to 51. Gene Vance had 15 and Andy Phillip 13 for the Illini, while Schadler topped the 'Cats with 17. In Iowa City, 14,400 saw the Hawkeyes humble the Hoosiers by a score of 68 to 46. Herb Wilkinson had 22 and his running mate at guard, Murray Weir, had 15, to pace the Hawks. And in Madison, 13,200 crammed into the fieldhouse to see their Badgers lose, 57 to 56, to a weak Ohio State team. Jack Underman had 18 for OSU in the victory, while Selbo and Lauterbach each had 12 for the Badgers.[8]

By the end of February, Wisconsin, Illinois and Indiana were the only teams with a chance to win the conference title. That may have been a reason that the Chicago Stadium double-header, with DePaul vs. Notre Dame and Northwestern vs. Ohio State, was so "under attended," with just 10,000 in the building on a Friday night. The Wildcats played poorly and were undone by 20 points. Wilfrid Smith reported on the game and his observations speak to the shooting percentages of the time, as well as the type of play. "Ohio scored 27 times in 76 shots. [This was viewed as good shooting!] Northwestern made 16 in 73, but Underman's hook throws from the pivot and the Buckeyes' follow-ups were accomplished from superior position."[9] Underman had 17, Amling 14 for OSU. Tourek had 14, Schadler 11 for Northwestern.

Both Wisconsin and Illinois then lost the next night, and a playoff was possible for the title. A most unusual situation had arisen, however. The previous week, when Wisconsin was at Purdue, with the Boilers leading the game at the half, bleachers in Purdue's fieldhouse collapsed and three people were killed. According to Bill Butterfield, as the teams were ready to take the floor for the second half, the stands slowly collapsed, as a result of poor anchoring of the stands to the floor.[10] The question before Commissioner Kenneth (Tug) Wilson was when and where the game would be completed, or whether it would be replayed from the start. The result would affect the title chase, since Illinois had ended its season at 8–4 in the conference and Wisconsin was 8 and 3. Wisconsin had lost in Minneapolis, before 16,519 Gopher zealots, 58 to 55. Illinois had been edged 43 to 41 by the slow-down tactics of Indiana, now 7–4 in Big 9 play. Despite the loss, Andy Phillip had set a new three-year scoring record in the conference with 516 points. The old record had been set the year before by John Kotz of Wisconsin with 512.[11]

Attendance continued to be great throughout the league, even for the bottom-dwellers. At Iowa City, 14,400 saw the Hawks top Purdue. Bloomington had 9,330 for the Illinois game. In a non-league game, Michigan topped Michigan State in East Lansing before 10,003.

The next day, the *Chicago Tribune* reported that the solution to the Wisconsin-Purdue game, and thus the Big 9 title, was still vexing to Commissioner Wilson. A poll of the athletic directors was that the game should be played from the completion of the first half, but the count was only five to four, making the result less than overwhelming. That evening, Indiana defeated Purdue, 54–38, in Indianapolis,[12] and the Hoosiers ended their season at 8–4 in Big 9 play, further complicating the decision, which would affect all of the District 4 NCAA possibilities for non-league teams, also.

After that game, it was announced that Wisconsin and Purdue would complete the second half of their game on a neutral floor on Saturday, March 8, at 8 p.m. The site would be Evanston High School, the home court of Northwestern for that season. With neither team playing at home, the crowd was quite small, fewer than 2,000. Perhaps because WGN Radio, which had a very powerful signal, carried the game (with Jack Brickhouse announcing it), Wisconsin and Purdue fans listened to the game at home, rather than travel the 125–150 miles for a 20-minute contest.[13]

After all the deliberation, the game turned into a Wisconsin romp in the second half, as they went from a 34–33 deficit to an easy 72–60 victory, led by Bobby Cook and Glen Selbo, who each scored 20 for the game. Neither team shot well, partly because of the fan-shaped wooden backboards that Evanston High School had. Most teams still had large square wooden backboards, which allowed players to shoot hooks (a common inside shot at that time) at a higher trajectory.[14]

Selbo, it should be noted, had played for Michigan the previous year, but was allowed to transfer to Wisconsin and play there for 1946–47. Selbo had started at Wisconsin and played there as a freshman in 1943 before entering the service. During the war he played for a year at Western Michigan University and at Michigan while still officially in the service.

The final Big 9 standings had Wisconsin at 9–3, Indiana and Illinois at 8–4, Minnesota at 7–5 and Michigan, 6–6. The rest of the league failed to get to .500. It was a sad ending for the four Whiz Kids, who had returned to Illinois with the hope of repeating their titles of 1942 and 1943, but they were each a step slower and they were not able to complete a dream season in 1947. Ed Smiley, rather than Phillip, was chosen by teammates as the Illinois MVP. The other team MVPs were Jim McIntyre of Minnesota, Ralph Hamilton of Indiana, Murray Weir of Iowa, Paul Hoffman of Purdue, Mac Suprunowicz of Michigan, Bernie Schadler of Northwestern, Jack Underman of Ohio State and Glen Selbo of Wisconsin. Despite Cook's leading the conference in scoring (15.6 per game, the lowest in six years and the last scoring leader to finish with fewer than 200 league points), his Wisconsin teammates selected Selbo as MVP, perhaps because of his maturity and leadership. Whatever it was, the Big 9 voters agreed, and he won the league's Silver Basketball as MVP on March 18. The *Chicago Tribune*, which awarded the trophy, noted that Selbo had the best shooting percentage of any guard in the league, 31 percent. That would be unlikely to get a player into the starting lineup today.[15]

The first team, All-Big Ten, consisted of Ralph Hamilton of Indiana, Cook and Selbo of Wisconsin, Jim McIntyre of Minnesota and Herb Wilkinson of Iowa. Second team was Vance and Smiley (IL), Hoffman (PU), Underman (OSU) and Lautenbach (WI).

### Final Standings and MVPs, 1946–47

| Team | Record | MVP |
|---|---|---|
| Wisconsin | 9–3 | Glenn Selbo (Big Ten MVP) |
| Illinois | 8–4 | Ed Smiley |
| Indiana | 8–4 | Ralph Hamilton (First team NCAA All-American) |
| Minnesota | 7–5 | Jim McIntyre |
| Michigan | 6–6 | Mac Supronowicz |
| Iowa | 5–7 | Murray Weir |
| Ohio State | 5–7 | Jack Underman |
| Purdue | 4–8 | Paul Hoffman |
| Northwestern | 2–10 | Bernie Schadler |

Wisconsin was selected to play in the NCAA tourney and would face City College of New York in New York on March 20, after the NIT had been completed there. The Badgers would meet CCNY, while Holy Cross would face Navy, with all games played in Madison Square Garden. Out west in Kansas City, Texas would meet Wyoming and Oklahoma would play Oregon. The Badgers were surprised by the Blackbirds of CCNY, who defeated Wisconsin, 70 to 56, after the Badgers had led by 15 at one point. CCNY then lost to Holy Cross and Bob Cousy, who defeated Oklahoma, 58–47, to win the NCAA tourney.

## The 1947–1948 Season

The 1947–1948 season would be a rebuilding year for both Illinois and Wisconsin, but even more so for the Hoosiers, who had lost all of their scorers, especially All-American Ralph Hamilton. Iowa and Wisconsin looked to be the teams to have the best chance to win the title because of their excellent returning players. Iowa had Murray Weir and Wisconsin had Bobby Cook back; the key would be how much each of them would be aided by their teammates in a quest for a title. Losing Selbo was a blow for Wisconsin, but Bobby Cook was the defending scoring champion. Michigan was a dark horse; Mack Suprunowicz would need help from his supporting cast to make an impact in the race. It promised to be a wide-open tussle for the title.

Opening weekend of the Big Nine season saw Wisconsin make a good first step with a victory, 52–47, over Illinois in Madison. Cook had 22 and Dike Eddleman led Illinois with 12. The Badgers made it two in a row with a 59–50 defeat of Minnesota, again in Madison. Cook led with 18, but sophomore Don Rehfeldt chipped in with 14, indicating good things to come for both the Badgers and himself. The Badgers went on the road and beat Indiana by four, 58–54, with Cook and Rehfeldt getting 16 and 13, respectively. Ritter had 22 for the Hoosiers. Iowa kept pace with a 60–49 win over Purdue, as Murray Weir got 27 points of the 60 that the Hawks scored.[16]

Wisconsin and Iowa met for an early, decisive game in Madison and 13,000 fans were there to cheer on their Badgers. The home team responded with a 60–51 triumph, paced by Rehfeldt's 20, matched by Weir for Iowa. Michigan finally beat Wisconsin in the next Badger game at home, by a 43–39 score. Rehfeldt with 10 and Cook with nine topped the Badger scoring in the slow-paced game. Bob Harrison had 16 and Don McIntosh had 12 for the victorious Wolverines. Iowa got back on the winning track by beating Indiana, 61–52, with Weir getting 26 points. Then, the Hawks took a giant step backwards in losing at Minnesota. Jim McIntyre had his way inside for the Gophers with 36 points, while Weir, all 5'9" of him, scored 30 for Iowa.[17]

Early on it was apparent that Northwestern would be at the bottom of the standings, along with Ohio State and Indiana. Halfway through the season, the Wildcats were 1–5, with OSU and Indiana at 2–4. At the top, as expected, were the Badgers and Hawkeyes, as well as Illinois. Just a half game behind were Purdue and Michigan. Michigan beat Northwestern to take over first place, then lost to OSU to fall back again. What was heartening to the Wolverines was that the supporting crew was aiding Mack Suprunowicz better than anticipated. Don McIntosh, Bob Harrison and Pete

Elliott were all performing well. In what was termed a "slow-moving game before 7,000," McIntosh led the Wolverines in scoring with 10 in the 53–37 win over Northwestern. In the upset loss to the Buckeyes in Columbus, Harrison had 20 and Elliott 17. The Wolverines then defeated Illinois in Champaign with McIntosh getting 17 and Harrison 15.[18]

At this time (February), the big news in the conference was that the Big Nine athletic directors and presidents would be meeting to discuss the so-called sanity code, recently adopted by the NCAA, which allowed off-campus recruiting, but prohibited financial assistance to athletes greater than that given to other students. This would be continually discussed throughout the winter and into the spring.[19]

Iowa was staying near the top of the league, thanks to Weir. In a 70 to 61 win over Illinois, Weir scored 34 points. The Illini were led by "Dike" Eddleman with 26. In their next game, the Hawks were beaten in Bloomington, 49–47, by the Hoosiers, although Weir had nearly half of his team's points (23). Michigan returned to winning that same night, topping Purdue easily, 69–56. The Wolverine balance continued with Suprunowicz picking up 17 and Harrison 13 in the victory.[20]

Near mid-season, Michigan leapt into first place after beating Indiana, while Wisconsin lost at Ohio State. Dick Schnittker, who would go on to the NBA in 1950 and play until 1958, led the Buckeyes in their upset with 24 points, while Cook (17) and Rehfeldt (13) had 30 of the 47 Badger points. For the Wolverines, Supronowicz had 21 and Harrison 18. The Hoosiers were paced by Lou Watson, future coach of the team from 1966 to 1971, with 19. Michigan followed this big win with another victory, winning at Minnesota, 56–45. The Badgers extended their losing streak in Iowa City, dropping the contest, 62–40; Murray Weir had 28 for the Hawks. In Minneapolis, Suprunowicz had 16, McIntosh 13, to lead the Wolverines.[21]

After nine games, Michigan, with a 7–2 mark, had a ½-game lead over the Hawkeyes at 7–3. Wisconsin had fallen to 6–4, while Purdue and Illinois were 5–5 each. It looked like the title was Michigan's to lose. They would not do so again, however. In West Lafayette, the Wolverines beat Purdue, who slowed down the game, as usual, 46–35. Harrison had 13, Suprunowicz 10. They clinched a title tie at home, beating Ohio State 40–36, but Iowa kept pace with a win against Minnesota, Weir scoring 28 of the 54 Iowa points in a 54–50 victory. Bud Grant led the Gophers with 15.[22]

At the end of February, Michigan gained a title tie with another slow-down win over Ohio State in Ann Arbor, by a score of 40–36. Suprunowicz and Harrison had nine each to lead the low-scoring game before 9,100 Michigan fans, the largest campus crowd for a basketball game ever. Iowa stayed close enough to still be able to tie, mathematically, after defeating Minnesota, 54 to 50, in Iowa City. Weir continued to top the Hawks and the league in scoring, as he poured in 28 points in the victory. Bud Grant had 15 for the Gophers.[23]

The next Monday (two days later), Iowa traveled to Ann Arbor for a chance to share the Big 9 title or for Michigan to clinch it outright. Another sellout crowd of 9,100 or more would be in place to cheer their Wolverines on. In a surprisingly one-sided contest, Michigan handed Iowa its fourth league defeat, winning by a score of 51 to 35. Suprunowicz led the balanced attack with 12, while Weir led Iowa, but was held to 14 points. The Wolverines would likely be headed on to the NCAA tourney, since "[B]y custom, the Big 9 winner is District 4 representative to the NCAA Tournament."[24] Michigan ended at 10–2, 16–5 for the season, while Iowa was 8–4 (15–4, overall), with Illinois and Wisconsin tied for third at 7–5.

The next day, the *Chicago Tribune* had the coaches' Big Nine first and second teams. Three Wolverines were named—Harrison, McIntosh and Pete Elliott (also an All-America quarterback on the football team, later Illinois coach and a defensive stalwart on the court)—as well as Murray Weir (the scoring leader and All-America selection) and Dwight (Dike) Eddelman of Illinois. The second team had Bobby Cook of Wisconsin, Dick Schnittker of Ohio State, Jack Burmaster of Illinois, Bill Berberian of Purdue and Don Ritter of Indiana. Weir was later named the winner of the Silver Basketball, emblematic of Most Valuable Player in the Big 9, after leading the league with a record 22.7 points per game.[25] Interestingly, Jim McIntyre of Minnesota was not named to either team, but was selected as an NCAA All-American.[26]

Bud Grant, most famous as the coach of the Minnesota Vikings, played three years of basketball at Minnesota, as well as football. He was Minnesota's MVP for the 1947–48 season (University of Minnesota Athletics).

### Final Standings and MVPs, 1947–48

| | | |
|---|---|---|
| Michigan | 10–2 | Pete Elliott |
| Iowa | 8–4 | Murray Weir (Big Nine MVP and First Team NCAA All-American) |
| Illinois | 7–5 | Jack Burmaster |
| Wisconsin | 7–5 | Bobby Cook |
| Purdue | 6–6 | Bill Berberian |
| Minnesota | 5–7 | Harry (Bud) Grant |
| Ohio State | 5–7 | Dick Schnittker |
| Indiana | 3–9 | Ward Williams |
| Northwestern | 3–9 | Chuck Tourek |

The Wolverines were invited, as expected, to the NCAA Tournament, where they met Holy Cross on March 19 in Madison Square Garden. The Crusaders were led by

All-American George Kaftan, future All-American Bob Cousy, and Joe Mullaney. They had won the 1947 NCAA championship, and easily topped Michigan, 63–45. Michigan defeated Columbia for third in the east regional by a 66–49 score. It was solace to Michigan, but not the ending that had been hoped for. Elliot got 15, Suprunowicz and McIntosh had 14 each.[27] Holy Cross lost to Kentucky in the eastern final and the Wildcats swamped Baylor, 58–42, to win the championship.

## The 1948–49 Season

The Big 9 season began with the defending champion Michigan Wolverines as the favorite, since they had Suprunowicz, Harrison and Elliott back, but their coach, Osborne Cowles, was gone, having taken the coaching position at rival Minnesota. Illinois had Dike Eddleman back, making them a threat, and Minnesota had Jim McIntyre return; he was joined by Myer "Whitey" Skoog, a 22-year-old sophomore, who had been a star at Brainerd (Minnesota) high school before the war. Minnesota won all eight of their non-conference games, referred to by Wilfrid Smith of the *Tribune* as "practice games."[28] Indiana would have Bill Garrett, the first African American to start and play significant minutes of varsity basketball in the Big 9.[29]

Bill Garrett started the first Indiana game in 1948–49 at a forward and scored eight points in a 61–48 victory over DePauw. Later in December, the 5–0 Hoosiers played in St. Louis against Washington University and stayed at the Chase Hotel. Their coach, Branch McCracken, had agreed to the Chase Hotel's terms that Garrett would not be allowed to eat in the hotel dining room because St. Louis was still a mostly segregated city. The players were not told, and when they went as a group after a team workout, Garrett was denied entry. Bill Tosheff said, "If Bill can't eat here, nobody does." From potential humiliation for Garrett came a bonding experience for the team, which would serve them well during the season.[30]

In an auspicious event that sadly presaged the scandals of the next year, a George Washington guard was arrested as one of four people attempting to bribe players to fix basketball games.[31] Illinois opened the league season on January 3, five days before the rest of the contenders, and topped Wisconsin, 62–50, in Champaign. Bill Erickson had 17 and Burdette Thurlby 12 for Illinois. The Badgers had balanced scoring with Doug Rogers getting 14, Don Page 13, and Don Rehfeldt 11.

Illinois won again five days later in Bloomington, in a double overtime contest. Again, Erickson topped the scoring chart with 16; Lou Watson was high man for the Hoosiers with 11. Minnesota won its opening game against Michigan, with McIntyre picking up 20 and Skoog 16. Harrison had 9 for the Wolverines.[32]

Both Illinois and Minnesota continued to win, the Illini on the road at Ohio State, and the Gophers at home. In Columbus, Walter Osterkorn had 18 and Bill Erickson 12 to lead the scoring for Illinois, while Dick Schnittker had 20 for the Buckeyes in a one-point 64–63 game. Minnesota had little trouble with the Badgers, 47–33, as Skoog had 14. Harold Foster, Wisconsin coach, complained about Minnesota's "slow-down" tactics, but his counterpart at Minnesota, Osborne Cowles, noted that Wisconsin had used the same tactic against Illinois early in that game, weaving and holding the ball and making no effort to score.[33] Michigan was upset by the Purdue Boilermakers in West Lafayette in a low-scoring contest, 45–36.[34] In that game Howard Williams and Norris Caudell each had 13 for Purdue, with Michigan's top scorer for the game (Bill Mikulich) getting seven.

The next weekend, in mid-January, Minnesota came into West Lafayette and pummeled the Boilers, 67 to 52, as McIntyre had 20, Skoog 18, and Bud Grant 14. Michigan beat Northwestern in Ann Arbor to get back on the winning track. Suprunowicz had 15 and Harrison 11; the Wildcat scoring was topped by Don Blasius with 15 and Bill Sticklen with 12. Wisconsin had 13,000 in their fieldhouse to watch the Badgers topple Indiana, 58–48. Don Rehfeldt, Badger center, had 27, and Bill Garrett had 15 for the Hoosiers.[35]

Minnesota moved into the early Big Nine lead two nights later with a 61–45 win in Iowa City. Skoog had 26 and was being called the best sophomore in the conference. He was supported by McIntyre's 15. Ohio State upset Wisconsin 57–54 as Raidiger had 23 for the Bucks and Rehfeldt 17 for the Badgers, before 13,000 in Madison.[36]

The Gophers came home and remained unbeaten after topping Indiana in a slow-down contest, 35–28. Skoog with 11, and McIntyre with 10, kept the 16,306 fans in "the Barn" happy. Bill Garrett had nine to lead Indiana. In Chicago Stadium, Northwestern defeated Iowa, reinforcing how far the Hawks had fallen. The two squads would end up at the bottom of the Big Nine that season.[37]

On the last weekend in January, Minnesota came into Champaign for what seemed to be the first "must-win" of the season for these top contenders. In a packed Huff Gym (6,905), the Illini held off the Gophers, 45 to 44. Fred Green, the 6'7" Illini center, and Jim Marks topped Illinois scoring with 10 points each. The Gophers got 38 of their 44 points from three players: McIntyre with 15, Skoog with 13 and Grant with 10. Michigan beat Ohio State in Ann Arbor, 54 to 48. Suprunowicz had 19 and Schnittker 15 to lead their squads in scoring.[38]

Two nights later, a middling Purdue squad edged Illinois in West Lafayette, 55–53. Minnesota defeated Northwestern and got back the game lost two nights earlier to the Illini. The next weekend, the Gophers gave it back at Ohio State. Marks had 13 and Dike Eddleman 11 in the 61–54 Illinois victory over Wisconsin in Madison, before 13,500. Don Rehfeldt had 20 for the Badgers.

In Columbus, the Gophers were held under 40 points, with Jim McIntyre getting 12 to top their scoring. The Buckeyes were led by Harvey Brown's 13 and Schnittker's 12 in the 48–39 win. Shooting percentages were given for the game and they reveal a lot about why games were low scoring. OSU shot 21 of 71 for 29 percent and Minnesota 17 of 61 for 28 percent. Both were considered average for that time.[39]

Halfway through the conference season, Illinois was 5–1, Minnesota 6–2, with only three other squads over .500: Michigan (3–2), Purdue (4–3) and Ohio State (4–3). The national basketball poll had both of the leaders in the top ten, Illinois at #4 and Minnesota at #7. Kentucky was ranked #1 in the nation and St. Louis (behind "Easy Ed" Macaulay) was #2. The two league leaders continued to win; Illinois routed Ohio State, 64–49, and Minnesota edged the Hawkeyes, 54–49, before 15,795 in Williams Arena on the Minnesota campus. Both winning squads were getting good balance from their five starters, making them harder and harder to beat.[40]

Michigan tried to make a run at the leaders, but in their first effort, in Ann Arbor on February 19, they lost to the Gophers, 54 to 47. A record crowd of more than 10,000 jammed the Michigan fieldhouse to see the contest. Bud Grant had 15 and Skoog, McIntyre and Gerald Mitchell each had 12 to nearly complete the Minnesota scoring. For the Wolverines, Harrison had 15 and Suprunowicz, 14. Two nights later, the Illini routed Iowa in Champaign, right after the Hawks had surprised Wisconsin by edging them in Iowa City, 61–60. The Illinois contest was not close with Coach Harry Combes clearing the Illini bench in the 80–49 victory. Dike Eddleman had 19 and Walt Kersulis, a backup center, had 13. Charlie Mason had 16 for Iowa. The Illini shot 31 of 83 for 37 percent, referred to in the *Tribune* as "their tops in conference play."[41]

Myer "Whitey" Skoog was an All-American guard at Minnesota and played six years for the Minneapolis Lakers, during which they won three NBA championships (University of Minnesota Athletics).

Five nights later, both leaders won again, Illinois in a romp over Northwestern, and Minnesota defeating Purdue, 58–48, before 16,202 in Minnesota. In the former game, played as part of a Chicago Stadium double-header that drew 17,095, Walt Osterkorn had 24 points and Eddleman 19 to lead Illinois's 81–64 triumph. In Minneapolis, McIntyre had 17 and Skoog 16 in the victory. At this point, with just two games left for Illinois and one for Minnesota, their records were 9–1 and 9–2, respectively.[42]

Illinois assured themselves of at least a tie for the conference title two nights later, with an easy victory over Indiana in Champaign. Eddleman had 23, Erickson 14, in the 91–68 win, with Don Ritter and Lou Watson leading the Hoosiers with 20 and 17, respectively.

The next day, conference tournament results were listed for some of the top conferences, and that illustrates another factor in how the Big Ten was the acknowledged top conference in basketball on a year-to-year basis. There was no Atlantic Coast Conference; it would not be created until 1953. The Southeastern Conference still included Tulane, and Kentucky was the only real power in the league. The Southern Conference included North Carolina, North Carolina State, Wake Forest and Maryland, but also George Washington, William & Mary, and Davidson.

On the last Saturday of the season, the Illini clinched the title as Minnesota lost to Wisconsin in Madison, 45–43, before 13,500 in the fieldhouse, which supposedly seated 11,500. Don Rehfeldt's 16 points led the Badgers, while McIntrye matched Rehfeldt's 16 and Bud Grant had 12. Rehfeldt also won the league scoring title with a total of 229 conference points, an average of 19.1 ppg. Iowa managed to avoid the league basement by edging Michigan, 63–62, behind Frank Calsbeek's 29 points. The loss left Michigan third in the league with a 6–5 record.[43]

Michigan got some solace two nights later by defeating the champions, 70–53, in Ann Arbor. Supronowicz had 18 and Vanderkuy 15 for the Wolves, with Green topping the coasting Illini with 14. The final standings had Illinois with a record of 10–2, Minnesota at 9–3 and Michigan 7–5, the only squads over .500.

The All Big-Ten first team consisted of Schnittker (OSU), Eddleman (IL), Rehfeldt (WI), Harrison (MU) and Williams (PU). The second team was Skoog and McIntrye (MN), Supronowicz and Elliott (MI) and Erickson (IL).

After leading the Illini to the conference championship, Dwight "Dike" Eddleman was named the winner of the Silver Basketball by the *Chicago Tribune* in recognition of his being named the Most Valuable Player in the Big Ten for 1948–49.

### Final Standings and MVPs, 1948–49

| | | |
|---|---|---|
| Illinois | 10–2 | Dike Eddleman (Big Ten MVP) |
| Minnesota | 9–3 | Harold "Bud" Olson |
| Michigan | 7–5 | Bob Harrison |
| Indiana | 6–6 | Lou Watson |
| Purdue | 6–6 | Howard Williams |
| Ohio State | 6–6 | Dick Schnittker |
| Wisconsin | 5–7 | Don Rehfeldt |
| Iowa | 3–9 | Charlie Mason |
| Northwestern | 2–10 | Bill Sticklen |

Eddleman was an amazing athlete, probably the best all-around athlete ever to attend the University of Illinois. Today, playing two varsity sports is unusual, but it was not in Eddleman's time. He, however, played more than that, earning 11 varsity letters. Eddleman was the punter on the football team, averaging 43.3 yards per kick, as well as playing halfback and averaging 32.8 yards per punt return. He won five of six indoor/outdoor Big Ten high jump titles, the 1948 NCAA title in that event (6'7"), then placed fourth at the 1948 Olympics in London with a jump of 6'4". He also played four years of basketball, scoring 329 regular season points (just over 14 per game), and led the Illini in scoring, then played four years in the NBA. In addition, he had fought in World War II for three years. He was named 2nd team All-America. As Wilson noted, "All this—and the Western Conference Honor Medal for Scholarship, as well."[44] Two other Big Ten players were named to the 15-person All-America squad; Dick Schnittker and "Whitey" Skoog were named to the 3rd team.

With their championship, the Illini received a bid to the eight-team NCAA tournament and were paired against Yale in the first game of the eastern regional. The two teams met as part of a Madison Square double-header on March 21, and the Illini were ten-point favorites against Tony Lavelli and the Elis. Neither Illinois nor Lavelli disappointed. He had 27 points, but the Illinois balance (Osterkorn 15, Sunderlage 15, Eddleman 11, Green 10) was enough to lead to a 71–67 Illinois victory. In the nightcap, defending NCAA champions Kentucky, led by Alex Groza, defeated Villanova and Paul Arizin, 85–72. Both Groza and Arizin had 30 points.

The next night another crowd of more than 18,000 saw Kentucky dismantle Illinois, 76–47, as Groza had 27, and no Illinois player had more than 7.[45] It was a disappointment, only slightly mollified by the Illini's joining Kentucky for a flight to Seattle for the NCAA finals the next Saturday. Illinois, led by Walt Osterkorn's 17 points, won the 3rd place game, 57–53, over Oregon. Kentucky repeated as NCAA champion with a 46–36 victory over Oklahoma A&M (now Oklahoma State).

Though disappointed, the Illini had held up the prestige of the Big Ten by finishing third in the nation (and fourth in the national polls). The league had accepted Michigan State as its tenth member in 1949, but they would not officially compete in the league until 1950–51. With the end of the 1940s, the era of returning servicemen to league competition was at an end. The 1950s would bring new perspectives and prospects.

# III

# Into the '50s

The new decade began with both optimism and fear. The war seemed finally in the past, but the damage in Europe would take years to rebuild. The relief at overcoming the Axis powers was muted by the rising fear of Communism in Eastern Europe and the continued uncertainties in the Far East. President Truman assured the U.N. that the United States would not send troops to Formosa to protect that bastion of Nationalist China from the advances of Mao Zedong and the Communists, who now controlled the mainland. The United States was still controlling Japan, but General Douglas MacArthur, the Supreme Commander of the Allied Powers in Japan, affirmed to the Japanese and the world that the rights of all citizens would be protected. President Truman promised more aid to West Berlin, now isolated behind what Churchill had termed "the Iron Curtain" in his famous speech in March of 1946 in Fulton, Missouri. The most discussed domestic policy change was the 50 percent rise in payroll/Social Security taxes from 1 percent to 1½ percent, the first rise since 1937.

Although there were still a small number of returning servicemen on Big Ten rosters, this would be the first season since the war that their number was greatly reduced. The defending champion, Illinois, had lost Dwight Eddleman, but Bill Erickson and Wally Osterkorn returned, and the Illini were seen as a contender for the 1950 conference title, along with Minnesota, Wisconsin, Northwestern, Ohio State, and possibly Indiana. Both Northwestern and Wisconsin had surprised UCLA, the Wildcats 64–58 in Chicago Stadium, and the Badgers 54–52 in Madison, just before the opener of the Big Ten season, making both seem to be definite threats for the title. Ab Nicholas, 65 years later, still spoke with pride and excitement about his team beating a John Wooden team (which went 25–7 that season) and Nicholas's contribution to that victory (12 points).[1]

New Year's Day in 1950 was on a Sunday, so the traditional start of the Big Ten season, usually the first Saturday in January, moved up a bit to Monday, January 2, when the defending champions, the University of Illinois, traveled to Madison to meet the Wisconsin Badgers before 13,510 screaming fans. The crowd size at the fieldhouse was largely, thought sophomore starter Ab Nicholas, because the local fire marshal did not enforce the fire regulations regarding size of the crowd and access to exits.[2] Those fans were not disappointed, but the Illini were, as they endured a 59–50 loss in the fieldhouse. Badger center Don Rehfeldt, the defending scoring champion in the conference, started the new campaign well with 27 points. He was supported by Bob Mader's 11, and 10 from Ab Nicholas. Bill Erickson was the only Illinois player to reach double figures with

19. That same day Ohio State suffered a non-conference defeat to Bradley University, one of the top teams in the country, by a score of 65 to 46, in Peoria.

Ohio State fell to 5–2 for the season, but there was a caveat in that Dick Schnittker, the leading scorer on OSU the previous season and a third team All-American, had not played in the game because he was busy at another venue, as an end on the victorious Ohio State football team that topped California in the 1950 Rose Bowl. Bob Donham and Fred Taylor led the Buckeyes in scoring in the loss, each with 11 points. Describing the Buckeyes in retrospect, Tug Wilson said, "Schnittker was the only super-star on the club, but had valuable aid from four other cool, poised players who were a perfect complement to his brilliance: Bob Donham at the other forward spot, Bob Brown and Bob Burkholder in the backcourt, and a smallish but rugged center named Fred Taylor...."[3]

In Bloomington, the Hoosiers went to 9–0, defeating Michigan State, a Big Ten opponent, not eligible for the title as of yet. Indiana was led by Lou Watson's 19 points in the 60–50 victory. Stauffer (12) and Rapchak (11) led the Spartan scoring.[4]

The next Saturday, the league went into full action with continued upsets; Northwestern defeated Purdue in West Lafayette, Illinois lost again, and Indiana defeated Wisconsin. For Northwestern, Ray Ragelis (17), Jake Fendley (16) and Wally Horavitch (15) were the bulk of the offense, while Andy Butchko (16) and Dick Axness (15) were the Purdue leaders. Illinois lost, 83–62, in Columbus, and Dick Schnittker returned to score 23 for the Buckeyes, while Bob Donham had 16, as the Bucks shot 43 percent (30/69) from the field. Illinois shot just 26 percent (23/87), with only Osterkorn (11) and Fletcher (10) scoring in double figures. Indiana won at home, despite shooting only 25 percent from the floor (24 of 94). Bill Garrett had 15 and Bill Tosheff had 11 to spark the Hoosiers. Rehfeldt had 25 of the 59 Badger points in the 61–59 contest. In the other conference contest, Michigan pounded Iowa, 66 to 46, in Ann Arbor. The leading scorer was Don McIntosh with 21, who had returned to the team after a year of academic ineligibility, a rare occurrence, in many ways, today.[5]

Don Rehfeldt was Big Ten MVP in 1950 for the Wisconsin Badgers and later played in the NBA (University of Wisconsin Athletics).

Indiana's unbeaten record (10–

0) had them ranked in the top five in the country that week, but things swiftly changed for them as they lost the next weekend to Michigan, and then at Iowa, 65–64. In the former game, Charles Murray (19) and Mac Supronowicz (16) led the Wolverines, while Lou Watson took games honors with 26 for the Hoosiers. "Murray buried a field goal right as time expired to give Michigan a 69–67 win in Ann Arbor."[6] In the Iowa game, center Franklin Calsbeek of Iowa had 32, while Bill Garrett led the Hoosiers with 18. Northwestern's swift start (2–0) was halted by Ohio State with a 10-point victory, 61–51, in Columbus. Schnittker had 22 and Donham 15, while Ray Ragelis led the Wildcat scoring with 17. The Buckeyes then pummeled Michigan, 74–58 (Schnittker had 28), and Illinois did the same to Northwestern, 76–50 (Bill Erickson had 24).

It was still January, but the Buckeye visit to Illinois the next weekend seemed of early season import in the conference. The Illini rose to the occasion and beat down the Bucks by 16 points, 66–50. Osterkorn (24) and Sunderlage (20) were the top scorers for Illinois, while Schnittker (16) and Taylor (10) were tops for Ohio State. Just under 7,000 squeezed into Huff Gym (seating capacity was just under that at the time; today it is 4,500). Indiana got back to winning against a weak Purdue team, 49–39, and Minnesota beat Michigan, 60–52. Two days later, Ohio State bounced back to defeat Iowa, 68–54, and take the early lead in the conference race.[7] The Buckeyes kept up the pace, topping two rugged rivals, Minnesota, 63–58, and Wisconsin, 61–47, in Columbus. The Ohio State scoring in these contests was quite balanced and was a key to their victories. Against the Gophers, Burkholder had 15, Taylor and Donham 14 each. In the victory over the Badgers, Taylor had 15, Schnittker 14, Burkholder 13.[8]

The victory over Ohio State seemed to energize the Illini, who went into Minnesota and defeated the Gophers, 67–57, before 13,527 in the Barn. Osterkorn led with 18, while Thurlby had 16 and Sunderlage 15, to propel the Illini. For Minnesota, Skoog had 18. Despite the loss to Illinois, Ohio State stayed focused and defeated Indiana in Bloomington, 56–55. Schnittker scored almost half the Buckeye points with 27, while Watson had 17 for the Hoosiers.[9]

Just when they seemed to be back to playing top basketball, the Illini lost to Iowa, 70–65, in Iowa City. Frank Calsbeek had 25 for the Hawks, while Illinois got 21 from Osterkorn and 14 from Thurlby.[10] Northwestern had reverted to form after taking their first two games and lost their fifth in a row, this last to Wisconsin in Chicago Stadium, 66–59. Don Rehfeldt scored 35 of the Badger points, hitting 12 of 17 shots from the field, mostly hooks and tap-ins. Minnesota also reverted, this time to what the *Tribune* called "snail-like" tactics that had served them well in the past. The result was not so good, however, as they lost handily to Indiana, 59–39, in Bloomington.[11]

The pattern for 1949–50 was a number of teams beating each other in the Big Ten, but one team, Ohio State, winning consistently. By mid–February, the Buckeyes were 8–1, with just three games to play. Wisconsin was 4–2 and three teams were tied at 4–3, Illinois, Iowa and Indiana. Indiana beat Illinois, 83–72; Wisconsin beat Iowa, 66–62 in overtime; but OSU kept winning. After a Chicago Stadium victory over Northwestern, the title was within reach. Buckeye coach Tippy Dye played a lot of players in the 68 to 46 victory, with Gene Browne (22) and Schnittker (18) topping the scoring. Wisconsin kept up minimal pressure with another victory over Iowa, 53–44, as Rehfeldt scored 25 to keep in the race for the scoring title of the Big Ten. Nicholas supported Rehfeldt with 12. OSU claimed at least a share of the Big Ten title with a victory over Indiana, 75–65. The Bucks shot 26 of 53 for 49 percent, called "phenomenal" by the *Tribune*. In that game, Schnittker again led with 20, while Jerry Stutteville had 14 for the Hoosiers.[12]

The individual scoring race at that point was between Rehfeldt and Schnittker, with the latter leading in total points because he had played more games, and the former having the better average, 23 pg to 20.5 pg. Trailing them were Osterkorn of Illinois, Skoog of Minnesota and Calsbeek of Iowa. Ohio State was ranked #3 in the country, while Indiana, the only other ranked Big Ten team, was at #17. These rankings were done by writers, with input from people around the country, since no one was likely to have seen all of the teams being ranked. The age of television would change all that.[13]

On February 25, the only team with a mathematical chance at catching the Buckeyes, Wisconsin, lost to Illinois, 76–58, and Ohio State claimed the 1950 Big Ten crown. Wally Osterkorn was the top scorer in the game with 26 for Illinois, and the Wisconsin point leaders were Don Rehfeldt with 17 and Ab Nicholas with 16. Rehfeldt and Osterkorn had been teammates at Chicago's Amundsen High School, and both would go on to have brief careers in the NBA. Iowa won in Bloomington, 59–53, to pull ahead of the Hoosiers in the race for third. Frank Calsbeek had 20 for Iowa and Jerry Stutteville had 18 for Indiana. Michigan continued a very disappointing year, losing to Northwestern in Chicago Stadium, 76–53. Ray Ragelis with 24, and Jake Fendley with 22, spearheaded the Wildcat attack; Supronowicz had 15 for the Wolverines.[14]

Ohio State would receive and accept what now was an automatic bid to the NCAA tournament, but would end their regular season February 27, with the NCAA tourney not beginning until March 23. The Buckeyes would have a long time between games. Some teams were entered in both the National Invitational Tournament (NIT) and the NCAA, but the Big Ten prohibited post-season games, other than in the NCAA tourney, with a total of 22 games the maximum in a regular season. The conference granted an exception to that in order to allow OSU to play two games before the opening of the NCAA tourney.[15]

The Bucks ended their league season with a victory in Ann Arbor, 69 to 58. Schnittker had 23, Taylor 16 for Ohio State, and Leo Vanderkuy had 19 for the Wolverines. The national poll of top teams had OSU as #2, with no other Big Ten team ranked. The Bucks ended the Big Ten season at 11–1.[16]

The rest of the league finished the season the next weekend with Illinois topping Northwestern, 69–52, to finish at 7–5; the Wildcats ended at 3–9, tied with Purdue for last once again. The Boilers lost to Michigan, 70–60, allowing the Wolverines to climb to 4–8, a huge disappointment after the 7–5 of the prior year. Minnesota, another disappointing team, defeated Iowa, 64–49, to drag the Hawks back to .500 (6–6), while the Gophers tied Michigan at 4–8. After a 60–52 defeat of Minnesota, Wisconsin finished at 9–3, two games behind OSU and two ahead of Indiana and Illinois. Rehfeldt had 21 and Nicholas 13 for the Badgers.[17]

For the second year in a row, Rehfeldt led the league in scoring (265 points, 22.7 ppg), followed by Dick Schnittker of OSU (20.8 ppg), Wally Osterkorn of Illinois (17.7 ppg) and "Whitey" Skoog of Minnesota (16.8 ppg). Bill Garrett of Indiana was named to the second team, all Big Ten, the first African American to receive such recognition. He would gain first team recognition the next season. Besides Garrett, there were also

Ragelis (NU), Calsbeek (IA), Osterkorn (IL) and Williams (PU). The first team was Schnittker and Donham (OSU), Rehfeldt (WI), Skoog (MN) and Watson (IN).

A week after the conference season ended, the Big Ten announced that the conference had approved, with the addition of Michigan State to the league schedule, a 14-game season for 1950–51, but would retain the 22-game limit on regular season games. The conference also codified the rule that allowed a team to play two extra "warm-up" games when it had been entered in the NCAA tournament. In addition, the Big Ten agreed to continue permission for post-game telecasts from film. Live television, as a conference policy, was still under consideration.[18]

Ohio State played two "tune-up" games before the NCAA tourney, defeating Butler 66–65, and then defeating DePaul, 70–63. The game against the Blue Demons was the third meeting of the year between the two squads, and Ohio State took the "series," two games to one. In the last game, Schnittker had 30 points to lead all scorers. That game was played on March 18 and the Bucks traveled to New York to play CCNY on March 23.[19]

CCNY, coached by former New York Celtic great Nat Holman, had won the NIT tournament the week before and was led by Ed Warner and Irwin Dambrot. As it turned out, both were among a number of players from top teams that year involved in point-shaving, so the final score of the OSU-CCNY game may be viewed with uncertainty, despite the 56–55 victory for the Beavers. Nevertheless, the *New York Times* lauded the play and intense competition at the time, while noting at least one "rock" that was made by Ed Warner in the closing minute of the one-point game. Warner also shot 3 of 16 from the field.[20] Was this part of the point-shaving? Very possibly. Floyd Layne was the point leader that game for the Beavers with 17. Schnittker had 26 and Donham 9, but both fouled out in the second half, sealing the fate of the Buckeyes. CCNY went on to win the NCAA tourney, defeating Bradley, as they had for the NIT title, but when both teams were implicated in the point-shaving scandal, the title was vacated. CCNY subsequently dropped from Division I to Division II basketball and has remained at the lesser basketball level since that time.[21]

The day after the Buckeyes were eliminated, the Big Ten announced that Don Rehfeldt was the winner of the Most Valuable Player award in the Big Ten, with Wally Osterkorn second, Bob Donham third, Lou Watson fourth, and "Whitey" Skoog fifth. Dick Schnittker was not considered because the nine nominees had been selected by their teammates on each of the teams and the Bucks had nominated Donham over Schnittker. Donham had led the league in field goal percentage, although Schnittker, the team MVP in 1948 and 1949, was all-conference and All-American (and sixth in the country in scoring).[22]

### Final Standings and MVPs, 1949–50

| Team | Record | MVP |
| --- | --- | --- |
| Ohio State | 11–1 | Bob Donham |
| Wisconsin | 9–3 | Don Rehfeldt (Big Ten MVP) |
| Indiana | 7–5 | Lou Watson |
| Illinois | 7–5 | Walt Osterkorn |
| Iowa | 6–6 | Franklin Calsbeek |
| Minnesota | 5–7 | "Whitey" Skoog |
| Michigan | 4–8 | Mack Supronowicz |
| Northwestern | 3–9 | Ray Ragelis |
| Purdue | 3–9 | Howard Williams |

## The 1951 Season

Ohio State saw Dick Schnittker and his starting teammates graduated and Coach "Tippy" Dye leave to take on the reins of the University of Washington basketball team. Wisconsin had lost Don Rehfeldt and three other starters, but Ab Nicholas looked capable of stepping into Rehfeldt's large, scoring shoes. At Iowa, there was coaching instability, but a fine class of young players. Illinois had Don Sunderlage ready to step up as a star for Coach Harry Combes, who had also lost four starters, and at Indiana, Bill Garrett was seen as a potential All-America player in his senior year. Even Northwestern, led by Ray Ragelis, was viewed as a threat for the first time in years. Michigan State would play a full slate of 14 games, and their addition to the league was difficult to predict. Teams would play five opponents twice and others once, for a total of 14 league contests.

The Big Ten opened the new year and the Big Ten season with Wisconsin hosting Illinois on New Year's Day, and the Illini edged the Badgers in overtime, 71–67. Bob Peterson, a 6'8" sophomore, topped the scoring with 19 points and Don Sunderlage had 16. For the Badgers, Ab Nicholas had 21, with James Clinton contributing 15.[23]

The rest of the conference began on January 6, with the most intriguing match-up being Michigan State at Northwestern in the Spartans' basketball debut (they would not play as a Big Ten football member until 1953) under first-year coach Pete Newell. The game was played at Evanston High School, as the Wildcats' new arena, McGaw Hall (later remodeled and expanded as Welsh-Ryan Arena), was not ready. Before a capacity crowd of 3,000, the Spartans stunned the 'Cats, 67 to 62, despite 25 points by Ray Ragelis, the Northwestern star.[24]

As an interesting aside,

Ab Nicholas was MVP of Wisconsin in 1952 and went on to establish a highly successful investment management firm (University of Wisconsin Athletics).

the Pacific Coast Conference (today's Pac-12) announced that they would ban their football games from being shown on television after determining that the three-year test of showing games was a "flop." What had resulted, they determined, was that attendance at games declined, not just at their games, but at high school, junior college and other college contests. With this kind of blame being placed on television for football declines in attendance, basketball would be even more hard-pressed to be shown on television.[25] Obviously, things would change over the next decade.[26]

In other contests, Illinois beat Minnesota, Indiana toppled Ohio State, Wisconsin topped Michigan, and Iowa defeated Purdue. In Champaign, the Illini were led in scoring by Sunderlage with 19 and Ted Beach with 18, while Maynard Johnson had 22 and "Whitey" Skoog 17, for Minnesota. In Columbus, the Hoosiers were relentless in their 77–62 victory. Bill Garrett had 23 to lead all scorers. The Badgers bounced back from their home loss to Illinois to defeat the Wolverines in Ann Arbor, with Anderson leading with 16 and Nicholas and Clinton chipping in with 14 each.

Michigan and Ohio State were looking weak early and the next weekend reinforced that view, as Northwestern beat Michigan, 67–64, in Ann Arbor and Minnesota easily handled the Buckeyes, 77 to 64, in Minneapolis. Illinois had an impressive victory in Iowa City, led by Peterson's 14 and Sunderlage's 13, while the Hawks got good performances from Calsbeek and Chuck Darling with 18 points apiece in the 72–69 contest. Illinois then manhandled Michigan, 68–47, in Champaign, and Indiana stayed undefeated in the league by beating Michigan State in East Lansing, 47–37, as the Spartans slowed things down. Northwestern surprised Iowa, 73–70, and Wisconsin kept the Buckeyes at the bottom of the league with a 74–67 victory, behind Ab Nicholas, who scored 27 points. The Wildcats were still playing home games before just 3,000 because of the limited capacity at Evanston High School, but they were the exception.[27] Most Big Ten basketball games were drawing over 10,000 on a regular basis. There was no question that they were the most popular conference in college basketball; they wanted to be the most successful on the court as well, since no Big Ten team had won an NCAA title since the 1940 and 1941 titles had been won by Indiana and Wisconsin, respectively.

Indiana staked a claim to a potential Big Ten title by topping Illinois, 64–53, in Bloomington on January 15. Bill Garrett had 21 and Sam Miranda 19 to dominate the Hoosier scoring and offset Don Sunderlage's 18 and Fletcher's 13 in the 11-point victory. That same night, Iowa won against Michigan State, 46–42 (an ugly game with 55 fouls), and Wisconsin beat Northwestern, 68–56.[28]

The Iowa game at Champaign was seen as another great early test for the Illini, but the Hawkeyes were doomed by the exigencies of playing in the Midwest in the 1950s' weather and difficult roads. After their flight was canceled because of an unexpectedly heavy snowfall, the Iowa team spent eight hours on a bus ride to Champaign, delaying their arrival and the start of the contest on Saturday night, January 20, by nearly three hours. They then played with "dead legs" and lost to the Illini, 69 to 53, falling to 2–3 in the league. Illinois went to 5–1, led by Don Sunderlage's 27 markers.

Indiana kept pace, easily defeating Purdue, 77–56, in Bloomington, and Northwestern pushed the Buckeyes deeper into the Big Ten cellar with an 81–75 victory at Evanston High. The Buckeyes played about as well as they could, shooting 16 of 28 in the first half (59 percent), but Ray Ragelis (26) and Don Blasius (17) pushed the Wildcats to the win. In a battle for the state, Michigan State won for the first time in Ann Arbor since 1933, defeating the Wolverines, 49 to 36. Neither team was very good, but it was still thrilling for the Spartans in their first year competing in the Big Ten.[29]

Two nights later, Indiana continued the season-long punishment of Ohio State with a 10-point victory, 69–59. They were led in scoring by Bill Garrett, referred to in the *Chicago Tribune* as "senior Negro center," who had 17, and Sam Miranda with 13. In a closer and more meaningful game, Iowa upset the Golden Gophers in Minneapolis by a 69–66 score. Chuck Darling and Frank Calsbeek led the scoring for Iowa with 22 and 18, respectively, while Maynard Johnson and John Wallerius had 11 each for Minnesota. The game was played before the usual crowd of over 12,000 in "The Barn."[30] At this point, with the season at the halfway point, the Hoosiers were 5–0, the Illini 5–1, the Badgers 4–1, with Minnesota and Northwestern tied at 3–2.

The next weekend, Northwestern pulled ahead of Minnesota as the Wildcats topped Purdue with a record 97–79 victory, in a run-and-gun battle, while Indiana won 32 to 26 over the Gophers as Minnesota played "slowdown." In the former game, NU center Ray Ragelis set a new Northwestern game-scoring mark with 36 points, most of them inside, with sidekick Blasius scoring 19, matched by Carl McNulty to lead Purdue scoring. In the latter contest, Bill Tosheff was the only double figure scorer in the game, leading IU with 12.[31] Ragelis (17), Blasius (17) and Jake Fendley (19), combined to push Northwestern to a victory two nights later in Columbus, against increasingly sad Ohio State, by a 78 to 67 margin.[32]

Into February and the Big Ten race seemed to be between three teams—Illinois, Indiana and Wisconsin—although both Northwestern and Iowa had mathematical possibilities to win, and many opportunities to be "spoilers." The Badgers edged Minnesota in a slow-paced contest, 47 to 44; Clinton and Nicholas both had 14 for Wisconsin and Whitey Skoog scored 13 for the Gophers. The contest in Williams Arena drew over 13,000. Ab Nicholas noted that Coach Ozzie Cowles of Minnesota often played a deliberate, slow-down game on offense and then a box and one on defense, with Nicholas being the one "honored" with the individual guarding.[33]

Meanwhile, Illinois was beating another of the Big Ten "punching bags," Purdue, 85 to 76, while Northwestern lost in Iowa City, 73–55. Rod Fletcher and Don Sunderlage continued to power the Illini offense with 21 and 20 points, respectively. In the Iowa-NU game, the "usual suspects" led their teams in scoring. Big Frank Calsbeek had 23, Chuck Darling 20, for the Hawks, while Fendley (17) and Blasius (12) led the Wildcats in the 73 to 55 rout.[34]

Despite the relative peace following World War II, the Korean War had begun in the summer of 1950, a result of the division of Korean along the 38th parallel. Korea had been occupied by Japan since 1910 and the split into two Koreas, one largely American-controlled and the other largely Soviet, made Korea the first place where the new Cold War became hot. The American effort to promote free elections throughout the entire country was rejected by the Chinese, who were acting in concert with the Soviets. At first, the fighting was more border skirmishing between the communist North and the right-wing government of the democratic South. When the Soviets boycotted the Security Council meetings on Korea, the United Nations voted to send troops to intervene there; these troops were largely American, although at least a dozen other countries also sent troops. In February of 1951, the conflict was so heated that fighting was reported in Seoul itself, and there was a grave danger of the Chinese/Korean troops overrunning the South before the U.N. forces repelled them at Chipyong-Ni.

The news from Korea was front page, but the sports page led with Indiana's loss at Minnesota, 61–54, and Illinois's victory, 63–52, over Wisconsin to propel the Illini into the Big Ten lead. In Minneapolis, Whitey Skoog (17) and Virgil Miller (14) were the scoring leaders for the Gophers, while Bill Tosheff (14) and Bill Garrett (11) led the losers. In the Illinois game, Ted Beach had 14, Clive Follmer 13, for Illinois as Sunderlage and Miranda were held in check. Markham, with 15, and Ab Nicholas, with 11, led the feisty Badgers. Iowa and Northwestern, meanwhile, won against weak Big Ten teams (Ohio State and Michigan) to stay above .500. The Monday games, two nights later, caused a further shake-out. Indiana went to Iowa City and won, 63–54, dropping the Hawks to 5–4 and lifting the Hoosiers to 7–1. Illinois toyed with Ohio State in a 20-point 79–59 victory. Purdue upset Wisconsin, 62–46, and Michigan State did the same against Northwestern, 52–48.[35]

The league standings on February 13 showed that two teams were pulling away, but two or three others were still hoping for a miracle:

| | |
|---|---|
| Illinois | 8–1 |
| Indiana | 7–1 |
| Wisconsin | 6–3 |
| Northwestern | 6–4 |
| Iowa | 5–4 |
| Michigan State | 4–5 |
| Minnesota | 4–6 |
| Michigan | 2–6 |
| Purdue | 2–7 |
| Ohio State | 2–9 |

Three weekends left to the season and on the ensuing one, Indiana and Illinois continued to win, over Northwestern, 94–63, and Purdue, 70–65, respectively, while Wisconsin lost its third in a row, 73–60, to Iowa, pretty much ending any title hope that they still had. Iowa, who beat the Badgers in Madison, was edging upward.

Two nights later, basketball was still dominating the sports pages, but not in a way anyone liked. Long Island University had called off the remainder of their games for the season after a point-shaving scandal was revealed. It was noted that college basketball had endured four such scandals since 1945 and the question was, "How much could be endured?" Unfortunately, things would get worse, when the LIU scandal expanded to include CCNY, the reigning NIT and NCAA champion, as well as Kentucky, Bradley and Columbia, but that was yet to come.[36]

On that same February evening, Indiana visited Champaign for what looked to be the most significant game of the Big Ten season, what with each having just one conference loss. Indiana had a lead at the half, 35–34, then built a second-half lead to 58–53 when Bill Garrett fouled out with 6:10 to play and Hoosiers ahead, 60–58. "Without Garrett to defend the post, Illinois pounded the ball inside for five point-blank field goals down the stretch and snatched away a 71–65 victory."[37] The Illini had four players in double figures led by Sunderlage's 18 and Fletcher's 13. For IU, Miranda had 18 and Garrett 16, despite missing almost half the game.[38]

The next weekend, both of the leaders, Illinois and Indiana, extended their winning ways, while Minnesota eliminated Northwestern, 73–68, and Iowa extended their recent winning streak against Michigan, 70–48, before 11,634 in Iowa City. Don Sunderlage had 34 points for Coach Harry Combes and the Illini, who won in Columbus, 89 to 69. Indiana won at home, defeating Purdue 68 to 53.[39]

In Madison, one of the worst-shooting games of the year was played in a 35–29 victory for Wisconsin over Michigan State. The winners shot just 16 percent on 7 of 45 from the floor, while the losing Spartans were a shade better with 19 percent on 12 of 61. Ab Nicholas was the only player in the game to achieve double figures with 10 points.[40]

Indiana stopped Iowa's winning streak two nights later with a ten-point victory in Iowa City. Bill Tosheff with 19 and Sam Miranda with 14 led the Hoosiers, who shot just 27 of 78 (35 percent) from the floor. Iowa was even poorer from the field, hitting just 19 of 82 (23 percent) with Chuck Darling scoring 20 of their 53 points in the 63 to 53 contest.[41]

The last weekend (Saturday/Monday) would determine the Big Ten champion, as Illinois maintained a one-game lead. On Saturday the Illini held off Northwestern, 80–76, in Chicago Stadium, before 18,890, to clinch a tie for the title. Sunderlage, with 27, and Ted Beach, with 21, were the Illinois top scorers, while Jake Fendley (21) and Ray Ragelis (14) led the 'Cats. Indiana matched the win with an easy triumph in Ann Arbor, 57 to 42. Tosheff and Garrett each had 14 for the winners, while Vanderkuy had 14 for the losers. The Wolverines lost the game at the free throw line, where they were particularly inept, making only 10 of 33 charity tosses.[42]

On to Monday, when the last games of the season were played: Illinois still had a one-game lead over Indiana. Indiana was playing Wisconsin in Bloomington, while Illinois had to take to the road and face Michigan State, 5–8 in the league. In the latter game, neither team could find the basket; Illinois was 17 of 65 for 27 percent, and MSU was 14 of 51 (28 percent). Illinois won the poorly played game, 49 to 43, relying on Don Sunderlage (16) and Rod Fletcher (12) for most of their scoring. Nevertheless, the victory clinched the Big Ten title, despite Indiana's win, 68–58, over the Badgers. Bill Garrett's 21 points led Indiana in scoring. He finished his career at IU as the all-time leading scorer with 792 points.[43] Iowa defeated Michigan to finish at 9–5, the only other Big Ten team over .500.

### Final Standings and MVPs, 1949–50

| | | |
|---|---|---|
| Illinois | 13–1 | Don Sunderlage (Big Ten MVP) |
| Indiana | 12–2 | Bill Garrett |
| Iowa | 9–5 | Franklin Calsbeek |
| Minnesota | 7–7 | "Whitey" Skoog |
| Wisconsin | 7–7 | Ab Nicholas |
| Northwestern | 7–7 | Ray Ragelis |
| Michigan State | 5–9 | Jim Snodgrass |
| Purdue | 4–10 | Carl McNulty |
| Michigan | 3–11 | Leo Vanderkuy |
| Ohio State | 3–11 | Jim Remington |

The all-Big Ten first team was composed of Sunderlage (IL), Ragelis (NU, who set a new Big Ten season scoring record of 277 points), Skoog (MN), McNulty (PU), Nicholas

(WI) and Garrett (IN). All but McNulty were also named All-American players.[44] Second team was Calsbeek and Darling (IA), Fletcher (IL) and Tosheff (IN).

The victory gave Illinois a record of 20–4, and they were the district choice for the NCAA tournament, which was to open in two weeks in three sites: Kansas City in the west, and Madison Square Garden and Reynolds Coliseum in Raleigh, North Carolina, in the east. The field was now 16 teams, and the collection of coaches in this tournament might match any that ever graced an NCAA field. In the west, Jack Gardner and his Kansas State Wildcats would face Arizona with Henry Iba's Oklahoma A&M squad waiting "down the road," along with Tippy Dye, former Ohio State coach, who had taken the Buckeyes to the 1950 NCAA Tournament, before leaving for Washington, where he would remain as head coach until 1959. His Huskies would face Texas A&M. Iba, a Hall of Fame coaching selection, as was Gardner, had already won two NCAA titles (1945 and 1946) and would win 655 games at Oklahoma A&M (renamed Oklahoma State in 1957).

In the East, Everett Case and his North Carolina State Wolfpack were set to play Villanova (coached by Al Severance, who won more than 400 games at the school) in the opener. Case, another future Hall of Fame coach, would win 374 games at N.C. State before taking early retirement in 1966 due to inoperable cancer. Frank McGuire, the coach of St. John's, would leave after the next season and go to Chapel Hill to coach at North Carolina until 1962, when he was hired to coach the Philadelphia Warriors. He returned to college coaching in 1964, coaching the University of South Carolina until 1980. He, too, was elected to the Basketball Hall of Fame. Adolph Rupp, the Kentucky coach, won NCAA titles in 1948 and 1949, and would win this tournament (and in 1958). He was also elected to the Hall of Fame. Illinois's coach, Harry Combes, won 316 games at Illinois, following a nine-year high school coaching career at Champaign High School that included two runners-up and one state championship.

At least three of the teams played practice games, allowed by the NCAA and their conferences, before the tournament as "tune-ups." Kentucky entertained Loyola and beat them, 97 to 61, as their big three (Spivey, 21; Hagan and Ramsey, 20 each) all scored at least 20. Illinois went to Manhattan to play Kansas State and the Wildcats devoured the Illini, 91 to 72. Jack Stone had 29 for KSU, while Illinois was led by Sunderlage with 18 and Beach with 12.[45]

Illinois was to open against Columbia, the Ivy League champion, who had gone 22–0 and won 31 in a row extending back to the 1949–50 season. The game would be part of a double-header in Madison Square Garden with Connecticut and St. John's playing game two. In a close contest, Illinois topped the Lions by eight points, 79 to 71. In describing the game, Wilfrid Smith lauded "Sunderlage's brilliant ball handling," Rod Fletcher's "effective dribbling" and Ted Beach's "startling long distance marksmanship." The latter entered the game with 9:20 left in the first half and made six of seven long-range shots, 10 of 17 for the game as he scored 22 points. Columbia led at the half by seven, but the Illini quickly tied the score in the second half and pulled away at the end. Sunderlage had 25 and Jack Molinas was the high scorer for Columbia with 20. Molinas would go on to a short pro career, but would be known more for his infamous involvement in the point-shaving and betting scandals of college basketball in 1961.[46]

St. John's, with their star Jack McMahon, later an NBA player and coach, defeated

Connecticut, 63 to 52, to win the right to play Kentucky, who had defeated Louisville, 79–68, in Raleigh. North Carolina State defeated Villanova, 67–62, to set up the other eastern semifinal match against Illinois. North Carolina State would be hampered by the loss of two starters (including Vic Bubas, later the coach at Duke from 1959 to 1969) who had played as freshmen, making them ineligible for the NCAA tourney since the NCAA had a ban on four-year varsity players, but that did not extend to each league's play. That would change the next year.

The NCAA was meeting at this same time and, amidst worries about gamblers getting too close to players, decided that the basketball tournament would head back to campuses and away from big-city arenas, starting the next year. NCAA Secretary-Treasurer Kenneth (Tug) Wilson, also the commissioner of the Big Ten, said that the move was "to protect the game." They also were considering "control of schedules and summer activities of players and abandoning the big arenas, such as Madison Square Garden." They would consider, at the June meeting, allowing freshmen to play varsity sports, without penalizing them for playing four years. Big Ten and the Southern Conference (which included most of today's ACC schools) had already voted to waive the freshmen rule. They would also re-examine the 16 slots for the NCAA tourney, which was 10 conference champions and six at-large berths (which did not allow for other conference competitors), since this alignment was "experimental."[47]

Meanwhile in the west, Kansas State edged Arizona, and Brigham Young defeated San Jose State, before 9,500 in Municipal Auditorium, Kansas City. Brigham Young and Kansas State would square off and Oklahoma A&M would meet Washington in the other Western semi. Kansas State and Oklahoma A&M won and met in the Western final, where the Wildcats romped over the Aggies, 68 to 44, and Washington topped BYU, 80 to 67 for third in the west.[48]

In the eastern semifinals, Illinois defeated N.C. State easily, 84 to 70, as Sunderlage scored 23, Fletcher 19, Beach 17 and Peterson 10. Kentucky topped St. John's by a 59 to 43 count. The low score reflected poor shooting; the Wildcats were 24 of 72 for 33 percent and the Redmen were 16 of 70 for 23 percent. Ramsey had 15, Spivey and Bobby Watson each had 12. For St. John's, Zeke Zawoluk had 15 and Jack McMahon had only 7.[49]

Kentucky was heavily favored to defeat Illinois, by both writers and coaches, but the game was expected to be close, and WGN in Chicago chose to televise the contest live from New York. In a tremendous battle, Kentucky edged the Illini, 76 to 74, before 16,425 in Madison Square Garden. Louis Effrat of the *New York Times* thought Illinois played well, but their foul shooting was off (22 of 35 for 63 percent) and the Illinois seven-point halftime lead evaporated. Spivey led the Wildcats with 28 points and 16 rebounds, but got some help from Linville with 14, Watson with 10 and Hagan with 8. Frank Ramsey shot 2 of 19 for just 5 points. The Illini were led by Fletcher with 21, Sunderlage with 20 and Irv Bemoras with 12. The shooting was pretty equal with Kentucky making 32 of 91 (35 percent) and Illinois 26 of 70 (37 percent).[50]

That same day, Tug Wilson, Big Ten commissioner, was testifying before the Kefauver Committee on Organized Crime, whose hearings during the entire month of March dominated the headlines across the nation. On this day sports and gambling came together in the hearing. Wilson expressed his firm opinion that no Big Ten referees were involved with gambling or gamblers, since the Big Ten did not announce their referees before the game and their names were not printed in the programs.[51]

The Kentucky victory sent them into the championship game the next week against Kansas State, while Illinois would meet Oklahoma A&M for third place. The games were to be played in "the Barn," Williams Arena, on the Minnesota campus on March 27. The Illinois and Kentucky teams shared a plane to Minnesota. In the third-place contest, Illinois pounded Oklahoma A&M, 61 to 46, with Sunderlage (17), Fletcher (14) and Beach (12) spearheading the scoring, as usual. It was a nice ending, but the elimination by Kentucky for the second time in three years in the tournament stung.

Kentucky, in an all-Wildcat final, went on to defeat Kansas State, 68 to 58; Spivey had 22 while Hagan had 10 and Ramsey 9.[52] The latter two were drafted by the Celtics and had long NBA careers, culminating in election to the Basketball Hall of Fame. Spivey was implicated, but never convicted of involvement, in the 1950 point-shaving scandals that rocked college basketball. He was blacklisted by the NBA, and he appealed numerous times, but was always denied and lost lawsuits against the league. His only opportunity in a top pro league was the short-lived American Basketball League, where he was first team all-league in 1961–62.[53] Lou Tsiopopolous, who became a starter the next two seasons, was also drafted by the Celtics and played three years in the NBA. Quite an impressive lineup, indeed.

Just as an aside, the game was reported on the sixth page of the *New York Times* sports section the next day, indicating how importantly it was viewed in the larger sports picture of the time. That same day another college basketball tournament was being played in Peoria, Illinois, at Robertson Field House on the campus of Bradley University. A crowd of 8,300 fans attended the opening of the National Campus Tourney, which was not played after that year, but did indicate an interest in many quarters for a more inclusive NCAA tournament; that would come years later.

## The 1952 Season

The NCAA decided to allow freshmen to play varsity basketball and to compete in the NCAA tournament as fourth-year players, and the Big Ten had its share of top freshmen. The rule was most likely a response to the Korean War and the potential shortage of top players, and it was rescinded the next year. Both the Southeastern and the Southern Conferences had this rule in place for at least two previous years and the Big Ten may have felt it was vital for attracting top players, especially football players. For 1952, Don Schlundt of Indiana, a 6'10" center, was clearly the best first-year player, and he made up for the graduation of Bill Garrett quite handily. His presence, as well as the ascension of top sophomore guard Bobby Leonard, made Indiana a team to contend with for the title.

"Schlundt was a tremendous offensive force, but his failings came on the defensive end. He was not as sharp as his teammates in denying ball possession and stopping his man from attacking the basket."[54] Nevertheless, Leonard felt that Schlundt would have been a star in the NBA. "The guy could really score. He had all kinds of inside moves,

... but he never chose to play pro ball, since he already had an insurance business while he was still in college. He definitely could have played. He was a scoring machine."[55]

Illinois had lost Don Sunderlage,[56] the winner of the Big Ten Silver Basketball for league MVP, but sophomore Johnny Kerr, who had played a lot off the bench in 1951, was ready to jump in and star for the Illini. With Fletcher, Bemoras, Bredar and Follmer all returning, the Illini still looked formidable and the team to beat. Peter Bjarkman, in retrospect, felt that this Illinois team was "the best of these great Illinois teams of the early 1950s."[57] Iowa would be difficult to beat, however, since Chuck Darling returned for the Hawkeyes. Ab Nicholas, a scoring machine in Madison, would make the Badgers tough, and both Minnesota, led by Dick Means, and Michigan State, coached by Pete Newell, were dark horses in the race.

The Illini began the season with seven straight victories, but Iowa was even better, winning its first twelve in a row. Illinois's seventh win was on the eve of the Big Ten opening day, in a double-header played in Milwaukee. The Illini topped Marquette, 68 to 57, and Minnesota defeated Arizona. The Gophers showed a strong balance with Kalafat getting 16, Gelle 15, and Means 10. The Illini also displayed balanced scoring in their win with Kerr leading with 15, but followed closely by Bemoras (11), Fletcher (9), Folmer (9) and Bredar (9).[58] Michigan State also started 7–0, defeating Notre Dame by 14 points to open the New Year. Gordon Stauffer and Bob Carey had 15 each, and Keith Stackhouse checked in with 15.[59]

Early scoring leaders nationally had three greats at the top: Clyde Lovellete of Kansas was averaging 27.3 ppg, Bob Pettit of LSU was scoring at a 25.6 clip, and Dick Groat of Duke (who ended up playing baseball and was 1960 MVP for the Pittsburgh Pirates) was scoring 25 ppg. The only Big Ten players in the top 20 were Darling at #6, 23.7 per game, and Kalafat, #20 at 18.4.

The Big Ten season opened with an important clash between Illinois and Minnesota and the Illini came away victorious in Minneapolis, by the score of 52 to 43. Rod Fletcher and Jim Peterson led the Illinois scoring with 14 and 12, respectively, while Bob Gelle had 18 for the Gophers. Iowa maintained its winning streak by edging Michigan State in East Lansing, 61 to 60 (ending the MSU winning streak at seven), as Darling had 20 and Bob Clifton, a 6'8" center, chipped in with 12. Indiana had an easy time defeating Michigan, 58 to 46. Bob Leonard had 18 and Sam Miranda 12, while Jimmy Skala, called "the game's most spectacular shooter," had 20 for the Wolverines. Northwestern, behind Larry Dellefield's 21, topped Ohio State at Evanston High School, and Purdue upset Wisconsin in Madison by 15 points, despite 24 from Ab Nicholas of the Badgers.[60]

Illinois had more trouble with the Badgers two nights later, but managed to eke out a win in Champaign, which Indiana could not do in Columbus, as they tumbled to the Buckeyes, 73–72. Iowa continued to win, defeating the Wolverines in Ann Arbor, while Michigan State humiliated Northwestern in East Lansing, 82 to 49. The Indiana loss was the most surprising, and it came despite a small crowd in Columbus (just 4,200) and good scoring from Leonard (19) and Schlundt (18). Paul Ebert, termed a "sofomore sensation," had 25 for the Buckeyes.[61]

The next week, the NCAA had their winter meetings and new changes for athletes were instituted. Approved were tougher academic standards for entrance to the institution, progress for degree timelines, and a revitalized "sanity" code, which had been discarded the year before by NCAA schools, addressing recruitment and scholarship support. The Big Ten adopted a version of it for the league. Basketball practice would be restricted to the period of December 1 to March 15, with only 20 out-of-season practices allowed in 24 days.[62]

Such restrictions would go into effect the next season. As for the current season, Illinois and Iowa kept up their winning. The Hawks beat Indiana by 19 in Iowa City, 78–59, and the Illini topped Michigan by 16 in Ann Arbor, 67–51. Minnesota also defeated Michigan State in Minneapolis, 55 to 49.[63] Chuck Darling (27) and freshman McKinley "Deacon" Davis (14) and Bob Clifton (12) led Iowa, while Schlundt (20), Leonard (16) and Miranda (10) carried the scoring load for Indiana. Irv Bemoras had 22 while Kerr and Bredar scored 11 each for the victorious Illini; Doug Lawrence had 12 to lead the Michigan Wolverines.[64]

A most disturbing incident occurred a couple days later when Purdue dropped a basketball player from the roster. This in itself was not news, but the player, Ernest Hall, had led his team to the Indiana State high school championship and was the "first Negro to make the Purdue varsity." Clearly, Purdue was not really comfortable with recruiting African Americans, and one perceived slip was enough to make Purdue act to rid itself of Hall. It would be at least three more years before another African American was on the Purdue roster, Lamar Lundy, who became better known as a football player for Purdue and the Los Angeles Rams.[65]

In an important match-up, especially for the Hoosiers, Illinois defeated Indiana, 78–66, in Champaign, to extend their space between themselves and Indiana in the league. Johnny Kerr had 18 for Illinois and Don Schlundt 23 for Indiana. Iowa stayed right with Illinois as they won their 11th in a row, defeating Northwestern by a score of 78 to 64. Chuck Darling had 24 to keep his league lead in scoring, while Frank Petrancek had 17 for the Wildcats, mostly from the inside.[66] Minnesota kept pace with a 10-point victory over Michigan in terrible conditions outside Minneapolis. Nevertheless, "5,584 fans braved sleet and ice" to see Weiss and Marcel (12 each) lead the Gophers to victory, 70 to 60.

Iowa made it 12 in a row the next weekend with a 76–59 victory over Minnesota in Iowa City. Darling had 34 and Bob Clifton 23 before 15,116 fans who packed the Iowa fieldhouse. Ed Kalafat (15) and Dick Means (13) led the Golden Gophers. Illinois was off for exams and Wisconsin topped Northwestern at Evanston High School by a score of 74 to 58. The Badgers hit 40 percent of their shots, which was heralded as quite good in the victory, while the Wildcats hit just 20 percent. Ab Nicholas had 16, while a freshman, Harold Grant, had 15 for Northwestern. Indiana stopped its three-game losing streak with a victory over the Boilermakers, 82–77, in West Lafayette before 10,000. Schlundt had 29 for the Hoosiers while Carl McNulty led Purdue with 22. In the battle for Michigan, in Ann Arbor, the Wolverines won 50 to 36 in a slow and sloppy game, played before 5,800.[67]

Two nights later, Indiana declared itself back in the Big Ten race with a hard-fought victory over Iowa, 82–69, in Bloomington. Schlundt (22) and Bob Leonard (18) were the main offensive weapons for the Hoosiers, while Darling continued his record-setting season with 31 points in a losing cause. "Deacon" Davis, the promising freshman, and the first African American to play for the Hawks in the Big Ten, had 19.[68] Ohio State spoiled Minnesota's night with a rally to edge the Gophers in Columbus by a score of 59 to 58. Paul Ebert tossed in almost half of those with 27 for the Buckeyes. Bob Gelle (15) and Dick Means (14) led Minnesota.[69]

Illinois came back from exam week to play a non-conference game against DePaul in Chicago Stadium the next weekend before 19,174, and the "rust" seemed obvious as the Illini eleven-game win streak was snapped by the Blue Demons, 69 to 65. Bob Peterson (16), Jim Bredar (13) and Rod Fletcher (11) led the sluggish Illini.[70] The loss had no effect, of course, on the league standings, and Illinois still led the league at the end of the month. The standings at the end of January:

| | |
|---|---|
| IL | 5–0 |
| Iowa | 5–1 |
| OSU | 3–2 |
| MSU | 3–3 |
| IND | 3–3 |
| MIN | 3–3 |
| NU | 3–4 |
| WIS | 2–3 |
| PU | 1–5 |
| MICH | 1–5 |

Northwestern moved to .500 directly after this time with an overtime win in Evanston over the Spartans, 86 to 76. Frank Petrancek, the 6'8" center, had 24, while Stauffer led MSU with 31, followed by Stackhouse's 16. Illinois remained undefeated in the league with a win over Ohio State, 66–62. Johnny Kerr led the Illini with 20, but Rod Fletcher had 17 to support him. Paul Ebert, OSU center, had 21 for game-scoring honors. The crowd of 8,565 was the largest at an OSU home game since 1939.[71]

The next weekend, most Big Ten teams were either off for exams or playing nonconference games. Iowa edged Butler, 58–57, as Darling scored 31, over half the Iowa points. St. John's defeated Purdue behind their two stars, Zawoluk and McMahon, who had 25 and 18, respectively. In the only Big Ten game, Minnesota pummeled Ohio State, which started off a big run by the Gophers toward the top of the league. In the 84–56 rout, Bob Gelle had 18, Dick Means had 17 and freshman Chuck Mencel 15.[72]

The AP poll of top teams in the nation had Kentucky at #1, followed by Kansas State and Illinois. The only other Big Ten teams in the top 20 were Iowa at #9 and Indiana at #18.

After the exam break, Illinois came back cold and lost to Iowa, 73 to 68, moving the Hawkeyes into a tie for the conference lead. The Iowa Field House was jammed way beyond capacity as 16,204 squeezed in to watch the game go down to the wire. With the score 70 to 66, the Illini fouled three times in four seconds, but Iowa declined to shoot the fouls, instead retaining the ball.[73] Iowa shot 19 of 27 free throws, but declined to shoot 18 times. Illinois had 39 fouls and all the starters fouled out. Chuck Darling had 26 points, Herb Thompson 15 and "Deacon" Davis 14 for Iowa, while Peterson had 16, Fletcher 13, and Bredar 10 for Illinois. Northwestern was edged by Michigan at Evanston High School, 71–69, while Indiana topped Purdue, 93 to 70, in Bloomington. Freshman center Don Schlundt had 35 for the Hoosiers and Carl McNulty had 36 for the Boilers. Minnesota continued winning, defeating Wisconsin 54 to 47. Chuck Mencel led the scoring with 19 for the Gophers.[74]

Two nights later Iowa and Illinois both won in easy games against Michigan (82–59) and Michigan State (84–62), respectively. Indiana lost ground by dropping a 74 to 61 game to Minnesota in Minneapolis. Mencel won the "battle of freshmen" with 20 points for the Gophers to 17 for Schlundt, who fouled out halfway through the third quarter. Leonard also had 17 for Indiana and Bob Kalafat had 18 for Minnesota.[75]

College sports were jolted a bit the next week when college presidents at the American Council on Education meetings ignored the NCAA's recommendations by supporting no awarding of strict athletic scholarships and demanding that eligibility be based on regular progress toward a degree. They also did not support freshmen on varsity teams and allowed a 3½-month basketball season between November 1 and March 15, leaving it up to the school to determine its season within that period. This would create new challenges for the next season.[76]

Iowa and Illinois won again on February 16, both with ease, once again over Purdue (90–67) and OSU (80–53), respectively. Indiana came back to beat Northwestern, 96–85, as Sammy Esposito, a future White Sox infielder, had 25 points for the Hoosiers. Minnesota continued winning (52–44 over Michigan), keeping close to the Big Ten leaders.[77]

The following Monday, Illinois pushed Indiana back with a victory, 77–70, in Bloomington, while Iowa beat Ohio State, 75–62, and Minnesota kept winning (60–58 over MSU). In the Illinois game, Johnny Kerr had 20 and Irv Bemoras 19. Leonard had 20 and Schlundt 14 for the Hoosiers. In addition to the 10,556 fans at the game, there were an estimated 250,000 fans watching on WGN television. In Columbus, Chuck Darling scored 26 to lead the Hawks, while Paul Ebert led OSU with 21. Ed Kalafat had 24 for Minnesota in their win at East Lansing.[78] In a game between two also-rans, Bob Skala had 15 and Don Eaddy 12, as Michigan defeated Wisconsin, 56–55. Eaddy and John Codwell were the first African Americans to play basketball for the Wolverines in this season.[79]

The most important contest of the season to date took place on February 23 in Huff Gym on the Illinois campus. Before 6,905 jammed-in spectators (and "thousands of televiewers"), Illinois defeated Iowa soundly, 78–62, to take a one-game lead over the Hawkeyes. Jim Bredar scored 20, Johnny Kerr 15 and Bob Peterson 13 for the Illini. Darling was the Iowa leader, as usual, with 22, and broke Ray Ragelis's one-year old scoring mark of 284 points, upping it to 291. Minnesota quietly kept pace with a 59–56 victory over Purdue, and Paul Ebert scored 40 points in an 80–67 OSU win over Michigan.[80] The Big Ten standings now had Illinois at 10–1, Iowa at 9–2, Minnesota at 10–3 and Indiana at 6–5, the only teams over .500 in league play.

After play ended on the first weekend in March, the logjam continued with some slight alteration. Iowa topped Northwestern, 77–68, in Evanston, Illinois defeated Purdue, 82–71, in West Lafayette, but Minnesota's win streak was ended by Indiana in Bloomington, where the Hoosiers won, 68 to 52. In this latter game, Dick Farley scored 23 points in a surprising performance, while Ed Kalafat had 26, 18 in the first quarter, for the Gophers. In Evanston, Chuck Darling upped his league scoring record with 23, mostly on a variety of hook shots and free throws.[81]

Two nights later, the title race ended as Iowa was upset by Wisconsin and the Illini defeated Northwestern easily, 95–74. The sold-out game in Huff Gym in Champaign was a blowout, with Johnny Kerr picking up 34 points (after entering for Bob Peterson with three minutes gone in the game) and Clive Follmer 19. Frank Petrancek had 28 for the Wildcats, but it wasn't enough. In Iowa City, the Badgers, led by Ab Nicholas with 25 points and 18 rebounds, were able to edge the Hawks, 78 to 75, despite Darling's 34 points, which set a league record for season scoring with 364 points (26 per game). Indiana also won, edging Michigan State in Bloomington, but that had no effect on the championship race.[82]

The season was over, although the Illini still had a meaningless game to play in Madison the next weekend. That week the All-America teams were announced and a Big Ten player made each of the first two teams. The first team consisted of Dick Groat of Duke, Clyde Lovellette of Kansas, Cliff Hagan of Kentucky, Mark Workman of West Virginia, and Chuck Darling of Iowa. The second team had Bob Zawoluk of St. John's, Frank Ramsey of Kentucky, Bob Pettitt of LSU, Don Meinecke of Dayton, and Rod Fletcher of Illinois. Kentucky was favored to repeat its NCAA title.[83] The first team All-Big Ten had Fletcher, Darling, Ab Nicholas (WI), Paul Ebert (OSU) and Carl McNulty (PU).

Two days later, Illinois endured an upset at Wisconsin, 58 to 48. Overall, poor shooting characterized the game, with Illinois shooting 23 percent and the Badgers 30 percent. Kerr was high scorer for the game with 16; Nicholas had 13 for Wisconsin. The game meant little, other than allowing Wisconsin to end their season with two big wins, to finish at 5–9 in league. That same day, Kansas rejected a bid by Illinois for a practice game before the NCAA, leaving the Illini to just practice among themselves for two more weeks before opening the NCAA tourney.[84]

### Final Standings and MVPs, 1951–52

| | | |
|---|---|---|
| Illinois | 12–2 | Rod Fletcher (Second team All-American) |
| Iowa | 11–3 | Chuck Darling—Big Ten MVP (First team All-American)[85] |
| Minnesota | 10–4 | Dick Means |
| Indiana | 9–5 | Bob Leonard |
| Michigan State | 6–8 | Bill Bower |
| Ohio State | 6–8 | Paul Ebert |
| Wisconsin | 5–9 | Ab Nicholas |
| Northwestern | 4–10 | Frank Petrancek |
| Michigan | 4–10 | Jim Skala |
| Purdue | 3–11 | Carl McNulty |

### The All Big-Ten Teams

First: Ebert, Darling, Nicholas, Fletcher, McNulty
Second: Irv Bemoras (IL), Ed Kalafat (MN), Bob Clifton (IA), Bob Leonard (IN), Don Schlundt (IN)

All this was announced at the Big Ten meetings, as well as the fact that the 1952–53 season would be 18 games, with each team playing two games against each league opponent. The season would begin about December 13 and end around March 9.

Little else made Big Ten basketball news until March 21, when the Illini opened the NCAA eastern regional in Chicago Stadium. In Game One, Duquesne, ranked 4th in the nation, beat Princeton, 60 to 49. The Illini, ranked #2 in the country, defeated Dayton (#11) in the nightcap, 80 to 61. Junior Jim Bredar led with 19, with sophomore Kerr picking up 13. In the other eastern site, Kentucky pounded Penn State, 82 to 54, and St. John's beat North Carolina State, 60 to 49.[86]

The next night, Illinois edged Duquesne to head to Seattle for the Final Four, by a score of 74 to 68. Bredar and Irv Bemoras had 16 each, while Duquesne was led by Jim Tucker with 29 and Dick Ricketts with 22, referred to by Ed Prell of the *Chicago Tribune* as Duquesne's "two gangling Negroes." Illinois chose to stall at the end and declined free throws seven times in the last free minutes, a common strategy under the rules of the period, when teams could choose to shoot free throws or get the ball back in the penalty period.[87]

In Raleigh, in the other eastern regional, Kentucky was upset by St. John's, 64–57, opening up the tournament for a new coterie of teams. Zawoluk had 32 and McMahon 18 in the victory for the Redmen, while Hagan had 22 and Ramsey 14 for the Wildcats. St. John's would play Illinois on March 25 in Seattle. In the west, Kansas had edged TCU, 68–64, then blasted St. Louis, 74–55, in Kansas City to set up a meeting with Santa Clara in Seattle. The Broncos had surprised UCLA, 68–59, and Wyoming, 56–53, to earn their trip to the Final Four.[88]

Kansas had no trouble with Santa Clara and future NBA star Kenny Sears, winning 74 to 55. Clyde Lovellette had 33, part of his Most Outstanding Player performance in Seattle, to lead the Jayhawks; Sears had 16 for the Broncs. The Illinois-St. John's game was much closer, but Illinois lost in the Final Four for the third time in four years, this time by 61–59. Zawoluk had 24 for the Redmen, while Bredar and Fletcher had 14 each, in the contest. It was a great season for Illinois, but another heartbreaking ending, despite the 67–64 victory (with Kerr scoring 26) over Santa Clara for third place, once again, two nights later. Kansas easily beat St. John's, 80–63, for Coach Phog Allen's only NCAA title in a tournament that he had helped create in 1939.[89]

# IV

# *The Big Ten in the New Age of Ike*

Liking Ike was all the rage in the fall of 1952, and it resulted in an overwhelming victory for Dwight Eisenhower in November. In January 1953 he was inaugurated as the nation's 34th president. Before that inauguration, he went to Korea and sought to speed up the armistice process. There were signs that the Korean War was winding down, at least for the American troops. South Korean troops were taking over on the front lines for the Americans in January, and troop withdrawals of American forces continued through the signing of the armistice in July of 1953 and the establishment of a Demilitarized Zone at the 38th parallel.

The draft continued, pulling athletes into service for a 21-month period. Basketball players were often too tall for the draft (being above 6'6" exempted a person), but, nevertheless, many were affected. The draft would continue until 1975, but the number of deferments grew during that period also. The response of many college leagues, and in 1951–52 for the Big Ten, was to allow freshmen to compete on varsity sports, but that was rescinded by the NCAA in 1952. The new season began with no first-year players eligible for the varsity, although those who had participated as freshmen the year before would not be penalized in any way at the end of their careers.

## The 1953 Season

The new Big Ten season would now be 18 games, and to accommodate that, the season began in mid–December, rather than the beginning of January. The initial favorites were Illinois, the defending champions, who had lost only Rod Fletcher from their starting five. Indiana was another team with top returning starters, as well as some impressive new players and early season wins. Minnesota was the last of the three Big Ten teams to be ranked nationally and thus to be seen as potential favorites for the Big Ten championship.

The opening game of the conference season saw Iowa top Michigan in Iowa City, 85–77, behind 22 points from Herb Thompson and 19 from Deacon Davis. Ray Eaddy, Michigan's first African American player, had 22 to lead the Wolverines, while Mead had 14.[1]

Two nights later, two more conference games were played as Wisconsin edged Iowa, 75–70, before 10,000 fans in Madison, and Illinois smashed Michigan 96–66 in Champaign. In the former game, Dick Cable with 25 and Paul Morrow with 12 topped the Badger scoring, while Deacon Davis had 23 and Ken Buckles 16 for the Hawks. Illinois's attack was led by Clive Follmer with 17 and Johnny Kerr with 16, although Kerr sat out almost the entire second half with four fouls. Milt Mead with 16 and Paul Groffsky with 14 were the Wolverines' top scorers.[2]

Indiana opened its conference season by routing Michigan, 88–60, and Purdue swung into action by edging Wisconsin, 65–59. The Hoosiers were led by center Don Schlundt with 24, while Groffsky had 15 to top Michigan scoring. Purdue's scoring was topped by Glenn Calhoun with 17 and Dennis Blind with 15. Wisconsin got 13 from Paul Morrow and 10 from Dick Cable in the loss.[3] Although Indiana's home game only attracted just more than 4,000 fans, WTTV in Bloomington estimated that more than one million fans viewed the game on television, the first of ten games to be telecast by that station.

Indiana continued its conference season with a surprisingly easy win in Iowa City, 91–72. Bobby Leonard had 27 on 13 field goals, all of which were beyond 20 feet. Don Schlundt had 23, including 11–11 from the line. Thompson (16) and Davis (13) were high scorers for the Hawks. That same night, Michigan had no trouble with Purdue, winning 88–73. Groffsky (25) and Eaddy (22) were the big scorers for the Wolverines. Runyan led Purdue with 19.[4]

The Illini were surprised by Minnesota, 77 to 73, on December 23 in Minneapolis. In an unusual occurrence, Minnesota "lived" at the free-throw line, shooting 45 and making 33, while Illinois was just 9 for 17. Bob Gelle had 19 for game and Gopher point honors, but was buttressed by Chuck Mencel and Buzz Bennett, each with 18. Irv Bemoras led Illinois with 15.[5]

Indiana had two early season defeats in non-conference play to Notre Dame, 71–70, and Kansas, 82–80; those losses would be remembered later in the year. In the last weekend of December, Illinois romped past Ohio State, 87–62, and Iowa defeated Wisconsin, 83–66, while Northwestern absorbed defeats from both Michigan State, 52–47, and Ohio State, 82–70.[6] Thirty-point individual games were seemingly common as Paul Ebert of OSU had 30 against Northwestern, Iowa's "Deacon" Davis had 30 against Wisconsin, and the season had just begun. Indiana's Don Schlundt would shatter that mark many times in the 18-game season.

Minnesota started 5–0, but lost to Marquette on New Year's Eve. They seemed to have an easy game on January 3 against a Northwestern team that had started the season at 1–4. The Wildcats, however, came into Williams Arena and defeated the Gophers, 71 to 65, before 10,162 fans. Larry Dellefield (17) and Don Blaha (16) topped the Northwestern scoring; Ed Kalafat had 22 and Chuck Mencel 14 for Minnesota. Indiana remained undefeated in the league with a tight win, 91 to 88, in Ann Arbor. Don Schlundt had 39 and Bob Leonard, a great point guard and shooter,[7] had 18 for the high-scoring "Hurryin' Hoosiers," while Don Eaddy had 25 for the Wolverines. Michigan State was making an effort at the Big Ten race and went to 2–1 in the league with a win against Ohio State, 68 to 57. Keith Stackhouse (20) and Al Ferrari (18) led the MSU scoring, but Paul Ebert, the high-scoring center for OSU, took game honors with 32 points.[8]

On the following Monday, Illinois won and Michigan State lost to Indiana, 69–62, in East Lansing. Minnesota beat Wisconsin, 64–53, in Minneapolis as Kalafat had 25 and Mencel 16, to again lead the Gophers. In West Lafayette, the Illini had an easy time in beating Purdue, 87 to 71. Johnny Kerr scored 25, Jim Bredar 23 and Max Hooper 20, to pace the Illini scoring. Indiana was led by their big guns, Schlundt (33) and Leonard (13) in their win against the Spartans, who shot just 25 percent from the floor. Al Ferrari had 22 for the losers.[9]

An early poll had Kansas State as the #1 team in the country, followed by Seton Hall, LaSalle and Illinois. Indiana was voted #7, and Minnesota was the only other Big Ten team in the top 20 at that point, checking in at #19.

The next weekend, Indiana played another of their toughest league contenders and again came out on top. Playing at home, Schlundt (17), Dick Farley (16) and Leonard (15) helped the Hoosiers, who needed two baskets by reserve Burke Scott in the last ten seconds to edge Minnesota, 66 to 63. Schlundt was benched for the fourth quarter to get more speed into the game for IU. The Gophers got 17 from Charley Bennett, 16 from Bob Gelle and 14 from Ed Kalafat, but it was not quite enough. Indiana remained undefeated in the league. Illinois stayed right on their heels with a win over Wisconsin, 71–61, and Michigan State stayed above .500 with a victory over Iowa in East Lansing.[10]

Northwestern topped Michigan 84 to 57 in newly completed McGaw Hall, which seated 7,000. Farewell to Evanston High School and "crowds" of 1500. Sophomore center Harold Grant had 19 after replacing Frank Petrancek, and Larry Dellefield had 17 for the 'Cats, while Don Eaddy (Ed Prell, the *Chicago Tribune* writer, referred to Eaddy as a "speedy Negro") led Michigan with 17. It was also noted that Northwestern's next game in Champaign on Monday, January 12, would be televised live on WGN.[11] Michigan State defeated Iowa, 68–61, to assert themselves even more in the Big Ten race. Bob Armstrong had 20 and Keith Stackhouse 15 for the winners, while Iowa got 18 from Deacon Davis.

In addition, the NCAA, from their annual conference, released a statement that they would no longer need help from the American Council on Education (ACE) or accrediting agencies like North Central Association of Colleges and Schools for their member institutions as they determined eligibility of programs and individuals. They also affirmed, ex post facto, that the University of Kentucky was suspended from basketball for the 1952–53 academic year for having used 10 ineligible players between 1948 and 1952. (Their three future NBA players, Cliff Hagan, Frank Ramsey and Lou Tsioropolous, all seniors, remained in school and played in 1953–54 as "seniors," despite being fifth-year students, having graduated the year before).

The televised game on Monday was a rout, 83 to 58, and it seemed to some that the Illini had run up the score (perhaps for television?). Irv Bemoras had 19 and Red Kerr had 18, while John Biever had 12 to lead the outmatched Northwestern Wildcats. Indiana, meanwhile, had their own rout, over Ohio State in Columbus, before a capacity crowd hoping for an upset, 88 to 68. Leonard had 22 and Schlundt 15, in limited minutes, while Paul Ebert topped Ohio State scoring with 22.[12]

The biggest Big Ten test for #6 Indiana came the next weekend when the Hoosiers hosted #4 Illinois in Bloomington. In a game worthy of pre-game hype, the action went to two overtimes before the Hoosiers prevailed by a score of 74 to 70, after ties of 61 in regulation and 66 after one overtime. Just under 10,000 squeezed into the old Fieldhouse to see Schlundt (22) and Leonard (18) lead Indiana in scoring. Bemoras (21) and

Kerr (15) paced the Illini, who dropped their second league game, and Indiana remained undefeated in the conference.[13] In other games, Wisconsin defeated Northwestern, 78–56, Minnesota topped Iowa, 65–58, and Michigan State edged Michigan, 66–64, in Ann Arbor.

On Monday, Indiana had little trouble with Purdue in West Lafayette and Illinois stopped Michigan State's winning with a 76 to 64 victory in East Lansing. In the latter game, Kerr (22) and Bemoras (15) were again top scorers, as was Al Ferrari (24) for MSU. Iowa defeated Northwestern in a fight-marred contest, 69–68, and Wisconsin won their third in a row, topping Ohio State 64–51.[14]

The next couple of weekends would have limited games because of the various final exam schedules at the Big Ten schools, but this allowed for some assessment of the season and the future prospects. Indiana was undefeated with eight victories and Illinois was at 6–2, with both Minnesota and Michigan State at 5–3. Wisconsin was at 5–4 and the rest of the league was under .500. Indiana would be hard to beat.

Bigger news than the Big Ten race was the first trial in the various charges brought for point shaving the previous years. There were 32 players named, and Bill Spivey, from the University of Kentucky, was the first defendant brought to trial. The New York City prosecutor charged him with perjury relating to his testimony regarding bribery and point shaving. After a two-week-long trial and 10½ hours of deliberation, the jury was deadlocked, 9–3, for acquittal, but unanimity was required for either conviction or acquittal.[15]

In early February, the Big Ten race finally got back its rhythm as the second semester began for all schools. The leaders continued to win and the bottom feeders continued to lose. Indiana met each new challenge with a victory. On February 7, they met a fired-up Northwestern team in McGaw Hall, before an overflow crowd of 8,710. The Wildcats took it to the Hoosiers before succumbing, 88 to 84. Schlundt led all scorers with 32, while Kurka (18) and Petrancek (16) led a balanced Northwestern attack. Two nights later, Indiana returned home and flattened Wisconsin by 18, 66–48. Illinois romped past Michigan, 92–62, and Minnesota and Michigan State moved into third by themselves with triumphs over Purdue, 74–50, and Iowa, 60–48, respectively.[16]

On Valentine's Day, neither Illinois nor Indiana felt loving toward Iowa and Michigan State, respectively. The 65–50 Hoosier win saw Schlundt get 30 and Leonard 15 to have most of the Indiana points. In Champaign, Johnny Kerr (17), Max Hooper (15) and Bob Peterson (14) led the 80–63 romp over the Hawkeyes.[17]

On February 16, Wisconsin duplicated Northwestern's hard-fought effort against Indiana, but the result was the same, a narrow victory for Indiana, this one by 72 to 70 in Madison. The shooting was not sterling, IU at 36 percent and Wisconsin at 32 percent. Both teams made 24 free throws, but the Badgers had a much better percentage (75 percent) than the Hoosiers (59 percent). Paul Morrow had his best game ever for the Badgers with 30 points, but Schlundt's 25 and Leonard's 15 pushed the Hoosiers to the win.[18]

The next weekend Indiana went 13–0 with an easy win over Ohio State, 81–67, but Illinois was upset in Iowa City, 67–62, reversing the Illinois romp of twelve days before, and the Hoosier title seemed almost assured. They were up three games with five to play. Michigan State kept winning, although against Purdue, the conclusion was likely foregone. Al Ferrari continued a fine sophomore season with 22 points in the 68 to 57 victory in East Lansing.[19]

The next day, however, Michigan State was slammed by the Big Ten for what were termed "recruiting violations." The Spartans were put on a one-year probation because of "funds raised by the alumni for athletic scholarships." A total of $33,500 was given to MSU, but only about $2500 was allocated and distributed, all to seniors (almost all in football) whose eligibility was spent. Despite that, this was seen as a recruiting violation, and recruiting, per se, was not allowed in the Big Ten. The Spartans were also being punished for poor record-keeping in this situation. Apparently, this fund-raising had begun shortly after MSU entered the Big Ten officially, in May of 1949.[20]

Indiana, meanwhile, not only continued to win, but to dominate, as evidenced by their massacre of Purdue in Bloomington on February 23. The score was 113 to 78, and various Indiana and Big Ten scoring records were broken. Schlundt played just over half the game and got 31 points; Leonard, playing about the same, had 16 in the rout.[21]

Illinois stayed alive, at least mathematically, by edging their closest foe, Minnesota, 83–82, avenging their earlier loss to the Gophers in Minneapolis. Johnny Kerr had 26 and Jim Bredar 18 to pace the Illini. Bob Gelle (27) and Chuck Mencel (16) led the Golden Gophers. Michigan State, fighting for third still, overcame Wisconsin and Coach Harold Foster's zone to win in East Lansing, 53 to 45. Ferrari (19) and Stackhouse (15) accounted for most of the Spartan scoring.[22]

Standings after 14 (or 15) of 18 games were these:

|  |  |
| --- | --- |
| Indiana | 14–0 |
| Illinois | 11–3 |
| Michigan State | 9–5 |
| Minnesota | 9–6 |
| Wisconsin | 7–8 |
| Iowa | 6–8 |
| Ohio State | 6–9 |
| Northwestern | 5–9 |
| Purdue | 3–12 |
| Michigan | 2–12 |

The first of March saw rumblings in the Middle East, which would be viewed in retrospect as ominous foreshadowing of later world troubles. The Shah of Iran left for Iraq for some rest, and Moslem insurgents then routed the prime minister, who managed to flee to safety. The incipient uprising was controlled by the end of the next day, but the seething of these insurgents did not vanish. Twenty-six years later, it would explode in the capture of the U.S. Embassy and the 444 days of hostage-holding that altered the Iranian government as well as the American presidency.[23]

Oblivious to such dealings, the Hoosiers captured the Big Ten title by beating the Illini in Champaign, 91 to 79. It was a most convincing victory, since the Illini had won 21 straight at home and needed the win far more than Indiana. Schlundt (33), Leonard (23) and Dick Farley (19) carried the load for the Hoosiers, who were continually whipped up by their coach, Branch McCracken. Even with a big lead, McCracken shouted at each time-out in the second half, "Remember you're never satisfied. We want 18 straight," referring to an undefeated Big Ten season, and the team roared back at each incitement. For Illinois, Follmer had 21, Kerr 19, and Bemoras 17, but the game was not close.[24]

Bobby Leonard recalled the game: "Huff Gym was a rough place to play. The seating put the fans right on top of you and they were on me from the start of the game, yelling things at me.... They were on me from the opening tip, and then I missed my first shot. Boy, were they going wild then. But then I hit seven shots in a row. I shut them up. It might have been the greatest game we ever played.... It was the best team game all the way around that we ever played while I was at Indiana."[25] And Phil Judson of Illinois recalled what a good shooter and player Leonard was, both in that game and overall.[26]

In the jostling for third, Michigan State defeated Purdue, 77–72, and Minnesota romped over Michigan, 83–69, leaving the Spartans ½ a game ahead of the Gophers, with one weekend to go in the season. Both teams had tough contests scheduled to end the season.

Indiana was obviously looking past Northwestern and its 5–10 record when they met the Wildcats two nights later in McGaw Hall. In what would have been a major upset, Northwestern took the Hoosiers into overtime before succumbing, 90 to 88. Schlundt (24) and Leonard (17) were the pacesetters for Indiana, while Biever (23), Dellefield (19) and Grant (18) had ⅔ of the 'Cat points. Illinois clinched second place with a 66–53 victory over Michigan State in Champaign. Max Hooper led Illinois with 17 points and Clive Follmer tossed in 16. MSU sealed their fate by shooting just 29 percent from the floor. Stackhouse and Ferrari each had 13 for the Spartans. Minnesota could not gain any ground on MSU, as they lost to Iowa 81–79 in overtime.[27]

The next weekend, McCracken's invective fell short as the Hoosiers were upset in Minneapolis, 65 to 63. Chuck Mencel hit a jumper with three seconds left to lift Minnesota to the win and send the record crowd of 18,114 home happy. In the process, Mencel also broke Whitey Skoog's school record for points in a season. Despite Mencel's heroics, Ed Kalafat (20) and Bob Gelle (16) were the high scorers for the Gophers. Leonard (17) and Schlundt (13) led the Hoosiers. The latter scored 12 points below his league average.[28] Illinois, Michigan State and Wisconsin were the other winners that Saturday.

On Monday, March 9, the season ended with Indiana winning over Iowa, 68–61, and Schlundt getting 22 points to end the season with a Big Ten record of total points (459; 18 games made this inevitable) and a 25.5 ppg average. (His overall season average was nearly the same, 25.4, seventh in the nation.) Wilson and Brondfield noted that he scored with "an amazing variety of hooks with either hand, tap-ins and soft sets."[29] Illinois solidified their second-place standing with a victory over Northwestern, 86–70, and Wisconsin defeated Michigan State, 58–51, to create a tie for third between the Spartans and Minnesota.

Schlundt and Leonard (IU), Bemoras (IL), Ebert (OSU) and Mencel (MN) were first team All Big-Ten. Second team was Kalafat (MN), Davis (IA), Kerr and Bredar (IL) and Ferrari (MSU). Schlundt led the conference in scoring, with Paul Ebert (22.6 ppg) and Chuck Mencel (17.2 ppg) trailing.

### Final standings and MVPs, 1952–53

| | | |
|---|---|---|
| Indiana | 17–1 | Don Schlundt—Big Ten MVP |
| Illinois | 14–4 | Irv Bemoras |
| Minnesota | 11–7 | Chuck Mencel |
| Michigan State | 11–7 | Al Ferrari |
| Wisconsin | 10–8 | Chuck Siefert |

| | | |
|---|---|---|
| Iowa | 9–9 | Herb Thompson |
| Ohio State | 7–11 | Paul Ebert |
| Northwestern | 5–13 | John Biever |
| Purdue | 3–15 | Jack Runyan |
| Michigan | 3–15 | Paul Groffsky |

Because the Big Ten season went so late, there was no need for Indiana to play any practice games before the NCAA tournament; their first game would be on March 13, a week after the season had ended. One of the eastern regional sites was Chicago, and Indiana would play in Chicago Stadium against the winner of DePaul and Miami of Ohio. The tournament had expanded to 22 teams with six first-round byes, one of which went to Indiana, which was ranked #1 in the country, although the NCAA did not seed teams at that time.

Indiana opened NCAA play March 12 with a victory over DePaul, 82 to 80, in Chicago Stadium before 15,984 fans, most of whom were rooting for the locals. Schlundt got 23 and Leonard 22 in the victory, but Ron Feiereisel of the Blue Demons took game scoring honors with 27. The next night, Indiana faced Notre Dame, one of three teams to defeat them in the regular season. Schlundt set a tournament record of 41 points in the Hoosiers' 79–66 victory. Said Bob Leonard, "Don just annihilated them."[30] The win earned the Hoosiers a trip to the Final Four in Kansas City. It was a sweet victory for Indiana, but more was to come.

In the west, Kansas had defeated Oklahoma A&M and Washington had topped Santa Clara to fill out the other half of the finals. Kansas then walloped Washington, #2 in the country, 79 to 53, to get to the final game.

Facing Indiana was LSU and their spectacular center, Bob Pettit; they had beaten Holy Cross in Raleigh, North Carolina, to reach the Final Four. The two teams squared off on March 17 and the Hoosiers toppled LSU, 80 to 67, as both Schlundt and Pettit had 29 points for their respective teams. Leonard had 22 and Dick Farley 10 to help Schlundt in the scoring.[31]

The championship and third-place games were played the next night and Washington defeated LSU, 88–69, as each

**Don Schlundt and Bobby Leonard, the stars of the 1953 NCAA champion Indiana Hoosiers (University Archives, Indiana University).**

team's top scorer had a great game. Bob Houbergs of the Huskies had 42 while Pettit had 36. In the featured game, it was back and forth with 14 ties in the game before "a pressure-packed free throw by Leonard with 27 seconds left finally iced the national championship" by a score of 69–68.[32] Leonard had been fouled by the Jayhawk captain, guard Dean Smith, who would go on to greater fame as a North Carolina coach. Schlundt took game-scoring honors with 30, followed by 6'9" center B.H. Born of Kansas with 26. Allen Kelley of KU had 20 and Chuck Kraak of the Hoosiers had 17. Born, who had also gotten 15 rebounds and blocked 13 shots, was named Most Outstanding Player of the tourney, but Indiana had avenged its early season loss to Notre Dame and finished at 23–3 with the national championship. Both Schlundt and Leonard were named All-America players.[33] McCracken won his second NCAA title, having piloted the Hoosiers to the 1940 title at the age of 31. He would be enshrined in the Naismith Memorial Basketball Hall of Fame in 1960 and retire in 1965.

## The 1954 Season

This new year saw the preparations for the midterm elections, almost always a disappointment for a sitting president. The fears of communism were rampant, both internally, with McCarthyism at its zenith, and externally, where the Soviet Union was extremely unstable. The death of Stalin in 1953 set off infighting for supreme power in the country. Turmoil continued until Nikita Khrushchev finally gained power in 1956, although his reign was still shaky until 1958. His greatest rival among a number of officials was Lavrentiy Beria, who was executed at the end of 1953 while Georgi Malenkov was Soviet premier.

The Big Ten wasn't quite as unstable, as the 1954 conference season began with Indiana, the reigning NCAA champions, the clear favorite to repeat as Big Ten champions, but Illinois and Minnesota were seen as major threats. This season the league returned to the 14-game slate, so once again conference play did not begin until January. All three of the pre-conference season favorites had performed as expected, with Indiana at 6–1, and both Illinois and Minnesota at 7–1. Both Illinois and Indiana would be "run and gun" teams. Illinois starter Phil Judson said that the Illini were expected to put up at least 75 shots per game by Coach Harry Combes. Teammate Bill Ridley said that the expected number was 100 shots per game.[34] Iowa was a real unknown as they returned just one starter, Deacon Davis. Five fine sophomores later to be dubbed the "Fabulous Five" were joining the team, but how good they really were remained to be seen.

By December 21, the unbeaten Indiana Hoosiers were ranked #1 in the nation and validated that with a 76–72 victory over #11 Oregon State 76–72, but the next night, the Beavers won in a game on the same court in Corvallis, Oregon, 67–51.[35]

Opening day of the conference season seemed to be easy for Indiana as they met perennial doormat Michigan in Ann Arbor, while Illinois and Minnesota met in Champaign. The Hoosiers were lucky to escape with a 62 to 60 victory as bad shooting characterized the game, with Indiana shooting 29 percent from the floor and Michigan just 23 percent. Don Schlundt (30) and Bob Leonard (16, including a 25-foot buzzer beater to win the game) had most of the Indiana points, while Jim Barron (21) and Paul Groffsky (16) led the upset-minded Wolverines.

The Illini were beaten by hot shooting (51 percent, deemed "remarkable" by the *Chicago Tribune*) by the Gophers in an 84 to 72 contest. The Illini always seemed to have trouble with the raised floor at Williams Arena.[36] Dick Garmaker, a junior transfer from Hibbing Community College, had 37 points to lead the Gophers with center Ed Kalafat chipping in with 14. For Illinois, Johnny Kerr had 31 and little (5'8") Bill Ridley, who was a good outside shooter and very fast dribbler, according to Phil Judson, had 13.[37]

Two nights later, the Illinois stumbling continued, but they escaped with a one-point victory, 66–65, in McGaw Hall over Northwestern. Kerr had 27, while Northwestern had three players in double figures: Lebuhn (15), Biever (13) and Kurka (12). The largest crowd to date in McGaw left excited, but disappointed. Indiana, meanwhile, returned home and squeezed by Wisconsin, 70 to 67, behind Schlundt (29) and Leonard (14) once more. Tony Stracka led the Badgers with 18. In Iowa City, a lineup of mostly sophomores for the Hawks defeated Michigan State, 73–63, led in scoring by their own top sophomore, Julius McCoy, who had 25 points in the 73 to 63 game. Iowa was led by Carl Cain and junior "Deacon" Davis, with 17 each.[38]

It was an exciting and unexpected opening weekend for the Big Ten, but the surprises continued the next weekend, as Illinois lost again, this time at East Lansing to the Spartans of Michigan State. Kerr led the Illini with 22 and Ridley had 13, but McCoy had 27 for MSU and Al Ferrari had 12 to top the Spartan scoring in the 60 to 59 victory. Indiana, meanwhile, traveled to Minneapolis, where Minnesota set a new record for an on-campus crowd in the U.S. as 18,872 attended the game, only to see Minnesota lose, 71 to 63. The Gophers were able to hold down Schlundt, but Leonard still had 20 and Dick White scored 17 off the bench (he had only 72 for the entire season). Garmaker led the Gophers with 18 and Chuck Bennett had 15. Iowa, looking better each week, defeated Wisconsin, 71 to 54, as sophomore Carl Cain scored 20 points and his classmate, Bill Logan, had 13.[39] In a game of no great significance in the Big Ten race, Robin Freeman had 32 for the Buckeyes in a 91–74 win over Purdue. He would be plagued by injuries during the year, but this was an auspicious start for the sophomore. Besides his great accuracy, Freeman shot the ball almost immediately upon catching it, making him that much more dangerous, noted Phil Judson, and Carl Cain called Freeman one of the best shooters that he ever saw.[40]

Another interesting and auspicious event occurred that day, to be reported the next day, when Jack Molinas, Detroit Pistons forward just selected for the NBA All-Star game, was banned from the NBA for betting. Molinas claimed that he had only bet on his own team and no claims were made to the contrary. By the end of the decade that would no longer be the case, as Molinas was integrally involved in the next big point-shaving scandal in college basketball, exposed in 1961.[41]

The top teams played the lower echelon teams in the next day of Big Ten contests with no upsets, highlighted by big scoring nights by Johnny Kerr against Ohio State (32 points), Don Schlundt against Purdue (30 points in 32 minutes) and Bill Logan, sophomore star of Iowa, with 32 against Michigan. The next weekend brought more meaningful games and, in the most significant, Minnesota defeated Iowa in Iowa City in a tight, low-scoring contest, 59 to 55. Kalafat had 20 and Garmaker 19 to dominate the Gopher scoring, while Iowa's two sophomore stars, Cain and Logan, were held to 10 and nine points, respectively. In Bloomington, the Hoosiers throttled Wisconsin by 16, 90–74, and Illinois edged Ohio State in Columbus, 82 to 78.

Victory in Columbus was made even more difficult by the venue, which was the Ohio State Fairgrounds Arena, woefully inadequate. According to opposition players, the visitors' locker room was cramped, cold, smelly and rodent-infested, making it difficult before even taking the floor.[42] Johnny Kerr had 23 for the Illini, but Robin Freeman took game scoring honors with 28 for the Buckeyes.[43]

Two nights later, Don Schlundt set a game scoring record in the Big Ten by going for 47, as Indiana routed Ohio State, 94 to 72. Iowa came back from their loss to Minnesota to topple Illinois in Champaign, 79 to 70, behind Cain's 24 points. Logan and Deacon Davis each had 14, while Kerr had 29 to lead the Illini.[44]

Indiana remained at the top, while the three "pretenders" kept knocking each other off. Mid-year exams arrived and the schedule was lighter for the next week or two. Minnesota and Iowa took turns defeating Northwestern and Purdue. Heading into February, the Hoosiers were still undefeated in the league, with Iowa and Minnesota close behind, with just one loss. Illinois and Wisconsin were 3–3 and the rest of the league was under .500. Indiana looked like they were heading to a second straight title, with only Iowa and Minnesota providing a bit of resistance.

The second half of the league season saw the top teams continue to win. Indiana had some trouble with Michigan State in Bloomington before winning 79 to 74. The score was tied eight times before the Hoosiers pulled away at the end. Leonard (26) and Schlundt (25) carried the load, while McCoy (23), Ferarri (20) and Bob Armstrong (16) provided the MSU offense. Illinois had no trouble with Michigan, 87–68, nor with Purdue, 89–55, two nights later. Minnesota struggled with Purdue in West Lafayette, winning 67–64, then was pummeled by Indiana, 90–77, on the Hoosiers' floor. In this game Schlundt set another record by going 14 for 14 from the free-throw line and 19 in a row over two games, both Big Ten records at the time. He had 36 points for the game, five more than Chuck Mencel for Minnesota.[45]

Then, the next weekend, the upper echelon of the conference was scrambled when Northwestern handed Indiana its first Big Ten loss, 100–90, and Iowa defeated the Golden Gophers, 86–82, in overtime. Illinois topped Wisconsin in overtime, 70–64, in Madison, and Purdue used only five players in its 64–50 defeat of Michigan State. This latter event was unusual anytime, but in the Big Ten, where forty fouls in a game was common, using just five players was nearly impossible. The Northwestern victory was spurred by the great offensive performances of Larry Kurka (28), Frank Ehmann (28) and Hal Grant (23), more than enough to offset Schlundt (27), Leonard (21) and Dick Farley (21) in a game where five players fouled out. Iowa's win in Minneapolis was led by the sophomores, Cain (16), Logan (15) and Bill Seaberg (14); Garmaker had 23 and Mencel 19 for Minnesota.[46]

The Big Ten had three teams in the nation's top 20 teams, according to the AP poll of mid–February: Indiana at #3, Iowa at #10 and Minnesota at #18. Duquesne was #1 and Kentucky #2. Iowa promptly lost at Ohio State, 77–69, diminishing their ranking, but Indiana, still reeling from the Northwestern loss, did manage to edge Michigan State, 63 to 61, in East Lansing on a Burke Scott 20-footer at the buzzer. High scorer was Charley Kraak with 16, his high game of the year; Don Schlundt had 15. Julius

McCoy had 20 for MSU. Illinois extended Iowa's losing streak in Iowa City with a 74–51 rout. Johnny Kerr had 26 to quiet a record Iowa crowd of 15,700.[47]

Iowa finally got back to winning in the most surprising manner, shellacking Indiana in Bloomington by 18 points, 82–64. Bill Seaberg had 21 and Bill Logan 17 to pace a balanced Iowa attack that held Schlundt to 20, with Farley following with 16. The Iowa balance would be the key to their success over the next three years. Carl Cain felt that they were the most balanced team in the country and made very few mistakes.[48] Minnesota topped Michigan, 79–70, behind Garmaker (26) and Kalafat (15), Illinois edged Wisconsin, 66–64, and the league race was close once again. With just one weekend of play left, the standings saw Indiana with a narrow lead:

| | |
|---|---|
| Indiana | 10–2 |
| Iowa | 9–3 |
| Illinois | 8–3 |
| Minnesota | 8–4 |
| Northwestern | 6–6 |
| Wisconsin | 5–6 |
| Ohio State | 5–7 |
| Michigan State | 3–8 |
| Michigan | 2–9 |
| Purdue | 2–10 |

Indiana, Illinois and Iowa all won on Saturday, February 27, to make the last Monday the possible decision date for determination of the league champion. Indiana's victory was easy, by 16 over Ohio State, 84–68, with Schlundt leading the way with 27, but getting unexpected assistance from Wally Choice with 20 in the 84 to 68 victory in Columbus. Paul Ebert got 24 points and, in the process, set a new season scoring record for OSU with 497 points (with one game remaining), an average of 23.6 ppg. In Ann Arbor, the Illini had little trouble in a 79 to 61 victory. Iowa struggled a bit in East Lansing before rallying to win 60 to 48 over the Spartans.[49]

On the following Monday, Iowa and Illinois won again to have just three losses, but Indiana was off until the next Saturday, when they would face Illinois, leaving the championship designation undetermined until that next weekend. Illinois was behind Northwestern the entire game before catching them with four minutes to play and outscoring them down the stretch. Illinois won the fourth quarter, 23 to 13, to take the game by two points, 84 to 82. Johnny Kerr had 32 to lead all scorers, while Northwestern's top scorers were Kurka and Ehmann with 16 each. The Hawkeyes had little trouble with Ohio State, despite the scoring of Freeman (21) and Ebert (19). Iowa got double-digit scoring from Logan (18), Sharm Scheuerman (17) and Cain (17) to win easily, 84 to 71. An interesting aside that had nothing to do with the league race occurred in Madison, where the Badgers, in the course of their 79 to 56 victory over Michigan State, set a new fieldhouse record for field goal percentage with 47.1 percent, long since broken a number of times. They also made 29 of 31 free throws for a Big Ten record.[50]

So Indiana would determine its own fate on March 6 as they faced the Illini in Bloomington. In a tight contest that featured poor shooting, Indiana edged the Illini, 67 to 64, to retain their Big Ten championship and prevent a three-way tie for the top spot. Schlundt led the Hoosiers with 25 and ended the Big Ten season with a record 379 points in 14 games, a 27.1 ppg average. In addition, teams were "so in their defensive zeal in trying to choke him off that they provided Schlundt with a new league high of 10.9 free throw attempts per game."[51] Bob Leonard had 22 and Dick Farley 11, while for Illinois, Kerr had 20, Jim Wright 19, and Paul Judson 11. The win put Indiana back in the NCAA tourney, which began first-round games two nights later, March 8. Indiana would play on March 12 against either Notre Dame, whom they had beaten by eleven in December in their fourth game of the season, or Loyola of New Orleans.[52]

Schlundt was followed closely in conference scoring by Johnny Kerr (25.9 ppg) Dick Garmaker of Minnesota (24.6 ppg), and the Ohio State duo of Paul Ebert (22.9 ppg) and Robin Freeman (21.2 ppg). Ebert (OSU), Schlundt and Leonard (IU), Garmaker (MN) and Kerr (IL) comprised the first team All-Big Ten. Second team was Cain IA), McCoy (MSU), Ehmann (NU), Freeman (OSU) and Mencel (MN).

### Final Standings and MVPs, 1953–54

| | | |
|---|---|---|
| Indiana | 12–2 | Don Schlundt (First Team All-American) |
| Iowa | 11–3 | Carl Cain |
| Illinois | 10–4 | John Kerr (Big Ten MVP) |
| Minnesota | 10–4 | Ed Kalafat |
| Wisconsin | 6–8 | Paul Morrow |
| Northwestern | 6–8 | Frank Ehmann |
| Ohio State | 5–9 | Paul Ebert |
| Michigan State | 4–10 | Al Ferrari |
| Michigan | 3–11 | Jim Barron |
| Purdue | 3–11 | Dennis Blind |

A new format for what were called the NCAA preliminary games was that two squads would have to each win two of three games to qualify for the rest of the tournament. Rice would face Texas for the Southwest bid, and USC would face Oregon State for the right to represent the Pacific Coast Conference. Also of note was that NBC had contracted to televise the NCAA championship game from Kansas City live on Saturday, March 20.[53]

Before the NCAA tourney started, all of the Big Ten squads held their award banquets at which they named the player the team voted as most valuable. One player would win the Silver Basketball as league MVP. The competition seemed to be between Don Schlundt, who had won the previous year, and Johnny Kerr of Illinois, with Paul Ebert a dark horse because of Ohio State's 5–9 record in the Big Ten. Kerr was a narrow winner before going on to a long and respected career as an NBA star, coach and broadcaster. The all-conference team consisted of Kerr, Schlundt, Leonard, Ebert and Dick Garmaker of Minnesota.[54]

Rice topped Texas in two straight to win the Southwest Conference berth in the NCAA tourney, and USC defeated Oregon State in two of three to join the Owls in the tournament. Kentucky, the winner of the Southeastern Conference, declined to accept a bid to the tournament because three of their starters, Hagan, Ramsey and Tsioropoulos, were ineligible under NCAA tournament rules since they were graduate students.[55] The SEC would be represented by LSU.

On March 9 in Fort Wayne, Indiana, Notre Dame defeated Loyola, 80 to 70, to set up a rematch with Indiana. In that same regional, Penn State defeated Toledo, 62 to 50. The next round of the regional was in Iowa City, and both first-round teams defeated the teams that had byes in the first round. Penn State defeated LSU, 78 to 70, and Notre Dame edged favored Indiana, 65 to 64. Bobby Leonard said, "That was a heartbreaker. We were devastated.... To this day, you know really, I haven't gotten over it. I feel like we should have gone into the books with two national championships."[56] The Irish held Schlundt to 10 and Leonard to 11 points, although Burke Scott had a great game with 20 to lead the Hoosiers as Notre Dame advanced to the regional finals. There they lost to Penn State, 71 to 63.[57] Leonard said, "Notre Dame had one game left in their system, and they saved it for us."[58] Penn State lost in the semis to LaSalle and Tom Gola, who defeated Bradley, 92–76, for the title.

The early exit by Indiana (which was still voted #1 UPI and #4 AP in the final polls) was a disappointment and a surprise, since there were many who felt the team was stronger than the national championship team of the previous year. The Hoosiers would lose Bob Leonard to graduation, but they would retain a solid core, including Schlundt, for the 1954–55 season.

## The 1955 Season

Just after the 1954 season had ended, the Senate began a series of hearings regarding the conduct of the U.S. Army and Senator Joseph McCarthy of Wisconsin. The Army-McCarthy hearings were nationally televised between April and June of 1954, and ultimately brought down McCarthy, as well as continuing to shine a light on possible communists in various sectors of the government.

Of more lasting significance was the *Brown v. Board of Education of Topeka* case, decided in May of 1954. As a result, the Civil Rights movement grew in various locations and intensities through the 1950s and 1960s. The Big Ten, which had just begun recruiting and playing African Americans in basketball, continued that growth incrementally over the next forty years.

The biggest sports story of 1954 was likely the World Series that had pitted the Cleveland Indians, who had set an American League record with 111 wins, and the New York Giants, who won the National League by five games over the Brooklyn Dodgers, who had won in 1952 and 1953. Cleveland, with its great starting pitching staff of Feller, Lemon and Wynn, were favored, but in Game One, Vic Wertz hit a deep drive to dead center with two on in a 2–2 tie in the 8th inning in the cavernous center field of the Polo Grounds, where the wall was 480 feet from the plate. Willie Mays managed to outrun the ball and caught it with his back to the plate, whirled and fired to the infield, and prevented any runs from scoring on a tag-up at second. The catch is still rated one of the greatest ever and fired the Giants to a four-game sweep of the Indians.

A month or so later, Big Ten teams started practicing for the new season. Two changes to college ball would have some effect on play. The first was relatively simple: a change from four quarters to two halves; but the second, a bonus free throw after the sixth team foul, could be decisive in some games. Many coaches were unhappy with the rule, and they were joined by prominent athletic directors like Edward "Moose" Krause of Notre Dame (who also been an All-America player in football and basketball in the 1930s), who said that the rule "will ruin the game."[59]

Minnesota and Iowa were seen as early favorites for the conference title with Indiana and Illinois, likely spoilers. Indiana started at 2–5 in non-conference play, while Illinois went 6–1, Iowa was 6–2, and Minnesota just 5–3. The Big Ten looked to be a bit weaker as a league and the league race was still a real question mark when conference play opened on January 1, 1955.

Almost immediately, there was an upset as Wisconsin toppled the Illini in Champaign by a score of 79 to 64. The lack of a strong inside presence to replace Johnny Kerr was obvious as Dick Miller (18 points) and Dick Cable (15) beat the Illini inside with regularity. Bruce Brothers and Paul Judson each had 11 to lead Illinois.[60]

Two nights later, the upsets continued as Northwestern defeated Minnesota, 74–72, while Indiana had an easy time with weak Michigan, 95–77. Schlundt had 30, while Jim Barley and Burke Scott had 19 apiece in the romp in Bloomington. Indiana shot 60 free throws, making 43. In Evanston, the Wildcats edged the Gophers as Grant (20), Mast (19) and Ehmann (18) scored all but 17 of the Northwestern points, while Dick Garmaker, with 32, had nearly half of Minnesota's points.[61]

Iowa, clearly unimpressed with the Badger upset of Illinois, pounded Wisconsin in Madison, 86 to 69, led by Seaberg (22) and Davis (21). Cable had 25 for the Badgers. Ohio State defeated Michigan State, 83–76, in Columbus as Robin Freeman, the nation's leading scorer, scored 39 points. Al Ferarri had 28 for the Spartans.[62]

Early basketball polling had Illinois (#12), Minnesota (#13) and Iowa (#14) in the top 20. The top-rated teams were Kentucky, Duquesne, North Carolina State, LaSalle and San Francisco.

The next week, Illinois and Minnesota seemed to rise to their ratings as the Illini crushed Indiana, 99–75, and Minnesota edged Iowa before 16,000 in Iowa City. Garmaker had 25, Chuck Mencel 20, to lead the Gophers, while Logan (24) and Cain (20) led the Hawks in a contest that saw the lead change hands 17 times before Minnesota won, 81 to 80. In Champaign, Bill Ridley had 20, Paul Judson 19, and a host of others scored in the win. Don Schlundt had 34 points for the Hoosiers, but had little help as only one other player, John Wood, scored in double figures with 10.[63]

In a nationally televised contest (on CBS), Michigan State blew out Wisconsin, 94 to 77, behind Julius McCoy and Duane Petersen, who each scored 19. Dick Cable had 25 for the Badgers. As college basketball began to take a firmer hold on television, pro basketball was still struggling for viewers. The NBA was also on television, but local stations could choose not to air it, and some big markets, like Chicago, did not do so; a movie often was shown instead.[64]

On Monday the three favorites all won, Illinois and Iowa, easily over Purdue and Michigan State, respectively, and Minnesota over Indiana, which was clearly not a good team for 1955. Schlundt had 30, but again had little help. Minnesota got 30 from Garmaker, while Mencel and Tucker each had 14 in the 88 to 74 victory.[65]

The next Saturday, January 15, was more of the same, with Minnesota embarrassing Purdue, 102–88, and Illinois edging OSU, 86 to 78, as Illinois found an inside presence with sophomore George BonSalle, who had 22 points. Iowa was idle, but defeated Illinois on Monday by 92 to 80 in Iowa City. Logan (19) and Cain (16) were the top scorers, with Ridley taking game honors for Illinois with 32. BonSalle had 13.[66]

The co-leaders, Minnesota and Iowa, lost the next Saturday, with Minnesota losing to Michigan State, 87–75, and Iowa to suddenly powerful Northwestern, 93–73. Ehmann (31) and Grant (26) led the Wildcat offense and completely dominated Iowa in Evanston. Michigan State got 27 points each from McCoy and Ferrari to spank the Gophers, who had 30 from Garmaker and 20 from Mencel. The Spartans hit 50 percent (37 of 74) from the field, a percentage worth noting.[67]

On Monday, both leaders (4 wins, 2 losses) got back on track; Minnesota got new help from their 6'11" center, Bill "Boots" Simonovich, who had 28, while Garmaker had 24 in their 102 to 82 pounding of Northwestern in Minneapolis. Iowa beat OSU easily in Columbus, as Robin Freeman missed the contest with an ankle injury. John Miller led the Bucks with 26, while Iowa continued its balanced scoring, led by Cain's 20 and Logan's 17.[68] Carl Cain noted that besides their balance, the Iowa team also really knew each other's moves. He remembered that he only needed to put one thumb up as the guards brought the ball upcourt, then would cut "back door" and he'd receive the pass and score an easy layup.[69]

In the last contest of January, as many schools were off for exams, Minnesota was taken to six overtimes by Purdue before finally beating the Boilermakers, 59 to 56. Minnesota played a zone and Purdue refused to try either to penetrate it or shoot from the outside. Neither team altered tactics and the score was at 47-all after regulation. Four overtimes were scoreless. Garmaker and Blind had 18 for Minnesota and Purdue, respectively. The victory gave Minnesota a ½-game lead as the season moved into February.[70]

Although Minnesota and Iowa were the leaders, the only Big Ten school in the latest top ten poll was Illinois at #10, with Kentucky and USF the top-rated teams nationally, as of early February. Big Ten action then resumed, and Iowa tied idle Minnesota for the lead with a 76–67 win over Purdue, which was nationally televised. Milt "Sharm" Scheuerman, who would become the Iowa coach from 1959 to 1964, led the Hawks with 23 points, five more than Bill Seaberg. In Champaign, the Illini defeated Northwestern, 104–89, in a foul-plagued contest. Paul Judson had 31 and Bill Ridley had 21 while the Northwestern "big three," Ehmann (27), Grant (26) and Mast (19), scored 80 percent of the Wildcat points. Ohio State got Robin Freeman back, and he scored 23 in the OSU victory over Indiana, a team heading in the wrong direction. Schlundt had 22, as did Jim Barley, and Burke Scott had 18, but the Buckeyes prevailed in Columbus, 90 to 87.[71]

Minnesota was back on the court on Monday and they made short work of Ohio State to take the Big Ten lead. Dick Garmaker had 27 and Chuck Mencel 18 in the 82 to 56 romp. Robin Freeman had 17 and Charlie Ellis 16 to top the Buckeyes. Illinois stayed close with a victory in Ann Arbor, 81 to 80. Football star Ron Kramer led the Wolverines with 25 points in the loss.[72] In an interesting aside, that day the *Chicago Tribune* ran a story that headlined the interest among colleges in adopting the NBA's 24-second rule. This was a bit ahead of reality, as the NCAA men finally adopted a shot clock in 1985 (45 seconds, altered to 35 in 1993). The NCAA women had adopted the 30-second shot clock in 1970.

The Big Ten standings, halfway through the season, looked thusly:

| | |
|---|---|
| Iowa | 5–2 |
| Minnesota | 5–2 |
| Illinois | 4–2 |

|             |     |
|-------------|-----|
| Michigan State | 5–3 |
| Northwestern | 4–4 |
| Ohio State | 3–4 |
| Michigan | 2–3 |
| Indiana | 2–4 |
| Wisconsin | 2–4 |
| Purdue | 2–6 |

The next weekend, two games were vital to the championship: Illinois was in Minneapolis and Iowa entertained Indiana, always a challenge with Don Schlundt. The Gophers and Illini went to two overtimes before Minnesota won, 86 to 81, before a national television audience on CBS. In Iowa, the Hawks won easily and held Schlundt to 17 in the 90 to 75 win. Seaberg (20), Logan (19) and Davis (19) paced the Iowa attack, but the game's high scorer was Indiana's Wally Choice with 29.[73] Indiana was no longer a factor, except as a spoiler, and perennial cellar-dweller Michigan was more assertive with the emergence of Ron Kramer.

Minnesota shut down Indiana in Bloomington, 80 to 70, with only the continued emergence of Choice as the leading Indiana scorer (26) of real interest in the game, despite Schlundt's (21) having topped 2,000 points for his career the week before. Iowa won neatly over OSU, 79–68, as did Illinois over Michigan State, 90 to 72. Michigan got 28 from Kramer in edging Northwestern in Ann Arbor, 72 to 70.[74]

The following Saturday, Minnesota beat Michigan, 74–65, and Iowa won 78–69 over Michigan State, the latter victory the first ever for the Hawkeyes in East Lansing. Northwestern continued Indiana's slide by defeating them in Bloomington, behind Ehmann's 29 and Grant's 25. Schlundt (29) got support from his new no. 2, Wally Choice, with 25, but they fell short, 85 to 78. Illinois routed Wisconsin. On Monday the Gophers and Hawks won again, against Wisconsin (71–69) and Illinois, respectively. Iowa was impressive in routing Illinois by 19, 89–70, in Champaign, to remain ½ a game behind Minnesota at 9–2 to the Gophers' 10–2 with Illinois back at 7–4.[75]

Two weekends left and it was a two-way race. Iowa won to tie for the lead on Saturday, and on Monday clinched a tie for the title with a big win in Minnesota, 72 to 70. Somehow 20,176 fans got into Williams Arena to watch the game and see five Iowa starters play the entire game. There were 17 lead changes before the Hawks, led by Logan's 25 and Cain's 16, were able to edge the Gophers, who were led by Mencel's 27 and Garmaker's 18. Illinois won to clinch 3rd in the conference.[76]

The monthly basketball poll now had San Francisco and Kentucky as #1 and #2 with LaSalle and Marquette just behind. Iowa was #12 and Illinois #17 in what was obviously a down year for the league. Still, Iowa had possibilities and they were able to ensure their visit to the NCAA tournament when Minnesota lost to Wisconsin, 78–72, the next Saturday. In a relatively meaningless game, Don Schlundt had 47 points in his final college game as Indiana defeated Ohio State, 84 to 66. Iowa, needing some rest, no doubt, after not playing their bench at all in the previous game, lost to Michigan, 71 to 58, with the starters only playing ⅔ of the game. Tom Jorgenson had 26 for the Wolverines.[77]

**Final Standings and MVPs, 1955–56**

| | | |
|---|---|---|
| Iowa | 11–3 | Bill Seaberg |
| Minnesota | 10–4 | Chuck Mencel (Big Ten MVP) |

| | | |
|---|---|---|
| Illinois | 10–4 | Paul Judson |
| Michigan State | 8–6 | Al Ferrari |
| Northwestern | 7–7 | Frank Ehmann |
| Purdue | 5–9 | Don Beck |
| Indiana | 5–9 | Don Schlundt |
| Wisconsin | 5–9 | Dick Cable |
| Michigan | 5–9 | Ron Kramer |
| Ohio State | 4–10 | John Miller |

League MVP was Chuck Mencel of Minnesota. He was a senior, so he got the nod from teammates over Garmaker, who had finished second (24.9 ppg) to Schlundt (26.4) in league scoring. Ehmann was right behind at 24.5. Iowa had no one standout and Mencel was from a team that had tied for second. Schlundt's great four years in which he never missed a game resulted in just one league MVP, with the Indiana collapse in 1954–55 a large factor in his not being voted MVP that year. Iowa, the conference champion, did not place a man in the league's top scorers, but four of their starting five averaged in double figures with the fifth averaging 9.5.[78] The all-conference first team consisted of Schlundt, Mencel, Garmaker, Robin Freeman (despite his missing six league games), Bill Logan of Iowa, Paul Judson of Illinois, and Frank Ehmann of Northwestern.[79] Bill Mokray had a slightly different take on this, probably reflecting the media and not the coaches. He listed the first team as Ehmann, Schlundt, Logan Garmaker and Mencel. The second team he had was Ferrari (MSU), Paul Judson (IL), Ron Kramer (MI), Scheurman (IA) and Freeman (OSU).[80]

The 1955 NCAA tournament was again 24 teams, with the Big Ten winner drawing a bye, as did the SEC winner (Kentucky), the Ivy League winner (Princeton), the Southern Conference winner (Duke), the Southwest Conference winner (SMU), the Big Eight winner (Colorado) and the Western Athletic Conference winner (Utah).

In the first round, Marquette defeated Miami of Ohio and Penn State topped Memphis to set up matches between Marquette and Kentucky, and Iowa and Penn State. These games would be in McGaw Hall on the Northwestern campus. In a major upset, Marquette defeated Kentucky, 79 to 71 to face the PSU-Iowa winner. The Hawks played a magnificent game in throttling Penn State, 82 to 53, with Cain scoring 21, Davis 19, and Seaberg 13. Iowa would meet Marquette the next day, March 12. In another fine team game, Iowa defeated Marquette, 86 to 81, to advance to the Final Four in Kansas City. Center Bill Logan had 31 for Iowa, but three other starters scored in double figures: Seaberg (12), Scheuerman (11) and Cain (10).[81]

Iowa (#5 in the nation) would meet defending NCAA champion LaSalle, led by Tom Gola. The Explorers (#3 in the nation) had defeated West Virginia 95–61, Princeton 73–46, and Canisius 99–64, to move on to Kansas City, where they were now installed as favorites to beat Iowa after sailing through the early rounds. The two teams met on March 18 and LaSalle edged the Hawks, 76–73, with Gola leading all scorers with 23 points. Logan and Cain led Iowa with 20 and 17, respectively.[82]

The next night, the western champion, University of San Francisco, led by Bill Russell and K.C. Jones, won its 26th game in a row to win the NCAA title. They had been pressed to the end by Oregon State and their 7'3" center, Harvey "Swede" Halbrook, and squeaked out a 57–56 victory in the western regional finals, but they had little trouble with LaSalle, winning 77 to 63. Bill Russell had 23 and K.C. Jones 24, overshadowing Gola with 16. In the third-place contest, Colorado pounded Iowa, 75–54, to end the Hawkeye season on a low note.[83]

Despite the loss in the Final Four, Iowa would be the favorite to win the Big Ten in 1955–56, since four of their starters would return. Minnesota would also have a good squad, as would Illinois, and some other dark horse might emerge.

# V

## *Sticking with Ike and the Traditional Powers*

The biggest sports story of 1955 was the victory of the Brooklyn Dodgers in the World Series, their first championship ever. The period was also one of shifting baseball franchises that reflected both economic changes and a new demographic, as a slow, steady movement to the west and South from the northeast and Midwest began among sports franchises. The Boston Braves became the Milwaukee Braves, the Philadelphia Athletics moved to Kansas City, and the St. Louis Browns bucked the trend and moved to Baltimore and became the Orioles.

The Civil Rights movement became more prominent, especially with the pronouncement of *Brown v. Board of Education of Topeka II* in 1955 that school desegregation proceed with "all deliberate speed." This emphasis was also seen in universities and their sports teams. The Big Ten in 1955–56 was still largely composed of white players, but the number of prominent African Americans was growing slowly, but steadily.

### The 1956 Season

Returning starters on both Iowa and Illinois (plus sophomore Don Ohl) made them the initial favorites for the Big Ten title, but Ohio State was seen as having good possibilities, since Robin Freeman would be back from an injury-shortened season, and he would be joined by rugged Frank Howard (future major league baseball star). In the December 1956 Holiday Tournament in Madison Square Garden, he set records of 32 rebounds for a single game and 75 rebounds for three games.[1] Michigan would return their MVP, Ron Kramer, but little else of note. Purdue would return Lamar Lundy, Joe Sexton and Frank Lorenz, a solid base to build upon. Regarding those basketball-playing footballers, Ron Smith, who sat on the Northwestern bench for two years, thought that Lundy was neither a good shooter nor defender, but took up so much space at 6'7", 270, that he was a useful rebounder. Kramer, on the other hand, was quite agile. He was also the strongest guy in the Big Ten and no one wanted to get in his way. Northwestern was seen by at least one magazine (*Dell Sports*) as the likely winner of the Big Ten.[2]

Illinois would rely on pressuring the ball and trying to put up 75 shots a game, according to Phil Judson of the Fighting Illini team from 1954 to 1956. They had what one might call a fluid offense and would simply shoot when they were open. Coach Combes didn't want too many passes before shooting and would never yell at a player for a bad shot, said Judson.[3]

The Big Ten season opened on January 2, 1956, with a televised game, Michigan State at Illinois. In Chicago, the game was shown on the ABC affiliate, WBKB, but the "network" was composed of independent channels, a total of nine, which could show the selected game each week, usually on Saturday afternoon, but beginning on a Monday night to begin the season.

Returning long-range shooters Paul Judson (23) and Bill Ridley (21) pushed the Illini to the win over MSU, 73 to 65, despite Julius McCoy's game-high 25 points. It was not a pretty game, as early season contests often aren't, and Illinois was down 10 at the half, after shooting just 21 percent in the period. It was "ragged basketball most of the way" (noted the *Chicago Tribune*), but the Illini were victorious.

Other games that night had Purdue winning in Madison, 78–66; Indiana defeating Northwestern, 94–81, in Bloomington, and Ohio State beating Michigan, 79–66, in Ann Arbor. Robin Freeman had

Lamar Lundy, one of the first African Americans to play basketball for Purdue, but who gained greater fame in football as a member of the Los Angeles Rams "Fearsome Foursome" in the 1960s (Purdue Athletics Communications).

28 for the Buckeyes, while top scorers for Indiana were Wally Choice with 26 and Charlie Brown with 22. Dick Mast had 28 and Glen Lose 25 for the losing Wildcats.[4]

The first Saturday of the league season brought what would turn out to be one of the biggest upsets, as Michigan State edged Iowa 65 to 64 in Iowa City. Iowa led 64 to 61 with 2½ minutes to go, but missed free throws and had turnovers to hand the game to the Spartans. Purdue went to 2–0 with an easy victory over Northwestern, 68 to 54. Michigan surprised Minnesota, 81–79, in overtime in Minneapolis, and Indiana beat Wisconsin in the nationally televised game on CBS, 75 to 71. Charlie Brown and Archie Dees had 19 each, but Brown and Paxton Lumpkin were both gone by the end of the month because of academic ineligibility, and Indiana's season would move steadily downward.[5]

Two nights later, Illinois became the early leader in the conference as they remained undefeated after topping Wisconsin, 96 to 77, while Purdue lost to Michigan, 74 to 67. Illinois was led by Bill Ridley (25) and center George BonSalle (26). Iowa defeated Ohio

State, 88 to 73, despite 37 points by Robin Freeman. Carl Cain and Bill Seaberg had 19 apiece for the balanced Hawkeyes. In Ann Arbor, Jim Shearon (18) and Ron Kramer (15) topped the Wolverine scoring, while Thornburg (16) and Lundy (15) led Purdue. Dave Tucker (23) and Jed Dommeyer (21) were the Gopher leaders as they edged Indiana, 77–71, in Minneapolis, despite 21 from Brown and 16 from Choice.[6]

The next weekend revealed a number of insights: Illinois could score a lot and would be a tough team to beat; Indiana would be mediocre (and this was before losing Lumpkin and Brown at the end of the semester); Robin Freeman would be one of the top scorers in the country; Iowa would give Illinois the toughest test in the league. The Illini won their third in a row and scored the highest point total by any visiting team in Bloomington with a 96 to 72 victory over the Hoosiers. George BonSalle led with 28, followed by Ridley's 22. Dees (22), Choice (15) and Brown (15) topped Indiana. Robin Freeman had 32 in a 100–98 OSU double-overtime win over Wisconsin in Columbus. Dick Miller, Badger center, matched Freeman's total. Iowa pounded Minnesota, 84–62, with the usual Hawkeye balance, led by Seaberg's 18 and Schoof's 16.[7] In the nationally televised game, Purdue squeaked by Michigan State, 66–62, in East Lansing. Joe Sexton had 21 for Purdue while Julius McCoy of MSU led all scorers with 24.[8]

The following Monday, Illinois repulsed the resurgent Boilermakers with a 92 to 76 thumping as BonSalle (21) and Judson (18) combined for 39 points. Sexton led Purdue with 24 from his guard's spot. In his last IU game, Charlie Brown led the Hoosiers to a 79 to 70 win over Michigan State. Brown had 19, but game-scoring honors went to McCoy of MSU with 34. At this same time, the 1956 Winter Olympics opened in Cortina, Italy, with the American delegation led by USOC Chair "Tug" Wilson, the Big Ten commissioner.[9]

Purdue went to 4–1 in conference play on January 21, upsetting Ohio State, 70 to 69, despite 24 points from Robin Freeman. Frank Howard chipped in 12 for the Bucks. The Boilermakers were led in scoring by Joe Sexton and Lamar Lundy, both of whom scored 21. Iowa kept pace with a 78 to 67 win over Michigan, with Logan (28) and Schoof (22) having big nights. Ron Kramer had 23 for the Wolverines. Two nights later, the two winners tangled in West Lafayette, and Iowa's "Fabulous Five" edged the Boilermakers by a 67 to 63 score. Logan led the Hawks in scoring once again with 21, while Sexton had 23 for Purdue. Ohio State bounced back to crush Northwestern, 92 to 41, as Freeman (30) and Howard (21) combined for 51 points.[10]

At this point in the season, the defending NCAA champion Dons of San Francisco, riding a two-year win streak, were the acknowledged #1 team in the country, with Dayton, Kentucky, North Carolina State and Illinois rounding out the Top Five. Despite winning the Big Ten, the previous year, advancing to the Final Four and returning four of five starters, Iowa was ranked only #13 at this point, and no other Big Ten teams were in the top 25. Iowa's strength was in having five players who were nearly interchangeable as each of the five could shoot, handle the ball and play inside or out, although they generally stayed in their positions. "They also were a real team, sharing the ball and playing together," noted Ron Smith.[11]

The nationally televised Big Ten game on January 28 was Northwestern at Minnesota, one of only two Big Ten games, because the schools were taking final exams for the fall semester. The other was Ohio State at Michigan State, and MSU won 94 to 91.

Big scoring was the order of the day, led by Freeman's 46 in a losing cause and McCoy's 40. Freeman was one point short of Don Schlundt's Big Ten record of 47. In the nationally featured game, Minnesota routed Northwestern, 83 to 67, before the smallest crowd to ever see a basketball game in Williams Arena (5,043).[12] This would surely cause the Big Ten to rethink their television agreement the next year.

The Gophers continued their home stand two nights later, meeting Illinois, who pounded them, 95 to 84. Both George BonSalle and Paul Judson had 24 and Bruce Brothers had 23 to account for ¾ of the Illini scoring. Jed Dommeyer had 27 for Minnesota to take game scoring honors. The other league game that evening saw Purdue top Northwestern, 78 to 68. Dan Thornburg topped Purdue with 22, while Jay Hook, the future Cincinnati pitcher, had 20 to lead the Wildcats.[13]

The start of the second semester saw some players' careers end abruptly because of academics, but overall, the league changed little regarding standings. Iowa and Illinois were the leaders with Purdue and Ohio State the other teams above .500. Northwestern was the only winless team in the conference. Wisconsin opened the month of February by extending Northwestern's winless streak, 79 to 55, while Purdue toppled Minnesota by eight points. In the nationally televised game, Robin Freeman scored 41 to lead the Buckeyes to a 100 to 82 coast over Indiana in Bloomington.[14] Both Bill Ridley of Illinois and Ron Smith of Northwestern agreed that Freeman was the best shooter in the Big Ten, in terms of both range and accuracy.[15]

The following Monday saw a number of big games, either for their league significance or for geographical "bragging rights." In East Lansing, the Spartans topped the Wolverines by 10, 86–76, for the Michigan "title." Julius McCoy had 41 to snuff out any Michigan hopes. The losers were led by Kramer's 20. In Madison, Iowa kept the pressure on Illinois by beating Wisconsin, 78 to 74. Bill Logan had 26 and he was aided by Bill Schoof and Bill Seaberg, who each had 16. Mueller (21) and Miller (19) led the Badger scoring. In a game that WBKB, the ABC affiliate in Chicago, televised, Illinois remained undefeated in the league with a 92–89 victory over Indiana in Champaign. Paul Judson had 30 while BonSalle and Ridley each tossed in 16; Indiana was led by Wally Choice with 34 and Archie Dees with 22.[16]

Robin Freeman was all–Big Ten in 1955 and 1956 and was Big Ten MVP his senior year. He averaged more than 30 ppg both years (The Ohio State University Archives).

The Winter Olympics continued, but a bigger story was the speculation on whether President Eisenhower would run for re-election that fall. He had had a significant heart attack during his first term and there were those who felt that he might return to his Gettysburg farm and leave the nomination to Vice-President Richard Nixon, or possibly Senator Robert Taft of Ohio. Ike said that he expected to announce a decision by March 1.

Eisenhower's decision would coincide with the end of the Big Ten race, which still looked to be a two-team contest, led by Illinois. Both the Illini and Iowa won twice the next weekend. Illinois routed Ohio State, 111 to 64, with Judson and Ridley peppering the Buckeyes for 23 each in a game where they played only ¾ of the contest. Frank Howard had 23 for OSU, but Ridley's harassing held Freeman to just 12, his low for the conference season. Iowa coach Bucky O'Connor played his starters the entire game in defeating Northwestern 70–65. Logan had 22 and Seaberg 17, while Northwestern countered with Dick Mast's 24, Jay Hook's 14 and Bill Schulz's surprising 15 and 23 rebounds. Northwestern remained winless.[17]

On Monday, February 13, Illinois swamped Michigan, 89–66, to go 8–0, in a game again seen on WBKB in Chicago. Ridley and BonSalle had 25 each, while Ron Kramer took game scoring honors with 26 for Michigan. In Iowa City, 14,800 were in attendance to see the Hawkeyes go 7–1 as they beat Purdue, who dropped to 6–3 in the league. Seaberg had 21 and Carl Cain had 15 for the Hawks. Purdue was led by Lamar Lundy's 25 and Joe Sexton's 15.[18]

The pattern for the league leaders continued the next weekend as Illinois went to 10–0 and Iowa to 9–1. Illinois toppled Michigan State in East Lansing by 20 points, 96–76, and then smashed Purdue 102 to 77 in Champaign. The former game was on national television and Coach Harry Combes cleared the bench in the rout. Paul Judson scored 18 and Bill Ridley had 16 to lead the scoring, but Julius McCoy took game honors with 26. Against Purdue, Judson (21) and Ridley (18) again led in the runaway, while Sexton (26) and Lundy (16) topped the Purdue scoring.

Iowa had no trouble with Wisconsin, 80 to 66, on Saturday the 20th, but struggled on Monday in Bloomington, edging the Hoosiers, 87 to 83. In the former game, Logan (19) and Cain (18) topped the scoring, while in the latter game, Cain and Seaberg each had 23. Indiana countered with 24 from Choice and 20 each from Thompson and Dees. Purdue's loss and Ohio State's victory over Wisconsin moved the Buckeyes to third, ahead of Purdue. In the Ohio State win, Robin Freeman had 27, to solidify his spot at the top of the league scoring race.[19]

On the next weekend, the league race was altered permanently, as Ohio State upended the Illini in Columbus by a score of 87 to 84. Bill Ridley, who had held Robin Freeman to 12 in their previous meeting, was slowed by a back injury, and Freeman went off for 43 points.[20] Frank Howard added 18 and 24 rebounds. George BonSalle had 34 points and 23 rebounds for Illinois and Paul Judson had 17, but the Illini could not overcome the Bucks and fell into a tie for first when Iowa won, 83–73, in overtime in Minneapolis. Cain (24), Seaberg (20) and Logan (18) were the top scorers for Iowa, while Tucker (25) and Dommeyer (20) led the Gophers. Bill "Boots" Simonovich, the big center, did not play for Minnesota, and Coach Ozzie Cowles offered no explanation. Purdue remained in fourth with a victory at home against Michigan State, 63–56. Joe

Sexton had 29 and 11 rebounds, and Lamar Lundy contributed 10 points in the victory. Julius McCoy had 19 for the Spartans.[21]

In a game with no championship implications, Indiana edged Northwestern in Evanston, 84 to 82, before a television audience of 96 stations. Dees (22), Bryant (18) and Choice (16) led the Indiana attack, but most impressive was the Hoosier free-throw shooting, 36 of 39, in the game.[22]

The following Monday, the 27th, both leaders won again, Iowa easily over Northwestern, 86–68, and Illinois rallying to win at home against Minnesota, 97 to 81. BonSalle with 34 and Schmidt with 23 were the big scorers for Illinois. Iowa had their usual balance in the victory, led by Logan (21) and Schoof (16).[23]

The Big Ten race would come down to the last weekend of the season, the first weekend in March. In the other "big race," President Eisenhower announced on the first of March that he would, indeed, stand for re-election in November and continue to enforce civil rights in higher education in the face of intransigence on the part of Southern states invoking issues of states' rights, allowing them to maintain segregation.

In a situation that could not have been planned better, Illinois and Iowa met in Iowa City on March 3 with the winner gaining a one-game lead, most likely the Big Ten title, and a trip to the NCAA tournament. The game failed to live up to the anticipation, as Iowa destroyed Illinois, 96 to 72. Logan (26), Seaberg (19) and Scheuerman (18) were instrumental in the win. George BonSalle had 34, but the next high scorer was Bill Ridley with 11 for the Illini. Iowa made 34 of 38 free throws, Illinois 12 of 21.[24]

Ohio State clinched third in a 96 to 84 victory over Michigan State as Freeman had 43 for the Bucks. Purdue seemed to have fourth clinched as they beat rival Indiana in Bloomington, 73 to 71. Joe Sexton had 23, which set a new Purdue career scoring mark, breaking the record set by Carl McNulty in 1952. Lamar Lundy had 17 to aid in the victory.[25]

The last Monday of the season saw Illinois needing a win to tie, but only if Iowa were to lose. That all became moot when previously winless Northwestern, playing five starters the whole way, upset the Illini, 83–82, before 8,500 in McGaw Hall. Glen Lose had a phenomenal game with 31 points and 15 rebounds, and Dick Mast was steady with 22 points for the Wildcats. For Illinois, BonSalle had 27 and Harve Schmidt 22, but that wasn't enough. With the pressure off, Iowa was able to coast to an 84–73 victory over Indiana in Iowa City. Wally Choice took game scoring honors with 25 for IU, while Seaberg (21) and Cain (18) topped the Hawkeye scoring. In the battle for third, Purdue ended up tied as Minnesota upset Ohio State, leaving both Purdue and OSU at 9–5 in the conference. In that latter game, Minnesota was paced by Dave Tucker with 28 and Jed Dommeyer with 26 in the 95–89 contest.[26] Robin Freeman had 33 to finish the season with 445 points (31.8 ppg), just six short of Don Schlundt's season record. Overall he averaged 32.5 ppg, second in the nation. Julius McCoy was second in the conference with 27.3 ppg (fifth in the nation) and George BonSalle averaged 22.9 ppg for third.

### Final Standings and MVPs, 1956

| | | |
|---|---|---|
| Iowa | 13–1 | Carl Cain |
| Illinois | 12–2 | Bruce Brothers |
| Ohio State | 9–5 | Robin Freeman (Big Ten MVP) First Team All-American |

| | | |
|---|---|---|
| Purdue | 9–5 | Joe Sexton |
| Michigan State | 7–7 | Julius McCoy |
| Indiana | 6–8 | Wally Choice |
| Minnesota | 6–8 | Dave Tucker |
| Wisconsin | 4–10 | Dick Miller |
| Michigan | 4–10 | Ron Kramer |
| Northwestern | 1–13 | Dick Mast |

The all-conference team had Cain, McCoy, Paul Judson and Freeman as unanimous choices. Bill Logan of Iowa and BonSalle alternated at center on most teams selected, and Bill Ridley received first team selection at guard.[27] Mokray listed the media choices as Cain, McCoy, BonSalle, Paul Judson, and Freeman. The second team was Wally Choice (IU), Joe Sexton (PU), Ron Kramer (MI), Bill Seaberg (IA) and Dick Miller (WI).[28]

Iowa would play in the second round of the NCAA tournament on March 15 against the winner of Morehead State and Marshall, which turned out to be the former. Iowa then defeated them, 97 to 83, to set up a meeting with Kentucky, who had overwhelmed Wayne State, 84 to 64. Carl Cain had 28 against Morehead, Bill Logan had 17 and Bill Schoof 15. It was not a pretty game with a total of 69 fouls, split nearly evenly between the two squads, 35 for Iowa, 34 for Morehead. Neither team dazzled at the free-throw line, with the Hawks going 35 of 52 for 67 percent and the Eagles 33 of 53 for 62 percent.

Bucky O'Connor coached Iowa from 1951 to 1958 before dying in a car crash. His Final Four starters are pictured: Milt "Sharm" Scheuermann, Carl Cain, Bill Seaberg, Bill Logan, Bill Shoof (Hawkeye Yearbook Collection, University Archives, The University of Iowa Libraries).

The Midwest regional was played in Iowa City, so this was a great advantage for Iowa, who met Kentucky the next night in a packed arena. In that contest, the Hawks knocked off Kentucky, 89 to 77, as Cain went for 34 and Scheuerman 22 in the win. This put Iowa in the NCAA Final Four to be played in McGaw Hall in Evanston, Illinois.[29]

In the east, Temple, led by their great guard tandem of Hal Lear and Guy Rodgers, defeated Canisius, 60–58, to gain the eastern title. In the west, SMU, led by Jim Krebs, overwhelmed Oklahoma City, 84–63, for the title, and in the far west, San Francisco continued its unbeaten skein by whipping Utah, 92–77, for the regional title. The four finalists would play on March 22 and the championships would be on March 23, 1956, in McGaw Hall, the Northwestern home court.

In the first national semifinal, Iowa defeated Temple, 83 to 76, to become the fifth Big Ten finalist in the 18 years of the NCAA tourney. Bill Logan scored 26, Carl Cain 20 (with 15 rebounds) and Bill Schoof 18 (with 18 rebounds) to spur the Hawkeyes to victory. Lear and Rodgers each had 32 points to total nearly 85 percent of the Temple scoring, but the Owls made only six of 17 free throws, compared to Iowa's 25 of 38. In the Western final, USF ran away from SMU, 86 to 68. Mike Farmer led the scoring with 26 and Bill Russell had 17 and 23 rebounds. Krebs led SMU with 24 points.[30]

The championship contest was USF all the way, as they completed an undefeated season and won back-to-back titles. Bill Russell had 26 points and 27 rebounds, but did *not* get the Most Outstanding Player of the tournament. Instead, it went to Hal Lear of the third-place Temple Owls, who scored 48 points in the meaningless game for third place, which they won, 90 to 81, over SMU. For Iowa, Cain and Seaberg each had 17 in the championship game.[31]

The USOC changed its manner of selecting basketball Olympians that year: rather than having the NCAA champions, an NCAA all-star team, the AAU champions and the military champions in a tournament, there was just the NCAA all-stars, the military all-stars, and the AAU champions and runners-up. The Phillips 66ers of Bartlesville, Oklahoma, coached by Gerald Tucker, won the tournament, handing Bill Russell his first loss in two years. Chuck Darling, the former Iowa star, was the big hero for the 66ers, getting 21 points and 10 rebounds in the 79–75 victory over the college all-stars.[32] There were then selections made from the other teams by the coach, and Russell and K.C. Jones from USF were chosen, as well as Carl Cain. The team played exhibitions in the summer and early fall since the Olympics did not begin until November in Melbourne's summer. Nevertheless, the American team easily won the Olympic Gold Medal and continued the unbeaten streak for the USA, which had begun with the opening of Olympic basketball in 1936.[33]

## The 1957 Season

The Olympics had taken place just after the Hungarian Revolution, and the tension between the Soviet Union and their oppressed puppet, Hungary, played out in bloody fashion in the pool of Olympic water polo, where the Hungarians defeated the Soviets, 4–0. The Cold War had gotten hotter and fears of world war were more prominent. Domestically, the United States continued in the midst of the Civil Rights Movement, now most prominently seen in the actions of Southern governors to prevent integration on their flagship campuses like the Universities of Mississippi, Alabama and Georgia.

The Big Ten had slowly but surely integrated their basketball teams over the four years since Bill Garrett had become a starter and star for Indiana. Three of the team MVPs from 1956 were African American and almost every team had at least one African American starter.

The first part of the 1950s had been dominated by the three "I" teams: Indiana, Illinois and Iowa. The 1957 season would be one of the tightest races in Big Ten history, and the winner would be a surprise in many ways. Illinois and Iowa were again favored to win the conference, and they started the non-conference season strong, going 5–1 and 3–1, respectively. Purdue was also 5–1 and was seen as another contender, as was Ohio State. Overall, the league was seen as weaker, following the graduation of many of its top stars. Iowa had lost five starters, their fabulous five who had taken them to the Final Four two seasons in a row. Illinois had lost Ridley and the Judson brothers, but still had BonSalle, Schmidt and Don Ohl. These retainees convinced the Big Ten coaches to pick Illinois to win the conference,[34] but both the Illini and Iowa opened the Big Ten season with losses. Iowa lost to Michigan State, 73–65, in a contest the Iowa players felt that they should have won, according to Nolden Gentry, who started for the Hawks in his sophomore year.[35] Northwestern, with mostly sophomore starters, won their opener against Wisconsin, 75 to 54. Purdue edged Michigan State in East Lansing and Indiana defeated Michigan.

Indiana's Archie Dees scored 26 points and had 20 rebounds in the 73–68 Hoosier victory over Michigan, which was led in scoring by Ron Kramer with 22. Lamar Lundy had 21 and Bill Grieve 17 in Purdue's 72–71 victory over Michigan State. The Spartans exhibited a balanced attack, with George Ferguson picking up 17 and Jack Quiggle and Chuck Bencie each getting 14, but they fell short at the end. Ohio State got 24 points from Frank Howard as the Buckeyes won, 72–60, in Iowa City, relying on superior rebounding (59–40) to solidify the victory. The big upset was Minnesota edging Illinois in Minneapolis, 91 to 88. The Gophers were led by their capable veterans, Jed Dommeyer (27), George Kline (26) and Dave Tucker (21), while Illinois countered with BonSalle (28), Schmidt (17) and Roger Taylor (15).[36]

In what seemed to be an early "must win," Illinois topped Iowa, 81–70, on the first Monday of the season, two nights later. Don Ohl had 21, Hiles Stout 17, to lead the Illini scoring while Tom Payne (28) and Clarence Wordlaw (11) led Iowa. Ohio State and Indiana each went to 2–0 with wins over Purdue and Wisconsin, respectively. Ken Sidle had 26 for the Buckeyes in the 75–68 victory, while Ed McCormick led the Boilers with 20. In Bloomington, Dees continued his great scoring with 28, while Litzow led Wisconsin with 19, in the 79–68 contest. Michigan evened its record and kept Michigan State winless with a 64–63 triumph in East Lansing. George Lee with 20 and Pete Tillotson (15) led the Wolverines, while Hedden (16) and Ferguson (15) topped the Spartans.[37]

The next weekend, a lot of teams went to 2–1 and Wisconsin continued its winless season with a pounding by Illinois. Michigan beat Northwestern, 64–63; Purdue topped Indiana, 70–64; and Iowa crushed Minnesota, 89–66. Tillotson (16) and Lee (15) again led Michigan, but Northwestern scoring was topped by two sophomores, center Joe

Rucklick with 27 and speedy guard Nick Mantis with 13. In West Lafayette, Lundy (15) and Grieve (13) led Purdue and were matched by Dees and Dick Neal, each with 15 in the tightly-defended game. Iowa ran away from Minnesota as Payne had 24 and Jim McConnell 22. The Illinois-Wisconsin game in Madison was the Big Ten game of the week, shown on WBKB, ABC-TV in Chicago, and in seven other states (the Big Ten states).[38]

The following Monday, Illinois seemed to be flexing its muscles as the Illini walloped Indiana, 112 to 91, in a contest that set Big Ten, Illinois and Huff Gym scoring marks. Ohl and Schmidt had 25 and BonSalle 20 to lead the Illini parade. Dees (28) and Neal (17) were tops for Indiana. Ohio State toppled Minnesota and Michigan kept Wisconsin winless, 71–62. The Ohio State game set a new attendance record for the recently opened St. John Arena with 12,250 on hand to watch the 85 to 73 victory, led by Frank Howard's 31 points.[39]

Michigan State went to 0–3 the next weekend, losing badly to Ohio State, 70 to 51, before 13,750 in Columbus, another St. John Arena record. Iowa and Minnesota beat the Big Ten doormats, Wisconsin (70–47) and Northwestern (73–62), respectively. Two nights later, Northwestern shocked Iowa with a 70 to 63 victory in McGaw Hall. Nick Mantis had 17 and Jay Hook 14 for N.U. Clarence Wordlaw led the Hawks with 23.[40]

There were only two league games the next Saturday, reflecting the uneven scheduling as the schools began final exam schedules for the fall semester. Ohio State remained unbeaten at 6–0 with a ten-point victory over Northwestern, 83–73, Frank Howard and Jim Laughlin each scoring 20. Michigan State gained its first victory by winning in Minneapolis, 72 to 59. Coach Fordy Anderson's squad got 23 points from Larry Hedden and 15 from sophomore center Johnny Green to secure the win.[41]

Ohio State appeared to be in the driver's seat halfway through the conference season, with a number of other teams right behind, but then Michigan State turned from doormat to tiger (to mix metaphors). After surprising Minnesota for their first league victory, they returned to East Lansing to face Ohio State, who had beaten them by 19 points just nine days before. Undeterred, the Spartans beat the Buckeyes, 73 to 64, to scramble the conference race and save Michigan State's season. Jack Quiggle had 21, Hedden had 17 and Johnny Green had 16 rebounds to go with nine points. Purdue beat Northwestern 81 to 77 in Evanston to move closer to the Buckeyes.[42]

As of February 1, the standings in the Big Ten were:

|  |  |
| --- | --- |
| Ohio State | 6–1 |
| Purdue | 4–1 |
| Illinois | 3–1 |
| Michigan | 3–1 |
| Indiana | 2–2 |
| Michigan State | 2–3 |
| Minnesota | 2–3 |
| Iowa | 2–3 |
| Northwestern | 2–5 |
| Wisconsin | 0–6 |

Illinois, tied for third, but still very much a factor with just one loss, was dealt a crippling blow when it was announced that George BonSalle, senior center, would be lost to the squad because of academics. He had failed a sociology course and would no longer be eligible, ending his college career. Hiles Stout would have to step in as the starter at center.[43] In the first game after that announcement, Illinois lost to Purdue, 85 to 74. Stout got 20 for Illinois and both Schmidt and Ohl had 14. Bill Greve had 26 for the victorious Boilermakers and Joe Campbell, a 5'7" guard, had 18.[44]

Michigan State won their third in a row, easily defeating Northwestern, 77 to 63. Ferguson and Andregg each had 16 for the Spartans, while center Joe Ruklick had 20 and Dick Johnson had 14 for Northwestern. That same day (February 2), Indiana defeated Iowa, 82–66, in the televised Big Ten contest, from Iowa City. Neal and Hudson had 21 each and Dees 18, while Iowa scoring was topped by Sebold with 19, and Payne with 13 (but only one of nine from the line).[45]

On the following Monday, George BonSalle played his last game as an Illini and went out with a 27-point performance as Illinois defeated the league-leading Buckeyes, 82 to 66, in Champaign. Roger Taylor chipped in with 20, while Frank Howard led Ohio State with 30.[46] Purdue lost to Michigan, 66 to 54, in Ann Arbor as the two future NFL greats, Kramer (17) and Lundy (14), led their respective squads in scoring. Indiana remained in third place, topping Northwestern, 74 to 56.

A tight Big Ten race became even more jumbled the next weekend as Indiana handed Ohio State another loss, 69–59; Iowa defeated Purdue, 74–67; Minnesota defeated Michigan, 82–62; and Michigan State topped Illinois, 70–64. Indiana's victory pushed them to the top of the league as the only team with just two losses. Dees (17), Bryant (16) and Neal (15) were the major contributors for the Hoosiers, who held Frank Howard to just nine points, although he did snare 19 rebounds. Michigan State won its fourth in a row as George Ferguson had 19, while both Larry Hedden and Johnny Green scored 14. Don Ohl (15) and Harve Schmidt (13) led the Illini, who were outrebounded 56 to 31. Clearly, BonSalle was missed.[47]

Two nights later, Indiana maintained its lead with a 91–72 win over Minnesota, while Michigan State won its fifth in a row to stay right on the heels of the Hoosiers. The Spartans edged Purdue in West Lafayette, 68 to 66. Illinois sprinted to victory over Northwestern, 104 to 97, setting a school and Huff Gym record by shooting 52 percent (40/77) from the floor. Schmidt had 34, Ohl 20, for the Illini, and Rucklick 33 for the Wildcats. Indiana's victory was much easier and Archie Dees was superlative with 29 points and 20 rebounds in the game.[48]

The next weekend, it became clearer that MSU and Indiana were the powers in the league. Both won on Saturday and Monday with convincing victories. Indiana beat Iowa (90–76) and Northwestern (87–74) handily, while Michigan State had no trouble beating Iowa, 77–67, but were pressed a bit in their victory over Illinois, 89–83.

In the midst of this race, the Big Ten revisited the sanitary code, particularly the question of athletic scholarships, rather than scholarships only based on need for athletes. In a narrow victory, finalized in March, the league presidents voted to retain their version of the sanitary code, basing athletic awards solely on need and limiting such awards to 100 athletes per year at any one school. This allowed the league to maintain the appearance of not being "football factories" (this really was about football, with the other sports just "hanging on"), like the Southeastern and Southern Conferences.

Virgil Hancher, the president of the University of Iowa, sent a six-page letter to

John Hannah, the president of Michigan State. Hannah chaired the Big Ten presidents' group, which was determining their position on athletic scholarships versus the "sanitary code's" strict awards based on need. Hancher's argument for athletic scholarship, which ultimately prevailed after many years, was pretty straightforward and sensible. He equated exceptional athletic skill and subsequent awards to those awarded for journalism prowess or excellence in arts and performance, which no one questioned. He mocked the efforts to copy the British notion of the amateur gentleman (and this from someone with a degree from Oxford) as hypocritical. He saw the temptations for "lawlessness" in the awarding of scholarships as unrelenting and advocated that the only way to "reduce temptation to the minimum is to make direct, above-board provision for room, board, tuition, books (to be paid for directly by the universities) and perhaps a small allowance for incidental expenses (the only money to be given directly to the athlete)." He also noted that this proposal was already being followed in the Big Seven (now the Big 12), but should not be precluded from being adopted because they did it first.[49] Alas, Hancher's letter did not alter the vote, and as noted, the charade of need-based scholarships would continue for a number of years, driven as always by football, with basketball and the other sports carried in its wake.

The next Saturday (February 23), Indiana and Michigan State continued to keep pace with one another. Indiana topped Wisconsin, 85–74, for their seventh win in a row, behind Dees with 21 points and 14 rebounds. Hallie Bryant had 20 points and 12 rebounds. Michigan State topped Minnesota, 70–65, for their eighth win in a row. Ferguson with 19 and Hedden with 16 paced the Spartans. On Monday, however, Indiana was surprised by Michigan, 87 to 86, in Ann Arbor, and Michigan State easily defeated Wisconsin, 78–62, to move the Spartans into a tie for the conference lead at 9–3. Johnny Green had 20 points and nine rebounds to lead the Spartans, while in Ann Arbor, Archie Dees had 39 points and 10 rebounds in defeat. M.C. Burton was the Wolverine leader with 21 points and 13 rebounds.[50]

In other games, Illinois made the ceremony highlighting the opening of St. John Arena less than happy for the 13,330 Buckeye fans by taking a 79 to 72 game. Don Ohl's 19 and Harve Schmidt's 16 offset a great game by Frank Howard, who had 23 points and 14 rebounds. This dropped Ohio State to 8–4, a full game behind the two leaders with one week to go in the conference season. In Minneapolis, George Kline had 40 points and 16 rebounds as the Gophers defeated Iowa, 102 to 81.[51]

In a fitting final weekend to the season, Indiana came to East Lansing to meet the Spartans in a battle for the conference title. In a surprisingly easy contest, Michigan State defeated the Hoosiers, 76 to 61, to clinch a tie for the title. The second largest crowd in Jenison Fieldhouse history (13,817) saw Larry Hedden get 22 points and Johnny Green 13 (and 19 rebounds) to offset Archie Dees's 28 points (and 12 rebounds). Ohio State managed to stay just a game back by defeating Northwestern, 84 to 70. Ken Sidle (22 points and 13 rebounds), Jim Laughlin (17 points) and Frank Howard (16 points and 15 rebounds) were the Ohio State stars, while Joe Ruklick (21 points, 13 rebounds) and Jay Hook (19 points) paced the Wildcats.[52]

The exciting weekend continued with more upsets on Monday. Michigan State's 10-game winning streak was broken at Michigan by the Wolverines, 81 to 72. Ron Kramer had 21 to lead Michigan, while Hedden had 22 for MSU; Quiggle had 15 and

Green 12 with 12 rebounds. Indiana rallied to beat Illinois in Bloomington, 84–76, and tie for the title. Archie Dees had 25 to end the season with an average of 25.5 ppg, tops in the league. (He was tenth in the country in overall scoring at 25.0.) Dees also garnered 13 rebounds in the game. Ohio State, also with a chance to tie for the title, lost in Minneapolis, 76 to 69, and Minnesota tied the Buckeyes for third in the league. Three Gophers (Kline, 20 points and 15 rebounds; Tucker, 15 points and 16 rebounds; and Dommeyer, 15 and 13) were the big heroes for Minnesota.[53]

For the first time ever, the Big Ten winner had as many as four losses, and the title was shared by Indiana and Michigan State. The two had only met one time during the season and MSU had won, but the stated reason for their getting the NCAA tournament nod was the same rationale used after that for the selection of Rose Bowl participants in football, i.e., MSU was selected because the Hoosiers had been to the tournament most recently.[54]

**Final Standings and MVPs, 1957**

| | | |
|---|---|---|
| Michigan State | 10–4 | George Ferguson |
| Indiana | 10–4 | Archie Dees (Conference MVP) |
| Ohio State | 9–5 | Gene Millard |
| Minnesota | 9–5 | Jed Dommeyer |
| Purdue | 8–6 | Lamar Lundy |
| Michigan | 8–6 | Ron Kramer |
| Illinois | 7–7 | Harve Schmidt |
| Iowa | 4–10 | Dave Gunther |
| Wisconsin | 3–11 | Bob Litzow |
| Northwestern | 2–12 | Joe Ruklick |

"It wasn't a big scoring year for Conference individuals and there was only one other (besides Dees) 20-point shooter in the league—Frank Howard (20.0), Ohio State's 6'8" strongman and magnificent rebounder at forward." All Big Ten were Dees, Howard, George Kline of Minnesota, Don Ohl, Jack Quiggle and Johnny Green.[55] Mokray listed Dees, Howard, Kline, Ohl and Quiggle, with Harve Schmidt (IL), Jerry Dommeyer (MN), Johnny Green (MSU), Hallie Bryant (IU) and Gene Millard (OSU) comprising the second team.[56]

Twenty-three teams were invited to the 1957 NCAA tournament. Michigan State received a bye for the first round and would face the winner of the Notre Dame–Miami (OH) game on March 15. The Irish defeated Miami, 89 to 77, and then squared off with MSU in Lexington, Kentucky, on the campus of the University of Kentucky. Johnny Green had a superlative game with 20 points and 27 rebounds to pace the Spartans to an 85–83 victory. Quiggle had 18, Ferguson had 16 and Hedden 13 (with 11 rebounds) to back up Green. In Game Two, the host Wildcats defeated the University of Pittsburgh, 98 to 92. John Cox had 26 and Vern Hatton 24 for Kentucky, heavily favored to defeat the Spartans the next night. In a stunning upset, Michigan State continued its improbable season by defeating #3-ranked Kentucky, 80 to 68, despite being down 12 points at the half. MSU held Cox to 17 and Hatton to 15, while Quiggle had 22, Ferguson 15 and Green 14 (with 18 rebounds). It was only Kentucky's fifth loss at home in 15 years! The Spartans would go to Kansas City as the Mideast representative in the Final Four.[57]

The games of the 1957 Final Four were some of the closest ever played in that situation. Michigan State was just a basket away from the championship game as they lost in the semifinals to North Carolina, the eastern regional champion. The Spartans were clearly the big underdogs, as evidenced by Richard Dozer's appraisal in the *Chicago Tribune*: "The Spartans, the 'poor cousins' of this 19th National Collegiate Athletic Association basketball tournament, will carry their 16 won and 8 lost record into Municipal Auditorium to battle the Proud Tar Heels, who have not been beaten in 30 games this season."[58] On that same day, the *Tribune*, with broad appeal and circulation in northern Indiana, as well as the Chicago area, had a photo of the "Hoosier Spartans": Chuck Bencie of Gary Froebel High School, Larry Hedden of Gas City Mississinewa High, Jack Quiggle of South Bend Central, and Coach Fordy Anderson, who had starred as a prep at Gary Emerson High.[59]

Michigan State had won 12 of their last 13, so they were not exactly destitute, but University of San Francisco, the two-time defending champion, had won 14 of 15 since regaining guard Gene Brown, who led the Dons in scoring, from an injury. The last member of the Final Four, the Midwest Champion, was the University of Kansas, led by Wilt Chamberlain.

The MSU-UNC game was called "the most thrilling game in school history" by Peter Bjarkman. As he went on, "The two scrappy clubs battled exhaustingly through three tense overtime periods that witnessed 21 ties and 31 lead changes in all."[60] Both squads had many opportunities to win, with MSU missing a free throw at the end of the second overtime that would have sealed the game. MSU led 54 to 49 with 5:42 to go, but could not hold on. Neither team shot well, the Spartans at 29 percent and the Tar Heels at 31.5 percent. Lenny Rosenbluth, the UNC All-America player, scored 31, but on 11 of 42 shots from the field (of UNC's 89). Jack Quiggle had 20 points for MSU and Johnny Green had 27 rebounds to go with his 10 points. The final score was 74 to 70, North Carolina.[61]

Meanwhile, Kansas and Chamberlain coasted to victory over USF, 80 to 56, as Wilt scored 31 points. KU would meet UNC the next night after MSU and USF played for third in the tourney. In the latter contest, USF topped the Spartans, 67 to 60, to end the MSU season on a sour note. In the championship game, KU and UNC played another triple overtime game before UNC edged the Jayhawks, 54 to 53.[62]

The college coaches met, as they usually did, at the tournament site and passed a number of rules for 1957–58, which would impact the game very much. First, they added the 1-and-1 free throw after the sixth foul for all college games. Second, goal tending was clearly defined and outlawed. Third, free movement on the end line out of bounds would be allowed under one's defensive basket after a made basket. Fourth, the clock would be stopped on all whistles. Fifth, there would no longer be a need for odd and even numbers on home and away jerseys, although many schools retained this.

## The 1958 Season

In October of 1957, the Soviet Union launched a rocket into space that contained a satellite named *Sputnik*, which changed the way the world viewed the Soviet Union, space technology and the future. The Soviets had "beaten" the USA into space, and there was scrambling at all levels of American institutions to overcome this "defeat."

Money for space technology, science generally, and education would flow for at least the next 20 years. The National Science Foundation, which had been established in 1950, saw its budget soar as America sought to catch up to the Soviets and win the space race. The ramifications would be felt politically as well as scientifically and educationally.

All this would mean little to the Big Ten basketball race, other than the fact that some thought Johnny Green might be capable of jumping into space, but that was speculation based on little empirical data. Green and his MSU Spartans were considered the co-favorites to capture the 1958 Big Ten title, along with Indiana and Ohio State, but the latter two had not exactly sparkled in the non-conference season. IU had gone 1–6 and OSU 1–7, hardly championship caliber, as the Big Ten went 44–31 in pre–conference season games. Of course, in 1957, MSU had started its conference season 0–3 before winning 10 of its last 11 contests to advance into the NCAA tournament, where they went to the Final Four. MSU was ranked in the Top 10 in the nation as the Big Ten season began.

*Sport Magazine* named three Big Ten players to their pre-season All-America team, lending some credence to the quality of the teams of those players. Selected to the first team (along with Wilt Chamberlain, Guy Rodgers, Elgin Baylor and Barney Cable) was Frank Howard of Ohio State, as the magazine noted: "No one in college today is any more rugged than this Buckeye star.... Right now, Ohio State has him and that one fact places the Buckeyes among the top contenders for the 1957–58 Big Ten crown."[63]

Archie Dees was selected to the second team, and *Sport* observed that he "figures to keep Indiana in contention against Ohio State and Michigan State for the conference title." A Michigan Stater, Jack Quiggle received an Honorable Mention and Nolden Gentry of Iowa was named a "sophomore to watch."[64] Quiggle and John Green were noted as "heading a fine cast" at Michigan State.[65]

Iowa added Nolden Gentry to its starting line-up, one of the first African Americans to start in the Big Ten since its integration by Dick Culberson in 1944 and, postwar, Bill Garrett in 1948. Gentry had enrolled at Iowa with an unusual "connection." His mother took piano lessons in Rockford, Illinois, from Deacon Davis's sister, so his "recruitment" had been somewhat subtle! His Rockford West team had won Illinois state titles in 1955 and 1956, and he and his high school teammate Bob Washington enrolled at Iowa, which was just a three-hour drive from Rockford.[66]

Besides the various rules changes described earlier, one additional rule was important to some schools. The NCAA tightened its rules for NCAA tournament play, decreeing that freshmen would be ineligible for playoffs, as well as seniors who had played as freshmen. This three-year participation limitation would affect more than those conferences that still allowed freshmen to play at the varsity level. For those leagues that continued to do so, their conference champions would no longer automatically qualify for the NCAA tournament.[67]

Only Northwestern had a significant change among Big Ten teams, as they had named Bill Rohr as their new coach, replacing Waldo Fisher, who had compiled a 35–75 record (21–53 in conference) in five years at the helm. Rohr had won 157 games at Miami (Ohio) in seven years, winning four Mid-American Conference titles.

The conference opened on January 4 with a full slate of games. In the one most potentially important to the conference race, Ohio State upset Michigan State in Columbus, 70–56. Larry Huston (14) and Frank Howard (13) were the leading Buckeye scorers, while Anderegg (16), Quiggle (15) and Kulas (11) led the Spartans. Joining OSU as winners were Illinois, Indiana, Minnesota and Michigan. The Illini beat a weak Wisconsin team, 64 to 59, in Madison, with Don Ohl (21) and sophomores Govonor Vaughan (16) and Manny Jackson (12), Illinois's first African American starters, leading the way.[68]

Indiana managed to stop Northwestern's upset bid in Bloomington, 68 to 65, as Jerry Thompson scored 23 and Archie Dees was held to 14. Willie Jones (20) and Joe Ruklick (17) were the high scorers for the Wildcats. Minnesota defeated Purdue, 83 to 76, in Minneapolis, and Michigan beat Iowa, 73 to 65, in Iowa City, in a game that Nolden Gentry thought the Hawkeyes should have won.[69] George Kline had 31 for the Gophers and M.C. Burton had 21 points for the winning Wolverines.[70]

On the following Monday, Iowa defeated Illinois, 70 to 68, to bring both teams to .500 records. Indiana lost to Purdue 68–66, to have those teams also at .500. Michigan went to 2–0 with a win over Wisconsin. The national poll saw West Virginia at #1; Kansas, #2; North Carolina, #3; Kansas State, #4; Mississippi State, #5; San Francisco, #6. The highest Big Ten teams were MSU at #14 and Illinois at #17.[71]

The Illini ranking would not last, as they lost to Indiana the following Saturday, 89–82. Dees had 26 and Pete Obremsky 23, to lead the Hoosier attack. Vaughan (28), Ohl (26) and Jackson (22) were nearly the entire Illinois offense. Michigan State got into the win column with a victory over Purdue, 84 to 75, as Larry Hedden had 29 for MSU, and Northwestern pounded Michigan, 93 to 72. Wisconsin surprised Ohio State with a 67 to 64 win in Madison, as Bob Litzow and Walter Holt led the Badgers to victory. Frank Howard had 24 for OSU.[72]

Northwestern continued to surprise on Monday night, January 13, winning in Iowa City, 82 to 80. Indiana defeated Minnesota, 85 to 64; Wisconsin kept Illinois spiraling downward with a win in Champaign, 72 to 70; and Michigan topped Ohio State, 72 to 63.[73]

Indiana's decisive victory seemed to make them the early favorite to win the league, but they were then upset by Iowa before 13,349 in Iowa City the next Saturday, 79 to 75, to bring them back to the pack. Dave Gunther, with the help of a lot of good picks from Gentry, had 22 points and 18 rebounds to lead the Iowa offense, and Archie Dees had 33 points and 19 rebounds in a losing cause. Michigan State beat Northwestern, 83 to 78, behind Johnny Green's 22 points and 22 rebounds. Ohio State and Purdue also won, against Minnesota, 95–79, and Wisconsin, 62–47, respectively.[74]

Tug Wilson called this season one in which "the league failed to produce a team that was truly the class of the conference. As a result, every night on the schedule was you-take-it-I-don't-want-it-night."[75] That pattern continued on January 20 as Wisconsin toppled Michigan State, 66 to 52. The usual one-two punch of the Badgers, Holt and Litzow, had 22 and 15, respectively, with Wisconsin shooting 38 percent (23/60) from the field. MSU shot just 27 percent (18/66) with Anderegg (16) and Green (10) their only players in double figures. OSU beat Iowa that same evening, 70 to 64, behind a great night for Frank Howard with 22 points and 18 rebounds.[76]

The Big Ten's relative weakness was illustrated the next weekend when Notre Dame defeated Illinois, 81 to 67, in Chicago Stadium. Former Chicago prep star and future

Minneapolis/Los Angeles Laker Tom Hawkins scored 39 points. Earlier in the year the Irish had pounded Indiana by 15 points.[77]

That same night, Michigan State defeated an improving Northwestern squad, 74 to 60, and Iowa edged Minnesota, 73 to 71, in Minneapolis. Johnny Green led the Spartans with 22 points and 16 rebounds, and Nick Mantis took game scoring honors with 25 for Northwestern. The Iowa win was the Big Ten televised game of the week, and Kline (30) and Ron Johnson (25) had 55 of the Gopher's 71 points. Gunther (19) and Wordlaw (16) led the more balanced Hawkeye offense.[78]

The next weekend Michigan State jumped back into the conference lead with an 88 to 64 victory over Minnesota, while Michigan lost to Purdue, 72 to 66, Iowa defeated Ohio State, 66–64, and Illinois beat Northwestern in overtime, 102–98. The Illini "run and gun" style, which Harry Combes's team had as a trademark, was exciting again, but a sad casualty was Coach Combes's father, who succumbed to a heart attack at the game. Indiana lost two nights later to Minnesota, 69–66, to keep the league a jumble.[79]

The national poll reflected the writers' perception of the Big Ten's weakness. Only one team, Michigan State at #15, was in the poll of top 20 teams. West Virginia and Jerry West continued as #1. Kansas and Wilt Chamberlain were still #2. Cincinnati and Oscar Robertson, #3, and Kansas State with Bob Boozer at #4, rounded out the top teams.

A new leader, Michigan, emerged the next weekend after beating Illinois, 88 to 81, in Ann Arbor. Indiana defeated Michigan State, 82 to 79, to knock them out of first. Purdue moved into second with an 83–63 romp over Ohio State. Jake Eison and Harvey Austin led the Boilers with 19 points each. In the Hoosier victory, Archie Dees had 21 and Jerry Thompson 19, although game honors went to Larry Hedden of MSU with 26. Green and Anderegg each had 16, and Green added 16 rebounds. For new leader Michigan, M.C. Burton scored 22, with support from George Lee and Pete Tillotson, each with 21. Don Ohl and Govonor Vaughan had 20 apiece, but the big difference was on the boards. Michigan outrebounded Illinois, 71 to 46.[80]

This was the end of the semester for all teams. The only announced casualties seemed to be on the Iowa team, which lost three players—starting sophomore center Larry Swift and two reserves, Payne and Bruns—for the season, because of academics. Iowa was in the middle of the pack, and this loss was unlikely to affect the Big Ten race much. In their next game they lost to Michigan State, 90–84, in East Lansing, which propelled the Spartans back into the league lead as both Michigan and Purdue lost to Minnesota and Illinois, respectively. Indiana beat Wisconsin, 93–87, moving the Hoosiers and Spartans back into a first-place tie. Hedden (27), Green (26 and 19 rebounds) and Quiggle (25) were the prime perpetrators for MSU in their victory, as they consistently beat Iowa on rebounds for second-chance points. Gunther (30) and Wordlaw (18) led Iowa scoring. For Indiana, Dees (30) and Obremsky (24) led the Hoosiers in Madison, where Litzow took game-scoring honors with 34 and Holt chipped in 24. Illinois won at home, 99 to 84, as Roger Taylor (29) and Don Ohl (22) led the fast-breaking Illini. Michigan succumbed, 80–69, as Minnesota's Kline led all scorers with 28.[81]

The next weekend found Michigan State's Spartans sweeping their two games, against Illinois (69–56) and Michigan (79–69), to plant themselves alone in first place.

Indiana lost its only contest, 93–83, to Ohio State. MSU got big games from Johnny Green, who scored 17 (with 17 rebounds) against Illinois and 18 (with 17 rebounds) against Michigan. Anderegg had 12 in the former game and 25 in the latter. Purdue struggled against Wisconsin in Madison, but escaped with an 81–76 win behind Greve's 21 and Eison's 20. Holt and Litzow each had 21 for the Badgers. Ohio State beat both Michigan, 85–76, and Indiana, 93–83, "holding" Dees to just 19 points.[82] The "parity" of the Big Ten continued to be reflected in the lack of high national rankings for members of the league. The latest national poll had Kansas State at #1, Cincinnati as #2, West Virginia #3, Kansas #4 and San Francisco #5. Michigan State was #12, the only Big Ten team in the poll listing. And the Big Ten standings were a jumble, as of February 22:

|  |  |
|---|---|
| Michigan State | 7–3 |
| Purdue | 6–4 |
| Ohio State | 7–5 |
| Indiana | 5–4 |
| Iowa | 5–4 |
| Northwestern | 5–5 |
| Michigan | 4–5 |
| Illinois | 4–6 |
| Minnesota | 4–7 |
| Wisconsin | 3–7 |

The following weekend, Purdue tied for the league lead by winning two games, one against Minnesota and the other against Michigan State. Michigan State defeated Wisconsin, 93 to 59, before losing to Purdue, 72–70. Indiana defeated Ohio State and Michigan, while Iowa also won two contests, against Illinois and Northwestern, to remain in the title hunt. Purdue's victories were keyed by Jake Eison, who had 25 points against Minnesota in the 88–79 win, and 19 (with 9 rebounds) in the showdown against the Spartans. In the latter game, Merriweather had 20 for Purdue (who only used five players), while Johnny Green (28 and 19 rebounds) and Bob Anderegg had 19 points for MSU. For Indiana, Dees was again the key with 33 points (and 19 boards) in the 88 to 83 win in Columbus (where Frank Howard had 14 points and 15 rebounds, despite fouling out with 10 minutes to go), and 27 points in the 95 to 88 win against the Wolverines. Burton (22) and Lee (23) were the Michigan leading scorers. Iowa's victories were led by Dave Gunther, who had 18 in the Illinois victory and 26 (with 15 rebounds) in the 86–78 victory in Evanston. In the former contest, the Hawkeyes were superior on the boards with Nolden Gentry getting 17 (to go with 16 points).[83]

Iowa kept its title hopes alive by beating Northwestern in Evanston, 86–78. The game was really won on the line, where Iowa went 28 of 35, while Northwestern was 14 of 28. Dave Gunther had 26 points and 15 rebounds for the Hawkeyes, and Joe Rucklick had 23 with 16 rebounds for the Wildcats. Rucklick could hook with either hand, so the defender had to try to keep him from getting too low in the post, but that was easier said than done.[84]

The last weekend of the season, the first in March, would seem to be the crucible for determining a champion in the Big Ten. Michigan State won over Iowa, 83–65, on Saturday and was off on Monday. Indiana won on both days, and the two teams were tied with records of 9–4. Purdue lost to Indiana and beat Iowa to end their season at

9–5. Northwestern closed with a victory over Wisconsin and Ohio State defeated Minnesota, leaving both winners with records of 8–6. For MSU, their win in Iowa City was easy, as Green had 20 (with 16 rebounds) and Hedden and Anderegg each had 18. Wordlaw had 25 for Iowa. Indiana ran away from Purdue, 109–95, as Dees scored 37 points. Purdue rebounded to defeat Iowa, 65 to 59. Indiana slammed Illinois, 96 to 86, as Dees scored 35 for the Hoosiers.[85]

The race was not settled, and one more date and game would be needed to decide the outcome. On March 8, Indiana traveled to East Lansing for the final Big Ten game of the season. The contest was the televised Big Ten Game of the Week, and turned out to be fitting for a championship clash. Indiana won 75 to 72, despite the Spartans' outrebounding the Hoosiers, 55 to 39, and making five more free throws (32 to 27) in a rough and rugged contest. MSU also held Big Ten scoring champion Archie Dees to just 14 points (Sam Gee led IU with 16), but MSU had more turnovers. The Spartans' Green had 23 points and Hedden 18 to take scoring honors for the game, but Indiana was advancing to the NCAA tournament and MSU would be sitting at home.[86]

### Final Standings and MVPs, 1957–58

| | | |
|---|---|---|
| Indiana | 10–4 | Archie Dees (Big Ten MVP) |
| Michigan State | 9–5 | Johnny Green |
| Purdue | 9–5 | Wison "Jake" Eison |
| Northwestern | 8–6 | Joe Ruklick |
| Ohio State | 8–6 | Larry Sidle |
| Iowa | 7–7 | Dave Gunther |
| Michigan | 6–8 | Pete Tillotson |
| Illinois | 5–9 | Don Ohl |
| Minnesota | 5–9 | George Kline |
| Wisconsin | 3–11 | Walter Holt |

The first team, All-Big Ten consisted of Dees, Green, Kline, Ohl and Frank Howard (OSU). The second team was Gunther (IA), Eison (PU), Ruklick (NU), M.C. Burton (MI) and Bob Anderegg (MSU). Dees led the league with 25.9 ppg, followed by Kline (23), Ohl (21.1), Gunther (20.8) and Rucklick (19.4). Nationally, Dees's average had him ninth. The top scorers nationally were Oscar Robertson of Cincinnati (34.58), Elgin Baylor of Seattle (33.96), Wilt Chamberlain of Kansas (30.14), and Bailey Howell of Mississippi State (27.80).[87]

In the Big Ten meetings, held in March, the conference increased aid to athletes of lower income (family income of $6,000 or less) and reduced the number of athletes able to receive aid from 100 to 75, noting that the conference average was 68 for the prior year. The league also raised the pay of basketball officials from $75 to $85 per game and from $125 to $135 for football officials.[88]

Indiana had an opening-round bye and would open NCAA play on March 14, playing the winner of the Notre Dame–Miami of Ohio game. That game would be two days earlier, in McGaw Hall on the Northwestern campus. Notre Dame, led by Tommy Hawkins, former prep star from Parker High School in Chicago, easily defeated Miami, 94 to 61. Early in the season, Notre Dame had routed Indiana by 15 points, but the feeling in Bloomington was that the Hoosiers had improved greatly since then. Their chance to prove it fell flat, as did the Hoosiers, 94 to 87, in Lexington, Kentucky. Hawkins had 31 and John McCarthy had 29 for Notre Dame. Dees led Indiana with 28, but his shooting was not good (9 of 27). Pete Obremsky had 18 for IU. The game wasn't as close as the score might seem to indicate, as Notre Dame led 94 to 81 with 32 seconds left, before IU scored uncontested and meaningless baskets.[89] Indiana salvaged third in the region the next night with a 98–91 victory over Miami. Dees had 24, Obremsky 20, and Wayne Embry had 36 for the Redskins (Redhawks as of 1997-forward).

It had not been a particularly impressive year for the Big Ten, but returning players made Michigan State, Purdue, Indiana, and even Northwestern as possible favorites for the conference title in 1958–59. The hope was that a strong team would emerge to make the Big Ten seem formidable once again.

# VI

## *Into the '60s in the Big Ten*

The Cold War continued, but some of the players involved had changed or were changing. Dwight Eisenhower was completing his second term, after earlier speculation that he would not continue, following his heart attacks. In the Soviet Union, Nikita Krushchev had become chairman of the Council of Ministers in 1958, but there were still power struggles within his nation. He constantly felt the need to show his strength and resilience and was unpredictable in his responses to Western actions or proposals. Harold MacMillan became prime minister of Great Britain in 1957 and served as a kind of "mediator" between the old and new of both the U.S. and the Soviet Union. It was a tense time.

In early January 1959, the long battle between the Cuban revolutionary forces and the dictatorship of Fulgencio Batista climaxed in the rebel victory and the flight of Batista and his claque, who took millions of dollars with them. Fidel Castro came into power with his revolutionary forces on January 2, supported by the bulk of the Cuban people as well as recognition by the American government (on January 8). That latter support would not last, of course.

As the season opened on college hoops, *Sport*, one of the two top regular magazines published on sports and the only monthly (*Sports Illustrated* was a weekly and only four years old), ran a major article on basketball recruiting by noted sportswriter Dick Schaap, in which he chronicled, anecdotally, the excessive payoffs and various offers being used in big-time college basketball to lure top players nationwide. At this time, most colleges recruited regionally, and even that was rather subdued, usually relying on high school coaches who had attended or were keen on a particular university to encourage their top players to attend or at least visit those schools. Big Ten rosters were almost totally filled with players from the particular university's home state or contiguous ones, but clearly that era of "laid-back" recruiting was coming to an end.

Schaap illustrated his thesis with examples of six top players, one of whom was Jerry Lucas, then a freshman at Ohio State. He noted his strengths in scoring, defense, academics and judiciousness, then presented a number of the excessive pressures that he had received from alumni of schools like Princeton, as well as the rumors of inducements that were made. The screening process created by Lucas's father and a local sports editor was noted, as well as how Lucas reduced the number of schools in which he was interested from 20 to ten and finally two, Cincinnati and Ohio State, before selecting the latter. The Lucas anecdote ended with a quote from an unidentified Midwest scout saying that Lucas had not taken the best deal (a straight-up academic scholarship consisting of room, board, tuition, books and fees). "He could have picked up a lot more cash from a dozen other places. I guess he wasn't looking for a payoff."[1]

## The 1959 Season

All of this seemed far removed from a new Big Ten season. Indiana, the defending champion, had lost most of its firepower and would rely on untested underclassman. The clear favorite was Michigan State, after finishing in a title tie in 1957 and a game behind in 1958. Their two top players, Johnny Green and Bob Anderegg, returned, along with a formidable cast of players to support them. Green was picked by *Sport* as a second team All-America player. The only other Big Ten players noted were Ron Johnson of Minnesota and Dave Gunther of Iowa as Honorable Mentions, not a ringing endorsement for the Big Ten in the upcoming season.[2] Other teams harboring championship hopes that were seen as viable were Purdue and Northwestern. In the pre–Big Ten season, only Michigan State emerged unscathed, but Northwestern, Iowa and Purdue all had good records and were seen as potential champions, if Michigan State faltered.

After a disappointing loss to North Carolina, 78 to 64, in late December, the Northwestern Wildcats, under second-year coach Bill Rohr, came back less than a week later to upset West Virginia and their star, Jerry West, 118 to 109, in double overtime in Chicago Stadium. West was held to 17, while Bucky Bolyard led the Mountaineers with 26 points. For the Wildcats, Joe Ruklick had 28, mostly on hooks and follow up shots, while Nick Mantis had 23. Northwestern looked to be "real."[3]

The 1958–59 University of Iowa team. Coach Sharm Scheuermann, far left, row three, helped the Hawkeyes win back-to-back Big Ten titles and Final Fours in the mid-1950s. Nolden Gentry is third row, second from right (Hawkeye Yearbook Collection, University Archives, The University of Iowa Libraries).

Purdue beat Notre Dame and their star, Tom Hawkins, in an Indianapolis doubleheader, and established firmer credentials for the Big Ten title. Jake Eison (20) and Willie Merriweather (26), Purdue captains, kept Hawkins in relative check (20 points), and he received little help from the rest of his Irish teammates in the 74–59 contest. In the other game, Butler downed Indiana, 81 to 76, although sophomore center Walter Bellamy (15 points) continued to look like a coming star.[4]

Michigan State lost its last game before the Big Ten season began (to North Carolina State), so no Big Ten teams were undefeated. Iowa may have been facing the biggest struggle as they tried to get used to new coach and former player, Sharm Scheuerman, who took over after the sudden and tragic death of Coach Bucky O'Connor in an auto accident in April of 1958. O'Connor was on the road a lot to speak at various basketball banquets, using his presence as a recruiting tool. Three days before his death he had been driven by Nolden Gentry to a banquet in Rockford, Illinois, which allowed Gentry to visit his folks while O'Connor spoke at a function; but the fatal trip was shorter, to Waterloo, Iowa, just 60 miles. O'Connor encountered a flock of birds on the road, swerved to avoid them, and crashed head-on into a semi going the opposite direction.[5] He died at the scene. Iowa was 3–5 after the non-conference season with their new coach, who, at 24, was the youngest among top universities. One loss, at Oklahoma, still rankled Nolden Gentry, over 50 years later. The Sooners pummeled, held and "just hammered us," but the refs had blinders on and Oklahoma won, 80–57.[6]

Ohio State also had a new coach, former center Fred Taylor, and the Buckeyes were seen as "most improved" by Richard Dozer, *Chicago Tribune* sportswriter.[7] Richie Hoyt and Larry Siegfried were top sophs who would step in and play well immediately.

In the first night of competition, both Michigan State and Northwestern won, although the Wildcats had to struggle with Iowa before prevailing, 80–77. Purdue was upset by Michigan, 82–75, Illinois edged Ohio State, 81–80, in Champaign, and Wisconsin headed for another year of woe, losing to Minnesota, 79 to 66. Purdue's loss was at home, compounding the pain, and Eison was held to 12 points with Merriweather getting 19. M.C. Burton spurred the Wolverines with 27 and 18 rebounds. Indiana was nosed out by the Spartans in East Lansing, 79 to 77, thanks to 23 points from Bob Anderegg and 17 from Horace Walker, who also snared 19 rebounds. The Hoosiers showed great scoring balance with Wilkinson and Radovich each getting 17 and Herbie Lee and Bellamy getting 16 each, but their efforts fell just short. The Illinois win was led by Mannie Jackson with 23 and Lou Landt with 17 off the bench. Larry Huston had 30 for OSU, but got help from two sophomores, Larry Siegfried and Jim Nieuhaus, who each had 14. Siegfried had led the state of Ohio in scoring his senior year in high school in Shelby, Ohio. He had chosen Ohio State over Kentucky, Northwestern, Indiana, Vanderbilt, Wisconsin and Tennessee in order to "be close to home so my mom and dad could watch the games and so I could get home to hunt and fish."[8] Northwestern's win was paced by Ruklick with 28, while Wordlaw had 23 for Iowa.[9]

On the following Monday, Northwestern remained undefeated, as Michigan State was upset by Iowa, 80–68. Purdue went to 0–2 with a loss to Indiana, 77–69, and Wisconsin also was winless after dropping a 77–51 game to Illinois. Northwestern won at Michigan, 83 to 78, and Willie Jones was the big star with 26 points while Nick Mantis had 23. The Wildcats shot nearly 50 percent from the field (47.7, to be precise), while holding Michigan to just 36 percent shooting. Burton had 24 and George Lee 21 for the Wolverines. Iowa's upset was led by their dynamic seniors, Clarence Wordlaw, with 23, and Dave Gunther, with 21. Bob Anderegg had 23 and Johnny Green 18 with 24 rebounds, but the Spartans fell short, 80 to 68.[10]

The next weekend, both Illinois and Northwestern picked up their first conference losses, to Michigan State and Indiana, respectively, while Michigan topped Ohio State in Ann Arbor. Purdue joined the many who would beat Wisconsin, by a score of 84 to 61. The MSU-Illinois game in Champaign came down to the last possession in the 97–96 contest. Johnny Green had 33 points and 19 rebounds, while Illinois was led by Jackson (23) and John Wessels (22). Indiana got 18 points from Herb Lee and 17 from Lindsey Flowers in the 76 to 69 victory in Bloomington. Nick Mantis had 22 and Joe Ruklick, 16, for the Wildcats.[11]

Illinois came back on Monday to top Iowa, 103 to 97, in Champaign, while Indiana edged Minnesota in Bloomington. Mannie Jackson and Roger Taylor each had 24 to lead the Illini, while senior leaders Gunther (19) and Wordlaw (18) topped the Hawkeye scoring. Indiana struggled before defeating Minnesota in Bloomington, 63 to 59. Walter Bellamy had 17 points and 20 rebounds for the Hoosiers.[12]

The next weekend, Northwestern seemed to be slipping behind quickly as they absorbed another loss, this time to Ohio State, 88 to 77, in Columbus. Larry Siegfried, the sophomore sensation, led the Bucks with 27 points and Rich Hoyt, another soph, had 22. Joe Ruklick led the Wildcats with 17. Iowa stopped Indiana, 88 to 78; Gunther (31) and Wordlaw (18) were the Iowa catalysts. Bellamy (18) and Radovich (14) were top Hoosier scorers. Purdue also saw their season slipping as they lost to Minnesota, 64 to 62. Tom Benson with 22 and Ron Johnson with 21, caused the most damage for the Gophers. Jake Eison had 24 for the Boilers.[13]

Northwestern ended the weekend with another loss (to Minnesota, 71 to 67) and Michigan State routed Ohio State by fifteen points, 92 to 77, to create a four-way tie for first (MSU, Michigan, Minnesota, Illinois). Paul Lehman (22) and Ron Johnson (18) led the Gophers, while Willie Jones (24) and Nick Mantis (20) were the leading Northwestern scorers. For the Spartans, Johnny Green had a superlative game with 26 points and 18 rebounds. Bob Anderegg and Horace Walker each added 16, and Walker also picked off 22 rebounds. Larry Siegfried, with 20, led the Bucks, who shot better than MSU (41 percent to 35 percent), but were destroyed on the boards as MSU grabbed 86 rebounds to 46 by Ohio State.[14]

A Chicago Stadium double-header highlighted the next weekend, including a Big Ten conference match, Iowa and Northwestern, which the Wildcats won, 99 to 96, in overtime. Joe Ruklick led the 'Cats with 30 and Nick Mantis had 23, enough to offset the 29 by Wordlaw and the 24 from Gunther. Illinois lost to Notre Dame in the opener, played before a disappointingly small crowd of 9,818.[15] Michigan State knocked Minnesota out of the logjam in first by defeating them, 82 to 76, in Minneapolis. Bob Anderegg had 21 to pace the Spartans. In West Lafayette, Purdue knocked off Ohio State, 86 to 69, as Willie Merriweather took game scoring honors with 27. Joe Roberts had 24 for the Buckeyes.[16]

Minnesota knocked Illinois out of the tie for first, 81 to 70, on Monday, while Ohio State defeated Iowa, 86 to 72, in Columbus. Ron Johnson had 28 and Roger Johnson had 14 for the winning Gophers, while Roger Taylor (20) and Mannie Jackson (18) led the Illini. Larry Siegfried had 22 for OSU ("We just didn't know how good he was," said Nolden Gentry, explaining how Siegfried was left open at times and drilled shots against the Hawks), backed by Joe Roberts with 21 and 15 rebounds. Dave Gunther led Iowa with 23 and 14 rebounds. More long-term disappointment was noted for both Indiana and Wisconsin. Indiana lost a starter, Bob Wilkinson, and two reserves to academics for the rest of the year, while Wisconsin lost three players to injuries, although all were expected back later in the season.[17]

Another big loss was suffered nationally by the state of Virginia, in its appeal to the Supreme Court to resist integration in its public schools, specifically Arlington, Virginia. As a result of that decision, the Virginia legislature passed bills to drop compulsory school attendance and to provide tuition grants for private schools. A number of other Southern states would follow suit, and these would be part of the concerns that continued to fuel the Civil Rights Movement.[18]

Michigan State continued to win, as various "pretenders" knocked each other off, a pattern that would continue for the rest of the season. The Spartans defeated Northwestern, 81 to 72; Anderegg had 21 and Green 17 with 19 rebounds. Ruklick had 29 for Northwestern. Purdue crushed Illinois, 102 to 81, as Merriweather (25), Eison (19 with 17 rebounds) and Harvey Austin (19) led the rout. The Boilers shot 59 percent (44 of 74) from the field. Ohio State beat Minnesota, 84 to 80, as sophomores Siegfried (30) and Jim Niehaus (16) were the top scorers. For Minnesota, center Ron Johnson scored 39 and captured 15 rebounds. In Iowa City, the Hawks edged Michigan, 78 to 74. The "usual suspects," Wordlaw (23) and Gunther (17) were top scorers. M.C. Burton had 24 for Michigan.[19]

Two nights later, a track meet disguised as a basketball game ensued in Columbus, and 214 points were scored as Indiana topped Ohio State, 122 to 92, setting various scoring records for the teams, the site (St. John Arena), and the conference. The Hoosier scoring was topped by Gary Long with 29 and Herb Lee with 25. OSU countered with Siegfried's 25 and Huston's 19. Michigan had a tougher time defeating Illinois in Champaign, 87 to 85, and Michigan State cleared their bench in routing Wisconsin, 88 to 57 in Madison.[20]

With the Big Ten season almost at midpoint, the standings were:

|  |  |
|---|---|
| Michigan State | 6–1 |
| Michigan | 4–2 |
| Indiana | 4–2 |
| Minnesota | 4–3 |
| Purdue | 3–3 |
| Illinois | 3–4 |
| Northwestern | 3–4 |
| Iowa | 3–4 |
| Ohio State | 3–5 |
| Wisconsin | 0–5 |

Nationally, Kentucky was ranked #1, followed by North Carolina, Kansas State, Auburn, Cincinnati, North Carolina State, Michigan State, Bradley, St. Louis and West Virginia. No other Big Ten teams besides the Spartans were ranked in the top 20.

Big Ten leader Michigan State lost, 85 to 81, in West Lafayette on February 7 and

Indiana defeated Michigan in Ann Arbor, 84 to 79, shrinking the MSU lead to a half-game and pushing Indiana into second by themselves. The Boilers got 24 points from Bob Fehrman, 20 from Jake Eison and 18 from Willie Merriweather. Johnny Green had 25 points and 18 rebounds for MSU, but fouled out with more than nine minutes to play and State leading. Indiana was led by three sophomores—Bellamy with 22, Lee with 21, and Long with 17. M.C. Burton had 31 points and 15 rebounds for Michigan.[21] A race for the title seemed possible once again, with a real logjam for the spots after second.

Two nights later (February 9), both Indiana and Purdue lost, giving MSU some breathing room and tightening the rest of the league. Illinois defeated the Hoosiers, 89 to 83, with Roger Taylor (26) and Mannie Jackson (21) the top scorers for the Illini. Johnson with 23 and Bellamy with 21 (and 18 boards) led Indiana, who outrebounded the Illini, 65 to 52, but were defeated by superior shooting. Purdue was embarrassed by Wisconsin, 91 to 86, in Madison, where just 3,000 fans even cared enough to attend. Rick Murray (27) and Jim Biggs (24) combined for 51 points to lead the Badgers to their first conference win of the year. MSU had two losses, but the next six teams all had either three or four losses.[22]

The Spartans felt the need to send a strong message to the rest of the league that they were, by far, the class of the conference, and that message was sent on Saturday, February 14, in the form of a record-setting victory in East Lansing. Michigan was the victim of a 103 to 91 sprint, with Anderegg (26), Green (24) and Walker (19) doing most of the damage. MSU, the top rebounding team in the conference, outrebounded Michigan, 71 to 49, with Green picking off 21. Purdue got back to winning by edging Northwestern in overtime in Evanston, 65 to 63. Indiana, led by Walt Bellamy's 18 points, kept pace with a 62 to 57 win in Minneapolis.[23]

On the following Monday, Indiana lost, but the rest of the top squads in the conference all won. MSU slipped by Northwestern in Evanston, 71 to 68, Purdue defeated the Hoosiers in West Lafayette, 94 to 89, and Michigan beat Iowa, 90 to 86, in Ann Arbor. Joe Ruklick (30) and Willie Jones (20) were nearly the entire offense for Northwestern, but it was not quite enough. Anderegg (18), Green (16) and Olson (15) countered for the Spartans. Rebounds were again a big factor in the victory as the Spartans led in that category, 60 to 47, with Walker (24) and Green (14) sweeping the boards most thoroughly. Purdue got a huge game from Jake Eison, who had 31 points and 16 rebounds to pace the Boilers. Michigan got 30 points from George Lee and 22 from M.C. Burton, as well as 20 and 24 rebounds, respectively, to hold back Iowa, led by Nolden Gentry's 20 points and 21 rebounds. The game also had a total of 132 recorded rebounds (68–64 Michigan). This game avenged Michigan's loss to Iowa two weeks earlier. Playing in Michigan's old fieldhouse was always a challenge, noted Gentry, because the floor had so many dead spots and the Wolverines seemed to know where all of them were to take advantage of the Hawkeye dribbling and steal the ball.[24]

In the latest national poll, North Carolina had taken over the top spot, with Auburn, Kentucky and Kansas State right behind. Michigan State had fallen to 9th, but both Indiana and Purdue had entered the poll with IU at #19 and Purdue at #20.

In one of the earliest "clinchings" in a number of years, Michigan State sewed up a title tie on February 21 with a 94–87 victory over Purdue, which gave the Spartans a conference record of 9–2 while every other team had at least five losses. MSU was led, as usual, by Bob Anderegg, with 29 points, and Johnny Green, who had 24 points and 25 rebounds. Merriweather (24) and Eison (19) led Purdue. The Spartans had a rebounding advantage, 71 to 49.

Northwestern toppled Michigan in Evanston, 87 to 84. Joe Ruklick had 32 points and 14 rebounds and M.C. Burton had 30 points and 20 rebounds for the Wolverines. In Champaign, the Illini deflated Indiana's title hopes with a 100 to 98 victory. Taylor (26), John Wessels (25) and Jackson (23) got most of the points; Bellamy had 26 and Radovich 22 for Indiana.[25]

In games with less effect on conference standings, Iowa beat Ohio State, 91 to 79, and Minnesota handed Wisconsin its ninth loss in ten games, 68 to 50. The Badgers' high scorer was Dale Hackbart, the starting quarterback on the football team, who later played 11 seasons in the NFL, with 11 points. For Iowa, Dave Gunther picked up 37 points and 15 rebounds.[26]

On Monday, a big shakeout occurred as three teams were officially eliminated from the Big Ten race. Northwestern beat Minnesota, 79 to 62; Iowa beat Purdue, 66 to 62; and Ohio State knocked off Indiana, 92 to 83. Larry Huston (26), Larry Siegfried (20)

**Walter "Big Bell" Bellamy snares a rebound for Indiana and keeps others at a distance. Bellamy was All-American both junior and senior years (1960 and 1961) and played on the fabulous 1960 U.S. Olympic basketball team before embarking on a 13-year NBA career (University Archives, Indiana University)**

and Joe Roberts (19 and 12 rebounds) keyed the OSU win. Bellamy did what he could with 25 points and 18 rebounds. Gentry had 18 and his Freeport (IL) High School teammate, Washington, had 16, for the Hawkeyes.[27]

The calendar turned to March, denoting the end of the Big Ten season and tournament time. Nationally, MSU had moved up to #6 in the rankings. The Soviet Union and their leader, Nikita Khrushchev, grew increasingly perturbed over the status and governance of the two Berlins and began making it more difficult through various "saber-rattling" actions. President Eisenhower, nearing the end of his two terms in office, was contemplating a response to the Soviet actions, which would ultimately lead to the Soviet construction of the Berlin Wall in 1961 in an attempt to isolate the city totally.

Meanwhile, the Spartans finally isolated themselves from the rest of the field by defeating Indiana in Bloomington on the Big Ten game of the week, shown regionally. The score was 86 to 82. Anderegg and Green each had 20 and Green snatched 16 rebounds, but surprisingly, Indiana outrebounded the Spartans, 51 to 47. The victory left MSU at 10–2 with Illinois second at 7–5, with just two games left in the conference season. Illinois had defeated Iowa, 72 to 70, in Iowa City, led by Roger Taylor's 28 and Govonor Vaughn's 18.[28]

Michigan State's victory took the tension out of the Big Ten race, but there were interesting and unusual occurrences to complete the season. Two nights after the clinching, Michigan beat Illinois, 101–95; Ohio State defeated Minnesota, 68–66, and there was a six-way tie for second in the league. Richard Dozer also did a biographical piece on Fordy Anderson, the MSU coach, who was from Gary, Indiana, where he played tuba in the band as well as playing basketball. Dozer noted that, as a result, Anderson used music and film a lot with his team, something unusual at the time.[29]

The Big Ten season ended on March 7 with a Northwestern victory over Illinois, 84–81, a Purdue win over Ohio State, 93–87, and an MSU victory over Iowa, 84–74, all of which created a three-way tie for second at 8–6, among Northwestern, Purdue and Michigan. Illinois, Ohio State, Indiana and Iowa were all at 7–7. Minnesota was 5–9 and Wisconsin 1–13. The continued abysmal play of Wisconsin led Coach Harold "Bud" Foster to tender his resignation after 25 years at the helm of the Badgers and three Big Ten titles, as well as an NCAA title (1941). His career record was 265–266, marred by his last four seasons, which were cumulatively 22–66.[30]

### Team Standings and MVPs, 1958–59

| | | |
|---|---|---|
| Michigan State | 12–2 | John Green (Conference MVP) |
| Northwestern | 8–6 | Willie Jones |
| Purdue | 8–6 | Willie Merriweather |
| Michigan | 8–6 | M.C. Burton |
| Ohio State | 7–7 | Larry Siegfried |
| Illinois | 7–7 | Roger Taylor |
| Indiana | 7–7 | Walt Bellamy |
| Iowa | 7–7 | Dave Gunther |
| Minnesota | 5–9 | Ron Johnson |
| Wisconsin | 1–13 | Bob Barneson |

First team All-Big Ten consisted of Green (MSU), Merriweather (PU), Ruklick (NU), Burton (MI) and Ron Johnson (MN). Second team was Anderegg (MSU), Gunther

(IA), Taylor (IL), Bellamy (IN) and Tidwell (MI). The team was long on centers and short of guards, but the voting was not done by position. Interestingly, Wilson and Brondfield claim that Gunther, rather than Burton, was on the first team, while Mokray lists both of them on a six-player first team.[31] M.C. Burton averaged 22.6 ppg to lead the conference in scoring, followed by Johnson and Rucklick, each with 21.9 ppg, and Siegfried of OSU with 21.6. Mokray's second team listing was Roger Taylor (IL), Bob Anderegg (MSU), Walt Bellamy (IU), John Tidwell (MI), Larry Siegfried (OSU) and Walter Eison (PU).

Michigan State headed into the NCAA tourney as a top team since they had finished sixth and seventh in the AP and UPI national polls. It was difficult to determine how good they were since the remainder of the Big Ten seemed so equal. Certainly, the Spartans were the class of the league and one of the top rebounding teams in the nation, topped by Johnny Green and Horace Walker. Add in Bob Anderegg's shooting and they had three reliable scorers, as well as two strong others in David Fahs and Lance Olson. They did not have a deep bench, and foul trouble, especially to Green, might lead to an upset. Nevertheless, they were a tough squad and they looked forward to their opener against the winner of Marquette and Bowling Green.

On March 10, Marquette, led by Don Kojis, topped Bowling Green, 89 to 71, and the Warriors of Marquette would meet MSU in McGaw Hall on March 13, with Louisville and Kentucky meeting in the other game. The Cardinals upset Kentucky, 76 to 61, and the Spartans struggled to defeat Marquette, 74 to 69. Anderegg had 23, Walker 20, and Green 14 (with 18 rebounds). Don Kojis had 17 for Marquette. The Spartans looked prepared to return to the Final Four, as they had done in 1957, but Louisville had not gotten that message and defeated the Spartans the next night, 88 to 81, behind John Turner's 22 points. Johnny Green had 29 and snared 23 rebounds; teammate Bob Anderegg had 22 points, but the Spartans fell short.[32]

The Spartan season was over and the Cardinals were headed home to Freedom Hall, where the Final Four was to be played. Louisville lost in the semis to West Virginia and Jerry West, which then lost in the championship game, 71–70, to an unheralded University of California team, which had beaten Oscar Robertson and Cincinnati, 64–58, in the semis. Michigan State was sort of represented in the finals, as the Cal coach was Pete Newell, the MSU coach from 1950 to 1954.

Michigan State had been led by seniors Anderegg (19.5 ppg) and Green (18.5 ppg and 16.6 rpg); their graduation left MSU with Horace Walker and a number of lesser players. Michigan State would not have a winning record again until 1964, and would not win another outright Big Ten title until 1978.

## The 1960 Season

The 1958–59 season had yielded a number of outstanding sophomores and juniors and they looked to be the strength of the league on teams like Indiana with Walt Bellamy (selected by the editors of *Sport* as a preseason second team All-America player[33]), Minnesota with Ron Johnson (selected by the editors of *Sport* as a preseason first team All-America player) and Illinois with Mannie Jackson, John Wessels and Govonor Vaughn.

Even more impressive, however, were the sophomores moving up to the varsity. At Purdue it was Terry Dischinger; at Iowa, Don Nelson; at Northwestern, Ralph Wells. The most dazzling promise, however, was in Columbus, where a team of freshmen who had strongly challenged the varsity in scrimmages, moved up, led by Jerry Lucas (selected by the editors of *Sport* on their preseason All Sophomore team), John Havlicek and Mel Nowell, considered the best recruiting class of the time and the second best of all time by *The Sporting News*.[34] They would join Larry Siegfried and Joe Roberts to form what looked to be one of the top teams in the Big Ten, if not the nation. The UPI rated them sixth in the nation in their pre-season poll.[35] Minnesota had convinced former coach John Kundla to take a college position after leading the Minneapolis Lakers to championships in 1947–1951 in three different leagues (the NBL, BAA and NBA).[36]

Back for what promised to be great senior years were Jerry West at West Virginia and Oscar Robertson at Cincinnati. Both had made it to the Final Four with their teams, but both had been thwarted in a quest for a national title. They were both eager to correct that before moving on to what promised to be great professional careers.

One highlight of the pre-conference season was the Bradley at Cincinnati game on December 22, 1959, which was the first colorcast of a collegiate basketball game. This contest was telecast locally in Cincinnati as well as in Peoria for those few fortunate enough to have color televisions at that time. The game wasn't as close as hoped, as the Bearcats, led by Robertson's 42, topped Bradley 86–71, despite 21 from Bobby Joe Mason and 16 from Chet Walker.[37]

At Christmastime, a number of tournaments were held, the best one being the Holiday Tournament in New York at Madison Square Garden. It included St. John's, coached by Joe Lapchick and featuring a spectacular shooting guard, Tony Jackson; Iowa with super soph Don Nelson, now the center who "could hook with either hand,"[38] and steady rebounder and scorer Nolden Gentry; and Cincinnati, led by the incomparable Robertson. Iowa polished off St. John's behind Gentry's 14 points and nine rebounds and Nelson's 12 points, but were topped by their 5'8" guard Mike Heitman's 22 points in the 91 to 84 victory, as the Hawks improved to 7–1. Tony Jackson had 26 for St. John's ("He could really shoot!" said Gentry). The Hawks went on to defeat NYU, led by Tom "Satch" Sanders, 80 to 75. Nelson (19), Gentry (18) and Heitman (14) led the Hawks again, while Sanders had 26 for the previously undefeated Violets. The win sent the Hawks into the finals against Cincinnati. On New Year's Eve, the Bearcats routed the Hawks, 96 to 83, as Robertson scored 50 points to more than offset Nelson's 25 and Ron Zagar's 21 for Iowa ("He had the quickest first step that I had ever seen," marveled Gentry).[39]

The Hoosier Classic pitted the four top Indiana teams in Indianapolis. The openers saw Notre Dame beat Purdue, 82–79, and Indiana top Butler, 91–85. Purdue got 31 from sophomore Terry Dischinger and the team shot 23 of 24 free throws, but it was still not enough to defeat the Irish, whose Mike Graney scored 31. Bellamy with 24 and Radovich with 21 led the Hoosiers. Ken Pennington took game honors for Butler with 36. The next night Indiana won the tournament with a 71–60 victory over Notre Dame. Purdue lost to Butler, 73–69, but Dischinger had 29 for the Boilermakers.[40]

In Los Angeles, both Illinois and Northwestern were playing in the Los Angeles Classic and lost to California teams, Illinois to NCAA champion Cal by 62–48, and

Northwestern to USC by a score of 81 to 62, making three losses in a row for Northwestern. Indiana won the Bluegrass Tourney in Louisville, defeating host Louisville in the championship, 90 to 71, behind 24 points by Walt Bellamy, as the Hoosiers upped their record to 8–1.[41]

In Columbus, Ohio State lost two early season games (to Kentucky and Utah), but were still seen as one of the three top teams in the Big Ten (Illinois and Indiana were the others). The loss to Utah was in Salt Lake City and the Utes were led by Billy McGill, who had 31; he would lead the nation in scoring in 1961–62. Lucas topped that with 32, but didn't get enough help from his mates.[42]

Iowa had a surprisingly good record (8–2) after their fine showing in the Holiday Festival. Ohio State was 8–1 and Jerry Lucas had scored 252 points in those nine games (28 ppg), so OSU prospects were tied to his success. The Big Ten had gone 49–35 in "pre-season" play—good, but not great—so it was difficult to ascertain how tight the league would be and how good it would be against later outside competition.[43]

The first games of the conference season included at least one upset with Purdue defeating rival Indiana, 79 to 76, in Bloomington, and Minnesota topping Iowa, 70 to 61, in Minneapolis ("We couldn't hit and they played well," noted Noland Gentry). Michigan State defeated Wisconsin, 91 to 79, but it was difficult to determine what that meant, since Wisconsin had been so poor the previous couple of years. In this latter game, the Spartan rebounding machine that had led to so many victories the previous years was still in business, as they snared 52 rebounds to Wisconsin's 31. Chief rebounders and scorers in the contest were Horace Walker, with 29 points and 17 rebounds, and Art Gowans, with 18 points and 14 rebounds. Tom Hughbanks with 19 and Bob Barneson with 18 led the Badger scoring. In Minnesota, Dick Erickson had 17 and Ron Johnson had 16, while the Iowa leaders were sophomore Don Nelson with 17 and senior Nolden Gentry with 12. Another soph, Terry Dischinger, was the star of the Purdue victory, as he scored 30 points, 21 in the second half, and grabbed 11 rebounds. Indiana was led by Frank Radovich with 21 points and 16 rebounds. Jerry Bass had 20 for the Hoosiers, who were stymied by a collapsing zone defense that negated the work of Walt Bellamy. The "Big Bell" had only 8 points, as the Hoosiers simply could not get the ball inside to him and shot just 35 percent from the field (to Purdue's 44 percent).[44]

Ohio State opened with Illinois and made short work of them, 97 to 73. Lucas had 30 points (11 of 15 from the floor) and 23 rebounds for the Buckeyes, complemented by Larry Siegfried's 20 points and John Havlicek's 14. Govoner Vaughn was the only Illini in double figures with 16. The Bucks also swept the boards, 59 to 35. Meanwhile, Northwestern surprised Indiana in Evanston, 61 to 57. Northwestern slowed down the Hoosiers and got 27 points from Bill Cacciatore in the victory.[45]

The next weekend (January 9–10) the Buckeyes faced Indiana in Columbus in what would be their first big test of the conference season. Larry Siegfried made a shot with six seconds left, his only bucket of the game, to help OSU nip Indiana, 96 to 95. Mel Nowell topped scoring with 26, and his sophomore teammates, Lucas and Havlicek, ably assisted with 22 and 21, respectively. For the Hoosiers, Herbie Lee had 23 and Walter Bellamy had 17.

Northwestern played in Iowa City and the Hawks trounced the Wildcats, 73 to 59, as Nelson (21) and Gentry (17) combined for more than half the Iowa points. Willie

Jones and sophomore Ralph Wells were nearly the entire Northwestern offense with 26 and 13, respectively. Illinois trimmed Minnesota, 90 to 82, with Jackson (25) and Vaughn (18) leading the Illini. Ron Johnson had 31 and Cronk 20 for the Gophers. Purdue had an easy time against Wisconsin, 99 to 69, and Michigan State also coasted, beating Michigan, 89 to 58.[46]

On Monday, January 11, the big excitement was Terry Dischinger's scoring 43 points in an 81–75 loss to Illinois. Iowa defeated Michigan State, 92 to 79, in Iowa City, with balanced scoring. Nelson and Gentry led with 17 and 13, respectively; Walker had 29 for the Spartans.[47] He was a fine ballplayer, good shooter and rebounder, but only 6'4", though he could really jump."[48]

Northwestern easily defeated Wisconsin, and then came to Columbus with an upset in mind on the next Saturday. Ohio State quickly disavowed that possibility with an easy 81 to 64 victory. Lucas had 28 and Nowell 16 for the hot-shooting Bucks (51 percent). Jones (28) and Campbell (17) led the Wildcats, who tried to play "slow down" against OSU, once holding the ball more than four minutes without a shot. Illinois topped Michigan State, 96 to 88, that same evening. John Wessels (25), Govonor Vaughn (24) and Mannie Jackson (17) led the Illini attack, while Walker (30 and 20 rebounds) and Olson (28 and 15 rebounds) were the top scorers and rebounders.

In Iowa City, the Hawks put the clamps on Dischinger and the Boilermakers, winning by a 63 to 54 score. The Hawk balance was again on display as four Iowa players were in double figures, led by Nelson's 13. For Purdue, Dischinger had 20 and Darrell McQuilty had 11. "They had Terry and that was it," said Noland Gentry, looking back on that game.[49] Minnesota won two in a row, defeating Michigan 74 to 58 on Saturday, then defeating Illinois 77 to 70 on Monday. Johnson and Ray Cronk were leading scorers for both contests.

In the AP poll for the week of January 19, two teams from the Missouri Valley topped the poll. Cincinnati was #1 and Bradley #2, followed by Cal-Berkeley, the defending NCAA champion, West Virginia and Ohio State. Both Illinois (#13) and Iowa (#15) were listed in the top 20.

Northwestern broke the short win streak of Minnesota on January 23, 62–61, on the next Saturday, while Ohio State easily defeated Purdue, 85 to 71. Dischinger took game-scoring honors with 32, but Lucas had 27 and Nowell 17, to offset that. For Northwestern, Willie Jones had 27 and Floyd Campbell had 11 to top their scoring. Michigan State defeated Iowa, 90 to 80, as Lance Olson (35 points,14 rebounds) and Horace Walker (20, 28) both had "double-doubles." Olson was a big guard who kept going into the post and isolating, then dominating the smaller Iowa guards, according to Gentry. Mike Dull led Iowa with 20, while Nelson had 19. Dull had started in place of Gentry, who had fainted on the plane and was feeling ill.[50]

On the last Saturday in January, Ohio State won another game that looked to be close and important by routing Michigan State, 111 to 79. Lucas had 25 points, playing less than ¾ of the game; Havlicek had 20, while Horace Walker took game honors with 27. Minnesota, after losing at Northwestern, came back to win two more in a row, against Iowa and Wisconsin, keeping them in second behind the undefeated Buckeyes.[51]

February opened with the Bucks winning their sixth in a row, routing hapless Michigan, 99 to 52. Indiana pounded Northwestern, 76 to 58, and seemed poised to make a run at the Buckeyes. Lee (16) and Bellamy (15) led the well-balanced Hoosier attack that shot 53 percent from the floor. The game was essentially over after the first half, wherein Indiana held Northwestern to 7 for 27 shooting (26 percent). Jones had 17 for the Wildcats. For OSU, Lucas had 23 and Nowell 19 in just under ¾ of the contest. Michigan State defeated Minnesota to push them out of second in the conference, 84 to 63. Walker and Olson each had 24 for MSU, while Ron Johnson had 22 for the Gophers.[52]

Ohio State got wins # 7 and #8 the next weekend, against Northwestern (77–58) and Wisconsin (106–69), as the rest of the conference battled for second and lower. Purdue defeated Michigan State, 68 to 65, in a tight contest in East Lansing. Northwestern topped Minnesota, 66 to 64, in Minneapolis, and Michigan State came back to defeat Illinois. Indiana managed to beat Iowa, 87 to 74, despite only getting 15 minutes out of Walter Bellamy, who drew four fouls within 10 minutes of the opening tap. The Northwestern win was unexpected, as the Wildcats battled back from being 11 down with 12 minutes left, led by Ralph Wells with 16 and Floyd Campbell with 15.[53]

Halfway through the conference season, the fight was clearly for second, unless Ohio State had an historic collapse. The standings:

| | |
|---|---|
| Ohio State | 8–0 |
| Purdue | 5–3 |
| Illinois | 4–3 |
| Indiana | 4–3 |
| Minnesota | 5–4 |
| Michigan State | 5–4 |
| Northwestern | 4–4 |
| Iowa | 4–4 |
| Michigan | 0–7 |
| Wisconsin | 0–7 |

Nationally, the top three teams were still Cincinnati, Bradley and Cal, but OSU had climbed to #4. Illinois still held at #20, the only other Big Ten team ranked in the AP poll.

The weekend of Valentine's Day saw OSU romp against two rivals: Iowa, 75 to 47, and Illinois, 109 to 81. Indiana also won twice, against Michigan, 86–69, and Wisconsin, 91–71. Wisconsin managed to get their first win, against Iowa, 63 to 58. Illinois defeated Purdue, 93 to 89, to push them out of second. Minnesota won twice, 82 to 73 against Michigan State, and 71 to 69 against Purdue.

Jerry Lucas continued to dominate play, even when he played just over half a game. He had 28 against Iowa, then 31 against Illinois. He broke Robin Freeman's Big Ten sophomore scoring record with five games to go. Ohio State also set a season attendance record with one home game to play. Terry Dischinger of Purdue got 36 in the loss to Illinois and 22 in the loss to Minnesota. Walter Bellamy of IU had 31 against Wisconsin and 26 against Michigan.[54]

On February 20, OSU clinched the Big Ten title on one of the earliest dates in conference history by winning its 11th in a row, over Michigan State, but it was a nail-biter, 84 to 83, in East Lansing. Lucas had 28 and Nowell 20 for the Bucks, while Walker had 23 and Olson 19 for the Spartans. Indiana and Minnesota stayed in mathematical contention with victories over Iowa, 79–64, and Michigan, 87–61, respectively.[55]

Indiana kept up the pressure on Monday with a victory over Illinois, 92–78, and Northwestern defeated Michigan State, 71–69, to stay in contention for third. Wisconsin got win #2, beating Michigan, 88–82. For the Hoosiers, Bellamy was overpowering with 42 points, but Jackson (28) and Vaughn (24) kept the game respectably close for Illinois until the end. The Northwestern victory was led by Bill Cacciatore with 20 and Ralph Wells with 15 (despite only hitting 3 of 9 free throws). Walker and Olson each had 22 for MSU.[56]

Ohio State had been off the previous Monday, so after a week of rest, they returned to action and pounded Wisconsin, 93 to 68, to win the Big Ten title outright. Despite that, the really big sports news that day came from Squaw Valley, where the Winter Olympics were being held. In the greatest upset in Olympic hockey history to date, the United States defeated the overwhelming favorites from the Soviet Union by a score of 3–2. The next day the USA defeated Czechoslovakia, 9–4, and were the gold medalists, with the Canadians second and the Soviet Union third.

With the victory by the Buckeyes, the battle was for second, although no Big Ten teams would be going to a tournament other than the Bucks, to the NCAA. Indiana, in the weekly televised Big Ten game, defeated Minnesota in Bloomington, 78 to 74, to make second place almost inevitable. Bellamy scored 26 in a battle with Ron Johnson of the Gophers, who tossed in 22 points. Northwestern won over Purdue, 68 to 66, creating a third-place tie with Minnesota. Terry Dischinger had game honors with 25, but the Wildcats had better balance with Jones scoring 21 and Brandt and Cacciatore tallying 13 each. Michigan managed to finally win a game, against state rivals Michigan State, by a score of 72 to 65. John Tidwell set a Wolverine scoring mark with 41 points, breaking the Yost Fieldhouse record of 39, set by Don Schlundt of Indiana in 1953. In his second to last home game, Mannie Jackson of Illinois scored 32 points to lift the Illini to victory, 85 to 70, over Iowa. In the last home game, the next Saturday, Govoner Vaughn followed Jackson's model and scored 30 points in his final home game to lead the Illini to a 90 to 61 win over Michigan.[57]

On Leap Day, February 29, the Indiana Hoosiers leapt over Ohio State to snap their winning streak and solidify the Hoosier grip on second place. It was the last game in the old Indiana fieldhouse and the Hoosiers played without Herb Lee, who had been suspended by the university administration for what was termed "misconduct." But Indiana was not to be denied, winning 99 to 83. Bellamy had 24 with 19 rebounds, Wilkinson had 21 and Long had 19 in the win. For OSU, Lucas scored 27 and grabbed 20 rebounds in playing all 40 minutes, while Havlicek had 25 with 11 boards.[58]

The battle for third ended in a tie for Minnesota and Northwestern as both lost the next weekend against Ohio State, 73–66, and Illinois, 84–77, respectively. Indiana finished at 11–3 by defeating Michigan State, 86–80, in East Lansing. Bellamy had 20 for the Hoosiers, but Horace Walker scored 29 and snared 26 rebounds in his last college game. For Illinois, Vaughn (25) and Jackson (15) combined for nearly half the Illini points in the 84 to 77 win, with Illinois shooting 51.5 percent from the floor. In Minneapolis, the Buckeyes were pressed by the Gophers, before pulling out a 73 to 66 win. Lucas had 23 and 19 rebounds and Joe Roberts followed with 18 tallies.[59]

### Final Standings and MVPs, 1959–60

| | | |
|---|---|---|
| Ohio State | 13–1 | Jerry Lucas (Big Ten MVP) First Team All-American |
| Indiana | 11–3 | Walt Bellamy |
| Minnesota | 8–6 | Ron Johnson |
| Northwestern | 8–6 | Willie Jones |
| Illinois | 8–6 | Govoner Vaughn |
| Purdue | 6–8 | Terry Dischinger |
| Iowa | 6–8 | Don Nelson |
| Michigan State | 5–9 | Horace Walker |
| Wisconsin | 4–10 | Fred Clow |
| Michigan | 1–13 | Lovell Farris |

The Big Ten scoring leaders were:

| | |
|---|---|
| Dischinger, Purdue | 27.5 ppg (seventh nationally, with 26.3) |
| Lucas, Ohio State | 25.9 (eighth nationally, with 26.1) |
| Walker, Michigan State | 25.0 |
| Johnson, Minnesota | 21.6 |
| Bellamy, Indiana | 21.5 |
| Tidwell, Michigan | 21.5 |
| Vaughn, Illinois | 20.0 |

First team All-Conference included Dischinger, Lucas, Bellamy, Ron Johnson and Walker. Dischinger, Lucas and Bellamy were all named All-Americans.[60] Second team was Tidwell (MI), Willie Jones (NU), Siegrfried, Lance Olson (MSU) and Governor Vaughn (IL).[61]

The NCAA opened for the Mideast on March 8, with Ohio University beating Notre Dame and Western Kentucky defeating Miami University in Lexington. The two winners advanced to Louisville, where they faced Georgia Tech and Ohio State, respectively, on March 11. Tech, helped by Roger Kaiser's 25 points, edged Ohio, 57 to 54, and the Buckeyes won easily over Western Kentucky, 98 to 79, as Lucas scored 36 and Havlicek picked up 17. This set up a Georgia Tech-OSU regional final for March 12 in Louisville. There, Ohio State had little trouble with the Yellow Jackets, defeating them 86 to 69. Lucas had 25 and Joe Roberts scored 19 for the Bucks, but Kaiser took game honors for Georgia Tech with 27.

In the east, West Virginia and Jerry West (34 points) were upset by Satch Sanders (28 points) and NYU in the Eastern final, 82 to 81, in overtime. Oscar Robertson scored 43 points in the 82 to 71 Cincinnati victory over Kansas in the Midwestern final. Cal, defending NCAA champion, defeated Oregon, 70 to 49 in the western final.[62]

The Final Four would match NYU v. OSU and Cal v. Cincinnati in the Cow Palace of San Francisco on March 18. OSU had little trouble with the Violets, winning 76 to 54 and holding Sanders to 8 points. Lucas and Siegfried had 19 each to pace the Buckeyes. They would meet defending champion Cal, who defeated Robertson and Cincinnati, 77 to 69. Darrell Imhoff took game scoring honors with 25 and Bill McClintock had 18 for Cal. The Golden Bears held the Big O to 18 points, followed by Paul Hogue's 14.[63] Robertson would "atone" in the third place contest, scoring 32 as the Bearcats topped NYU and Sanders (25 points), 95–71.

The championship game, unexpectedly, was not close. Ohio State came out hot and led 37 to 19 at the half, after sinking 16 of 19 field goals. Cal shot only 8 of 27 for the first half and the game was essentially over. Ohio State had been a bit concerned because Havlicek had cut two fingers on his right hand the night before the game, but his offensive slack was picked up by Nowell with 15, and Havlicek was still a terror on defense. Lucas led with 16, but every starter was in double figures. Dick Doughty was high for Cal with 11 in the 75 to 55 OSU win.[64]

## The Ohio State Juggernaut

The OSU victory was the start of three straight championship appearances and the contention by many that this was the greatest team in Big Ten, if not NCAA, history. The entire starting five from 1959–60, Lucas, Havlicek, Nowell, Siegfried, Roberts, all went on to play professional basketball, and two, Lucas and Havlicek, are in the Naismith Memorial Basketball Hall of Fame, as is coach Fred Taylor. One of the first two off the bench was Bob Knight, another Hall of Fame coach, and Gary Bradds, class of 1965, was Lucas's back-up in 1962, before stepping in and becoming Big Ten Player of the Year in 1963 and National Player of the Year in 1964.

Fred Taylor, who was the architect of this juggernaut, played high school basketball for just a season in Zanesville as the tenth man, but returned (after 36 months in World War II, where he greatly improved his athletic skills) to Ohio State and starred at center for the 1950 Big Ten champion Buckeyes. Taylor was a better baseball player and signed with the Washington Senators after graduation, but only played in 22 major league games at first base (behind All-Star Mickey Vernon) in three years before leaving baseball. He was freshman basketball coach for five years, then became head coach in June 1958 at the age of 33, replacing Floyd Stahl. (Both Lucas and Nowell had announced for OSU in May.) Taylor won seven Big Ten championships in his 18 years at the helm, was National Coach of the Year in 1961 and 1962, and was enshrined to the Naismith Memorial Basketball Hall of Fame in 1986.

Joe Roberts, the only senior starter, averaged 11 ppg and was drafted and signed by the Syracuse Nationals for the 1960–61 season. Marquette had been his first choice for college, but their coach, Ed Hickey, was too busy with a European tour to pursue him. Roberts was interested in both Georgia Tech and Ohio University, but the former didn't recruit blacks and the latter had racial "guidelines" in the town of Athens. So he went to Ohio State.[65] At OSU, he played mostly inside, so it was an adjustment to small forward in the NBA. He played behind Dolph Schayes, Johnny Kerr, Dave Gambee and Barney Cable, but managed to get into 68 games and average nearly five points and four rebounds a game. He upped that to about eight points and seven rebounds in an average of 20 minutes a game the next season, but the addition of both Len Chappell and Chet Walker, in 1962–63, cut his playing time and totals to 5.5 ppg and just two rebounds a game, and he appeared in just 33 games. Roberts left the NBA after that season and went into coaching, first at the college level and then in the NBA, and was an assistant coach on the 1975 NBA champion Golden State Warriors. He stayed in the Bay Area and later was a real estate broker and coached at Alameda County's Juvenile Hall.

Larry Siegfried had been the leading scorer (21.6 ppg) for the Buckeyes in 1958–59, but modified his game to fit into the winning-team concept infused by the three sophomore starters in 1959–60. He scored 13.4 ppg (second on the team) and ran the offense. In 1960–61 he averaged 15.2, again the second leading scorer, as the Buckeyes went undefeated until the NCAA championship game. He was drafted by both Cincinnati of the NBA and Cleveland of the newly formed American Basketball League; he signed with the latter, where he became part of the championship team. He was coached by both John McLendon and Bill Sharman at Cleveland, and this made him an even better player. He averaged nine points a game and was second in assists for the Cleveland Pipers, who folded after the initial ABL season, despite winning the first and only league championship. He was cut by the St. Louis Hawks, but signed by the Celtics for the 1963–64 season at the strong urging of his former OSU teammate, John Havlicek, and stayed with the Celtics for seven seasons, averaging between 12 and 14 points the last five seasons. He was selected by Portland in the expansion draft, then immediately traded to San Diego, where he played one season; he then played with Houston and Atlanta in 1971–72 before retiring. He led the league twice in free-throw percentage. He coached for a number of years, then counseled prisoners. He died of heart failure at the age of 71 in 2010.

All-American Jerry Lucas rebounds and looks to outlet the pass to John Havlicek of the OSU Buckeyes (The Ohio State University Archives).

Mel Nowell was a starter from his sophomore year and averaged 13.3 ppg, third on the team in 1960–61. The next year he averaged 13.6, then 12.5 his senior year. He was drafted by the Chicago Zephyrs in 1962 and played 39 games, averaging 5.9 per game. He was not on an NBA roster the next season and played for Wilkes-Barre of the Eastern League. He was then out of pro basketball until 1967, when he made a brief comeback try with New Jersey of the American Basketball Association, where he averaged 9.6 points per game. He later became a businessman, was the state of Ohio's budget director for nearly three years, and went into real estate, construction and retail sales.

John Havlicek was the second leading rebounder on Ohio State behind Lucas, all three years. He averaged 12.2 ppg his sophomore year, 14.5 his junior year and 17.0 his senior year. He was drafted by the Boston Celtics in the first round in 1962, then played on eight championship teams in his 16-year NBA career, all with Boston. He averaged 20.8 ppg and 6.8 rpg lifetime, and was named one of the top 50 all-time NBA players in 1996. He was elected to the Naismith Memorial Basketball Hall of Fame in 1984.

Jerry Lucas may have been the greatest player in Big Ten history (according to, among others, Peter Bjarkman and "Tug" Wilson),[66] and he was the scoring and rebounding force of the team. He averaged 24.3 ppg over three years, as well as 17.2 rpg. He also shot .624 for his career, and that and the rebounding records are still his at OSU. He was voted AP, UPI and USBWA Player of the Year for both 1961 and 1962. After his storied career, Lucas was drafted by the Cincinnati Royals of the National Basketball Association (NBA) and the Cleveland Pipers of the American Basketball League (ABL), owned by George Steinbrenner. Although he had initially said that he was not interested in playing pro basketball, Lucas signed a personal services contract with Steinbrenner, and when the ABL was foundering and Cleveland dropped from the league, Lucas was left with a contract, but no team.[67]

Lucas worked out with the Buckeyes, helped with the freshman team, and took some graduate courses in business and management during his "off year." He was not one to let his mind or body rest, having achieved a nearly all "A" average in the School of Business and Commerce. His memory was phenomenal, and he ultimately wrote a number of memory books and lectured on memory improvement, following his basketball career.

A deal was worked out between Steinbrenner, the Cincinnati Royals, and Lucas, and he became a Royal starting in 1963, playing with Oscar Robertson. The Royals improved by 13 games, winning 55 (second best in the league), and Lucas was Rookie of the Year. Robertson was voted MVP. The Royals were eliminated by the Celtics, and that pattern continued, even as Lucas continued an amazing pattern himself. For the six full seasons that he was a Royal, he averaged between 17.7 and 21.5 ppg and 17.4 and 21.1 rpg. In 1969 he was traded to the Warriors, where he played for two seasons before being traded to the New York Knicks for Cazzie Russell in 1971. In his three seasons in New York, they lost in the championship round, won the NBA championship, and were eliminated in the eastern finals. Lucas was no longer a starter, but a solid contributor off the bench, and finally had an NBA ring. He continues to lecture on memory and has written a number of children's books.

It was an Olympic year in 1960, and the formation of the U.S. basketball team was still a result of a tournament in which the winner's starters were selected and players were then added from the other seven teams. The tournament was won by the NCAA All-Stars, whose coach, Pete Newell, was then named as the Olympic coach. Seven NCAA All-Stars were named, four AAU players and one Armed Forces player. This was a kind of compromise in the AAU-NCAA tussle for control of USA Basketball (and for amateur sport, generally in the U.S.). The Big Ten was well-represented on the All-Stars and thus the team, which included Walt Bellamy, Terry Dischinger, and from the NCAA champions, Jerry Lucas. John Havlicek was not named to the team. Other top college players were Oscar Robertson, Jerry West, Darrell Imhoff and Bob Boozer. This was the best Olympic team ever, until the Dream Team of 1992, the first year that professionals were officially allowed in the Olympic Games. The 1960 team won its eight games by an average of 42 points, and the championship against Brazil was a 27-point victory, 90 to 63.[68] Clearly, American basketball was superior, and of the returning college players from the U.S. Olympic team, three of the five were from the Big Ten.

## The 1961 Season

As defending Big Ten and national champions, the Buckeyes of Ohio State were clearly the favorite for the 1960–61 Big Ten championship, but there would be at least one other team, Indiana, who was seen as a title possibility. *Dell Sports Basketball* picked Lucas as first team All-American and OSU as #1 in the nation; Indiana was ranked 18th. *Sport* did not pick teams, but did say, "Lucas shoots and rebounds with the skill of a pro and … is expected to lead the Buckeyes to their second consecutive NCAA tournament championship."[69]

Besides the three Big Ten Olympians, *Dell Sports Basketball* also selected John Tidwell, Don Nelson, Ray Cronk, Mel Nowell, Larry Siegfried and John Havlicek as Midwest all-regional players. All were juniors or seniors, but Midwest "sophs to watch" included Illinois's Bill Burwell, Dave Downey and Billy Small. From Indiana, Tom Bolyard, Jimmy Rayl and Ray Pavy were noted. Michigan State had Lonnie Sanders, the final soph mentioned.

The December UPI ratings had OSU as #1, Bradley as #2 and Indiana as #3. No other Big Ten teams were mentioned. An early test of league and league members' strengths would be holiday tournaments. Ohio State was in New York City to play in the Holiday Festival, and they won that easily with a romp against Seton Hall, 97–57, a tight 70–65 win over St. John's, and a struggle against St. Bonaventure and Tom Stith, 84–82. Against Seton Hall, Jerry Lucas had a season-low 16 points, but his teammates showed why the Bucks were so dangerous: they were incredibly balanced. Havlicek and Siegfried also had 16, Mel Nowell had 15, and Bob Knight 12. The win made OSU 7–0. They got 32 points and 21 rebounds from Lucas to defeat the Bonnies, as Stith, on fire, even against the defense of John Havlicek, scored 35.[70]

Purdue, meanwhile, hosted the Hoosier Classic, where they topped Notre Dame, 78–58, led by Terry Dischinger's 32 points. Butler defeated Illinois in that tourney, 70–68, not a good omen for the Fighting Illini, who got 17 from both John Wessels and Jerry Colangelo (future Phoenix Suns general manager and president and director of USA Basketball). Sophs Bill Burwell and Dave Downey got 14 each. In the championship, Butler edged Purdue, 65–63, despite 34 points from Dischinger.

In Los Angeles, Iowa defeated Cal in the Los Angeles Classic with Don Nelson picking up 32 points. UCLA crushed Michigan State, 98–61, USC defeated Minnesota, 75–52, and Indiana edged Stanford, 58–50.

It was not just fun and games at the start of 1961. In fact, it had a most ominous beginning as President Eisenhower, soon to leave office, warned the North Vietnamese about incursions into Laos, noting that the U.S. was ready to help protect that part of the world from communist invasions.[71] Despite that warning, the North Vietnamese did enter Laos, but Eisenhower decided to leave further decision-making on this issue to his successor, John F. Kennedy, who would be inaugurated in two weeks.[72]

The Big Ten season opened on January 7, and Richard Dozer felt that Iowa (8–1) was now the Buckeyes' chief challenger for the championship. He also found Purdue (6–3) "erratic, but talented and explosive." Indiana was also 6–3.[73]

True to Dozer's form, the three teams all won on Saturday, as did Indiana and Wisconsin. The Bucks had their way with Illinois, 91–65, in Columbus. Lucas had 35 points on 14–17 from the floor and snared 13 rebounds. Siegfried had 18. For Illinois, soph Burwell had 15 and senior Colangelo, 14. In West Lafayette, Dischinger had 41 points to lead the Boilermakers to a 79–64 victory over Northwestern, who were led by Brad Snyder with 16 and Bill Cacciatorre with 14. Iowa had no trouble with Minnesota, winning 71–46; the Gophers were handicapped by the loss of potential All-American Ray Cronk to academic ineligibility. Indiana topped Michigan, 81–70, and Wisconsin defeated Michigan State, 74–71.[74]

On the next Monday, Indiana and Iowa won again, IU over Michigan State, 79–55, and Iowa over Wisconsin, 76–68, in Madison. Bellamy (24) and Bolyard (19) led the Hoosiers, and Frank Allen (24) and Nelson (20) led the Iowa win.[75] There were no other Big Ten games, although Ohio State played and defeated Evansville, 86–59. That was not news, but the fact that Jerry Lucas sat out with a sprained knee certainly was. Five days later, the fear was gone as Lucas picked up 30 points and Siegfried 16 in a 79–45 romp over Northwestern. Illinois ended their early season losing streak with an easy win over Michigan, 84 to 64. Sophomore Dave Downey had 24 and Jerry Colangelo 18 for the Illini. Iowa won its ninth in a row, defeating Michigan State, 86 to 72, behind Don Nelson's 18 points. Purdue handed Minnesota its second loss in a row, 65 to 64. Terry Dischinger led all scorers with 29 points for the Boilermakers. The game was played at a snail's pace with just a total of 40 rebounds in the contest.[76]

Iowa defeated Illinois, 78–71, on Monday to keep their win streak intact. Don Nelson had 25 and Ron Zagar 18 for the Hawks. Colangelo led the Illini with 20. Northwestern lost to Minnesota, 66–54, and shot just 20 percent from the field (14–69) in doing so. MSU won the meaningless battle of Michigan, defeating the Wolverines 81–69. The UPI rankings that week reflected what seemed obvious by now, i.e., four teams were the only serious contenders for the Big Ten title. OSU was ranked #1, Iowa #4, Indiana #15 and Purdue #20. Rounding out the top five were St. Bonaventure, Bradley and Louisville.[77]

On January 21, 1961, John Fitzgerald Kennedy was sworn in as the nation's 35th president and the youngest to be elected. It was a time of excitement, and Kennedy's interest in sports was quickly emulated by the rest of the nation. The Big Ten race had that excitement. That same day, Purdue ended the Iowa win streak, 47 to 41, in a deliberate game with poor shooting played in West Lafayette. Dischinger (19) and Dick Mitchell (11) were the Boilermaker scorers. Iowa was topped by Nelson's 13 in a game that had a 23–14 halftime score. Ohio State coasted by Minnesota, 75–56 in Columbus. Lucas had a typically great game with 22 points and 19 rebounds. Overall the Bucks outrebounded the Gophers, 55 to 26.[78]

Purdue's share of the Big Ten lead was short-lived as Northwestern surprised them two nights later in Evanston. Led by Ralph Wells (21) and Brad Snyder (14), the Wildcats won 64–62, holding Dischinger to 17 points. Jerry Berkshire led the Boilers with 20. Minnesota pummeled Michigan State, 89–70, in Minneapolis.[79] The next weekend, the

Gophers topped Northwestern, 66–59, while Ohio State crushed Purdue, 92–62, to hand the Boilers their second loss in a row. Dischinger took game-scoring honors with 26, while Siegfried (21), Lucas (17) and Nowell (17) led the Buckeye romp.[80]

The next week (January 31, 1961) started with Ham the chimp taking the headlines as he rode an American rocket 155 miles into space and back. The space program had been started by President Eisenhower, but was accelerated by President Kennedy, who vowed to get an American to the moon within 10 years. On Monday, the Buckeyes continued their own rocket ride against hapless Wisconsin, 100–68, while Indiana lost to Minnesota, 66–58. The race was becoming more and more a runaway for Ohio State, rather than a real horse race.[81]

Ohio State kept winning and maintaining its hold on the #1 spot in the national basketball rankings. They breezed by Michigan, 80–58, then trounced Indiana, 100 to 65. The big "showdown" was all OSU as Lucas had 34 (and 14 rebounds), Siegfried 27 and Havlicek 22 (plus 13 rebounds). Walter Bellamy had 19 points and 19 rebounds for the overmatched Hoosiers, who were outrebounded, 54–34.[82]

Iowa had moved to #8 in the country and Indiana was still #14, despite their pounding by the Buckeyes, illustrating how much respect the Big Ten had, despite the dominance of OSU. The next week, OSU was still #1, but Iowa had dropped a bit to #9. Purdue at #17 had replaced Indiana in the top 20.

Iowa won at Indiana, 74–67, while Ohio State continued to go undefeated. In Big Ten play, they were 7–0, Iowa was 4–1, Purdue 5–2 and Indiana 3–2. To make matters worse for Iowa, they lost four starters, Frank Allen, Ron Harris, Ron Zagar and Dave Maher, at the beginning of the second semester because of academic ineligibility. An unnamed member of the physical education department, in reference to this issue, made an unusual comment, stating that grades in that department "are not given on the basis of merit, but on the basis of need."[83] The four starters all failed at least one course because "under Big Ten rules, failure to pass one course makes an athlete ineligible."[84]

Ohio State won its 23rd in a row on February 13, defeating Northwestern, 89 to 65. Mel Nowell led the scoring with 27. Iowa edged Wisconsin, 63–61, and Purdue defeated Indiana, 64–55. For the Hawkeyes, Nelson had 24 and Matt Szykowny, the starting quarterback for the Hawkeyes, had 22.[85]

Terry Dischinger was an All-American all three seasons at Purdue and led the Big Ten in scoring his senior year (Purdue Athletics Communications).

At this point, mid–February, the Big Ten standings looked like this: OSU 9–0, Iowa 6–1, Purdue 7–2, Illinois 4–3, Minnesota 5–4, Indiana 3–4, Northwestern 3–6, and Wisconsin, Michigan, and MSU all 1–6. With five or six games to play, both Iowa and Purdue were theoretically in the race, but the likelihood Ohio State would lose a game, let alone the Big Ten title, seemed remote. Iowa had lost four starters at the semester, but Purdue had a solid lineup led by Dischinger, Garland and Berkshire.

Ohio State survived its biggest scare on February 18, when they rallied to beat Iowa in Iowa City, 62–61. The Buckeyes were down at the half 34–24, down 59–52 with 3:36 to go, and trailed for 38 minutes, before gaining four points on steals by Knight and Gearhart in the last two minutes. Don Nelson, the only Iowa starter over 6'3", missed a shot, and there were two unsuccessful Iowa tips as time expired. Lucas had 25 and Havlicek 17, while Nelson matched Lucas with 25.[86]

Purdue also had a scare that day, as they edged Michigan 65–64 in Ann Arbor. Dischinger had 26, Darrel McGinley 23 to lead the Boilermakers, while Scott Maentz (18), John Tidwell (15) and Jon Hall (15) led the upset-minded Wolverines.[87]

Two nights later Iowa kept the pressure on OSU with a 50–46 victory in Ann Arbor and the Bucks responded with a 73–69 win in Bloomington for their 26th victory in a row. Nowell (27) and Siegfried (17) carried the scoring load. Lucas battled Walt Bellamy, his Olympic teammate, outscoring him 16 to 13. They each had 17 rebounds, but Indiana outrebounded Ohio State, 57–50. The Buckeyes were 11–0 in the conference. Nelson (22) and Szykowny (16) had almost all the points in the Iowa win.[88]

On the following Saturday, OSU clinched at least a tie for the championship with an easy win over Wisconsin, 97–74. Purdue stayed close with an 85–74 win over Michigan State as Dischinger scored 52 points, a new Big Ten record. Iowa kept pace with a 61–43 victory in Minneapolis as Nelson scored 30. Also of interest was the Indiana victory over Illinois, 93–82, in Bloomington, which had been hit with a blizzard that kept the crowd to just 1,800. High school officials had to be used in the contest, in which IU outrebounded the Illini, 74–47.[89]

Ohio State was off on February 27, but Iowa defeated Purdue, 73–62, in Iowa City, to take second place in the conference. Nelson had 26, Syzkowny 20, for the Hawks, while Dischinger had 35 with 21–29 free throws, causing four Hawks to foul out. Purdue shot just 27 percent from the floor (16–59), while Iowa hit 22 of 49 (45 percent). Ohio State ended the drama the next Saturday by winning their 28th in a row, 23 for the season, in defeating MSU, 91to 83. Havlicek had 26 points and 10 rebounds, while Lucas had 23 points and 20 rebounds.[90]

The Buckeyes ended the Big Ten season undefeated on March 11 with an easy victory in Champaign, 95–66. That same day, Fred Taylor was named college basketball's "Coach of the Year" after receiving 45 percent of the votes cast. Eddie Donovan of St. Bonaventure was second, with Sharm Scheuerman of Iowa third. Purdue tied Iowa for second in beating Wisconsin, 88–81.[91]

### Final Standings and MVPs, 1960–61

| | | |
|---|---|---|
| Ohio State | 14–0 | Jerry Lucas (Big10 Player of the Year) First Team All-American |
| Iowa | 10–4 | Don Nelson |
| Purdue | 10–4 | Terry Dischinger (First Team All-American) |

| | | |
|---|---|---|
| Minnesota | 8–6 | Dick Erickson |
| Indiana | 8–6 | Walter Bellamy |
| Northwestern | 6–8 | Brad Snyder and Ralph Wells |
| Illinois | 5–9 | Dave Downey |
| Wisconsin | 4–10 | Ken Siebel |
| Michigan State | 3–11 | Art Schwarm |
| Michigan | 2–12 | John Tidwell |

Terry Dischinger led the league in scoring with a 28.9 average. The next five scorers were Lucas (24.6), Nelson (22.9), Bellamy (21.1), Downey (19.3) and Tidwell (18). First team was Lucas, Havlicek, Dischinger, Bellamy and Nelson. Second team was John Tidwell (MI), Dave Downey (IL), Mel Nowell (OSU), Larry Siegfried (OSU) and Bob Griggas (MN).

The NCAA tourney opened on March 14 with first-round games for 16 teams, while the remaining eight would face winners of the opening games. OSU was the #1 team in the country and had a bye in the first round. Louisville defeated Ohio University in the first round in Louisville and would play Ohio State in Freedom Hall on March 17. That contest was surprisingly close as the Buckeyes edged the Cardinals, 56 to 55. Louisville sagged on Lucas with as many as three men and held him to two of seven from the field and nine points. Havlicek went eight of 13 and 17 points, plus he hit a 25-footer with six seconds to go for the win.[92] "Lucas told *Sports Illustrated*, 'I was guarded so tightly I thought I was in jail.'"[93]

Ohio State's victory sent them into the regional finals against Kentucky, who had defeated Morehead State, 71 to 64, in the second game of the double-header in Louisville. The winners met the next night and OSU won easily, 87–74. The only weak part of the OSU game was their greater number of fouls, giving Kentucky a free-throw advantage (30–39 for UK, 17–28 for OSU). The Buckeyes shot better from the field, 59.3 percent, while Kentucky was just 31.9 percent. Jerry Lucas had 33 points and 30 rebounds to dominate play, while Larry Siegfried had 20 points. A key in the second half was when Bob Knight had two 3-point plays in less than a minute. Roger Newman was high for the Wildcats with 26, with 18 of 22 free throws.[94]

OSU would head to Kansas City to meet eastern regional winner St. Joseph's, on Friday night, March 24. The other contest would pit Utah, who had beaten Arizona 88 to 80 behind Billy McGill's 31 points, against Cincinnati, a 69–64 winner over Kansas State. In those semifinals, OSU trounced St. Joe's, 93–69, and Cincinnati defeated Utah, 82–67. OSU's win was their 32nd in a row, 27th of the season, while Cincinnati's victory was their 21st in a row, after a 5–3 start. The Bearcats got 21 from Carl Bouldin and 18 from Paul Hogue, after getting 22 from Bob Weisenhahn and 16 from Tom Thacker in the semifinals. They were a well-balanced team, a fitting opponent for the national title against the Buckeyes. OSU's win over St. Joe's was again led by Lucas with 29 (10–11 from the floor and 9–10 free throws) and Siegfried with 21.[95]

The next night one of the most memorable games in NCAA finals history was played, as Cincinnati defeated OSU in overtime, 70 to 65. Despite the excitement of a NCAA title game, there was no national television coverage. In fact, Eddie Einhorn, who packaged and sold this game for $6,000, could only get stations in Ohio and Kentucky to show the contest.[96] That game had been preceded by a record-setting third-place contest as St. Joe's defeated Utah in four overtimes, 127–120. In the final, OSU led at the half, 39–38. In the second half, OSU led 52–46 with 11:46 to play, but only scored nine points the rest of the half. The game went to overtime at 61–61, and was still a one-point contest with 47 seconds to go, but Cincinnati outscored the Buckeyes by four in that time to win 70–65. Lucas had 27, Siegfried 14, and Nowell 9, and the Bucks shot 50 percent (25–50), but were outrebounded, 30–24. Cincinnati had four players in double figures and Hogue with nine. They did not shoot as well as OSU, 29–64 for 45.3 percent. OSU also hit 15 of 16 free throws, while Cincinnati was 12 of 19. A couple of OSU errors spelled doom at the end as Siegfried threw the ball away and went one of two at the line in the last seconds of the game.[97]

The Cincinnati victory over Ohio State was a shock to most basketball observers, but it was hard to see OSU's loss as a failure. Coach Fred Taylor noted, "They simply outhustled us. Our kids have nothing to be ashamed of, I told them that."[98] Lee Caryer called it "the most difficult defeat of the Golden Age, probably in Ohio State basketball history."[99]

Despite the devastating loss, OSU had the next year to look forward to, since Havlicek, Lucas, Nowell, Gary Gearhart and Knight would all return as seniors. They would be heavily favored to repeat as Big Ten champions and return to the NCAA finals, but it would be a long summer of reflection for the Buckeyes.

# VII

## *The Coaches*

Obviously, the players play the game and determine the actual outcome, but many games are won before the tip-off by insightful scouting, focused preparation, timely substitutions and insightful play-calling. These practices are those of the coach and his staff. In this chapter, a number of coaches from the period of 1910–1970 will be presented, with at least one from each of the original nine Big Ten teams. Most of the coaches that worked in the Big Ten during that period will *not* be discussed, simply because of space limitations. Rather, these brief biographies will examine those considered the best or the most influential coaches in the league for the periods in which they toiled.

The earliest basketball coach to find consistent success in the Western Conference was L.J. Cooke, who began at the University of Minnesota in 1897. Admittedly the sport was just in its infancy, but Cooke won five conference championships (1906, 1907, 1911, 1917, 1919) and coached 27 years at Minnesota, during which time he compiled a record of 244–135.[1]

One of the first great Big Ten coaches was Walter "Doc" Meanwell, who coached at the University of Wisconsin from 1911 to 1917, then again from 1920 to 1934 (having taken time out for World War I), followed by a two-year coaching stint at the University of Missouri. Meanwell was born in Leeds, England, in 1884 and moved with his family to Rochester, New York, in 1887, where he graduated from Rochester High School and competed for the Rochester Athletic Club in wrestling, baseball and basketball, captaining the latter two teams. He graduated from the University of Maryland Medical School in Baltimore in 1909, interned at Maryland General in Baltimore before being named athletic director of a Baltimore park, then supervisor of recreation for the city of Baltimore, and after that, athletic director for Loyola University in Baltimore. He developed the short pass pattern that would characterize his teams, while coaching in the Baltimore Public Athletic League. His team could only use a small amount of space in the settlement house gym in which they played, and the short pass became first a necessity, and later a trademark of his teams.[2]

Meanwell was named the coach of the University of Wisconsin basketball team for the 1911–12 season and his short pass, criss-cross offense, which emphasized ball control, brought some patterns to what had generally been helter-skelter offense at Wisconsin, as well as the conference. He also emphasized tight defense and this combination led to an undefeated season, 15–0. His team was named national champions by the Helms Foundation, and they followed up that season by going 14–1 and winning their second consecutive Western Conference (Big Ten forerunner). The next season the Badgers went 15–0 once again, 12–0 in conference, to win their third consecutive title, and were again named national champions. They repeated as national champions in 1916 after a year hiatus.[3] Meanwell's team went 20–1, 11–1 in conference, for the last title, and he was 92–9 in six years in Madison.

During that time he also was also working for a doctorate in public health, which he received in 1915. In 1917 he left for Columbia, Missouri, and led the Tigers to a 17–1 record and the Missouri Valley Conference title. He then captained a medical corps during World War I. He returned to Missouri and coached in 1919–20, leading the Tigers to another Missouri Valley Conference title with a record of 17–1.

In 1920 Meanwell returned to Wisconsin as coach and remained in that position until 1934. During that time his teams tied for four Big Ten basketball titles in 1921, 1923, 1924 and 1929. He also trained a number of players and assistants who went on to great coaching careers, adopting and adapting the "Meanwell or Wisconsin system." These included his successor at Wisconsin, Harold "Bud" Foster, as well as Harold Olsen, who coached at Ohio State and later Northwestern.[4] Meanwell's overall record at Wisconsin was 246–99, 158–80 in conference.

Walter "Doc" Meanwell, a native of Leeds, England, was an early basketball coach in England, then coached Wisconsin for 20 years (1911–17 and 1920–34), winning four Big Ten titles (University of Wisconsin Athletics).

Meanwell retired from coaching in 1934 to practice medicine exclusively. In 1959 he was enshrined in the Naismith Memorial Basketball Hall of Fame.[5]

Ralph Jones began his Big Ten basketball coaching career at Purdue in 1909, having already coached at Butler and Wabash. Jones was born in 1880 and was considered the first high school basketball coach in Indiana, having formed a team while a student at Indianapolis Shortridge High in 1899. In his second year at Purdue, he led them to their first Big Nine championship in 1911, then repeated in 1912. He went 32–9 at Purdue before moving to the University of Illinois in 1912. He took a mediocre program and led it to a Big Nine title in 1915, as well as a Helms National championship title. The Illini won another Big Nine title in 1917, before Jones left Illinois after the 1920 season with a record of 85–34. He became basketball coach at Lake Forest (IL) Academy in

1920 before becoming coach of the Chicago Bears and leading them to the NFL championship in 1932. He then returned to Lake Forest, but this time as coach of Lake Forest College, where he remained until retiring in 1948.[6]

The last of the oldest "old-timers" to be profiled is Ward "Piggy" Lambert, the coach at Purdue from 1916 until he entered the U.S. Army in World War I, then again from 1918 until 1946, when he retired at the age of 57. He died in 1958 at the age of 69. Lambert was born in Deadwood, South Dakota, but raised in Crawfordsville, Indiana, where he played all sports before attending Wabash College in Crawfordsville. There he led the basketball team in scoring in his sophomore year, added coaching the local high school team to his resume in his junior year, and was the college head coach in his senior year. He also played football and baseball on the Wabash teams. He graduated in 1911 and enrolled in graduate school at the University of Minnesota in chemistry, but left in less than a year and returned to Indiana as the basketball coach of Lebanon High School. After four successful years there, he was hired to be the Purdue baseball and basketball coach and assistant in football in 1916. "When Piggy Lambert took over at Purdue, the Boilermakers had been suffering through hard times.... Purdue sank slowly through the ranks until 1916 when, coachless, they finished last."[7]

Lambert returned after the war to lead the Boilermakers to 11 Big Ten championships and a Helms Foundation National title in 1932, when the team was led by All-American guard John Wooden. Lambert's Purdue squads won 371 games and lost 152; his 228 wins in Big Ten play are second to Bobby Knight and Gene Keady.[8]

"Lambert possessed the extraordinary ability to take players with average ability and transform them into fundamentally sound performers.... Much of Lambert's success can be traced to his innovative style of play and his ability to recruit suitable players to execute his strategy."[9] That required three key elements: a big man who could snare defensive rebounds and get the ball out to streaking guards quickly; guards and forwards who were excellent ball-

John Wooden was an All-American all three seasons, 1929–32, at Purdue (Purdue Athletics Communications).

handlers; and perimeter players who played aggressive defense to deny opponents unguarded shots at the bucket. These same characteristics were woven into the coaching of John Wooden, and he credited Lambert with that. His run-run offense had and has had a continued influence on the way the game is played. He retired from coaching because of ill health and became commissioner of the National Basketball League in 1946. He was instrumental of the merger with the Basketball Association of America in 1949 to form what became the National Basketball Association. Lambert was enshrined in the Naismith Memorial Basketball Hall of Fame in 1960, two years after his death. His Hall of Fame biography notes that his "coaching methods greatly influenced Wooden and his Pyramid of Success. Lambert pioneered the fast-breaking style of hardwood play and his teams were always noted for their great speed."[10]

Harold Olsen was from Rice Lake, Wisconsin, located in the northwestern part of the state, and attended the University of Wisconsin, where he played basketball under Doc Meanwell, captaining the1916–17 squad. After graduation he enlisted in the Army Air Force and served three years before his discharge and acceptance of the head coaching position at Bradley University. From 1920 to 1922 he coached at Ripon College, then was hired in 1923 as the head basketball coach at Ohio State University. He remained in that position until 1946, when he resigned to accept the position of head coach of the Chicago Stags in the newly formed Basketball Association of America (BAA) pro league.

Olsen's record at Ohio State was 259–197 and included five Western Conference championships (1925, 1933, 1939, 1944, 1945). He implemented the "Meanwell system" and it paid off hugely. In later years, his former players disagreed on how good a coach he was, but all asserted what a great, honest person he was.[11] Olsen was instrumental in the formation of the NCAA basketball tourney, chairing the NCAA playoff committee for eight years, which was originally organized and run by the National Association of Basketball Coaches (NABC), of which Olsen was president in 1933.[12] His Ohio State squad won the eastern half of the first tournament in 1939 in Philadelphia, and then lost to Oregon, 46–33, in the NCAA tournament championship game.

Olsen coached the Chicago Stags for three years, compiling a record of 113–76, winning the BAA Western Division in 1947, but losing in the championship series to the Philadelphia Warriors. When the BAA merged with the National Basketball League (NBL) to form the National Basketball Association (NBA) in 1949, Olsen left the pro ranks. He returned to coaching the next season as Northwestern head coach and compiled a record of 19–25 in two seasons before being forced to retire because of ill health. He died in 1953 and was elected to the Naismith Basketball Hall of Fame as a contributor in 1959.[13]

In 1925, Everett Dean was appointed coach of the Indiana University Hoosiers. Dean had been born and raised in Indiana and enrolled at Indiana University in 1917, where he played football, basketball and baseball as a freshman. He turned down several offers to pursue a career in baseball and captained the Hoosiers basketball team as a senior. After graduation in 1922, he coached at Carleton College in Northfield, Minnesota, for three years, then returned to Indiana to be both basketball and baseball coach beginning in the 1924–25 seasons; he coached both for 14 seasons. His baseball teams won three conference titles and were runners-up four times, while his basketball squads won Big Ten titles in 1926, 1928 and 1936. His record as basketball coach was 162–93.

In 1938 Dean moved to Stanford and coached them to an NCAA title in 1942, with a Jim Pollard-led squad. Dean's overall record at Stanford was 166–120 in 11 seasons. His baseball teams won three Pacific Coast Conference titles in seventeen seasons. He retired in 1955 and was elected to the Naismith Memorial Basketball Hall of Fame in 1966 and the Baseball Coaches Hall of Fame that same year.[14] He served as Bobby Knight's Honorary Coach for the 1984 Olympic basketball team in Los Angeles.

Dean emulated Meanwell's system of patterns and ball control. "Indiana played ball-control basketball under Dean although [Branch] McCracken set a league scoring record in his All-American senior season, despite the system."[15] Dean died in 1993 at the age of 95.

Arthur "Dutch" Lonborg was born in Gardner, Illinois, in 1898, but moved to Kansas at a young age since his father worked for the Atchison, Topeka and Santa Fe Railroad. He played basketball for "Phog" Allen at the University of Kansas from 1916 to 1920, with time out in 1917–18 for military service. Lonborg was all-Missouri Valley Conference in football in three seasons, as well as all-MVC in basketball two years and second team All-American in 1919–20. He graduated in 1921 with a law degree, but postponed a legal career for a year to try coaching. He never went back to law. He coached all sports at McPherson (Kansas) College for two years, then went to Washburn University (Kansas) for four years, during which time his squad became the last college team to win the AAU basketball championship in 1925.[16]

Arthur "Dutch" Lonborg, head basketball coach at Northwestern from 1927 to 1950 (Northwestern University Archives).

Lonborg's teams were 63–15 at Washburn in four years and his success propelled him to the Northwestern head coaching position, which he assumed for the 1927–28 season. Within four years, he had made the Wildcats Big Ten champions in 1931, and again in 1933. Lonborg utilized a set-play offense, but his team could and did run when it had the opportunity.

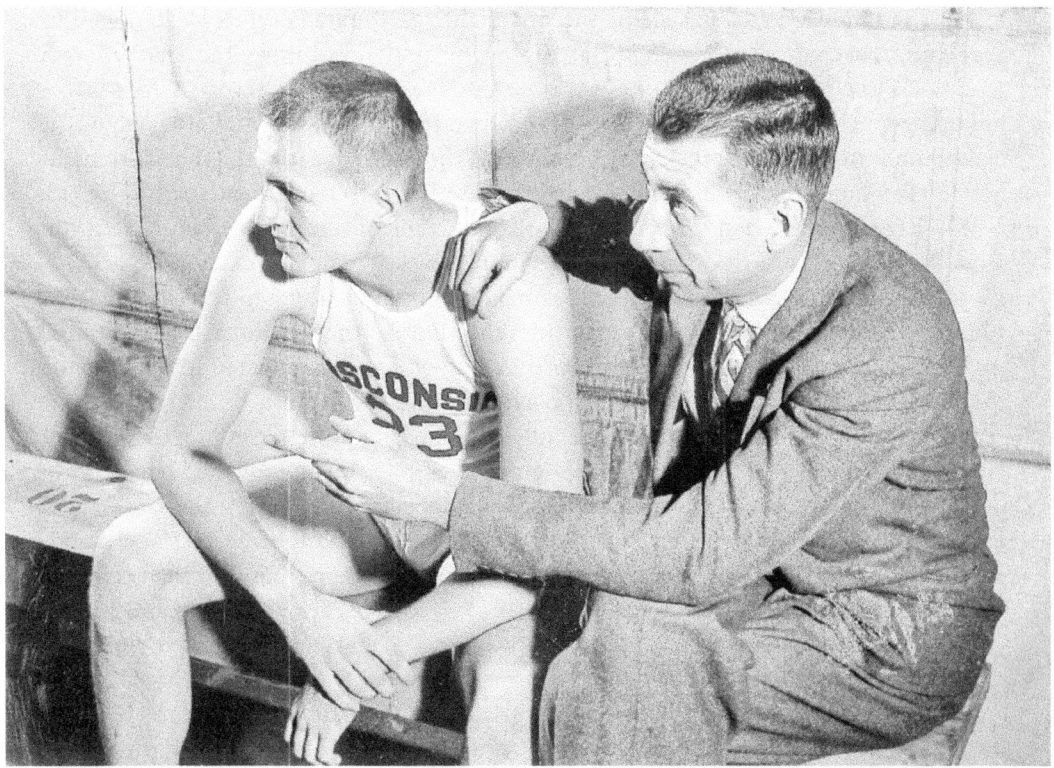

Coach Harold "Bud" Foster, shown with Don Rehfeldt, won 266 games in 25 years as head coach of the Badgers, three Big Ten titles, and the NCAA title in 1941 (University of Wisconsin Athletics).

Lonborg is the all-time winningest Northwestern coach with 236 victories in 23 seasons. In 1950 he went back to his alma mater, the University of Kansas, as athletic director and was an active builder of teams and facilities. He retired in 1964 as athletic director, but continued as director of events until 1973. He was enshrined in the Naismith Basketball Hall of Fame in 1973, and also was elected to Northwestern and Kansas Sports Halls of Fame. He died in 1985.

Meanwell was succeeded at Wisconsin by one of his former players from 1928–30, Harold "Bud" Foster. "Foster played in only eight losing games for the Badgers (13–4 in 1928, 15–2 in both 1929 and 1930) and captained the 1930 team."[17] He then played professional basketball for four years in various Midwestern leagues before being hired in 1934 to succeed Meanwell at Wisconsin, where Foster emulated the pattern offense of his mentor.

Foster won three Big Ten titles (1935, 1941, 1947), as well as the third NCAA championship in 1941. Foster won 265 games at Wisconsin, stepping down from the head coaching post in 1959. He then served 17 years as professor of athletics and director of grants-in-aid for the university, retiring in 1976. He was elected to the Naismith Memorial Hall of Fame, as a player, in 1964.

Branch McCracken was another former great player who succeeded his mentor and returned to coach at his alma mater. McCracken had been an All-American player in 1930, led the Hoosiers in scoring three straight years under Everett Dean, and upon graduation, became head coach at Ball State University in Muncie, Indiana, where he was 93–41 in eight seasons. In 1938 he succeeded Dean and went 87–17 in five seasons, including an NCAA championship in 1940, when IU finished second in the league, but champion Purdue refused the NCAA bid. It was the second year of the tournament and McCracken holds the distinction of being the first Big Ten coach to win an NCAA title.

In 1943 he enlisted in the Navy and rose to the rank of commander before returning after the war to his position as head coach for the 1946–47 season. He then won 277 games and lost 157 over the next 19 seasons, winning four Big Ten titles (1953, 1954, 1957, 1958) and another NCAA title in 1953, led by the fabulous Don Schlundt. McCracken retired in 1965 with a total of 364 victories and was elected to the Naismith Memorial Basketball Hall of Fame as a player in 1960.

McCracken's teams ran whenever they could, earning the nickname the Hurryin' Hoosiers. Their plan was to play hawking defense, grab the ball off the boards, throw one outlet pass and break as much as possible. Bobby Leonard, All-American for Indiana, recalled, "Branch believed in full-court pressure, rebounding, a fast break and a simple offense."[18] They rang up enormous point totals of more than 100 many times in McCracken's years, and his All-Americans included Schlundt, Bob Leonard, Dick and Tom Van Arsdale, Bill Garrett (the first African American in the Big Ten conference), Jimmy Rayl, Hallie Bryant and Jon McGlocklin. After retiring in 1965, McCracken served in an administrative capacity until his death in 1970.[19]

Coach Branch McCracken congratulates senior star and future Indiana coach Lou Watson in a 1950 contest (University Archives, Indiana University).

Illinois and Indiana were the top teams in the Big Ten in the late 1940s and early 1950s. The Illini were coached by Harry Combes, starting in 1947. Combes had grown up in Monticello, Illinois, then attended the University of Illinois, where he played on the basketball team from 1934 to 1937 and helped them win two Big Ten titles under Coach Doug Mills. He graduated in 1937 and coached at Champaign High School from 1938 to 1947, with seven state tournament appearances; over his last three years there, his team was second in the state (1945), state champions (1946) and second once again (1947). It was at this point that he was hired by the University of Illinois as the head coach.

Over his first five years, Combes compiled a most enviable record, as the Illini won three Big Ten titles (1949, '51 and '52). In addition, his teams finished third in the NCAA tournament each of those years, losing in the semifinals to champion Kentucky in both 1949 and 1951 and to St. John's in 1952.

Combes compiled a record of 316–150 in 20 years at the Illini helm and was the winningest coach in Illinois history when he was forced into retirement in 1967. He also won a Big Ten title in 1963. Combes was crushed by the slush fund scandal of 1967 and never fully recovered from that. He died ten years later at age 62.

One would be remiss to not mention one of the most noted coaches of the era, Bennie Oosterbaan, who was an All-American football and basketball player at the University of Michigan in the period 1925–28 and led the Big Ten in scoring in basketball in 1927–28. He also was all-Big Ten in baseball. He turned down offers to play professionally because of his Dutch Reformed background, which prohibited working or playing sports on Sunday. Instead, Oosterbaan became a coach, assisting at Michigan in football from 1928 to 1947, before ascending to head football coach in 1948. He went 63–33–4 in nine seasons with three conference championships and a Rose Bowl victory in 1951, before stepping down in 1958. He was an assistant coach in basketball from 1928 to 1938, then was head basketball coach from 1938 to 1946, compiling a record of 81–72 with his up-tempo style. Oosterbaan was not an exceptional basketball coach, but his amazing overall coaching record deserved being noted. From 1959 to 1972 he served as director of athletic alumni relations before retiring.[20]

For a short time in the 1950s, Iowa ruled the roost in the Big Ten, and the Hawkeyes were led by coach Frank "Bucky" O'Connor. O'Connor followed a most circuitous path to his position. He had played basketball at Newton (IA) High and Drake University (captain his senior year), despite his poor eyesight and slight frame. After graduation he coached at two Iowa high schools before enlisting in World War II and rising to the rank of captain in the Army Air Corps. He returned to high school coaching before going to the University of Iowa as freshman basketball coach and head golf coach in 1948. In the 1949–50 season, Iowa head basketball coach Harrison had to step down temporarily because of illness. O'Connor took over on an interim basis and had a 6–5 record. Harrison was then fired in April of 1950,[21] and O'Connor was ultimately hired as permanent coach for the 1951–52 season after Assistant Athletic Director and former coach Rollie Williams served for one year. In seven full seasons at the Hawkeye helm, O'Connor compiled a record of 114–59 (.659) and a Big Ten record of 72–41 (.637). In his first five years, his teams were either first or second in four of those years, and in 1955 and 1956, his Iowa squads were in the NCAA Final Four, finishing second in 1956 to the undefeated University of San Francisco Dons.

O'Connor employed a run-and-gun style and had great players in Chuck Darling, Bill Logan and Carl Cain. In O'Connor's last two years (1956–57 and 1957–58), his teams were down, but he was rebuilding for another great season when he was killed in a highway accident in April of 1958 at the age of 44, after attending a dinner in his honor held in Waterloo, Iowa.

In 1958, Floyd Stahl, the Ohio State basketball coach and an associate athletic director and former baseball coach, resigned as basketball coach at the age of 59 to focus on administration totally. In his place as basketball coach, the university selected Fred Taylor, another multi-talented athlete, who had starred as both a first baseman in baseball and a leading scorer on the basketball team while an OSU undergrad between 1946 and 1950. Taylor had spent three years in the Army Air Force after graduating from Zanesville High in 1943. After college graduation he failed to get a basketball coaching job and played in the Washington Senators' minor league system, appearing in 22 major league games in three years.[22] After one more year in the minors, Taylor ended his baseball career and returned to Ohio State as the freshman basketball coach, the first ever. He remained in that position until Stahl's resignation and his hiring as head coach in June 1958.[23]

After an 11–11 first year, Taylor added three top sophomores to his starting lineup: Jerry Lucas, Mel Nowell, and John Havlicek. They joined Joe Roberts and Larry Siegfried to propel the Buckeyes to the Big Ten (13–1) and NCAA championships. A reserve on the team was Bobby Knight. "Over the course of three seasons the Bucks dominated in all facets of team play, losing but two league games over the three-year span."[24] Four more championships in a row followed, as well as two more NCAA championship games (losing both times to the University of Cincinnati). Taylor also led OSU to Big Ten championships in 1968 and 1971 before retiring from coaching in 1976 after a 6–20 season. He was a really good teacher of the inside game, said at least one of his former players, later a successful coach, Dave Merchant.[25] His record at OSU was 297–158 (.653). "Taylor twice was named Coach of the Year by the U.S. Basketball Writers Association and UPI and was elected to the Naismith Memorial Basketball Hall of Fame in 1985."[26] He died in Columbus in 2002 at age 77. No less an authority than Bobby Knight said, "As a head coach Fred Taylor did more to determine how basketball would be played in the Big Ten than any coach in any other conference. Coaches changed their approach to defense and their thinking on shot selection because they couldn't beat Ohio State if they didn't."[27]

Fred Taylor led his Buckeyes from 1958 to 1976, winning seven Big Ten championships and the NCAA title in 1960 (The Ohio State University Archives).

## VII. The Coaches

During the mid-1960s, Taylor's Buckeyes were briefly outperformed by Dave Strack's University of Michigan Wolverines. Strack was a graduate of Indianapolis Shortridge High School and the University of Michigan, where he played basketball for Bennie Oosterbaan, and was basketball MVP in both 1943 and 1945. He played briefly for the Indianapolis Kautskys of the National Basketball League before returning to Michigan as freshman coach in 1948. After a few years in that position he became varsity assistant, then left to take the head coach job at the University of Idaho in 1959. In 1960 he returned to Michigan as the head basketball coach. He was 13–35 in his first two seasons, but managed to recruit Cazzie Russell in 1962, and Michigan and Strack's fortunes turned around. Over the next four years his Michigan teams went 77–25, 43–13 in conference, and won three consecutive Big Ten titles, 1964 (tie) to 1966. They went to the Final Four twice, finishing third in the nation in 1964, and losing to UCLA in the championship game in 1965. Strack was named UPI Coach of the Year for the 1964–65 season.

After two losing seasons, Strack resigned to become athletic business manager, then associate athletic director. He went to Arizona in 1972 as athletic director and hired the first African American coach in the Pacific Ten, Fred Snowden. He resigned in 1982 and was a professor of physical education. He died in 2014 at age 90.

Strack was succeeded by Johnny Orr in 1968, who stayed in that position for 12 seasons, winning 120 games in the Big Ten while losing 72 and going 209–113 overall. He won only one outright Big Ten championship, but tied for a second, and his Michigan team went to the Final Four in 1976. By that time the NCAA had expanded the field to include more than one league representative, and Indiana and Michigan came into the 32-team field. The two teams were placed in different regional brackets and they met in the championship game. Indiana was undefeated and had beaten Michigan twice in the season. The third time was indeed a charm as the Hoosiers topped the Wolverines, 86–68, for Bob Knight's first title, Indiana's third. That was as close as Orr would come to a national championship.[28]

Orr had been an Illinois high school legend as a player at Taylorville High School, leading them to a state championship and an undefeated record in 1944. Orr enrolled at the University of Illinois and played three sports as a freshman, but withdrew to join the U.S. Navy after his freshman year. After leaving the service, he went to Beloit College to play for his high school coach, Dolph Stanley, who was the coach and athletic director. Upon graduation, Orr played for the St. Louis Bombers and Waterloo Hawks of the early NBA, but taught and coached at Milton (WI) High School, then Dubuque (IA) High School starting in 1951. In 1959 he became an assistant coach for John Erickson at the University of Wisconsin, and four years later gained his first head coaching position at the University of Massachusetts, where he remained for three seasons.

Orr was a great recruiter and enthusiastic bench coach, usually pumping his fist in excitement. He preferred a running style to the game and recruited players who could handle that. Orr left coaching for one season to be an insurance executive, but returned in 1967 to be an assistant for Dave Strack. After Strack's resignation, Orr accepted the head coaching position. He left in 1980 to take over the head coaching position at Iowa State, a team down on its basketball luck. He retired from that position in 1994 at the age of 67 and died in 2013 at the age of 86.[29]

# VIII

## *The Big Ten Up for Grabs*

The end of the first year of John Kennedy's presidency was dominated by the tensions of the Cold War. In August the East German government began building an enclosure for East Berlin. First would be a wire perimeter fence, with the actual concrete wall not built until 1965. In December of 1961, President Kennedy reassured West Berliners that the United States stood with them: "We shall stay," he said.[1]

### The 1962 Season

The college basketball season opened with Ohio State and Cincinnati ranked as numbers 1 and 2. "*Sports Illustrated* predicted that Ohio State would be the first Big Ten team to win three consecutive titles since Wisconsin did it in 1914."[2]

The Buckeyes began with five straight wins, one an 85–62 win over #5 Wake Forest, with sophomore Gary Bradds making his first significant contribution (15 points). In late December, OSU returned to the Los Angeles Classic and scuffled a bit before defeating the University of Washington, 54–49. Jerry Lucas had 20 points and 21 rebounds. The Bucks then romped over UCLA, 105–84, and won the championship with a win over USC, 76 to 66. Lucas had 30 against UCLA on 11 of 13 shooting, and 38 against USC, going 16–26 for 38 points. He was named MVP of the tournament.

Purdue defeated West Virginia that same night, 86–79, with Terry Dischinger scoring 32 points. Wisconsin looked strong in pounding Dayton, 105 to 93, in the ECAC tournament in New York. Ron Jackson had 33 and Tom Gwyn 29 for the Badgers. Illinois defeated Manhattan, 61–56, in that tourney with Bill Burwell (18), Dave Downey (16) and Jerry Colangelo (14) leading the scoring. Iowa defeated Penn in Philadelphia, 72–64, with Don Nelson getting 17, Andy Hankins 13, and Dave Roach 12.

On December 30, Loyola, the nucleus of the 1963 NCAA champion, defeated Indiana, 95–90, despite 30 points from Jimmy Rayl and 23 from Jerry Bass. Wisconsin came back to earth with a crushing loss to Cincinnati, 101 to 71, as Ron Bonham had 25 and Paul Hogue 23 for the Bearcats. Don Hearden (18) and Ron Jackson (16) led the Badgers. Iowa also lost that evening, to Villanova, 69–58, so the Big Ten did not seem as strong as in prior years, making OSU's road to the championship seem relatively easy. Richard Dozer echoed those sentiments, calling OSU's road to #1 undisturbed, noting that the Big Ten was good, but not great.[3]

Indiana routed Notre Dame on January 2, 1962, 122 to 95, but the Hoosiers were still seen as a middle-of-the-pack team, behind OSU, Purdue and Iowa. McCracken said, "If we can play like that against the Big Ten teams, we'll give 'em fits in the league."[4]

Both Wisconsin and Illinois had played well, noted OSU coach Fred Taylor.[5] Ohio State had little trouble with the Northwestern Wildcats, and the game attracted over 8,800 fans to Evanston, despite a heavy snowstorm. The Bucks led 30–12, then coasted to an 85–62 victory behind Havlicek with 27 and Lucas with 16 and 18 rebounds. Bill Cacciatore (17) and Ralph Wells (10) led NU. Illinois had no trouble with Michigan, winning by 20. Wisconsin also won easily over Iowa, 91–79, despite Don Nelson's setting a new Wisconsin Field House record with 39 points. Minnesota surprised Purdue, 81–69, despite Dischinger's 31. Eric Magdanz had 27 for the Gophers.[6]

Nelson continued his hot shooting two nights later, with 36 points against Northwestern, in a 74–69 Hawkeye win. Dischinger was even better, scoring 45 against Illinois as Purdue won its first Big Ten game, 96 to 89. Minnesota went to 2–0 with a 104–100 track meet against Indiana. Magdanz had 30, Ray Cronk 25 for the Gophers. Jimmy Rayl had 32 for IU.[7]

The next weekend the NCAA held its annual meetings and adopted a rule that would alter off-season basketball. The NCAA adopted an amendment (by one vote) that would forbid players from participating in organized basketball competition outside of the regular season. This basically meant AAU teams and leagues, one year after the AAU split with the NCAA. The NCAA envisioned it, so it said, as an anti-bribery action, but there were those who saw it as a retributive power display.[8]

In game action, Ohio State had little trouble in subduing Michigan, 89–64, for the Buckeyes' 12th win in a row. Purdue thwarted Northwestern's zone defense in a 90–74 victory as Tim McGinley led the Boilers with 25 points, followed by Dischinger's 20. Rich Falk emerged as a Northwestern weapon with 26 points for the 'Cats. Iowa handed Minnesota its first conference loss, 65–63. Illinois edged MSU in East Lansing, 66–65, behind Downey's 28 points.[9]

Except for the steadiness of Ohio State, the Big Ten kept going topsy-turvy among its other members. Michigan surprised Iowa in Ann Arbor, edging the Hawks, 56 to 55. Neither team shot well (Iowa, 33 percent; Michigan, 31 percent), but the Wolverines held on to win. In East Lansing, Purdue dominated Michigan State, 89–74, solidifying the Boilermakers as the early #2 team in the league.[10]

The next weekend, Iowa topped Northwestern, 72–60 (Nelson had 25 for Iowa), Michigan State beat in-state rival, Michigan, 80–74, and Ohio State coasted to their 13th win in a row, 90–76 over Minnesota. The Bucks then sent Purdue running in a game hyped for its potential for upset. OSU won 91–65 behind Lucas's 32. Havlicek held Dischinger to just nine points. Wisconsin's hopes of making a good showing in the league received a blow at the end of the first semester when center Ron Jackson, from Chicago's Tilden Tech, was declared academically ineligible for the second semester.[11]

With OSU not coming close to losing a game, the battle for second and individual achievements took on more prominence. Jimmy Rayl of Indiana took a lot of the spotlight with his shooting. Against Minnesota, he scored 56 points, a new Big Ten record, in a 105–104 overtime victory for Indiana. Coach McCracken called it "one of the greatest exhibitions of outside shooting that I have ever seen."[12] In a final game, Ron Jackson scored 21 to lead the Badgers in an upset victory over Purdue, despite Terry Dischinger's 50 points for the Boilermakers. The month of January ended with Wisconsin, without Jackson, beating Illinois, 85–81 (Ken Siebel had 23 for the Badgers) and Ohio State pounding Purdue again, 94–73 in West Lafayette, as the Bucks shot 54 percent (36–67) to the Boilermakers' 39 percent (24–61).[13]

Ohio State was still #1 in the national poll, followed by Kentucky, Cincinnati, Kansas State, USC and Duke. Wisconsin was in at #14 and Illinois #19.

February began with a rout for Ohio State over Northwestern, 97–61, win #16 in a row. It was also 21 Big Ten wins in a row, a modern record and close to Wisconsin's 23 in a row in 1913. Wisconsin beat Minnesota, 94–88, Illinois topped Indiana, 96–85, and Purdue had an easy time with Michigan State, 86–64.[14]

OSU routed Iowa, 89–63, with Lucas scoring 24 and Havlicek 16, but Don Nelson took game honors with 29. Michigan upset Wisconsin 81–74 in Madison, a game in which the Wolverines put on a 3½ minute stall and shot five free throws to close out the scoring. Illinois crushed Minnesota, handing them their sixth loss in a row, 89–80, behind Downey's 28 points.[15]

Big Ten standings had OSU (7–0), Wisconsin (5–1), Illinois (4–2), Indiana (3–2), Iowa (3–3), Purdue (4–4), Michigan (2–3), Minnesota (2–6) and Northwestern (1–6). Illinois beat Iowa to move closer to Wisconsin and separate themselves further from Iowa. Terry Dischinger set another record in the victory over Indiana, 105–93. His three-year total was 1,068, breaking the career Big Ten record held by Paul Ebert of Ohio State in the early 1950s.[16]

Ohio State continued on its merry way, defeating Michigan, 72–57, for its 24th in a row in the Big Ten. The minutes and points were shared by the Buckeyes, Havlicek leading with 15 and Lucas and Nowell having 13 each. Lucas also took 18 rebounds. Wisconsin adjusted easily to Indiana's "race horse" style (and Jimmy Rayl's 44 points) and defeated the Hoosiers, 105–94. Purdue beat back Iowa, 82–75, as Dischinger got 38 points and McGinley 23 for Purdue, and Nelson 21 for Iowa.[17]

Wisconsin, the Buckeyes' closest competitor, made things a bit easier by losing to Michigan in Ann Arbor, 84–65. Purdue moved a bit closer to Wisconsin, led by Dischinger's 45 points in a Purdue victory over Illinois, 100 to 88. Illinois tried to upset Wisconsin the next Monday, but fell short, 103–101. Wisconsin was 8–2, OSU 10–0, and Purdue 7–4. Wisconsin came back two nights later to edge Illinois, 103–101, as Ken Siebel (26) and Tom Hughbanks (25) kept the Illini and Bill Burwell (31) at bay.[18]

The big news that week was the three orbital flights of John Glenn around the earth. He returned to terra firma and was honored by President Kennedy on February 24, 1962. Basketball would have to take a back seat to the courage and daring of this Navy commander, who would later be elected to the United States Senate from Ohio.

The team from Ohio had gone to 11–0 in conference with a 102–79 win over Illinois. All the starters scored in double figures and the bench had 31 points. The Bucks went on to Iowa City and went 12–0 with a 72–62 victory.[19] Wisconsin was 9–3, so the title was no longer in question. Another undefeated league season, however, was still possible.

"As Ohio State prepared to travel to Wisconsin to play out the schedule, they were leading the league in scoring with 87.7 points per game and defense, allowing 66.7

points per contest. The winning margin was 21 points per game. Lucas led the league and the nation in field goal percentage, Havlicek was sixth in the nation and fourth behind Lucas, Nelson and Dischinger-in the Big Ten."[20]

Wisconsin hosted Ohio State on March 3 in a game that meant nothing in the standings, but turned out to be a point of pride for the Badgers as they upset the Buckeyes, 86–67. Before 13,472, who turned out in temperatures lower than 20 degrees below zero, Wisconsin shot 50 percent from the floor, while the Bucks seemed in a state of torpor because of the cold, shooting just 32 percent. Don Hearden, a sophomore averaging 10.9 points per game, had 29 points on 14 of 23 from the field. Veteran forward Ken Siebel had 22, Jerry Lucas had 23 on eight of 18 shooting, Nowell had 19 on nine of 21, while Havlicek shot just three of 15 from the floor.[21] Despite the loss, OSU remained #1 in the country, but Cincinnati closed the gap at #2. Wisconsin moved up to #16.

Other games saw Iowa beat Illinois, 88–78, as Don Nelson (32) and Jerry Messick (28) combined for 60 of the Iowa points. Jimmy Rayl had 37 points and the Hoosiers held Terry Dischinger to just 21 in the 88–71 Indiana victory in Bloomington. Eric Magdanz had 30 for Minnesota as they ran to a 98–91 win over Michigan State.[22]

Magdanz (42) and Rayl (37) continued their hot scoring in their next contests, both high-scoring victories for their respective teams. Minnesota beat Michigan, 102–80, as Magdanz set a new Minnesota scoring record; Rayl led Indiana to a 104–92 win over Illinois.[23]

Even in the heat of the conference race, the Cold War was not far from the nation's thinking. On March 6, Colonel Francis Gary Powers testified before a Senate committee regarding his May 1, 1960, U-2 crash over the Soviet Union and his subsequent 21 months in a Russian prison. Powers had been released as part of a prisoner swap on February 10, 1962, and this was his first public speaking appearance.

The last day of the Big Ten season was March 10, and teams were playing for pride and position since the race had long before been decided. The Ohio State seniors played their last contest in St. John Arena and crushed Indiana, 90–65. Lucas scored 20 points and snared 30 rebounds, Mel Nowell scored 22. Terry Dischinger had 30 in his final game as Purdue edged Michigan, 77–75. Dischinger's Big Ten average for the season was 32.8 points per game, which broke Robin Freeman's mark of 32 ppg set in the 1955–56 season. In his final game, Don Nelson scored 35 points as Iowa humbled Wisconsin, 81–64.[24] He finished third in conference scoring at 26.9 ppg, just behind Rayl with 32.4 ppg. Eric Magdanz (25.1) and Jerry Lucas (22.3) rounded out the top five scoring leaders.

### Final Standings and MVPs, 1961–62

| | | |
|---|---|---|
| Ohio State | 13–1 | Jerry Lucas (Big Ten MVP) First Team All-American |
| Wisconsin | 10–4 | Ken Siebel |
| Purdue | 9–5 | Terry Dischinger (First Team All-American) |
| Illinois | 7–7 | Dave Downey |
| Indiana | 7–7 | Jimmy Rayl |
| Iowa | 7–7 | Don Nelson |
| Minnesota | 6–8 | Ray Cronk |
| Michigan | 5–9 | John Harris |
| Michigan State | 3–11 | Art Schwarm |
| Northwestern | 3–11 | Ralph Wells |

The first team, all-Big Ten was Lucas, Havlicek, Dischinger, Nelson, and Rayl. The former three all made All-American also. Dischinger and Lucas were the first two men from the same league to make All-American three years in a row.[25] Second team was Downey (IL), Tom Bolyard (IU), Eric Magdanz (MN), Nowell (OSU) and Ken Siebel (WI).

Ohio State would once again represent the Big Ten in the NCAA tourney and would have a bye in Round One. They would play the winner of Western Kentucky and Detroit in Iowa City on March 16. Kentucky would meet the winner of Butler and Bowling Green in the second game in Iowa City. Ohio State had little trouble with Western Kentucky, who had beaten Detroit, 90–81, and defeated the Hilltoppers, 93–73. Doug McDonald led the Buckeye scoring with 21; John Havlicek had 17. Lucas, saddled with four fouls and triple teaming, had just nine points on four of 13 shooting. The Bucks would meet Kentucky, who had beaten Butler, 81–60.[26]

For the second straight year, OSU and Kentucky met in the Mideast regional finals and, for the second straight year, Lucas scored 33 points in leading Ohio State to victory with the score this time 74–64. Adolph Rupp, the legendary Kentucky coach said, "It's awfully nice that all those people [14,500] got to see Mr. Basketball tonight, the only way to stop a monster like Lucas is to graduate him."[27] Lucas was 12–21 from the field, 9–10 from the free throw line and had 15 rebounds. Havlicek had 13 and had 10 rebounds, and had also held Cotton Nash, averaging 23.8 ppg, to just five of 19 shooting and 14 points. Larry Pursiful had 21 for the Wildcats.[28]

In the east, Wake Forest, led by All-American Len Chappell, defeated Villanova, 79–69, and would face Ohio State in Louisville. Cincinnati had crushed Colorado, 73–46, to return to the Final Four, where they would play the western champion, UCLA, who had easily defeated Oregon State and Mel Counts (24 points), 88–69.

Wake Forest had won 12 games in a row and was 21–8, but the Demon Deacons were no match for the Buckeyes, despite Chappell's 27 points and 18 rebounds. Havlicek had 25 and 16 rebounds and Lucas 19 and 16 rebounds, in the 84–68 OSU win. But there was a price to pay. Lucas had sustained a severe knee sprain late in the game when he was bumped in the air grabbing a rebound, twisted his heel upon landing and hurt the knee. At that time the semis were played on Friday night and the finals on Saturday night, so he would have less than 24 hours to recover. There was no question that he would play, but how effective would he be against the massive Paul Hogue and the long, quick George Wilson? That remained to be seen.[29]

The Bearcats had beaten UCLA, 72–70, on a 25-footer with three seconds to play by Tom Thacker, his only basket of the game. Hogue had scored 36 and sophomore Ron Bonham 19. Cincinnati had inside and outside scoring, as well as their usual stout defense, the best in the nation.

In warmups, Havlicek could see that Lucas was not as effective as usual. His knee was clearly bothering him, but Lucas never said so, nor did he use that as an excuse in the 71–59 Cincinnati victory. Lucas was just 5–17 from the floor, scored 11 points and gave way to Bradds at times as Gary led the team in scoring with 15. Havlicek had 11. It was the backcourt that actually dominated, however. Thacker had 22 and Tony Yates 12, while Nowell had just nine on four of 16 shooting. Reasbeck had two and Gearhart eight. Hogue, with 22 points and 19 rebounds, was voted the tourney Most Outstanding Player, the first time that Lucas had been in a college tournament and not won that distinction.

One of the saddest aspects of the game was that on that same evening, ABC telecast a fight for the welterweight championship between Emile Griffith and Benny "Kid" Paret, one that resulted in Griffith's fatally battering Paret in the twelfth round. Paret died ten days later from a brain hemorrhage. The great NCAA final was lost in the horror of the first boxing death shown on national television. In fact, the great final was not shown live on television except in Los Angeles, where the *Los Angeles Times*' television station, KTTV, managed to score a coup by getting the rights to show it live. The rest of the country had to wait until the next day to see a compressed 90-minute version on *ABC's Wide World of Sports*. The game was not broadcast live on radio except to local OSU and Cincinnati stations. Quite a contrast to today.

The loss of the five seniors at Ohio State was notable for many reasons. The graduating team had claimed the national title, the two national runners-up titles, the distinction of never having lost a home game in three years, three Big Ten titles, and an overall record of 78–6 in those three years. Ohio State and the Big Ten would not be able to replace such a squad, but their graduation seemed to throw the league wide open for the 1962–63 season.

## The 1963 Season

The 1962–63 basketball season had a two-time defending national champion (Cincinnati) returning with a strong squad that would be considered the national favorite until proven otherwise. A similar, but different, position was found in the Big Ten race. There was a three-time Big Ten champion and three-time NCAA finalist in Ohio State, but there the similarity ended. Graduated were Lucas, Havlicek and Nowell, as well as back-ups Gary Gearhart and Bob Knight. They had accounted for 69 percent of the points and 74 percent of the rebounds in 1961–62. Doug McDonald, the OSU captain for 1962–63, speaking at a tip-off dinner, said, "We hope to give you the kind of basketball you are used to. We know we're missing some players—what are their names?"[30] Disingenuous, but the line hit close to home. The Buckeyes would have McDonald, Dick Ricketts, Dick Reasbeck, Jim Doughty, Dick Taylor and Gary Bradds as their top six, a line up that wasn't making the rest of the league quake. Bradds had led the team in scoring in the NCAA championship game with 15 points, but he had played at a very small Ohio high school in Jamestown and had only 103 points his sophomore year, playing in fewer than 20 games. So there were a lot of unknowns in the Buckeye future.

The favorites for the Big Ten title seemed to be Illinois or Minnesota, with Indiana and Michigan also highly rated. The Illini returned Dave Downey, Bill Burwell, Bill Small and Bob Starnes, and would welcome sophs Tal Brody, Skip Thoren and Bogie Redmon. Minnesota would be led by Tom McGrann, Eric Magdanz and Mel Northway, with sophomore Terry Kunze predicted to do great things. Indiana's roster had returning top scorers Jimmy Rayl and Tom Bolyard, plus a couple of sophomore swing men, twins Dick and Tom Van Arsdale. Jon McGlocklin, a future star, was not able to do much playing on this talented Hoosier squad. Michigan would be led by powerful Bill Buntin, with support from Tom Cole and John Harris. Northwestern had high hopes, but they faded after center Jim Pitts tore up his knee stepping off the McGaw Hall raised court after pre-game warmups in an early season non-conference game.

Nationally, Cincinnati was the odds-on favorite to win their third consecutive national title. Paul Hogue was graduated, but four starters returned for the Bearcats, and each player was selected for one of the four teams named to the All-American pre-season squad by *Sports Review Magazine*'s basketball issue. *Sport Magazine* also named the four—Tony Yates, Tom Thacker, Ron Bonham and George Wilson—to their All-America teams. The only Big Ten players mentioned were Dave Downey of Illinois, Ken Siebel of Wisconsin, Jimmy Rayl of Indiana, and Eric Magdanz of Minnesota. *Sport* also named an All-Sophomore team, and the Van Arsdale twins, Dick and Tom, were named from Indiana. *Sport* did not rank teams, and *Sports Review* only evaluated teams within a region. In the Midwest, that magazine's writers predicted that the Big Ten would see "its tightest race since Ohio State began its string of three straight championships ... in 1960.... The way should be open for Illinois, Wisconsin, Minnesota, Indiana and Ohio State to fight for the crown."[31]

Illinois showed itself to be a top team after taking the Holiday Festival Tournament in Madison Square Garden in late December of 1962. After crushing a good Penn team, 90 to 66, the Illini thrashed a very good West Virginia team, led by Rod Thorn, 92 to 74, to win the championship of the tournament. Dave Downey and Bill Burwell led the team in scoring and rebounding, respectively, but the team was playing very well together, overall.[32]

The Associated Press poll had Cincinnati as #1 (8–0), Ohio State #2 (6–0), Loyola of Chicago #3 (7–0) and Illinois #4 (5–0). Both Indiana and Michigan received votes, but only the top ten teams were ranked in order.

Minnesota did not fare well in holiday contests, losing at Wichita, 79–62, and at Drake, 67 to 65. Only Eric Magdanz scored in double figures in either game. Wichita, led by Dave Stallworth, also surprised Ohio State, defeating them 71 to 54.[33]

Notre Dame upset Illinois, 90 to 88, in Chicago Stadium on New Year's Eve, and the new year began with a Notre Dame defeat of Indiana and a Purdue win over Drake in a double-header played in Fort Wayne. Indiana was led by Jimmy Rayl (21) and Tom Bolyard (19), but the Hoosiers fell short, losing to the Irish, 73 to 70. The Purdue win was in overtime, 83 to 79, and senior guard, Mel Garland, led all scorers with 30 points. Ron Hughes chipped in 15 for the Boilers.[34]

Three nights later (January 5), the Big Ten season opened, and Illinois began a new win streak with a victory in Iowa, 85 to 76. Bill Small had 25, while Tal Brody and Dave Downey had 17 each, to lead the Illinois attack. Dave Roach (20) and Jim Rodgers (18) were leading scorers for the Hawks. Indiana, Ohio State, Michigan and Wisconsin also opened the conference season with victories. Indiana won at Michigan State, 96 to 84, and shot 55 percent from the floor, while the Spartans shot just 42 percent. Rayl scored 44 points and Bolyard 25, more than 70 percent of the team scoring. Sanders and Schwarz each had 15 for MSU. In Columbus, OSU edged Minnesota, 78 to 76. Gary Bradds, called "Ohio's new Jerry Lucas" by Richard Dozer of the *Tribune*, scored 25 (on 12 of 16 field goals) and Dick Reasbeck had 22 for the Buckeyes. For Minnesota, Tom McGrann had 22, Mel Northway and Eric Magdanz had 16 apiece. Bill Buntin scored

33 and Tom Cole 14, to allow the Wolverines to escape from Northwestern, 78 to 75, in Ann Arbor. Richie Falk and Rick Lopossa had 21 each to top the Wildcat scoring. Finally, the Badgers defeated the Boilers in West Lafayette, 74 to 66, behind 21 from Jack Brens and 19 from Ken Siebel.[35]

On the first Monday of the season, Indiana and Michigan won, but the biggest win was in Champaign, where Illinois handed Ohio State its second loss of the season, 90 to 78. Brody (23), Small (22) and Downey (21) led a balanced Illini attack. The 6'8" Gary Bradds "put the clamps on Burwell (14 points), who moved out and fed teammates to open lanes inside." Bradds also had 33 points, but got little assistance from his mates, as Ricketts was the only other scorer in double figures with 12.[36] The Buckeyes led 37–36 at the half and led 48 to 45 with 15 minutes to play, before Illinois went on a 16 to 2 run to ice the game. Illinois shot 47 percent from the floor, OSU, 34 percent.

The Indiana victory in Bloomington was over state rival Purdue, 85 to 71, and Rayl (25) and Bolyard (15) were the scoring leaders. Ron Hughes took game honors with 27 for Purdue. In Iowa City, Michigan had an easy time in an 88 to 77 win. Buntin had 34 and Oosterbaan 18 for Michigan. Roach and Messick had 15 and 11 respectively for the Hawks.[37]

Cincinnati and Loyola were now the only undefeated teams among major basketball powers, and they were ranked #1 and #2 after the first week of January, with Illinois #3 (9–1), Arizona State #4 (12–1) and Ohio State #5 (9–1, before the loss to Illinois). Wisconsin was the only other rated Big Ten team at #19. The Big Ten was viewed as one of the top two conferences in the nation, along with the Missouri Valley, which boasted highly rated Bradley and Wichita State, in addition to Cincinnati.

The second week of the conference season saw Ohio State beat back another pretender, Michigan, 68 to 66, with Bradds scoring 33 and Reasbeck 16. The Wolverines countered with 17 from Cole and 16 each from Bob Cantrell and sophomore center

Gary Bradds led the Big Ten in scoring and was Big Ten MVP in 1962–63 and 1963–64 for Ohio State, and was also national Player of the Year in the latter year (The Ohio State University Archives).

Bill Buntin, but it was not enough. Illinois, meanwhile, remained unbeaten in the league with a 106–82 thrashing of Purdue. Almost every Illini played, with Downey (22) and Bogie Redmon (18) leading the scoring parade. Garland (27) and Hughes (19) led the Purdue attack. Minnesota looked formidable in trouncing Iowa, 83 to 58. Bob Bateman, averaging 9 points a game, exploded for 25, and Terry Kunze had 17 for the Gophers. Leading scorer Eric Magdanz had just nine on four of 17 shooting, but the outcome was never in doubt. Dave Roach had 15 for Iowa.[38]

The next Monday's games contained at least a couple of near upsets, with the biggest being Illinois edging Northwestern, 78 to 76, on Dave Downey's 55-foot shot as the clock ran out. The game, played at McGaw Hall, was close the entire way, with Rich Falk (21) and Rick Lopossa (20) keeping the Wildcats in it until the heartbreaking end. Downey had 20 for the Illini, but Bob Starnes led the scoring with 26. Another tense contest was in Ann Arbor, where the Golden Gophers defeated the host Wolverines, 66 to 63. Sophomore Terry Kunze was the star for the Gophers with 28 points, on 14 of 15 field goals. Magdanz had 20. For Michigan, Bill Buntin led with 21. The other game that evening saw Iowa rally to defeat Wisconsin in Iowa City. Dave Roach had 17 and Joe Reddington 14 to lead Iowa, while Bob Johnson topped the Badgers with 12 points[39]

The next weekend, there was a major upset in the conference as Iowa defeated Ohio State in Iowa City, 81 to 74. Andy Hankins had 22 and Joe Reddington 21 to pace the Hawks' win. Bradds scored 26 and had 14 rebounds, but got little help from his teammates other than Jim Doughty's 19 and 11 rebounds. The guards for OSU shot a collective 14 percent, with the starters, Reasbeck and Ricketts, shooting six for 31(19 percent).[40]

Also on that night, Northwestern lost to Michigan State, 80 to 68, and Minnesota topped Purdue, 82 to 73. Ted Williams (23) and Marcus Sanders (18) were the big guns for MSU in their Northwestern victory, with Falk (18) and Woislaw (14), leading the 'Cats. In West Lafayette, Eric Magdanz dropped in 25 and Mel Northway 17, to offset the superb game by Purdue's Mel Garland, who had 39 to lead all scorers.[41]

On the next Monday, there was only one game, and Iowa, coming off their upset of OSU, defeated MSU in East Lansing, 60 to 59, in a deliberate contest. Jimmy Rodgers and Andy Hankins each had 15 for the Hawks, while Pete Gent (who would later play pro football for the Dallas Cowboys and author the bestselling novel, *North Dallas Forty*) led MSU with 14 and Jack Lamers had 13.

On Saturday, January 26, a number of schools were engaged in semester final exams, and the conference had just a couple games. Northwestern won its first conference game, over Purdue, 96 to 82. Rick Lopossa picked up 26 and Rich Falk, 22, to pace the Wildcat attack. For Purdue, Hughes had 26 and Mel Garland 21 in the game, played before just 2,500 fans at McGaw Hall. In Minneapolis, the Gophers failed to hold home-court advantage, losing to Michigan State, 61 to 59. Pete Gent was the top scorer for the game with 20, leading the Spartans, and he was backed by 12 points from Bill Berry. Magdanz had 19 for Minnesota and McGrann had 14. The biggest games that night, however, were in Chicago Stadium, where a double-header had three of the nation's top teams playing. In the first contest, Cincinnati defeated Illinois, 62 to 53, and in the second, Loyola topped Santa Clara, 82 to 72. Illinois got 15 from Downey and 11 from Burwell, but could not contain Ron Bonham and Tom Thacker, who scored 26 and 20, respectively, to lead the Bearcats.[42]

## VIII. The Big Ten Up for Grabs

The second semester of Big Ten play began on Monday, January 28, and Ohio State edged Northwestern, 72–70, in Columbus, while Indiana defeated Purdue, 74–73, in West Lafayette. Gary Bradds had 35 points for OSU, but Rich Falk nearly matched him with 32 for Northwestern. Reasbeck and McDonald supported Bradds with 12 each, but Falk had no teammate in double figures. Jimmy Rayl had 25 and Tom Bolyard 19 in the IU victory, with newly eligible Bill Jones leading the Boilermakers with 22 and Mel Garland contributing 20 points. Northwestern overcame the OSU loss to upset Indiana on the following Saturday, 100 to 87, in a classic "run and gun" game. Falk had 35 and Woislaw 20 for the 'Cats, while Bolyard (28) and Rayl (21, on just 9–30 shooting) led the Hoosiers. Purdue bounced back from their loss to IU, but not quite far enough, as they tried to surprise Ohio State, but were edged 97–96 by the Buckeyes in West Lafayette. Bradds had 38 to lead the win and maintain his hold on the Big Ten scoring lead. Mel Garland had 34 for Purdue, who shot 40 of 62 (65 percent) from the floor.[43]

In the other games that day, Minnesota slipped by Wisconsin, 69–68, and Michigan did the same to Michigan State, 72 to 71. Ken Siebel had 25 and Jack Brens 15 for the Badgers; Eric Magdanz had 21 for the Gophers. In East Lansing, Tom Cole had 23, John Harris 16, and a limping Bill Buntin just five. Pete Gent led the Spartans with 20.[44]

After a turbulent first month, the conference standings had only Illinois undefeated in the league (4–0), Indiana at 3–1, Minnesota and OSU tied at 4–2. The rest of the league was Michigan (3–2), Iowa and Minnesota (both 3–3), Northwestern (2–4), Wisconsin (1–3) and Purdue, winless in seven tries.

Illinois remained undefeated the next Monday, but just barely, as they engaged in an exhausting 104–101 victory over Indiana. Sophomore Tal Brody, from New Jersey, one of only two non–Illinois natives on the squad (Bill Burwell from Brooklyn was the other), scored 22 points, Bob Starnes 21, and Dave Downey 20. For Indiana, Tom Bolyard had 35 and Jimmy Rayl 31. Purdue finally won a game, but had to hit 56 percent from the floor to top Michigan State, 103 to 81. Mel Garland dropped in 34 points and Bob Purkheiser 23, on nine-for-nine shooting from the floor. MSU was led by Sanders with 18 and Lamers with 16. In Ann Arbor, the Badgers topped the Wolverines, 81 to 78, behind Jack Brens's 22 and Dave Grams's 19 for Wisconsin. Despite continued knee problems, Bill Buntin led Michigan with 20 points.[45]

The two undefeated powers, Cincinnati (17–0) and Loyola (20–0), remained at the top of the latest AP poll in the first week of February. Duke was now #3, just ahead of Illinois and Arizona State. Ohio State had fallen to #12.

There were other concerns nationally, most pressing being the possible placement in Cuba of nuclear missiles that could reach the United States. Since the revolution and Fidel Castro's strong alliance with the Soviet Union, the United States had been closely monitoring ships heading to Cuba, hoping to deter the placement of Soviet-made missiles there. Both Cuban and Soviet governments denied that there was such a plan in the works.[46]

The second semester began with a controversial contest: Iowa defeated Northwestern, 66–65, in two overtimes, but only after a basket at the halftime buzzer, by Rich Falk of the Wildcats, had been disallowed. At the time, it seemed relatively unimportant since the 'Cats led at halftime. But Iowa put on a great defensive performance in the second half and forced overtime. Falk (23) and Lopossa (19) led Northwestern. Roach (19) and Reddington (12) topped Iowa scoring in a balanced attack.[47]

Ohio State had little trouble with Wisconsin, winning 94 to 70, behind 31 from Reasbeck and 26 from Bradds. Michigan defeated Indiana 90–86 behind Bill Buntin's 36 points. Rayl had 26 and Bolyard 22 for the Hoosiers. Minnesota overcame their own sluggishness to win at home, 80 to 73, over Purdue. Magdanz led the Gophers with 26 points, while Bob Purkhiser took game honors with 29 for Purdue. Illinois struggled to defeat Michigan State, 91–86, in Champaign. Starnes and Small had 20 and 19, respectively, but Marcus Sanders was the high scorer for the game with 29 for Michigan State.[48]

On a Monday with just two games, a weak Wisconsin team, with only one conference victory, dealt the Illini their first conference loss, with an 84 to 77 contest in Madison. Ken Siebel (26) and Jack Brens (25) played their best game of the season in leading the upset. Wisconsin led all the way, dominating the boards 64 to 39, with Brens taking 22 and Gwyn 19. Wisconsin won at the line with 18 of 27 free throws, to Illinois's 9 of 16. Small had 29 for the Illini.

Minnesota had their title hopes undermined by Indiana, who topped the Gophers in Bloomington, 89 to77. Jimmy Rayl had 32 and was supported by Dick Van Arsdale with 20 (and 11 rebounds). This was another game with free throws making the difference, as Minnesota was 17 of 22 and Indiana 29 of 39.[49]

Saturday, February 16, was upset day for the major powers. Cincinnati lost to a very good Wichita team, 65 to 64, with 46 of the Wichita points coming from Dave Stallworth. Loyola lost to Bowling Green, featuring Nate Thurmond and Howie Komives, 92 to 75. Illinois lost their second game in a row, to Indiana, 103 to 100. Dave Downey scored a Big Ten–record 53 points on 22 of 34 shooting, but Illinois could not overcome Indiana's free throw advantage (37–48 v. 14–19) and the scoring of Bolyard (34) and Rayl (30).[50]

In other, less surprising Big Ten contests, Wisconsin defeated Northwestern, 78 to 65; OSU won at Michigan, 75–68; Iowa topped Purdue, 73–64; and Minnesota won in East Lansing, 75–70. The Badgers' win was sparked by Dave Grams, who had 26 points, after only scoring 58 points all year. Bradds had 34 to lead the Buckeyes in the Michigan contest, while Buntin topped Michigan with 21. Roach (15) and Messick (13) led for Iowa, and Purkhiser (16) and Garland (15) for Purdue. Magdanz (19) and Northway (17) topped the Gopher scoring, while Gent (22) and Williams (19) were brutes inside for MSU.[51]

Monday's games returned to a more normal mode with Illinois winning at Purdue, Ohio State defeating Michigan State, and Minnesota crushing Wisconsin, 72–48. Iowa was edged at home by Indiana, and Northwestern pulled a mild surprise by topping Michigan in Evanston. This latter game saw Michigan missing shots to win at the end of the game after Northwestern blew a 12-point lead, and both teams missed too many free throws. Northwestern was 15 of 24 (62.5 percent) and Michigan 10 of 17 (59 percent). Falk had 23 for the Wildcats and Marty Riessen, future Davis Cup tennis player, had 12. Buntin (21) and Cole (13) led the Wolverines.[52]

Illinois and Ohio State each scored 87 points in their victories, with Small (32) and Downey (18) leading Illinois, and Bradds (31) and Reasbeck (16) topping OSU. Purdue had 74 and MSU had 77 in the two games that were not close. Iowa's game, however, was close, as the Hawks could not hold home court advantage in the 72–71 defeat by Indiana. Tom Bolyard was huge for the Hoosiers with 29, who got only two points from Jimmy Rayl.[53]

With just over two weeks left, the Big Ten standings were now even more jumbled. Illinois and OSU were tied for the top spot at 7–2; Minnesota was right behind at 7–3; Indiana was 6–3, while Iowa sat at 5–4. The bottom was also bunched with Michigan and Wisconsin at 4–5; Northwestern, 3–6; and MSU, 3–7. Only Purdue, at 1–10, seemed to have a position locked. Three or four teams were still in contention for the title and the NCAA berth that accompanied it. On that same day, a bid to the tournament was offered to Loyola, who immediately accepted. They would play March 11 on Northwestern's McGaw Hall court against an unnamed opponent. Today, with the great hype around the day that NCAA bids are offered on national television, such an action seems hard to imagine. But at that time, more than half the bids to the 25-team tournament were open (not tied to a league), and the bids for those teams were made on a rolling basis starting in late February.

The Illini and Buckeyes won twice the next weekend, keeping the race tight, but Minnesota lost to Northwestern on Saturday, 71–66, and to Illinois, 81–70, on Monday, making it essentially a two-team race. Indiana also split two games and fell back to the middle of the pack, but Jimmy Rayl managed to come back from his terrible performance of the week before and score 56 points in a 113–94 win over Michigan State, breaking Downey's recently established conference scoring record.[54]

Marty Riessen was a starting guard for Northwestern in the early 1960s and was an All-American in tennis, later playing on five Davis Cup teams from 1963 to 1981 (Northwestern University Archives).

The Illini victory, 89–77, over Wisconsin, was led by Downey with 22 and Burwell with 21. Ken Siebel took game honors for Wisconsin with 26. On Monday, Illinois defeated Minnesota, 81 to 70 in Minneapolis, with Downey (24) and Burwell (19) again leading the scoring. Sophomore Terry Kunze had 22 for the Gophers. Ohio State won on Saturday, 83–70, getting their revenge against Iowa, with Bradds getting 40, then were slowed down against Northwestern before winning 50–45 on Monday. Bradds had 25, half the Buckeye scoring, as both teams shot poorly (OSU, 33 percent, NU, 30 percent).[55]

Michigan won twice, beating Purdue, 71–53, and Iowa, 78–70. The Wolverines suddenly looked as good as anyone in the league, but they had come together too late. It did bode well for the next year, however.[56]

So the Big Ten season was down to 10 days and three league contests to determine a champion. The first games of March brought excitement and possibly some resolution. Ohio State had no trouble with hapless Purdue, winning 95–75 in their final home game of the season. Coach Taylor let Bradds and Reasbeck play long enough to get a big lead, then pulled them for the obligatory ovations, as Reasbeck scored 32 (on 14 of 23 shooting) and Bradds 29. Junior Don DeVoe, starting in place of Doughty, out with the flu, had nine points and 11 rebounds.[57] DeVoe would go on to an acclaimed college coaching career. Illinois, however, fell to the onrushing Michigan Wolverines, 84–81, in Ann Arbor, giving OSU a one-game lead with two to play. Buntin and Cole led Michigan with 27 and 22, respectively, while Downey had 28 for Illinois, who had only one other player in double figures: Brody, with 12.[58]

Reflecting the latest outcomes, the AP poll had Cincinnati #1, followed by Duke, Loyola, ASU and OSU. Illinois fell to #7. The Big Ten standings had OSU 10–2 and Illinois 9–3. Minnesota, Iowa and Michigan each had five losses, so it was a two-team race now.

On Monday, March 4, Ohio State clinched a tie for the title and Illinois won, to remain mathematically eligible to tie. A tie for the Illini would actually be a win, since they would end up representing the Big Ten at the NCAA tourney, because OSU had been there more recently (the prior year). Illinois, playing at home, defeated Northwestern, 79–73. Downey and Brody had 19 and 16, respectively, with Lopossa (19) and Gibbs (17) leading Northwestern. It was the first game ever in Illinois's new facility, Assembly Hall, and 16,137 fans jammed the building. Ohio State, led by Bradds (25 points) and Ricketts (23), had little trouble defeating Minnesota, 85–65.

The rest of the games had no effect on the title race, but there was jostling for lower positions. Indiana topped Michigan, 104–96. Bolyard (31), Tom Van Arsdale (26) and Rayl (23) led the "run and gun" Hoosiers to victory to clinch at least tie for 4th in the conference. Wisconsin topped Iowa, 75–69, on a night that saw Ken Siebel set a new Badger record for career points with 1,060. He had 18 and Jack Brens had 20 in the Wisconsin win.[59] Purdue won its second Big Ten contest, defeating Michigan State, 94–93. Jones and Garland each had 22, while Ted Williams had his best game for the Spartans with 35.[60]

The conference season ended on Saturday, March 9. Illinois, playing at home, defeated a stubborn Iowa team, 73–69, giving them 11 wins, already the Ohio State total. In Bloomington, Ohio State led 36–34 at the half, but a second-half surge sent the Hoosiers ahead, 52–47, midway through the period. Then, Ohio State ran off ten straight points to lead 57–52, and stretched the lead to 71–60 with just over six minutes left in the game. Ohio State tried to slow the game down, but Indiana applied pressure in the person of Tom Bolyard, who scored 11 straight points for IU, while OSU totaled just two, making the score 73–71, Buckeyes. At 79-all, Coach Taylor called a play for Bradds, a foul line jumper with Reasbeck passing him the ball. Bradds turned, saw an open lane, and drove to the hoop, but was called for charging Rayl at the bucket. The call fouled out Bradds and sent the game into overtime. Reasbeck and McDonald had preceded Bradds to the bench. Indiana won, 87–85, after a bench-clearing near-brawl with two seconds remaining. Bradds finished with 32 points and 14 rebounds. Bolyard had 29 for the Hoosiers. The Ohio State loss made them co-champions with Illinois, and since the NCAA prohibited playoffs until 1968, Illinois would go to the NCAA tourney.[61] Tug Wilson, in commenting on the season, noted, "[I]t had been a beautifully co-ordinated Illinois team which carved out—and deserved—a share of the league championship honors."[62]

### Final Standings and MVPs, 1962–63

| | | |
|---|---|---|
| Illinois | 11–3 | Dave Downey |
| Ohio State | 11–3 | Gary Bradds (Big Ten MVP) |
| Indiana | 9–5 | Tom Bolyard |
| Michigan | 8–6 | Bill Buntin |
| Minnesota | 8–6 | Eric Magdanz |
| Wisconsin | 7–7 | Ken Siebel |
| Northwestern | 6–8 | Rich Falk |
| Iowa | 5–9 | Jerry Messick |
| Michigan State | 4–10 | Ted Williams |
| Purdue | 2–12 | Mel Garland |

In addition to Bradds, the rest of the All-Big Ten team were Downey, Buntin, Bolyard, Garland of Purdue, and Rayl (who was eighth in the nation in scoring with 25.3 ppg). Bradds led the league in scoring with 30.9 ppg (and was fourth in the country with 28.0 ppg.). Buntin led the conference in rebounding with 12.7 rpg.

Illinois would go the NCAA tournament for the first time since 1952, when they had finished third in the nation. Their opening-round opponent would be the winner of Notre Dame-Bowling Green. The Mid-American conference champions defeated the Irish and met Illinois on March 15. In an historic double-header, Illinois defeated Bowling Green, 70–67. Burwell had 20 against rugged Nate Thurmond, who was held to 15. Downey had 20. Howie Komives led the Falcons with 25. Bowling Green outrebounded the Illini 51 to 49 because of Thurmond's 19, but Downey (12), Skip Thoren (12) and Burwell (11) all worked hard on the boards for the Illini, whose free-throw shooting nearly lost them the game. They were 18 of 26, missing consistently in the closing minutes of the contest, while BGSU was 17 of 19.

The real historical moment of the games that evening, however, was having the all-white Mississippi State team sneak out of Starkville, avoiding an injunction, in order to play a team with African Americans, four of them starting. Loyola defeated the Mississippi State Maroons, 61–51, but this was the first significant chink in the wall of segregation that surrounded many of the Southern schools.[63]

With their victories, Illinois and Loyola would play the next night in East Lansing for the Mideast regional title and a trip to the Final Four in Louisville's Freedom Hall the next week. Led by Mideast MVP Jerry Harkness, who had 33 points, Loyola downed the Illini, 79–64. Downey (20) led the Illini in scoring, but the dominance in team rebounding was more significant. The Ramblers had 65 rebounds with Vic Rouse (19), Les Hunter (15) and Ron Miller (11) all in double figures. Illinois had 49 rebounds with no one in double figures. The Illini also committed 20 turnovers.[64] Loyola would go on to win the title, defeating two-time champion Cincinnati, 60–58, in Louisville.

The abrupt ending to the year was a surprise and disappointment for the Illini (who finished seventh and eighth in the final polls), but with most of their team back for 1963–64, they figured to be back in the championship mix for the following season. That assessment was less true for the Buckeyes, but having Gary Bradds back would have made any team dangerous. Michigan would not only have Buntin back, but would have help from rising sophomores Cazzie Russell and Oliver Darden. Indiana would lose Bolyard and Rayl, but the Van Arsdales and Jon McGlocklin would be returning. Minnesota had Kunze and Northway returning, plus expected help from rising sophs Lou Hudson and Archie Clark. It promised to be another competitive year for the rugged conference.

## The 1964 Season: More of the Same?

After the tie of Ohio State and Illinois for the 1963 Big Ten championship, both teams would be seen as contenders for the title once again, but they would have big holes to fill, Illinois having lost Downey, Burwell and Small, and OSU having to replace starters Jim Doughty and Doug McDonald. Certainly Indiana, Minnesota and Michigan looked to be formidable, but they would have to show that on the court, not just on paper. *Complete Sports Basketball, 1964* selected Cincinnati as the #1 team in the country in the pre-season. The highest-ranking Big Ten teams were Michigan at #7 and Minnesota at #12. As for top players, the magazine picked Gary Bradds for its first team after he averaged 28 points and 13 rebounds in his junior year. Bill Buntin was selected as a 3rd-teamer. The magazine's all-sectional picks for the Midwest included Mel Garland of Purdue and Rich Falk of Northwestern.

*Dell Sports* selected Loyola to repeat as national champion, just ahead of NYU, with Duke 3rd. The top Big Ten teams were Ohio State at #11, Northwestern at #12 (really) and Michigan at #13. Big Ten players on their All-American choices were Gary Bradds (1st team) and Bill Buntin (3rd team). Their all-sectional team (of ten players) for the Midwest included Mel Garland of Purdue and Rich Falk of Northwestern. The "Sophs to Watch" in the Midwest listed Cazzie Russell and Jim Myers of Michigan; George Peeples of Iowa; Dave Schellhase of Purdue; Jim Pitts of Northwestern (noting that the conference gave him an extra year because of his knee injury the previous year); Al Peters and Dick Renick of Ohio State; Don Freeman of Illinois; Max Walker of Indiana; Lou Hudson, Tom Barnhorst and Archie Clark of Minnesota; and Stan Washington of Michigan State.[65]

As for almost all of the rising sophs, there had been few or no games in their freshman year. Dave Schellhase said that the freshmen played a game before each varsity home game. It was really a scrimmage with 16 players rotating in and the better players getting "double shifts." Big Ten scholarships were limited to six per year, so Schellhase was one of just six on the squad of 16 with a scholarship. Despite these limitations on play, Schellhase said that he thought he improved more in his freshman year than any other season, due to good coaching, better competition and his overall maturity.[66]

After the surprise of the prior year, both AP and UPI picked Ohio State as #7 in the country, but *Sports Illustrated* did not rate OSU in the top 30 teams in the country. They did, however, mention both Northwestern and Minnesota as teams "not in the top 20, but [that] bear watching." They also noted that "the three top sophomores for

Minnesota, Lou Hudson, Archie Clark and Don Yates, were all Negroes, the first to ever play for Minnesota."[67]

By mid–December of 1963, there were some impressive patterns for Big Ten squads. Michigan State went undefeated until losing to Tulsa on December 18. Illinois routed Butler on December 19. Minnesota won its first three games, then lost to both Bradley and Wichita from the Missouri Valley. Kentucky pounded Wisconsin 108–85 on the same night that Michigan State lost to Cal in Tempe. Indiana went to Corvallis and lost 70–57 to Oregon State as Mel Counts had a monster game with 42 points and 22 rebounds. Notre Dame edged Northwestern, 70–68, but Rich Falk had 28 points in defeat and Jim Pitts had returned from his knee injury and scored 14 for the Wildcats.

Ohio State was edged by a powerful Duke squad, led by Jeff Mullins, at the West Virginia Invitational, then lost to an equally powerful Davidson team led by Fred Hetzel, Terry Holland and Dick Snyder. The score was 95–73 and was the first OSU home loss since 1959 after 50 straight victories. Missouri made it two straight before the Bucks played "their best game of the pre–Big Ten season" in defeating Wichita State and Dave Stallworth (25 points and 12 rebounds), 78–60. Bradds had 29 points and 17 rebounds, while Jim Shaffer played center and had 15, and Dick Ricketts had 14.[68]

Princeton topped Wisconsin, 90–87, as Bill Bradley scored 47 for the Tigers. In a more decisive contest, Michigan, already ranked #2 in the country on the basis of the great development of sophomores Cazzie Russel and Oliver Darden, crushed Duke, 83–67. Buntin had 14 points and 18 rebounds, while Russell had 21 points and 15 rebounds. All American Jeff Mullins scored 22 for the Blue Devils. Purdue lost to Evansville, small college #1, by the score of 110–84. "They were really good and beat a lot of good teams," remembered Dave Schellhase.[69]

In late December, Illinois and Michigan were both in the L.A. Classic. Illinois topped West Virginia, 92–86, with Don Freeman scoring 23 points and four other Illini scoring in double figures. Michigan defeated NYU with their two All-American players, Barry Kramer (11) and "Happy" Hairston (35), 83–74. For the Wolverines, Russell had 26, Buntin 18, Cantrell 14, and Tregoning 11. The next night the Illini beat Pitt, 83–76, and Michigan took its first loss to go 8–1 as UCLA (8–0) won 98–90. Gail Goodrich had 30 and Fred Slaughter had 16 for the Bruins, while Darden led Michigan with 25. Both Buntin and Russell were held to 11 points each. Michigan came back to defeat Pitt, 95–80, as Buntin had 26 and Russell 18.

Northwestern traveled to Philadelphia for a tourney and played their neighbors from Chicago, Loyola, losing to them 88–82, but Rich Falk scored 36 for NU. Minnesota defeated St. Joseph's in Madison Square Garden, 69–63, behind 20 from Don Yates and 19 from Lou Hudson, but then lost to Villanova two nights later, 77–73, despite 26 from Hudson. Villanova was led by Wally Jones with 31. Also in the Garden, Purdue played 16 players and romped over Dartmouth, 101–53, to end a five-game losing streak.

In a New Year's Eve double-header in Chicago Stadium, Illinois defeated Notre Dame, 87–78, and Loyola defeated Indiana, 105–92. Skip Thoren led the Illini with 33 and three others scored in double figures. For Indiana, Dick Van Arsdale had 36, his brother Tom 17, and Jon McGlocklin 17, but they needed more inside help. Also on New Year's Eve, Michigan crushed Detroit, 117–87, as Russell had 36, Buntin had 29 and 14 players scored for the Wolverines. In St. Louis, Ohio State absorbed its fifth loss of the season (5–5) to the Billikins, 91–89 in two overtimes, despite 25 from Bradds and three others in double figures.

After a very rugged pre-conference season, the Big Ten season opened on January 4 with Michigan the unanimous choice to win the league and Minnesota (7–3) the pick for #2. Michigan State and Illinois were each 6–3, and only two teams (Indiana, 4–5 and Purdue, 3–5) were under .500 heading into the conference season.[70]

Michigan opened its season against Northwestern, which had added Marty Riessen to their squad as soon as he returned from Davis Cup doubles play. In this, his first game, he scored nine points and was the ball-handling guard setting up Falk (17 points) and Lopossa (29), but the Wildcats fell short of the powerful Wolverines, 85–73. Russell (23), Buntin (22) and Tregoning (18) were the major contributors for Michigan.[71]

Illinois set Michigan State back in Champaign with an 87–66 victory, led by Tal Brody with 29 and Skip Thoren with 16. Stan Washington had 20 and Fred Thomann had 17 for the Spartans. Iowa edged Indiana in Bloomington, 72–71, and Ohio State had little trouble with Wisconsin, defeating them 101–85. Bradds started his final Big Ten season with 32 points. Minnesota struggled to beat Purdue, 97–93. Lou Hudson shot 16–25 from the floor and scored 36 points. Dave Schellhase had 29 for the Boilermakers.[72] Schellhase remembered that Hudson wore a kind of turban during the game, having hit his head on the bottom of the backboard and opening a large cut.[73] After that, colleges were required to put a strip of padding on the bottom of the backboards.

Despite its three future NBA players, this was not to be Indiana's year. Northwestern hit them with a partial zone, designed to keep the Van Arsdales off the boards, according to Coach Larry Glass, and it led to a 79–65 Northwestern victory.[74] Rich Falk had 26 and Rick Lopossa 21 for the Wildcats. Tom Van Arsdale had 18, but shot only 7–19 from the floor. Brother Dick had 17 on 7–15 field goals. Michigan State raced past Wisconsin, as most teams would ultimately do, 106–90.[75] Northwestern duplicated that the next Saturday with a 76–63 win, and Michigan State did the same to Indiana, 107–103.[76]

In two contests that were much more meaningful, Ohio State defeated Minnesota, 85–73, and Michigan won at Purdue, 77–70. In the former game, Bradds, with 27, and Ricketts, with 21, led

Rick Lopossa shoots one of his beautiful jumpers for Northwestern in a 1963 contest (**Northwestern University Archives**).

all scorers, while Hudson topped Minnesota with 19. In the latter game, Buntin had 23 and Russell 17 for the Wolverines. Schellhase had 20 for Purdue.[77]

The next week the Big Ten altered its traditional calendar and had the first Big Ten game on a Tuesday night, rather than just Saturday-Monday contests. In that game, played in Minneapolis, Minnesota defeated Michigan State, 103–82. Hudson (23), Northway (21) and Clark (18) led the Gopher scoring, while Stan Washington was the game's leading scorer for MSU with 26. Fred Thomann, the 6'9" Spartan center, missed the game with an injury.[78]

Michigan faced another big challenge the next weekend when they hosted Ohio State, but the Buckeyes were not up to the test, falling to the Wolverines, 82–64. Buntin and Russell each had 27, as did Bradds for OSU, but the next highest scorer for the Bucks was Don DeVoe with 14. Minnesota edged Northwestern in Minneapolis, 76–74, behind Hudson (19) and Clark (17). Rick Lopossa was high for the game with 29, while Falk and Don Jackson had 15 each.[79] Michigan followed up the decisive win with an equally decisive one against Minnesota, 80–66. Russell had 25, Buntin 23, while Northway had 19 and Hudson 17 for the Gophers. It was more of the same the next weekend, this time against Michigan State, 91–77. Russell (34) and Buntin (25) were again the scoring leaders, while Gent (23) and Thomann (18) led the Spartans. Michigan also outrebounded the Spartans, 52–35. Northwestern toppled Minnesota, 82–76, to keep in the race, at least for second. Lopossa (29) and Falk (22) outscored Clark (17) and Hudson (14) for their respective teams. Ohio State was still a factor and showed it by topping Purdue, 98–87, as Bradds went for 47 points.[80] "He may have been the best player that I ever saw in the Big Ten," marveled Schellhase.[81]

At this point, Michigan and Illinois were both undefeated in the conference, but Michigan was 5–0 and the Illini, through a scheduling quirk, were 2–0. OSU was 3–1, Northwestern 3–2, and Minnesota 3–3. The rest of the league was under .500: MSU 2–3, Purdue, Iowa and Wisconsin all 1–3, and Indiana 0–3.

Bradds followed up his 47-point outburst against Purdue with 48 against Michigan State, but it was not enough for a Buckeye victory in East Lansing as the Spartans won, 102–99. It was a rough game, with Dick Ricketts (OSU) and Stan Washington (MSU) both ejected for fighting. Marcus Sanders had 27 and Bill Schwarz 22 for MSU.[82]

The calendar moved into February and the Wolverines were still undefeated in the conference and 15–1 for the year. They had little trouble with MSU in Ann Arbor, but were upset in Columbus, 86–85, on February 3. Indiana finally won after eight losses in a row, topping Illinois 104–96 in Bloomington. Purdue went to 3–3 in conference with a 101–98 win over Michigan State, despite 26 from Gent and 25 from Sanders. Schellhase (38) and Garland (23) powered the Boilermakers. In the OSU win, Bradds had 42 while Russell (30) and Buntin (26) were the usual leaders for Michigan. Indiana's victory was a function of superior rebounding as they took 60 to the Illini's 44 caroms. Tom Van Arsdale had 27 points and 13 rebounds, his brother Dick had 25 and 15 rebounds, and Jon McGlocklin had 27 points and 11 rebounds. Skip Thoren led Illinois with 26 points and 18 rebounds.[83]

Michigan followed its first conference loss with a victory over Illinois, 93–82. Buntin had 37 and Russell 28 for 65 of the points. Brody (26) and Thoren (22) led Illinois. Northwestern defeated Michigan State, 93–86, and the Wildcats displayed great balance in doing so. Falk had 22, Jackson 20, and both Riessen and Lopossa had 19. Minnesota won at Iowa, 76–71, in what the *Chicago Tribune* called a "raggedy game." Yates and Northway led the Gophers with 18 each. Ohio State won in overtime at Indiana, 98–96, as Bradds scored 40 and Ricketts 24. Tom Van Arsdale and Jon McGlocklin had 27 each for the Hoosiers. Wisconsin essentially ended Purdue's title hopes, weak as they were, by defeating the Boilermakers, 81–80, in Madison, despite 35 points from Dave Schellhase. Ken Gustafson had the game of his life with 31 for the Badgers.[84]

Gary Bradds stayed hot two days later, scoring 49 points against Illinois in a 110–92 OSU win. It was his fifth 40-point performance in a row and the most points scored in a Big Ten game by anyone up to that time. Another game of significance had Northwestern topping Wisconsin to tie for 3rd in the conference, the Wildcats' highest standing in years, with a 5–2 record. The Associated Press poll that week had UCLA at #1, Michigan #2, Kentucky #3, Davidson #4 and Duke at #5. Ohio State was mentioned among other teams receiving votes. Another disturbing action was the arrest of a number of bookies at Chicago Stadium during Chicago Black Hawk games. Admittedly, this was hockey, but the venue was used as much for basketball, and after the point-shaving scandals of the past few years, there was new fear that this might extend once again into college basketball.[85]

Michigan and Ohio State rolled on, the former with an easy 99–87 win over Indiana, the latter with six in a row, this time over Wisconsin, 92–74. Bradds had 40 once again. In the Michigan contest, Russell and Buntin each had 23 (plus 14 rebounds for Cazzie and 15 for Bill) to offset the 24 from McGlocklin and the 21 each from the two Van Arsdales. Michigan outrebounded Indiana, 59–28. Minnesota remained close with a 92–81 win over Illinois. Archie Clark had 20, Bill Davis 19, and Lou Hudson 18 for the Gophers. Northwestern fell back with a 93–84 loss in West Lafayette to Purdue. Schellhase had 32, Garland 25 for the Boilermakers, while Falk had 23 and Lopossa 17 for Northwestern.[86]

On February 17, Iowa managed to "hold" Bradds to 30 points, but OSU still won easily in Iowa City, 99–82. Don DeVoe picked up the "slack" for OSU with 23 points. In his six-game 40+ streak, Bradds shot 93 of 160 from the floor for 58 percent.[87] The NCAA began issuing at-large bids at that time, and eight of the ten were announced that day. These were Loyola, Louisville, Villanova, Providence, Creighton, Texas Western, Oregon State and Utah State. There would be two more at-large berths, plus 15 conference champions in the tournament.[88]

The most prominent domestic issue of the time was the Civil Rights bill, which had gained President Johnson's support, after the death of President Kennedy, who had initially proposed it. The bill was lengthy and had arcane sections, so the clarification of the bill and its implications was vital to its passage in the Senate after clearing the House of Representatives.[89]

Michigan played at Minnesota in one of the new Tuesday night contests and the Gophers handed the Wolverines their second conference loss, 89–75. Minnesota burst out to a 43–25 halftime lead and never were threatened in the second half, as 17,019 fans cheered wildly. The Gophers shot 21–37 from the floor, and the Wolverines just 11 of 41. Rebounds were even, and each team made nine free throws. Hudson and Terry Kunze led Minnesota with 19 each, but four others were in double figures for the

Gophers. Russell had 26 and Buntin 22 for Michigan.[90] The loss dropped them into a two-way tie for first with Ohio State. The standings were: OSU and MI, 8–2; Minnesota, 7–3; Northwestern, 5–4; Purdue, 4–4; Michigan State, 5–6; Illinois, 3–5; Iowa, 2–6; Wisconsin and Indiana, 2–7.

Every game was key now and both the Buckeyes and the Wolverines won on the next Saturday. Ohio State topped Northwestern, 72–61, but it was an ugly win. Bradds was three of 21 from the floor and scored 12 points. Northwestern outrebounded the Bucks, 48–47, as they stayed in a tight zone the entire game. Jim Shaffer saved the Buckeyes with 23 points. Both Falk and Lopossa had 20 points. Michigan romped over Wisconsin, 103–59, and Minnesota fell back with a loss at Illinois, 86–78. Senior captain Bill Edwards had his best game as a collegian, scoring 21 to lead the Illini.[91]

Two nights later, Rich Falk tied Bradds's recently set Big Ten mark and set a new Northwestern and McGaw Hall record with 49 points in a 98–76 win over Iowa. The Wildcats moved to 6–4 in league play, but would not win another contest that season.[92]

On February 28, the sports pages were dominated by the upset of Sonny Liston by Cassius Clay in Miami Beach. The victories by both Ohio State and Michigan were expected, as they defeated Indiana and Illinois, respectively. With their victory, Michigan went to 19–3 for the season. Illinois played as well as they could, shooting 54 percent from the floor, but still lost, 89–83. The most notable part of the 73–69 OSU win at home was that Indiana played a box and one the whole game and managed to hold Bradds to 15 points.[93]

Two nights later, Ohio State topped Illinois, 86–74, and grabbed a ½-game lead in the Big Ten over idle Michigan. Bradds had 34. On March 7, Michigan won, but Ohio State was upset at home against Michigan State, 81–80. Bradds had 31, which set a new Big Ten season mark of 474 points, breaking the old mark set by Terry Dischinger in 1962. Bradds's 174 field goals also set an OSU mark, breaking that of Robin Freeman (163) set in 1956. Michigan State went out to a 10–1 lead, but OSU came back to lead at the half, 46–39. Down the stretch, the Bucks still led, 72–66, but went cold and MSU took the lead at 79–78. With 31 seconds left, Dick Ricketts, the shortest man on the court, had a rebound basket to give OSU the lead, but Pete Gent hit a long jumper with 10 seconds to go to give MSU the win. Michigan won against Iowa, 69–61, and looked to have the Big Ten title clinched, but Purdue upset the Wolverines, 81–79. Purkhiser (26) and Schellhase (25) were a better one-two than Russell (27) and Buntin (19), and the Boilermakers shot 53 percent to Michigan's 43 percent from the floor. Schellhase remembered that (Earl) Brown guarded Cazzie and "knocked him down" early in the game, and the Boilermakers fed off that, not backing down in the game against a more powerful foe.[94] The loss dropped Michigan into a tie for the Big Ten title, but because of the "Rose Bowl rule," Michigan would be the conference representative in the NCAA tournament and the Buckeyes would stay home.[95]

### Final Standings and MVPs, 1963–64

| | | |
|---|---|---|
| Michigan | 11–3 | Cazzie Russell |
| Ohio State | 11–3 | Gary Bradds (Big Ten MVP) First team All-American |
| Minnesota | 10–4 | Bill Davis |
| Michigan State | 8–6 | Fred Thomann |

Rich Falk drives the lane for the Northwestern Wildcats in 1963. Falk was All-Big Ten his junior and senior seasons and an All-American his senior year. He was later head coach of the Wildcats from 1978 to 1986 (Northwestern University Archives).

| | | |
|---|---|---|
| Purdue | 8–6 | Dave Schellhase |
| Northwestern | 6–8 | Rich Falk/Rick Lopossa |
| Illinois | 6–8 | Skip Thoren |
| Indiana | 5–9 | Tom Van Arsdale/Dick Van Arsdale |
| Iowa | 3–11 | Jim Rodgers |
| Wisconsin | 2–12 | Ken Gustafson |

In addition, Gary Bradds, the lightest center in the conference at 6'8", 195 pounds, was the unanimous choice of the National Association of Basketball Coaches for Player of the Year. Besides his scoring records, he led the Big Ten in field goal percentage (.535) and rebounding (13.2 pg).[96] Bradds, Russell, Buntin, Schellhase and Dick Van Arsdale were first team All–Big Ten. Russell, at 26.1 ppg, and "Buntin, at 24.6, formed the highest scoring tandem in Big Ten court history."[97] Russell also had broken Michigan records in total points, field goals and foul shots.[98]

Michigan would open NCAA play against the winner of the Loyola/Murray State game, which was won by Loyola, 101–91, in Minneapolis. Loyola was the defending NCAA champion, but they had lost captain Jerry Harkness and were simply not as strong a team as Michigan, and so lost to the Wolverines in a close contest, 84–80. Bill Buntin had 26, Cazzie Russell had 21. Loyola had all five starters in double figures, led by Les Hunter's 25, but their shooting was their demise. The Ramblers shot 33–88 (38 percent) from the floor and 14–23 from the line (61 percent), while the Wolverines were 32–73 (44 percent) and 20–27 (74 percent) from the stripe. Michigan was fortunate to escape from a very difficult second-round opponent.[99]

The victory sent Michigan into the Mideast regional championship game against Ohio University, who had surprised coach Adolph Rupp's Kentucky Wildcats, 85–69. Michigan ended the upset hopes of the Bobcats with a 69–57 victory. Russell had 25 and Buntin 15, but the game was won at the line as OU made just five of 11 and Michigan was 17 of 19. The victory sent Michigan into the Final Four the next weekend in Kansas City.[100]

The rest of the field would include east champion Duke, led by Jay Buckley and Jeff Mullins, who had crushed Connecticut, 101–54, in Raleigh; Midwest champion Kansas State with Willie Murrell (28 points), who had toppled Wichita, despite Dave Stallworth's 37 points, 94–87, in Wichita; and western champ UCLA, led by Walt Hazzard and Gail Goodrich, who had come from eight down at the half to defeat San Francisco, 76–72, in Corvallis, Oregon.

There was no national television coverage of the NCAA semifinals; rather, the game was sold to individual stations through a packager. WGN in Chicago carried the games live Friday and Saturday, for example, but there was no live coverage in many markets, especially the smaller ones. In Atlanta, the semifinals were not carried and the championship was carried on WSB, an independent station. In Washington, an ACC market, only the Duke semifinal was carried on Channel 5, WTTG, also independent, but now a Fox station. After Duke's victory, the championship game was also carried on WTTG. In New York, the NIT tourney was far larger in media coverage, and only the NCAA championship game, on Saturday night at 10, was carried by independent Channel 5, WNYW, now also a Fox station. In Los Angeles, the semis and finals were carried by the *Los Angeles Times* independent station KTTV, Channel 11, now a Fox station. In all of these markets and more, the NIT semis and finals were carried as afternoon weekend games on NBC affiliates.

In the first NCAA semifinal contest, Duke topped Michigan, 91–80, avenging an early season win by Michigan over Duke, 83–67. In the latest game, Jay Buckley had 25 and 14 rebounds for the Blue Devils, outplaying Bill Buntin, who had 19 points. Cazzie Russell had 31 for game honors against Jeff Mullins, who had 21. Duke edged the Wolverines 46–45 in rebounds.[101]

A third-place game was still being played in 1964, and Michigan defeated Kansas State, 100–90, to end the Wolverine season on a winning note. Buntin had 33, but Russell missed the game with what were termed "sore feet." Bob Cantrell had 20 for the Wolverines.[102] In the championship, UCLA began their historic run of championships with a 98–83 romp over Duke. Walt Hazzard won the Most Outstanding Player (MOP) Award.

Despite the lack of a championship, Michigan had acquitted themselves and the Big Ten well with their third-place finish. Their prospects for the next season were excellent, with all starters returning and their sophomore starters more experienced.

Ohio State would lose Bradds, the AP and UPI Player of the Year, who would be drafted by the Baltimore Bullets as the #3 pick in the 1964 draft, but played just eight minutes a game and averaged just over 3 points per game. The next year he was cut after three games and played in the North American Basketball League for the 1965–66 and 1966–67 seasons. With the start of the American Basketball Association, Bradds found new life. He averaged in double figures for three straight years for the Oakland/Washington franchise, but averaged just 5.5 points per game in 1970–71, his last year in the league. He then became a teacher and school principal in his hometown of Greenview, Ohio, but died at age 40 of cancer.

# IX

## Michigan Muscles the League

After UCLA's inspired run to the 1964 NCAA championship, they lost only Walter Hazzard to graduation, but he was the Most Outstanding Player in the tournament. Michigan, the third-place finisher, which retained its strength with an intact back line and Cazzie Russell, was picked by most preseason pollsters as #1 in the nation. *Basketball Yearbook, 1965*, edited by Zander Hollander with Contributing Editor Phil Pepe adding credibility, had Michigan as #1, UCLA #2, Davidson #3. The only other rated Big Ten team was Minnesota at #18. Russell was picked as a first team All-American with seven Big Ten players picked among the "50 Top Sophomores." These were Gary Lovemark and Paul Presthus of Minnesota, Tom Niemeier of Purdue (all bad choices in retrospect), Rich Mason and Jim Burns of Northwestern, Keith Stetler of Wisconsin, and Ron Sepic of Ohio State.[1]

*Complete Sports Basketball, 1964–65* saw Michigan as #1 in the nation with UCLA and Davidson following. Minnesota was ranked #14, the only other Big Ten team listed in their top 20. The *Complete Sports* All-Americans listed only Russell and Buntin as Big Ten representatives among the ten players selected. The all-sectional team of the Midwest had both Van Arsdales and Dave Schellhase as three of the five players selected.[2]

*Sports Illustrated*'s "College Basketball 1965" issue predicted Davidson as #1 in the country followed by Michigan, UCLA, Kansas and Duke. Minnesota was seen as #9. In a section called "A Few Surprise Packages," a number of teams were named that might be much better than most anticipated. Of the ten teams noted, two were from the Big Ten: Purdue and Northwestern, with six sophomores ready to impact the Wildcats.[3]

The 1964–65 season opened with high expectations for four Big Ten squads with significant returning starters. Michigan, of course, had Russell and Buntin returning, but also Oliver Darden and Larry Tregoning, and they were the favorites to repeat as champions and to go on to possibly win the national title. Indiana had the Van Arsdales and Jon McGlocklin returning, but sophomore Butch Joyner, counted on at forward, broke his ankle in pre-season and missed the entire year.[4] Minnesota had Lou Hudson, Archie Clark, Tony Yates and Mel Northway back for another season, and Illinois had veterans Skip Thoren, Tal Brody, Bogie Redmon and Don Freeman. Illinois made an early season impression in December when they routed UCLA, 110–83, but UCLA soon shook off the loss and won 14 games in a row before losing to another Big Ten team, Iowa, in late January. Despite their record of five Big Ten titles in a row, Ohio State was not seen as a threat with the loss of Gary Bradds, although the Buckeyes had been underestimated when they had lost Lucas, Havlicek and Nowell in 1962, and, had ridden Bradds to two more title ties following that. This time there was no "Braddslike" hero who would emerge.

The rest of the league was mediocre—Iowa, Purdue, Ohio State—or less than that—Northwestern, Michigan State, and Wisconsin. The initial estimates would prove to be true, although that did not mean that there would not be upsets along the way. After the usual early season "warmup" contests, the end of the first academic semester sent most of the Big Ten squads around the country to participate in various holiday tourneys.

As those tournaments began play, the United States announced a big international surprise, i.e., that the United States planned to cut a new canal in the Central American region to accommodate the need for deeper, wider locks for world shipping. Four sites were described as potential locations, two in Panama, one in Nicaragua and one in Colombia. Civil unrest in the latter countries made those locations difficult to secure, and other problems led to the abandonment of the new Panama sites, but in the 1960s, expectations were still high for many things.[5]

The holiday tournament at the University of Kentucky had Illinois defeating the University of Dayton, 104–86, then upsetting the host Wildcats the next night, 91–86. In the former game the Illini shot 56 percent from the floor with Don Freeman (25), Tal Brody (24) and Skip Thoren (23) providing most of the scoring. Against Kentucky, the Illini continued to shoot well (48 percent), while holding Kentucky to 36 percent shooting. An "overflow crowd" of 11,800 saw Thoren have 27 points and 22 rebounds and Brody pick up 25 points to lead Illinois. Kentucky had six players in double figures, led by Louie Dampier with 16 and Pat Riley with 14, but they were just not able to keep up with Illinois on the boards or in shooting.[6]

In Charlotte, Ohio State fell badly to highly ranked Davidson, 87–64, as Fred Hetzel with 28 and Dick Snyder with 22 led the Wildcat assault. Dick Ricketts had 16 as the new leader of the Bucks. OSU was 4–2. Northwestern lost to a mediocre Creighton team in McGaw Hall, 82–70. There were just 3,800 fans, no band, no cheerleaders, and no shooting accuracy as the Wildcats shot 11 of 45 (24 percent) in the first half and Jim Pitts was out with knee problems once again.[7]

Minnesota looked sharp in an easy victory over Utah State before just under 10,000 in Minneapolis, 88–69. Lou Hudson led all scorers with 33, but Wayne Estes, Utah State All-American, who would die tragically at 22,[8] scored 28 for the Aggies. Wisconsin and Michigan State began their descent into oblivion, 1965, with losses to Marquette and Butler, respectively. Iowa was surprised by Providence in Iowa City, 71–70, despite good scoring from Chris Pervall (21), George Peeples (15) and Gerry Jones (14). Indiana stayed undefeated by topping Notre Dame before 10,000 in a tournament in Ft. Wayne, 107–81. The Hoosiers had four in double figures, led by Tom Van Arsdale with 21 and Ron Peyser with 18. Purdue defeated a highly regarded Ohio University squad, 79–73, in West Lafayette. Dave Schellhase with 41, and Bob Purkhiser with 26, scored all but 12 of the Boilermaker points.[9] Despite this, Purdue never really got a rhythm going in their play that year. Schellhase said that Coach Ray Eddy, who was a fine man and a good coach, was nearing retirement and had little patience with the players. One mistake and a player was pulled; rhythm, flow, was impossible to sustain.[10]

Minnesota stayed unbeaten by toppling Loyola 89–75 in Minneapolis with all five starters scoring in double figures, led by Archie Clark and Mel Northway's 19 each. Michigan also stayed undefeated with an easy victory over Butler in Ann Arbor, 99–81. Cazzie Russell had 21 and Bill Buntin 19 for the Wolverines, the #1 ranked team in the nation.[11]

Illinois spent its holiday in Philadelphia at the Quaker City Tourney and opened with a win over NYU, 102–79. Thoren had 25 and Freeman 20 for the Illini. They then were toppled by the host, St. Joseph, which was also ranked in the top ten in the nation, 75–71, before 9,244 at the Palestra. Indiana remained unbeaten with a romp over St. Louis in the Memphis State Invitational, 98–68. Jon McGlocklin scored 29 for the Hoosiers with double-figure scoring by both Van Arsdales and Steve Redenbaugh. The Hoosiers won the tournament by beating Memphis State, 91–68, before 6,839 fans. Tom Van Arsdale led the scoring with 21.[12]

Michigan, playing in the ECAC Holiday Festival tournament in Madison Square Garden, opened with a 90–77 win over Manhattan. Russell had 36 and Buntin 19. In the semifinal contest, Michigan met Princeton and their great star, Bill Bradley. In the first half Russell had an ill-fitting shoe and missed periods of the game while the Michigan staff tried to adjust his footwear. Bradley was pushing the Tigers to build a lead; at the half, he had 23 points. He continued to score throughout the contest, but also picked up four fouls. When he fouled out with 4:37 left in the game with 41 points, Princeton was up by 12, but the Wolverines swiftly ate away at the lead, and with three seconds left, Cazzie made a jumper from 15 feet to give Michigan a victory, 80–78. He finished with 27 points. In the finals, Michigan met St. John's and the Redmen (now the Red Storm) upset the Wolverines, 75–74, before a sellout crowd of 18,449. Michigan blew a 68–52 lead as Sonny Dove led St. John's with 23 points and 18 rebounds. Russell had 24, Buntin 16, for Michigan.[13]

Minnesota went to California to play in the Los Angeles Classic, where they lost their first game of the season to UCLA, 93–77, before 14,861 fans. Seven Bruins scored in double figures, led by Gail Goodrich with 22. For the Gophers, Hudson had 26 and Northway 18. The Gophers returned home to beat Detroit, 80–66, behind Hudson's 25 and Yates's 19.[14]

The Big Ten's 14-game season would open with one undefeated squad (Indiana, 9–0), but four clearly outstanding teams in Michigan, Minnesota, Indiana and Illinois. The uneven schedule seemed to favor no one team, as Michigan played top teams Iowa and Indiana, as well as bottom-feeders Northwestern and Wisconsin, just once. Minnesota and MSU only met each other once and each played Purdue once.

Illinois topped Wisconsin, 70–56, to begin the conference slate, then handed Indiana its first loss, 86–81, before 16,128 in Champaign's new Assembly Hall. Three Illini had at least 20: Brody, 23; Thoren, 21; and Redmon, 20, while five Hoosiers were in double figures, led by Peyser and McGlocklin with 19 each.[15]

The Illinois victory set up a key early season clash for them in Ann Arbor five days later, and the Wolverines were victorious, 89–83, crushing Illinois on the boards, 62–42. Buntin and Russell each had 30 points and Buntin added 18 rebounds. For Illinois, Freeman had 27, Thoren 24, and Brody 21. Iowa defeated Michigan State, 85–78, behind 24 from Chris Pervall and 19 from Jimmy Rodgers in a foul-plagued contest (50 were called, 27 on MSU and 23 on Iowa) in East Lansing. Indiana set a Big Ten free-throw record by hitting 20–21 from the line in an 86–73 win over Northwestern in Bloomington.[16]

With Iowa at 2–0 and Indiana 1–1, their game in Iowa City was vitally important to both squads. With three players topping 20 points (Redenbaugh 22, McGlocklin/Dick Van Arsdale, 20 each), the Hoosiers disappointed the 12,500 Hawkeye fans with an 85–76 victory. Chris Pervall and George Peeples each had 23 for the losing Hawks.[17]

Michigan had slipped to #2 nationally this week as UCLA reclaimed the top spot, with Wichita #3, St Joseph's #4 and Indiana #5. Both Minnesota and Illinois were listed as "others receiving votes." Michigan, Indiana and Illinois all won that next weekend. The Wolverines had no trouble with Northwestern, winning 90–68. Russell had 36 in the game to lead all scorers. Illinois won a key match-up with Minnesota in Champaign, 75–72, as five Illini scored in double figures, led by Don Freeman's 19. The Gophers had four in doubles, led by Hudson's 18. In Columbus, the Hoosiers made Ohio State 0–2 in the conference with an 84–72 win.[18]

Nationally, two stories continued to shake and shape American life—Vietnam and the Civil Rights Movement. The 1964 Civil Rights Act was now the basis for a series of voter registration and voting discrimination cases brought by the U.S. Department of Justice and for a series of demonstrations for voter rights in many venues throughout the South. Dr. Martin Luther King Jr. was often at the forefront of those demonstrations and marches, such as the ones in Selma, Alabama, that were occurring at this time.

A week after Indiana defeated Iowa in Iowa City, the Hawkeyes returned the "favor," topping the Hoosiers 74–68 in Bloomington. Pervall and Gary Olsen each had 20 for the Hawkeyes, while Redenbaugh and Dick Van Arsdale led the Hoosiers with 18 points each. Jon McGlocklin missed the contest with an ankle injury sustained in the defeat of Ohio State two days before. Only 3,278 saw the game because the fire marshal ruled that exit space was insufficient for the capacity of 10,388. There was a lot of unhappiness over that, as well as with the game, and both would be dealt with quickly.[19]

The next Saturday brought no surprises as Michigan, with five players in double figures, routed Purdue, 103–88, Minnesota topped Ohio State, 97–77, and Northwestern edged Michigan State, 76–75. On Monday, Minnesota handed Purdue its first home loss of the season, 85–81, after scoring 51 second-half points. Minnesota had five double-figure scorers and Schellhase took game scoring honors with 32 for the Boilermakers.[20]

The weekly AP and UPI polls showed little movement on January 27 with UCLA and Michigan topping both polls. The next three were St. Joe's, Providence and Wichita, in various orders. Indiana was #9 in the AP and #10 in UPI. AP listed Minnesota and Illinois as "others receiving votes," while the UPI rated through twenty positions and had Illinois at #12 and Minnesota at #13.

It was quite a surprise when Michigan came into East Lansing to face the downtrodden Spartans, who then took the Wolverines into overtime, before sanity and Michigan prevailed, 103–98. Cazzie Russell had 40 points, including eight of the 15 Michigan points in overtime. Oliver Darden had 19. For Michigan State, Bill Curtis had the game of his life and scored 36 points, and Marcus Sanders had 29. Michigan would not be so overconfident playing their next game in West Lafayette. They drubbed Purdue 98–81 and held Schellhase to just eight points. Bill Jones, the Purdue center, who had had eligibility problems previously, had run into them once again, and this would be his last college game, as he had become academically ineligible for the spring semester of his senior season.[21]

Northwestern, with three sophomore starters and hopes for the future, sent Michigan State to a 77–75 defeat in a televised game on Big Ten compiler stations. Ohio State beat Wisconsin, 98–86, in Columbus. The standings at the end of January had Michigan at 5–0 followed by Iowa (4–1), Illinois and Minnesota (each 3–1), Indiana (3–2), Northwestern (2–2), Ohio State (1–3), Purdue and Wisconsin (each 1–4) and Michigan State (0–5). No big surprises here. Michigan was the class of the league, but Iowa was playing better than had been predicted under new coach Ralph Miller, who had had great success at Wichita, where he had won 220 games in 13 seasons. Cazzie Russell was the class of the league and continued to play like it, but so did the Van Arsdales, Thoren, Freeman, and surprising junior college transfer Chris Pervall, who fit perfectly into Ralph Miller's "run and gun" scheme.

February began with the Gophers having difficulties with Northwestern in Minneapolis, before finally beating the Wildcats, 70–66, before 8,039. The shooting was poor by both squads, 32 percent for each. Northway and Clark had 18 apiece for the victors, while sophs Jim Burns (18) and Ron Kozlicki (17) led Northwestern.[22]

Things were heating up in Vietnam, where Viet Cong forces killed eight G.I.s, wounded 62 and shot up 21 planes in attacks on U.S. compounds at Pleiku. Things were heating up in Champaign, too: the Illini and Boilermakers scored a record 214 points, as Illinois routed Purdue, 121–93. How was this possible? Dave Schellhase said that "defense wasn't as tough as it is today."[23] The 121 points were second to Indiana's one-game total of 122, set in 1959. Skip Thoren had 25 in the first half on the way to a 37-point performance, and Schellhase led all scorers with 41 in a losing cause.[24]

Iowa also stayed hot, winning their fifth in a row, defeating Northwestern in Iowa City, 78–72, before 12,500 Hawkeye fans.

Archie Clark, one of the first African Americans to play for Minnesota, was an All-American and played in the NBA for 10 seasons (University of Minnesota Athletics).

It was not a pretty game, as 57 fouls were called, 21 on Iowa, and 36 on Northwestern. The Hawks made the most of it, hitting 36–49 from the line and just 21 field goals. Northwestern was 12–25 from the line, a big factor in their loss. Minnesota kept pace with a victory in East Lansing, 88–79. Lou Hudson led all scorers with 32 points.[25]

Iowa's win and their surprising victory over UCLA made their next contest in Ann Arbor a test of their real strength, and Michigan showed that the Wolverines were clearly the class of the league with an 81–66 victory, their 19th straight win. Buntin and Russell each had 19, but Gerry Jones (a teammate of Russell's at Carver High School in Chicago) took game honors for Iowa with 26. Illinois tied Minnesota and Indiana for the second spot in the league with an 86–71 win in Columbus, the first victory there for Illinois since 1957. Thoren (27) and Brody (24) led the Illini scoring. Indiana was still a game behind after routing Michigan State, 112–94.[26]

Vietnam and the Civil Rights Movement continued to be the top stories. The U.S. retaliated against the Viet Cong with a big victory at the Da Nang airfield, and thousands of African Americans prayed for their adversary, Sheriff Jim Clark of Selma, who had been hospitalized with chest pains.[27]

In the Big Ten, Illinois lost ground to Minnesota when the Gophers thumped them in Minneapolis before 8,200 fans, 105–90. Indiana kept pace with a win in Evanston, 86–76. Iowa scored with three seconds to go to beat Ohio State, 82–81, and Michigan had little trouble with Michigan State in their rematch, 98–83. Russell scored 22 second-half points and a total of 32 for the Maize and Blue. In Minnesota, Hudson had 29 and Yates 20, but Tal Brody took game honors for Illinois with 31. Iowa's victory was won at the line, where they were 28–33; OSU hit 19 of 28. Iowa had six players in double figures. Indiana's win was also due largely to free throws, of which they made 22 of 29. Northwestern was only 14–25, but the Wildcats were huge on the boards, with 80 rebounds (Jim Pitts had 29!) to Indiana's 57.[28]

Two nights later, Michigan came into Bloomington and faced 9,300 Hoosier fanatics, who saw Indiana blow a seven-point lead with 56 seconds to go, as the game went to two overtimes before Michigan squeaked out another victory, 96–95. Russell and Buntin had 23 points apiece and Tregoning 20. Indiana had five in double figures, led by Tom Van Arsdale with 27 and his brother Dick with 21.[29] Minnesota and Illinois stayed a game behind Michigan with easy victories over Wisconsin (101–91) and Ohio State (95–72), respectively.

Michigan won its ninth Big Ten game in a row, defeating Ohio State 100–61, but both Minnesota and Illinois stayed close with wins. The Gophers beat Northwestern, 88–77, while Illinois set a new fieldhouse record in East Lansing, winning 113–94 over the host Spartans.[30]

On February 22, Purdue defeated Indiana, 82–70, before 9,265 in West Lafayette. Besides the pleasure of beating their in-state rivals, Purdue also became the first second-division team to beat a first-division team in the Big Ten in the 1964–65 season. Big Ten scoring leader Dave Schellhase had 32 for the Boilermakers.[31]

The next night saw two crucial battles, one in Minneapolis, where the Gophers hosted Michigan, and the other in Champaign, where Illinois entertained Iowa. Neither was close. Illinois sent 13,387 fans home happy with a 97–80 victory. Don Freeman had 33 and Tal Brody 24 to top game scoring. In Minnesota, Michigan pounded the Gophers,

Lou Hudson, going high for a rebound, was one of the first African Americans at Minnesota. He played in the NBA for 13 seasons and was an NBA All-Star six times (University of Minnesota Athletics).

91–78, despite the imploring of 17,600 rabid Minnesota fans. Cazzie Russell led all scorers with 27, while Lou Hudson led the Gophers with 25.[32]

With these latest contests, there was a bit of a shake-out in the league standings. Michigan still led at 10–0, with Illinois and Minnesota tied for second at 8–2. They were followed by Iowa (7–3), Indiana (6–4), Purdue (4–6), Ohio State (3–7), Northwestern and Wisconsin (each 2–8), Michigan State (0–10). With two weeks and four league games left for most teams, Michigan was still in control, but Illinois and Minnesota had hope, despite their inability to beat Michigan in head-to-head match-ups. The next important meeting would be on February 27 in Champaign, and WGN in Chicago was to broadcast the contest.

At this time, the NCAA began sending out bids to teams that had either clinched their conference or to independents. (DePaul was feted in the *Tribune* for receiving a bid.) This was done, most likely, because the NIT still operated independently and was inviting teams to play in that tournament, so the NCAA probably felt it needed to make moves early or lose some teams, since the only teams bound to the NCAA tournament were the conference champions of 12 conferences.

The big clash between Michigan and Illinois was all that it was cracked up to be, but the result was the same: a victory for Michigan, 80–79, before 16,128 and the WGN television audience. Buntin had 30 points and 13 rebounds, while Russell had 23 points, including the last five for Michigan. Bogie Redmon had 24 to lead the Illini, with Tal Brody marking 18. Minnesota kept their hopes alive with a big 100–88 victory over Indiana in Minneapolis. Hudson (31) and Clark (25) were a potent duo, although McGlocklin (25), Tom Van Arsdale (21) and Dick Van Arsdale (20) all had impressive games. Iowa fell out of contention with a loss at Purdue, 76–68.[33]

Now more than ever, it looked as if the league was playing for second behind the powerhouse Wolverines. On March 2, Michigan made it official, rolling over Wisconsin, 98–75, to claim at least a tie for the Big Ten title. Minnesota defeated Iowa, 78–70, in Iowa City, to stay in theoretical

**Dave Schellhase drives to the bucket in a game against Wake Forest in December of 1964 (Purdue Athletics Communications).**

contention. Almost as big a story as the Michigan win, however, was the news from Indiana that Branch McCracken would retire at the end of the season after 25 years at the helm. He would be losing all five starters, including the Van Arsdales and McGlocklin, so this may have had some bearing on his decision. After being an All-Big Ten player, McCracken had coached at Ball State from 1930 to 1938 before taking over at Indiana for the 1938 season. He won an NCAA championship in 1940 and another in 1953. After enlisting in World War II in 1943, McCracken returned to retake the head coaching reins in 1946. He stepped down two months short of his 56th birthday and died five years later of heart failure at the age of 61.[34]

Indiana won its last two contests after McCracken announced his retirement, but that only gave them a record of 7–5. In both games, the Hoosiers had five players in double figures, a real team effort. In the final game, against Purdue, they managed to avenge a loss to the Boilers in West Lafayette two weeks earlier. Purdue seemed lifeless, and the next day, Head Coach Ray Eddy also announced his retirement, joining McCracken in stepping away. Illinois closed with an easy victory over Northwestern in Evanston, 93–70; a loss in Iowa City before 10,500, 94–84; and a romp over Michigan State, 121–89. In the win over Northwestern, Thoren had 32 points and 18 rebounds. In the Iowa loss, he had 22 points and 14 rebounds, and Illinois had five in double figures, but they were outgunned by Chris Pervall with 38 and George Peeples with 23. Against Michigan State, the Illini had five in double figures again, topped by Freeman with 27 and Brody with 24.[35]

Minnesota closed with an 85–84 overtime victory over Iowa in Minneapolis, before 11,430 Gopher enthusiasts. Hudson (27) and Clark (23) thrilled the fans and gave them something to look forward to the next season. Michigan, having already clinched a tie for the title, defeated the Gophers, 88–85, in Ann Arbor behind Russell's 24 and Darden's 18. Hudson had 31 for the Gophers. Two nights later, with Russell out with a 101-degree fever and sore throat, and the Wolverines looking towards the NCAA tourney, the Buckeyes of Ohio State upset Michigan, 93–85. It was the highlight of the OSU season, as the five-time defending champions finished 6–8 in the conference. Ricketts had 32 and sophomore Ron Sepic 16 for the Bucks, who had five players in double figures. The loss prevented Michigan from going undefeated in conference and ended their regular season at 21–3, still ranked #1 in the country.[36]

As the NCAA tournament loomed, call-ups to Vietnam increased, with 3,500 Marines sent to guard the big U.S. airbase at Da Nang. This brought the total to 27,000 ground troops in Vietnam. Things would only get worse there. They also were bad in Selma, Alabama, where President Johnson, saying that he wouldn't be "blackjacked" into using force, barred sending troops to protect civil rights marchers there. The 2014 film *Selma* dramatized this period of history, and brought the Civil Rights Movement back to the consciousness of 21st-century America.[37]

The NCAA tourney began before the Big Ten season had ended: Princeton defeated Penn State, Providence topped West Virginia, St. Joe's beat Connecticut, all in the east. Houston edged Notre Dame in the Midwest and Oklahoma City defeated Colorado State in the west. DePaul pounded Eastern Kentucky and Dayton edged Ohio University in the Mideast. These games were played on March 8 and 9. The Big Ten finished its season on March 9.

### Final Standings and MVPs, 1964–65

| | | |
|---|---|---|
| Michigan | 13–1 | Cazzie Russell (Big Ten MVP) |
| Minnesota | 11–3 | Lou Hudson |
| Illinois | 10–4 | Skip Thoren |
| Indiana | 9–5 | Dick and Tom Van Arsdale |
| Iowa | 8–6 | Jimmy Rodgers |
| Ohio State | 6–8 | Dick Ricketts |
| Purdue | 5–9 | Dave Schellhase |
| Wisconsin | 4–10 | Jim Bohen |
| Northwestern | 3–11 | Jim Pitts |
| Michigan State | 1–13 | Stan Washington |

It had been a rugged Big Ten season, but the final results were no surprise: the Wolverines of Michigan were as dominant as predicted, and the Gophers of Minnesota good enough to play in the NCAA tournament, if today's format had been in place. Illinois and Indiana also might have been in an expanded NCAA, and surely in the NIT, if the Big Ten had allowed such participation at that time.

The final polls (taken at the end of the season, before the NCAA tournament) had Michigan as #1, UCLA #2, St. Joe's #3, Providence #4, Vanderbilt #5, Davidson #6, Min-

The 1963–64 Michigan team, anchored by Cazzie Russell, Oliver Darden and Bill Buntin. They won three straight Big Ten titles, 1964–66 (Bentley Historical Library, University of Michigan).

nesota #7, Villanova #8, BYU #9 and Duke #10. Consensus first team All-Americans were Bill Bradley (30.5 ppg), Cazzie Russell (25.7 ppg), Gail Goodrich (24.8 ppg), Fred Hetzel of Davidson (26.5 ppg), and Rick Barry of Miami (37.4 ppg). Second team was Bill Buntin,[38] Dave Schellhase, Clyde Lee of Vanderbilt, Dave Stallworth of Wichita,[39] and Wayne Estes of Utah State.[40]

Michigan, with a first-round bye, would open against Dayton in Lexington, Kentucky, on March 11 and soundly defeat the Flyers, 98–71, with Buntin (26) leading the way as five players scored in double figures. Henry Finkel had 22 for Dayton. The Wolverines would face Vanderbilt, an 83–78 winner over DePaul, the next night for the Mideast regional title.[41]

Vanderbilt was led by All-American Clyde Lee, who would go on to a fine NBA career. Against Michigan he had 28 points and 20 rebounds, but did not get quite enough support from his teammates as the Wolverines pulled out an 87–85 win. Russell and Buntin each had 26 points, and Buntin also snared 14 rebounds. It would not have been as close if Michigan had hit their free throws, going just 15–29, while Vandy was 15–21. The AP reporter for the game noted, "Michigan is not the best defensive team in the nation. A team can get good shots on the Wolverines and tonight Vanderbilt got more than one at a time...." A lack of familiarity with the Wolverines (something that could not happen now with all of the access to media coverage of teams) led to the Vanderbilt coaches' actually asking the media who to foul at the end of the game. Unfortunately for the Commodores, they chose the wrong guy—Cazzie—who was 8–10.[42]

Meanwhile, in other regionals, Bill Bradley was pushing his Princeton team to victory in the east as he scored 41 points in the 109–69 win over Providence before 12,653 in College Park, Maryland. In Manhattan, Kansas, Wichita defeated Oklahoma State, 54–46, for the Midwest title in a slow-down contest, brought about by Okie State's fear of the Wichita running game. Out west, UCLA ran past San Francisco, 101–93, in Provo, Utah, as Gail Goodrich (30) and Keith Erickson (29) combined for 59 points. Ollie Johnson had 37 for USF.

The national semifinals would pit Michigan against Princeton and Wichita against UCLA on March 19 in Portland, Oregon's Memorial Coliseum. That same day the Voting Rights Act was being reviewed in a House of Representatives hearing. The lack of a major television contract meant that the games could be bought by independent stations in various markets, but in the Eastern and Central Time Zones, the contest would start or end out of prime time. Because Michigan's Cazzie Russell was from Chicago, WGN contracted to carry the games in the Chicago market, with the championship telecast beginning at 9:45 p.m. CST. In Philadelphia and New York City, independent channels (WFIL, Channel 6, and WNYW, Channel 5, respectively) were carrying the one semifinal contest that featured "local" favorite Princeton, plus the finals the next night. In Los Angeles, local station KTLA (Channel 5) would carry both semifinals and the finals. But these were the exceptions. In Atlanta, for example, a city with a metropolitan population of about 1.75 million, there would be no coverage of any NCAA games because Atlanta had only three television stations—all major network outlets with network and local commitments. This latter situation would be true for much of the nation, and basketball fans would miss some of the most memorable tournament games ever.

In the first semifinal contest, Michigan overwhelmed Princeton, 93–76, despite

Bill Bradley's 29 points. Cazzie Russell had 28 and Bill Buntin 22 and the Wolverines hit 25–32 free throws and outrebounded the Tigers, 52–32. In the second semifinal, UCLA had no trouble with Wichita, winning 108–89. Six Bruins scored in double figures, led by Goodrich's 28 and Edgar Lacey's 24 points. Jamie Thompson had 36 for the outmanned Shockers.[43]

The semis set up a dream match between #1 and #2 in the nation, as well as an intriguing third-place contest, since these were still being played at that time. In this latter game, Bradley scored 58 points on 22–29 field goals and 14–15 free throws as the Tigers ran away from Wichita, 118–82. Bradley was named the NCAA tournament's Most Outstanding Player, edging Goodrich. He was also named Player of the Year by both wire services, the *Sporting News* and the USBWA. He and Goodrich were chosen as Helms Foundation co-players of the year. He would accept a Rhodes Scholarship and said, " I'm not planning on turning professional."

The championship game saw UCLA run out to a 13-point halftime lead (47–34), then keep Michigan at bay the rest of the game, winning 91–80. Goodrich led all scorers with 42 points, while Russell had 28. The shooting was fabulous with UCLA hitting 33–58 (56.9 percent) and Michigan 33–64 (51.6 percent). UCLA won the game at the line, hitting 25–33 charity tosses to Michigan's 14–17.[44]

Michigan had come so close, but UCLA was faster and shot better to win their second NCAA title in a row. After a hiatus of a year, they would win seven in a row from 1967 to 1973. Michigan was hopeful of returning to the NCAA title hunt, despite losing Buntin, Tregoning and Pomey, since they returned Russell, Darden and John Clawson. No super sophs were coming up, but reserves Jim Myers and John Thompson were expected to step in and be big contributors. Minnesota and Iowa had at least three returning starters each, and the 1965–66 race was not being conceded to the Wolverines, even with Cazzie Russell still there.

Coach Dave Strack, who was named the UPI Coach of the Year, was a key to the continued Wolverine success. Strack was a true Michigan man, having played there from 1943 to 1946, then coached as an assistant from 1948 to 1959. He was head coach at the University of Idaho for the next year before returning to Michigan as head coach in 1960, upon the resignation of Bill Perigo.

## The 1966 Season

Michigan was the pre-season #1 for most observers, and the Big Ten was also seen as having a number of strong teams. *Basketball Yearbook 1966* had Michigan #1, UCLA as #2, St. Joseph's as #3, Providence #4 and Brigham Young #5. The only other Big Ten team ranked was Minnesota at #11. The editors also saw Iowa, Northwestern and Ohio State as filling out the rest of the Big Ten's upper division. Cazzie was picked a first team All-American and Schellhase as a second teamer.[45]

*Complete Sports 6th Annual Basketball, 1965–66*, also had Michigan and UCLA as #1 and #2, but selected Providence as #3, followed by St. Joe's and Duke. Minnesota was their pick as #9. Their All-American team included Russell and Schellhase as part of the five selected, with Oliver Darden, Lou Hudson and Chris Pervall making up ⅗ of the Midwest all-sectional team.[46] *Dell Sports* made no predictions for top rankings, but in their "Midwest Roundup" picked Minnesota to dethrone Michigan in the Big Ten, with Iowa a possible surprise in the league. Their All-American picks had Cazzie on the 1st Team, Dave Schellhase on the 2nd team, and Lou Hudson on the 3rd team.[47]

*Inside Basketball 1966*, produced by the editors of *Sport Magazine*, picked no All-Americans and ranked no teams, but did predict league rankings. They saw Minnesota, Iowa, Michigan, Ohio State and Michigan State as the top five teams in the Big Ten.[48]

Despite the early wire service polls that had at least three Big Ten teams in the top ten (Michigan, Minnesota and Iowa were seen as #3, #6 and #9, respectively, in the AP poll of December 21), it would become readily apparent by the end of the pre-conference season that the Big Ten not only did not have a dominant team, but that the league was on a decidedly down year. The week of December 28, Michigan was ranked #7 and #10 and Minnesota #9 and #10 in the two polls. By January 4, no Big Ten teams were ranked in the Top Ten; in the next week, none were ranked in the top 20 teams.

*Sports Illustrated* had the most "aberrant" of predictions with St. Joe's as #1, Kansas #2, Duke #3, Vanderbilt #4, UCLA #5, and Michigan #6. Most surprising was their prediction of Ohio State as #8 in the nation on the basis of the development of junior Ron Sepic, whom the magazine compared favorably to Cazzie Russell, and Iowa as #14, largely because of sophomore additions Ben McGilmer and Huston Breedlove.[49]

The beginning of December brought sobering news regarding Vietnam and the continued troop buildup there. Secretary of Defense Robert McNamara announced that the U.S. would be increasing troops on the ground there each week with an expected total of 200,000 in country by January 1, 1966.[50] He refused to speculate on what the final total might be. Within a year, it was over 350,000.

By holiday tournament time, both Iowa and Minnesota were playing well, although Michigan absorbed an early season overtime loss to #1-ranked Duke on December 21, 100–93, in Detroit. Jack Marin had 30 and Bob Verga 27 for the Blue Devils, who had already beaten UCLA twice. Iowa went to 7–0 after topping a good Drake team on December 18, 69–51. George Peeples had 19 and Chris Pervall 17 for the Hawks, with Bob Netolicky leading Drake with 12. Minnesota was in the top ten after beating Creighton, 89–77, but they also lost Lou Hudson for at least six weeks with a broken right wrist as a result of a fall. He had scored 32 against Creighton and kept playing after the fall that broke his wrist. Later X-rays revealed the fracture.[51]

The December 22 Associated Press Poll had Duke at #1, followed by St. Joe's, Vanderbilt, Minnesota and Michigan, with Iowa tied for ninth with Kentucky and votes for Michigan State. That same day, Michigan was upset by Butler, the second loss for the Wolverines in two nights, three in the first month of the season. The next day, Vanderbilt was lucky to escape from McGaw Hall with a 59–58 victory in the last ten seconds over Northwestern, putting the Commodores at 8–0. Clyde Lee led them with 14 points, while Jim Burns topped game scoring with 19 for the Wildcats. In their first game without Hudson, Minnesota lost badly to Utah State in Logan, 97–72.[52]

It got worse for Michigan, in Portland for the Far West Classic, as they lost to Arizona State, 89–87. Cazzie had 35 and Jim Myers had 23 for the Wolverines, but it was fouls and free throws that were the difference. ASU had only 15 fouls to Michigan's 27, and the free throws showed that, with ASU going 27–35 from the line and Michigan

11–15.⁵³ In Philadelphia at the Quaker City Classic, Minnesota finally got back to winning, but just barely, edging Cornell 84–82. Clark led with 25 while Paul Presthus had 18. Illinois, playing in the ECAC Holiday Festival Classic in New York City, defeated Georgetown, 96–94, behind 33 points from Don Freeman and 30 from Rich Jones.⁵⁴

The last UPI poll of the calendar year still had Duke as #1, but Vanderbilt had jumped to #2, Brigham Young to #3, Bradley to #4 and Kentucky to #5. Iowa slipped into #6, Michigan was at #9 despite a record of 4–3, and Minnesota was #10. There clearly was respect for the league that led to these votes for the three Big Ten squads. The AP voting had Duke, Vandy, Bradley and Iowa as the top four, with Michigan at #7 and Minnesota #9, and St. Joe's in between them at #8. That night (December 29) the Hawks of St. Joe's routed the Gophers at the Quaker City Classic, 91–66. The winners had five in double figures, led by Billy Oakes with 20. The losers were led by sophomore Tom Kondla with 21 and Archie Clark with 18. Iowa managed to stay undefeated in El Paso, at the Sun Carnival Tournament, beating UCLA 77–75. In Portland, Michigan won a consolation game, 83–74, over the Air Force Academy.⁵⁵

Minnesota won the next night against LaSalle, 92–87, at the Quaker Classic, while Illinois lost to Army, 78–69, in New York, as Mike Silliman topped the Mules with 26 points. Freeman had 30 for Illinois. In Portland, Michigan topped Washington State, 93–81, behind 32 points from Russell and 19 from Darden. Iowa was upset by Texas Western in El Paso, 86–68. The Miners had six scorers in double figures, led by Neville Shed with 17. Pervall and Peeples had 18 each for the Hawkeyes. As the season progressed, this game looked less and less like an upset, as the undefeated Miners rose in the polls.⁵⁶

The first poll of the new year came out on the eve of the Big Ten season,⁵⁷ and Duke was #1, Kentucky #2, Vanderbilt #3 and Iowa #7, the only Big Ten team in the top ten. Indiana, Michigan and Michigan State were among others receiving votes. Overall, there were no great surprises in the play of the top Big Ten teams, with the Hawkeyes playing as expected and the Golden Gophers a bit disappointing. Michigan played Minnesota and Michigan State just once in their uneven conference schedule, but that was true of those two teams also. MSU and Minnesota only played Iowa once each, so the schedule would not be a significant factor in determining the champion of the conference.

On January 8, Iowa lost again, dropping their conference opener to Wisconsin, 69–68, in Madison. Iowa shot themselves out of the game, going 27–76 from the floor (35 percent), while Wisconsin shot 26–47 (55 percent) from the field. Northwestern topped Purdue as Jim Burns hit for 37 and Jim Pitts 23, while "holding" Dave Schellhase to 26 in the 111–97 victory. Purdue had a new coach, George King, described by Schellhase as the best coach for whom he ever played.⁵⁸ Illinois went to 2–0 with a 98–84 defeat of Indiana in Bloomington. Butch Joyner, who usually guarded Schellhase for Indiana, was not impressed with him as a player, though he saw him as a great shooter. Schellhase, said Joyner, directed his teammates where to go, often to get him a shot.⁵⁹ Three Illini had at least 20: Freeman with 28, Jim Dawson with 21, and Rich Jones with 20.⁶⁰

Michigan topped Ohio State, 83–78, in Columbus, the first Wolverine victory at that venue in 19 years, indicating both the strength of Michigan and the relative weakness of OSU. Russell (32) and Darden (25) had 57 of the 83 points in the win. Sophomore Bill Hosket topped OSU with 24. Michigan State routed Minnesota, 85–65, in East Lansing, to establish themselves as legitimate title contenders. Bill Curtis (23) and Stan Washington (18) led the Spartans, while Archie Clark led the Gophers with 27. The Spartans also dominated on the boards, 51–30.[61]

Two nights later, the two Michigan teams won again, over the two Indiana teams. The Spartans beat Purdue, 89–78, in what the *Chicago Tribune* called a "ragged game" with 43 fouls. The Wolverines crushed Indiana, 88–68, with Russell (27), Myers (24), and Darden (19) combining for 70 of the points. Free throws told much of the story as Indiana was 7–13, and the Wolverines 28 of 34. In Iowa City, 12,185 cheered on their Hawks to a 70–58 victory over Northwestern. Chris Pervall (24) and Gerry Jones (22) led the Iowa scoring.[62]

Illinois kept their winning streak alive, defeating Wisconsin for a second time, 80–64, but then lost in West Lafayette to Purdue, 93–87. Schellhase had 38 for the Boilermakers. Illinois was outrebounded and often forced to foul inside, resulting in a free-throw advantage of 14 points. Purdue was 35–44 from the line, and Illinois 21–34. Michigan State beat Ohio State (as most would do this year), 80–64. Minnesota beat Indiana, 91–82, in a game most notable because Lou Hudson returned for the Gophers and scored 20 points while wearing a cast on his wrist and forearm. Butch Joyner said that Hudson learned quickly how to use the cast as a cudgel, when referees were not able to see what he was doing. At the end of the Minnesota games, Joyner said that he was covered with bruises from guarding Hudson.[63] Michigan had a surprisingly difficult time defeating Northwestern in Evanston, 93–86. Twice the Wildcats led by 13, but they finally succumbed to Cazzie Russel's relentless scoring (he had 39 points). Northwestern was led by Jim Burns with 29 and Ron Kozlicki with 27.[64]

Two days later, Indiana surprised Iowa in Bloomington with a 73–61 Hoosier win before just 4,282 Hoosier fans. Little (5'9") Vern Payne (whom Butch Joyner called "a great teammate and shooter"[65]) had 23 and Max Walker 17 for Indiana. Iowa got 15 from Gerry Jones and 14 from Ben McGilmer, the sophomore *Sports Illustrated* had been so high on, getting his first significant playing time.[66] The AP Top Ten had Duke as #1, Kentucky as #2, followed by St. Joe's, Providence and Vanderbilt. Texas Western (12–0) was #8. Three Big Ten teams (Iowa, Michigan and Michigan State) were listed as "others receiving votes."

The next weekend Michigan claimed the top spot in the Big Ten. Before just under eight thousand fans in Ann Arbor, they topped Minnesota, 97–85, as Cazzie had 40 and got great help from Oliver Darden (16 points and 17 rebounds) and Jim Myers (12 points and 21 rebounds). Michigan overwhelmed Minnesota on the boards, 64–36. Archie Clark had 30 for the Gophers, while Hudson had just 12. Iowa handed Michigan State their first conference loss, 90–76, with five Hawks scoring in double figures, led by Denny Pauling's 21.[67]

Vietnam was now the only constant story in the daily headlines and the news was almost never good. On January 25, the headline on page one was, "46 GIs Die in Viet Crash," describing the crash of a troop plane shortly after taking off from an American airbase. The Midwest headlines addressed a bitter cold snap and Purdue seemed to succumb to that in a loss in East Lansing, 92–74. Matthew Aitch, a muscular junior college transfer (a rare occurrence in the Big Ten at that time), led the Spartans with 23 points and 12 rebounds, and Stan Washington had 21 points and 14 rebounds to offset Schellhase's 25 for Purdue. Iowa struggled with Ohio State in Iowa City before winning 98–89, but OSU was now showcasing some top sophomores, notably Bill Hosket, who had 28 points to lead all scorers.[68]

Michigan's rebounding and running were proving too much for Big Ten teams, so new strategies were being tried to eke out wins over them. Wisconsin tried slowing the pace as the game wound down, but succeeded only in making the score closer as the Badgers fell, 69–67, in Madison. Neither team shot particularly well (Michigan 39 percent, Wisconsin 38 percent) and Wisconsin held a surprising advantage on the boards (55–43), but Michigan eked out the win.[69] A month into the conference season and the standings had Michigan still undefeated and atop the league at 5–0. They were followed by Michigan State at 5–1; Illinois, 3–1; Iowa, 3–2; Minnesota, 2–2; Ohio State, Wisconsin and Indiana, all at 1–3; Northwestern and Purdue at 1–4 each. The only constant in the conference seemed to be Michigan, with the rest of the league a toss-up at this point.

The United Nations sat down on February 1 to debate Vietnam. Illinois and Minnesota settled their debates, defeating Michigan and Northwestern, respectively. The Wolverine loss, in Ann Arbor, was their first home loss in two years. Don Freeman matched Cazzie Russell with 33 points and Rich Jones had 31 for Illinois as they won, 99–93, before 7,300 stunned fans. Minnesota was outrebounded by Northwestern (43–37), but outshot the 'Cats, 43 percent to 29 percent for the win. Archie Clark led the Gophers with 26 points, but Mike Weaver took game honors with 28 for Northwestern. Jim Pitts had 18 points and 14 rebounds for Northwestern.[70]

The next weekend had Michigan, Michigan State and Illinois win, as expected, over Indiana, Wisconsin and Ohio State, respectively, although the Illini victory, before 9,388 in Assembly Hall, was a heart-stopper. OSU led for the first 34 minutes, before Illinois finally took a lead and edged the Buckeyes at the end, 78–77. Minnesota beat Purdue before 15,191 in Minneapolis, 66–61, as the Boilermakers tried an unsuccessful slowdown game. Schellhase had almost half the Purdue points (27).[71]

Northwestern handed the Illini their second league loss in Champaign, 80–77, in a game won on the boards by Northwestern, 57–48. Mike Weaver had 30 points and 16 rebounds for the Wildcats. The loss dropped Illinois to 5–2, third behind Michigan and Michigan State, both at 6–1. The UPI national rankings now had those three Big Ten teams in the top 20: Michigan #10, Illinois #18 and Michigan State #20.[72]

The tie at the top was broken once again on Lincoln's birthday when Michigan routed Wisconsin, 120–102, but Minnesota topped Michigan State, 81–77, before an enormous crowd of 17,039 in Minneapolis. Illinois stubbed their toes against Indiana, losing 81–77 in Champaign. Two days later, there was only one game and it was of little consequence as Indiana beat Ohio State, 81–61. What was more significant that day was a short piece announcing that Wisconsin had hired a "Negro coach" as an assistant on the football team. The article noted that the new hire, Lewis Ritchersen, was one of two Negro coaches in the Big Ten, the other being Frank Gilliam of Iowa.[73] That evening the Hawkeyes dampened Minnesota's title hopes with a 96–87 win in Iowa City, pleasing the 12,900 fans who jammed the arena. Pervall (28), Peeples (25) and McGilmer (22) combined for all but 21 of the Iowa points. Hudson had 26 and Clark 23 for the Gophers.[74]

The war in Vietnam was not just controversial in the United States, where the Secretary of State challenged the Senate Foreign Relations Committee to vote on the administration's war policies, but in other countries. In Australia, demonstrators shouted "war monger" at Vice-President Hubert Humphrey in Canberra, as he visited on an official state visit.[75] In a small item, the *Chicago Tribune* was noted that Joe Paterno, Rip Engel's top assistant coach, had been appointed to be his successor as the new head football coach at Penn State.[76]

Michigan solidified its hold on first by beating Purdue, 128–94, while Minnesota and Michigan State both lost, the former to Illinois, 100–89, and the latter to Wisconsin, 78–77. In the Michigan romp, Dave Schellhase scored 57 points, a new Big Ten record, breaking the mark of Jimmy Rayl, who had scored 56 in one game twice, in 1962 and 1963. Schellhase shot 23–42 from the floor. Wisconsin's upset, before 10,073 in East Lansing, was their third Big Ten victory, all by one point.[77]

Two nights later, the Wolverines lost their second Big Ten contest and sixth game of the year, to Iowa, 91–82, before 13,100 Iowans. Russell had 31 and Myers 19 for the Wolverines, but Iowa's McGilmer (26) and Pervall (20) countered that, as did the 37–28 Iowa advantage on rebounds and the 53 percent Iowa shooting. It was the first Iowa victory over Michigan since 1962.[78] Michigan now led the Big Ten with a record of 8–2, with Illinois and Michigan State at 6–3. Iowa was 6–4, the only other team over .500. Nationally, only Michigan (#9) was in the top 20, with Kentucky, Duke and Texas Western holding the top three slots, and only two teams, Kentucky and Texas Western, undefeated.

Halfway through the conference season, Michigan was holding to its lead, but Michigan State and Illinois were still formidable and had a shot at the title. Cazzie Russell, Lou Hudson, Archie Clark, Don Freeman and Dave Schellhase played like All-Americans, and they were.

For the three conference leaders, each game was vital. Michigan State made the first big move with a victory over Illinois, 68–66, to claim sole possession of second. Bill Curtis (23) and Stan Washington (17) led the Spartans, while Don Freeman (23) and Rich Jones (16) were the high scorers for the Illini. Michigan kept their lead with an easy 105–85 win over Purdue, despite 37 points from Schellhase; Cazzie had 33 for the Wolverines. Illinois lost again, this time to Minnesota, 94–92, pretty much ending any Illini hopes for the conference title. Clark, with 25, and Hudson, with 19, were the chief tormentors of Illinois, who got 35 from Freeman.[79]

Michigan closed February by closing out Iowa, 103–88, in Ann Arbor before 7,265 fans, about capacity for Yost Fieldhouse, which would be replaced the next year by Crisler Arena (nicknamed the House that Cazzie Built), seating over 12,000. Cazzie had 31, going over 2,000 points for his Michigan career, and Jim Myers had 23. The Wolverine shooting was deadly, 42–66 (64 percent), and they also outrebounded the Hawks, 42–29. Iowa was led by Ben McGilmer with 27 as the Hawks also shot well, 35–68 (51 percent). Michigan State stayed close with a 98–79 win at Ohio State before 8,065. Washington (26) and Curtis (20) led the Spartan scoring. Illinois, despite their virtual elimination, kept pace with a 98–81 victory over Purdue. Rich Jones had 30,

Don Freeman had 26, but game honors went to Dave Schellhase with 38 for the Boilermakers. His 2,014 career point total broke the Purdue career scoring record of Terry Dischinger set from 1959 to 1962.[80]

In "lesser" games, Minnesota defeated Indiana, 96–90, in Bloomington, where only 4,200 viewed the game. The bigger story, however, would turn out to be that Johnny Orr, the head coach at the University of Massachusetts (and Illinois high school scoring legend at Taylorville High School in the 1940s), had quit his position to go into the insurance business in Illinois. That new career never seemed to materialize, as he was soon signed on as an assistant coach for Dave Strack at the University of Michigan, whom he ended up replacing in 1969 when Strack moved into administration at the age of 45.[81]

The national polls now had Kentucky #1 and Texas Western #2, followed by Duke, Loyola, Vanderbilt and Kansas. No Big Ten teams were in the ranking, although Michigan was among the "others receiving votes."

For their final home game and Cazzie's final game in Ann Arbor, the Wolverines clinched the Big Ten title by bombing Northwestern, 105–92, and Cazzie set a new Michigan scoring record for a game with 48 points. Butch Joyner said that Russell was "just strong, as well as a good shooter and smart player."[82] Jim Burns had 38 for Northwestern. Michigan State rolled over in Bloomington, losing to the Hoosiers, 86–76, as Indiana outshot the Spartans, 55 percent to 36 percent. Michigan State was superior on the boards, 51–32, but their shooting doomed them to defeat. Illinois honored Don Freeman in his last game in Champaign, and he responded with 32 points to lead the Illini to a 106–90 victory over Iowa. Illinois lost its last contest, to Northwestern, 84–76, ensuring Northwestern would finish in the first division of the Big Ten, a rare accomplishment for the purple-clad Wildcats. Minnesota lost in Columbus, 94–89, and OSU had some hope for the future as Bill Hosket had 33 and Ron Sepic had 22, but then the Buckeyes ended their season with a loss at Purdue, 92–86, despite 32 from Hosket. In that game, Schellhase's 31 brought him the national scoring title with an average of 32.54 in 24 games. Russell was third at 31.2, but won the Big Ten scoring title 465 points to 451.[83] Don Freeman of Illinois scored 27.8 ppg, good for seventh in the nation.

In a game that meant nothing in the standings, but a lot for in-state rivalry, Michigan State defeated the Wolverines, 86–77, in East Lansing before 12,283 MSU rooters. Curtis had 26 and Washington 23 for the Spartans, who had already clinched second in the league. Russell had 34.[84] The loss dropped Michigan to 11–3 in conference.

### Final Standings and MVPs, 1965–66

| | | |
|---|---|---|
| Michigan | 11–3 | Cazzie Russell (Big Ten MVP) First Team All-American |
| Michigan State | 10–4 | Stan Washington |
| Illinois | 8–6 | Don Freeman |
| Iowa | 8–6 | Dennis Pauling |
| Minnesota | 7–7 | Archie Clark |
| Northwestern | 7–7 | Jim Pitts |
| Wisconsin | 6–8 | Paul Morenz |
| Ohio State | 5–9 | Bob Dove |
| Indiana | 4–10 | Max Walker |
| Purdue | 4–10 | Dave Schellhase First Team All-American |

All of the MVPs were seniors, voted on by their teammates.

The Michigan loss had no effect on the determination of their opening game in the NCAA tournament, which began that same night. The Wolverines would play the winner of the Loyola–Western Kentucky contest, which surprisingly went to Western Kentucky, 105–86. They would meet Michigan on March 11 in Iowa City. The final UPI poll had Kentucky at #1 (23–1), Duke #2 (21–3), Texas Western #3 (23–1), Kansas #4 (21–3) Loyola #5 (22–2, before their loss to WKU), St. Joseph's #6 (22–4) and Michigan #7 (17–6). No other Big Ten team was mentioned.

Michigan had their hands full with the Hilltoppers of WKU, edging them 80–79 on two free throws by Cazzie with 11 seconds left. The foul call was controversial since it came on a jump ball after a missed WKU free throw with 14 seconds left. On the jump ball, it was ruled that Greg Smith of WKU jumped into Russell, who got two free throws that won the game. Free throws were the difference as Michigan was 18–22 from the line and WKU 9–17. Russell had 24 points, backed by Darden and Clawson with 18 each. Steve Cunningham led WKU with 24 and Wayne Chapman had 22.[85]

Michigan would meet #1 Kentucky, who had defeated Dayton, 86–79, for the Mideast regional championship. In other regions, Duke won the east, 91–81, defeating Syracuse. Texas Western won the Midwest, edging Kansas, 81–80, after slipping by Cincinnati, 78–76. In the west, Utah defeated Oregon State, 70–64.

On March 13, the lead story nationally was "Governors Back Viet War" in a vote of confidence to President Johnson on his handling of the war in Vietnam. In a White House conference, 39 state governors and three from U.S. possessions gave unanimous approval for LBJ's war plans and implementation of those plans.[86]

The big basketball story was the defeat of Michigan, 84–77, by the Wildcats of Kentucky before a capacity crowd of 13,500 in Iowa City. Kentucky's fine shooting (51.4 percent) and the mediocre shooting of Michigan (38 percent) doomed the Wolverines. Both teams distributed the scoring well, with Kentucky having five players in double figures and Michigan four. Pat Riley and Cazzie Russell led their teams with 29 apiece.[87]

Both Kentucky and Texas Western won in the semifinals, setting up the legendary Texas Western victory, 72–65, over Kentucky in the NCAA championship contest. The game, in which Texas Western started five African Americans (the first time that had occurred; Loyola had started four in their 1963 championship victory) against Kentucky's all-white roster, had much greater implications than just a basketball contest and remains one of the most storied of NCAA championship games ever.[88]

The end of the tournament brought final disappointment for Michigan and Cazzie Russell, after finishing third and second in the nation in his three years of play, then losing in the Mideast championship. Michigan was only the third team in Big Ten history to win three straight Big Ten basketball titles. Michigan would certainly be weaker in 1966–67, losing Russell, the consensus national Player of the Year, and Michigan State might be much stronger. As for the rest of the league, it was hard to say, depending on the rapidity of player development and good fortune.

# X

# The 1967 Season: A Year to Forget for the Big Ten

The 1966–67 basketball season was, according to all pundits, to be the year of UCLA, led by their amazing sophomores, particularly Lew Alcindor. *Sports Illustrated* decided to no longer make predictions about which teams would be in the top twenty of the nation; instead they just ranked the teams in each top conference. Their lead basketball story was on UCLA, however, and Alcindor was on the cover. Their Big Ten ranking had Michigan State as the top squad, followed by Michigan, then Illinois, who would be led by Rich Jones, Jim Dawson, and sophomore star Steve Kuberski. They saw "hope" for Northwestern, as well as for Iowa, largely because of a junior college transfer, Sam Williams. Michigan State's success was not just linked to the players, but to the fine coaching leadership of John Bennington, who had taken a 5–19 team and, in his first year, produced a record of 17–7. He was runner-up for national coach of the year in 1965–66.[1]

*Basketball Yearbook 1967*, edited by top basketball writer Zander Hollander, selected UCLA as the top team, followed by Duke, Kentucky, Louisville, Dayton, Providence, Houston and, at #9, Michigan State. No other Big Ten team made the top twenty teams. In Big Ten coverage, the outlook was Northwestern as a potential #2 team in the league, followed by Illinois, Iowa, Indiana, Michigan, Wisconsin, Minnesota, Purdue and Ohio State.[2]

The early AP and UPI polls were very similar. Both had UCLA as #1 and Texas Western as #4. Louisville was #2 and North Carolina #3 in the AP poll, and those positions were reversed in the UPI poll. Both had Michigan State as #5. The AP only ranked ten teams, then listed others alphabetically. These latter included Illinois and Northwestern. The UPI poll had Illinois at #13 with Northwestern among the others receiving votes, not in the top 20. Illinois defeated Kentucky, 98–97, in Lexington in early December, a win that made an impressive statement to the rest of the college basketball world.[3]

Some other early season games were encouraging for the Big Ten. At that time most teams played a number of games against teams in other top conferences, or independents, as well as some so-called cream puffs. Indiana lost a December contest, 82–69, to Kansas State, in Manhattan, which was disappointing. Michigan had a relatively easy time defeating Butler, 91–80, in Ann Arbor. Wisconsin drew 10,241 fans to Madison to see the Badgers defeat Iowa State, 80–73, despite 27 points from Jon McGonigle and 25 from Don Smith of the Cyclones. Purdue defeated perennial power St. Joseph's of Philadelphia, 98–65.[4]

On December 16, it was announced that the Big Ten was investigating the possibility of a "slush fund" at the University of Illinois, involving both football and basketball players. No players were mentioned, but the tone was certainly ominous. This aura of foreboding would last throughout the season for the Illini, and the Big Ten would also feel this discomfort.[5]

The Big Ten investigation was initiated at the request of University of Illinois President David Henry, according to Big Ten Commissioner Bill Reed, who was quoted as saying:

> [C]ertain irregularities with respect to grant-in-aid assistance to athletes had been brought to his [Henry's] attention.... A reliable source indicated Friday that football coach Pete Elliot and basketball coach Harry Combes had been put on secret probation and banned from recruiting for a year by Henry.
> Henry reportedly took the action after discovering the existence of a "slush fund." The fund, which was built up by money donated by local businessmen and well-to-do alumni, was reportedly used to give financial aid to top-rated athletes. Star football and basketball players appear to have bad the greatest opportunities to use the fund.[6]

Regarding that fund, when questioned, "a few athletes commented that they didn't know of it or 'it was a well-kept secret.'"[7]

Despite the overall weakness anticipated for the conference, December 17 was a night of only victories for the league: Indiana topped Loyola, 83–73, as Butch Joyner scored 26 for the Hoosiers; Wisconsin edged South Carolina, 88 to 84; Purdue defeated Washington with five players in double figures, 85–70; Minnesota slipped by Ohio University; and, most impressively, Iowa beat Drake, 83–75. This latter win was keyed by Sam Williams with 27 points and Tom Chapman with 22. Future ABA star Bob Netolicky had 29 for Drake, with Andre McCarter chipping in 15.[8]

Two nights later, for the second year in a row, the Big Ten season started with a single December game, the reason being that the two teams, Wisconsin and Illinois, could not find a mutually agreeable time for the contest after the first of the year. The Illini defeated the Badgers in Champaign, with Jim Dawson (22) and Rich Jones (19), leading the attack. Sophomore Chuck Nagle was high for Wisconsin with 22 points. Northwestern showed that they had the offensive firepower to warrant the high ranking that they had received from some Big Ten observers, as they defeated Tulane, 121–116. Ron Kozlicki, with 26, and Jim Burns, with 25, were the biggest contributors.[9]

Two of the top-rated Big Ten teams had opposite results the next night as Michigan State lost to Loyola of New Orleans in the New Orleans Classic, while Indiana topped rugged Notre Dame, 94–91, in Fort Wayne. Butch Joyner said that this win gave the Hoosiers a lot of confidence and they felt that they could win the Big Ten, despite finishing last the year before.[10] In the former game, sophomore Lee Lafayette led the Spartans with 19 points. In the latter contest, Jack Johnson had 18, Vern Payne and Bill Russell had 16 each.[11]

The AP and UPI polls had the same top five teams: UCLA, Louisville, North Carolina (reversed with Louisville in one poll), Texas Western and Michigan State. Illinois was ranked #13 in the UPI and among "others" in the AP poll, as was Northwestern in both polls. Nevertheless, it would soon become clear that the belief in a strong Big Ten, as was usually the case, was in fact ill-placed.

Illinois defeated Stanford in Champaign, 74–71, with Ron Dunlap (19) and Rich Jones (18) high scorers. Still in New Orleans, Michigan State defeated Tulane, 76–66, as Matthew Aitch (19) and Heywood Edwards (18) led the scoring.[12]

The Stanford contest would be the last for both Jones and Dunlap as they were implicated by name on December 23 in the slush fund scandal. The two, plus sophomore Steve Kuberski, were declared ineligible because of receiving illegal aid, and their ultimate punishment, as well as the details of the involvement of others, would come out over the next few months, putting a pall over the Illini season.[13] Playing without these three and with a head coach, Harry Combes, who had offered to resign in light of the situation, Illinois still managed to win in overtime in Chicago Stadium, 97–87, over the University of California. Captain Jim Dawson had 23 and two new starters, Deon Flessner and Dave Scholz, had 24 and 22, respectively. In Iowa City, Stanford continued its Big Ten road trip with another loss, this one to Iowa, 77–74. Gerry Jones had 26 and Tom Chapman 20 for the Hawks.[14]

On Christmas Eve, the University of Illinois received a very unwelcome Christmas "present," the naming of the other two basketball players alluded to in the initial accusation of those receiving illegal payments (there were five basketball players and seven football players accused). Sophomore Steve Spanich and freshman Randy Crews were both declared ineligible, pending further investigation. Like a festering sore, information on this situation would seep out over the rest of the season.[15]

The students of the university were on break at this time, but the first *Daily Illini* issue after the break expressed bitterness for both Assistant Athletic Director Mel Brewer (who revealed the existence of the fund to President Henry) and both coaches, Elliott and Combes. In a column, student Bob Strohm noted:

> Brewer was not just a bad guy (as a tattle tale), but also Elliott and Combes were "bad guys." No one would argue that they thought what they were doing was legal.
>
> The most unfortunate part of this whole business is not that Illinois's basketball team has been severely impaired this season or that the future of Elliott's football team is uncertain, at best, but that Elliott and Combes are sympathized with and Brewer is being blamed for the whole situation.[16]

It was the season of holiday tournaments and Big Ten teams were spread out over the nation. Northwestern was in New York for the Holiday Festival. Indiana and Minnesota would play in the Far West Classic in Portland, Oregon. Illinois, Michigan and Wisconsin were part of the L.A. Classic, Michigan State was at the Quaker City Classic in Philadelphia, and Purdue was participating in the Rochester Classic. The Big Ten had gone 41–18 in December, "one of its best December marks in history," but that would be a deceptive figure, as it turned out.[17] The latest AP and UPI polls indicated the growing lack of confidence in the strength of the Big Ten. The top teams remained the same, but only Michigan State remained as a listed Big Ten team, #7 in the UPI and #10 in the AP.

Illinois, with its new lineup and a tightly bonded team, defeated Arizona in Los Angeles, 93–77. Dave Scholz had 22, Deon Flessner had 20 and Jim Dawson 19, as five players scored in double figures. In Philadelphia, the Spartans were edged by the Villanova Wildcats, 66–63. Steve Rymal with 18, and Aitch with 16, led the MSU scoring. In Portland, Indiana tripped up Oregon State, 71–60, for a win. Butch Joyner led the Hoosiers with 18.[18]

The next night, December 28, Northwestern lost to Providence in a packed Madison Square Garden of nearly 18,000 fans. Jimmy Walker dazzled the 'Cats with 38 points, although it was on 16–41 shooting. Jim Burns (26) and Ron Kozlicki (21) led the Northwestern forces. Purdue started off in Rochester with a loss to Georgetown, 104–82. Michigan State lost again, this time to Bowling Green in the Quaker City consolation game, 75–67. Aitch had 24 for the Spartans. In Los Angeles, things were no better. Wisconsin was thumped by the best team in the nation, UCLA, 100–56, while Michigan lost big to Georgia Tech, 101–70. Lew Alcindor, playing about half the game, had 24 for the Bruins. Chuck Nagle led the Badgers with 16. Center Craig Dill, 6'10", topped the Wolverine scoring with 20 against the Yellow Jackets. Minnesota "kept pace," as it were, by losing to Oregon in Portland, 67–60, despite 16 from Tom Kondla, 14 from Wayne Barry and 13 from Paul Presthus. Only Iowa stopped the Big Ten bleeding with a 94–76 win at home against Wichita State. Tom Chapman had 28, Gerry Jones 23, and Sam Williams 23 for the winning Hawks.[19]

The next night was slightly better for the conference. In Los Angeles, Illinois and Wisconsin lost, but Michigan won, although the latter win was not as triumphant as it might have been, since Michigan defeated league foe Wisconsin, 98–88. Craig Dill led the Wolverines with 24, while Mike Carlin led the Badgers with 22. Illinois was edged by USC, 73–72. Scholz (22) and Dawson (17) were high scorers for Illinois. Purdue won against their overmatched host, the University of Rochester, 112–73. In Greensboro, North Carolina, Ohio State managed to slip by Duke, 83–82, despite Bob Verga's canning 41 points for the Blue Devils. Sepic (22) and Hosket (16) led the OSU attack, but Denny Meadors clinched the game by canning a one-and-one with 17 seconds left to play.[20]

Tournaments and holiday contests continued the next night. Iowa played in Chicago Stadium in one of the big double-headers and defeated Cincinnati, 78–69, behind 23 points from Tom Chapman. Northwestern lost again in the Garden, 91–87, this time to Rhode Island, before a crowd of 18,499. Burns and Weaver led the 'Cats with 24 and 19, respectively. In Los Angeles, Illinois, Wisconsin and Michigan all won. Illinois topped Georgia Tech, 83–71, with Scholz (27) and Flessner (26) leading the charge. Wisconsin pounded Arizona, 104–77, as Joe Franklin led four other teammates in double figures with 32 points. Michigan topped Arkansas, 82–77. In Oregon, Indiana took third in the Far West Classic with a 102–64 win over Oregon. Vern Payne (22) and Butch Joyner (18) led the parade of Hoosier scoring. Minnesota beat Oregon State, 60–54, also in Portland.[21]

In Charlotte, Ohio State was destroyed by North Carolina, 105–82, which was not surprising, considering the compositions of both teams, but Fred Taylor was miffed because the Bucks had played a tough game the night before against Duke while North Carolina was fresh, having not played for nearly a week. When he agreed to schedule the UNC game, it was with the proviso that the Tar Heels also played a Big Ten opponent on Friday night, which Dean Smith had agreed to. When the schedules were released, UNC had no Friday game scheduled. Taylor tried to cancel the UNC game, but the contracts were already signed, and he was told by Athletic Director Dick Larkins, "Ohio State will honor the contract." So much for honor among coaches.[22]

Most Big Ten teams were off until the start of the Big Ten season on January 7, 1967. Northwestern started fast and ran Michigan's Wolverines out of their own gym in Ann Arbor, 93–73. Burns had 27 and Kozlicki 22 to lead the rout. In Champaign, the Spartans edged the Illini, 76–74, before just over 11,000 Illini supporters, a disappointing number in the 16,000-seat arena. Aitch and sophomore Lee Lafayette each had 24 for Michigan State, while Scholz (23) and Dawson (21) were the high scorers for Illinois. Iowa knocked off Indiana in Iowa City before a near-capacity crowd of 11,586 elated fans. Sam Williams had 25 and Tom Chapman 21 for the Hawks. The Hoosiers were led by Butch Joyner with 19 and Vern Payne with 18.[23]

The Hoosiers returned home on Monday and topped Minnesota, who had lost to Ohio State on Saturday. Joyner had 23 in the 83–68 victory, played before just 5,448 in Bloomington. IU shot 47 percent from the floor to Minnesota's 32 percent, but free throws kept the Gophers within hailing distance, as they shot 24–34, while Indiana had just 13–23.[24]

The first polls of the new year had little change at the top: UCLA, Louisville, New Mexico, North Carolina, and Houston were the top five in both polls. Iowa and Michigan State were "others receiving votes" in the AP poll. In the UPI poll, Iowa tied for #20. Not a strong showing for the Big Ten, to be sure.

The next night Northwestern defeated Illinois, 104–96, and Wisconsin beat Michigan, 98–90, in Madison. In Evanston the Wildcats had six players in double figures, led by Burns with 28. Illinois got 29 from Dawson to lead all scorers, and he was followed by Preston Pearson with 17. Michigan's loss to a mediocre Wisconsin team indicated how bad the Michigan year would likely be. It was.[25]

On January 13, the lead headline was "Mao's Edict: Purge Away." This was the signal, as it turned out, for the Cultural Revolution, which wracked China for the next few years and reverberated for even longer. Mao appointed his wife, Chiang Ching, as the adviser to a new group, to oversee changes in the country. It was a lethal appointment for many.[26]

The weekend of January 15 saw Illinois have a tough time with Michigan, but still prevail, 99–93, thanks to Dawson (27), Flessner (26) and Scholz (22). Craig Dill had 24 for the Wolverines. Michigan State set back Iowa in East Lansing, 79–70. MSU had five in double figures, led by Lee Lafayette's 17. The score would not have been as close if MSU could have shot free throws at a decent rate; they hit nine of 20. Gerry Jones had game honors with 27 and Sam Williams was right behind with 26 for the Hawks. Ohio State was defeated by Indiana, 81–80, in Columbus, and the *Tribune* saw it as an upset, assuming that Indiana would be near the bottom of the Big Ten standings, as they had been the year before. Bill Hosket had 32 and Jeff Miller had 21 for the Bucks, but they had little help from their mates. IU had more balance, led by Butch Joyner's 22 and Irv Inniger's 19.[27] It was this balance that would characterize Indiana basketball for the entire season. Joyner said that the IU team that year was "a great *team* [his emphasis], close knit," willing to always make the extra pass, not caring who scored.[28]

The national rankings were shaken the next week when Louisville lost to the #1 small college team in the country, Southern Illinois,[29] who had also beaten Wichita State. This SIU team was led by Walt Frazier and Dick Garrett and would go on to win the NIT in the spring, but at this time, the whole notion of "small college" versus "big college" teams and ranking seemed almost up for grabs. It is similar to how the five power leagues may be viewed versus the rest of the larger conferences starting in 2015, as they control more of their own destinies and the influence and money that goes with that.

Northwestern defeated Iowa, 90–88, to start the next weekend and became the last unbeaten team in the Big Ten at 3–0. It was not a pretty game, as 52 fouls were called and six players fouled out, four for Iowa, two for Northwestern. The Wildcats were led in scoring by their reliable trio of Burns (20), Kozlicki (19) and Weaver (19), while Sam Williams was the Iowa offense with 39, followed by Gerry Jones with 13. Michigan State was surprised in Ann Arbor by Michigan, 81–59. The Wolverines dominated in every aspect of the game, outrebounding MSU 54–37, despite the Spartans being the Big Ten rebounding leader. MSU hit just 7–15 free throws, while Michigan was 15–20. Craig Dill was the high scorer for the game with 18, followed by Jim Pitts with 17, the same total for Matthew Aitch and Steve Rymal of MSU.[30]

Iowa rebounded from their loss to defeat Michigan two nights later in Iowa City, their 18th home win in a row. Tom Chapman had 24 and Sam Williams 20 in the 91–81 win. Ohio State defeated Purdue in Columbus, 82–72, in a "game marred by fouls and a near riot" after a scramble under the basket got more heated. There were 54 fouls called. Bill Hosket and Herm Gilliam each had 28 for their respective teams.[31]

One of the hazards of Midwestern life and Big Ten basketball manifested itself on January 27 as 23 inches of snow fell in 29 hours in the Chicago area, combined with 50 mph winds, a storm that paralyzed the city. The Northwestern-Ohio State game was postponed and played in Evanston three nights later. The Wildcats remained undefeated in the conference, crushing OSU 100–77. Burns and Weaver each had 20 for the Wildcats, but Bill Hosket was high for the game with 27.[32]

Vietnam was never far from the front page and, for those of draft age, it was never completely from one's thoughts. Around this time, rumors began to float about an end to the war, but the rumored feelings from North Vietnam were squelched by President Johnson on February 2, who said that no talks to end the war were going on or imminent.[33]

Northwestern's undefeated run ended on February 4 when the Illini topped them in Champaign, 93–83. It was a close game, but Illinois, led by Dawson and Scholz, who each scored 26 points, pulled away to win. Burns led all scorers with 29 for Northwestern. That same night, UCLA was slowed to a crawl by USC before winning 40–35, making the Bruins 17–0.[34]

Indiana grabbed a share of the Big Ten lead two nights later with a big win over Michigan State, 82–77, in Bloomington before less than half the capacity of Assembly Hall's 16,000. Irv Inniger hit 12 of 16 shots for 24 points to pace the Hoosiers, who hit 55 percent as a team. MSU was led by Aitch with 20.[35]

The nation's top teams, as determined by the AP poll, changed little with UCLA (17–0), North Carolina (14–1), Louisville (18–2), Princeton (17–1) and Houston (15–2) topping the list. There were no Big Ten teams mentioned anywhere in the rankings.

Northwestern was fortunate to return home to play weak Michigan, whom they trounced, 105–82. Walt Tiberi and Dan Davis were high scorers for the 'Cats with 19 apiece, while Dill led Michigan with 25. Free throws were a real factor in the game as Northwestern went 29–40 and Michigan 14–29. Indiana kept pace with Northwestern by winning over Wisconsin, 93–81. Five Hoosiers were in double figures, led by Inniger's

18. Illinois dropped a 93–81 contest to Minnesota in Minneapolis before only 8,317. Tom Kondla had 32 for the Gophers to lead all scorers, while Jim Dawson had 22 for Illinois. The Gophers won the game on the boards, outrebounding Illinois, 47–29. Iowa stayed close to the top with a 73–72 victory in Columbus. Sam Williams had 29 for Iowa, while Bill Hosket topped the Bucks with 21.[36]

Playing a week after their loss in Bloomington, Michigan State returned the favor, stopping the Hoosiers' five-game win streak with an 86–77 victory in East Lansing. Lee Lafayette led the Spartans with 24 points, followed by Steve Rymal's 19. Butch Joyner had 25 for Indiana.[37]

The Big Ten standings now had four teams still with viable claims to the title. Northwestern (5–1), Indiana and Michigan State (each 5–2) and Iowa (4–2) were the only teams with winning records in the league at this point. They were followed by Purdue and Illinois (each 3–4); Ohio State (3–5); Wisconsin (2–4); with Minnesota and Michigan bringing up the rear (each 2–5).

Northwestern promptly lost at Iowa, 80–75, and there was a four-way tie for first in the conference. The Iowa fieldhouse rocked, with nearly 13,000 fans cheering on Sam Williams, who responded with 24 points and 10 rebounds; Gerry Jones, who had 22 points; and the rest of the Hawks, who really won the game at the free throw line. They were 22–30, while Northwestern was 15–19. Jim Burns had 21 for Northwestern.[38]

Northwestern came home, only to lose again, this time to Indiana, 81–79, disappointing the 8,232 fans who packed little McGaw Hall, but saw bad shooting by both teams. IU shot 39 percent, the Wildcats, just 32 percent. Irv Inniger was out with an injury, so Bill Russell stepped into the breach and got 20 points for the Hoosiers, and Vern Payne 16. Payne, however, missed three free throws in the last minute, each time enabling Northwestern to take the lead, but they were unable to do so. Mike Weaver had 21 and Jim Burns had 20, but his shooting (6–23) summed up the Wildcat frustrations for the day.

Near the end of the nip-and-tuck contest, Earl Schneider, a sub, was fouled under the basket and a timeout was promptly called. Coming out of the huddle, Schneider said to Joyner, "You shoot 'em." So Joyner went to the line, assuming that the little ruse would be noted by the refs or the scorers, but no one seemed to notice, and he made both free throws, a difference in the final score. Three weeks later, the Hoosiers were playing in the NCAA tournament at the regional, being held in McGaw. Joyner and some of his teammates got into an elevator with Tex Winter, Northwestern coach, and some of his staff. They made teasing remarks to Joyner, by now obviously having seen the game films and catching the ruse that had been perpetrated.

Despite the victory, Butch Joyner said that McGaw was one of the toughest places to play. "It was so dark, the locker rooms were terrible and the raised floor was not fun."[39]

Iowa also fell from the top with an upset loss in triple overtime at home, to Wisconsin, 96–95. Free throws were again a significant factor in the game as Wisconsin was 24–29 and Iowa 15–20. Chuck Nagle and Jim Johnson each had 26 for the Badgers, while Iowa's Williams was high for the game with 28, and Chris Phillips had a career-high 27. Michigan State won over Minnesota on a disputed basket, 67–66, in East Lansing. With four seconds left, a 45-foot heave by a Spartan player went off the board and was dunked by a teammate as the buzzer sounded. Coach Johnny Kundla of Minnesota protested vehemently, calling the basket goal-tending, but there was no review possible and the call stood. The MSU crowd left quite satisfied. Lee Lafayette had 19 and John Bailey 18 for MSU; Tom Kondla, the Big Ten scoring leader, had 32 for Minnesota.[40]

As noted, Kondla was the scoring leader in the conference with 230 points (28.7 ppg), followed by Sam Williams of Iowa with 226, Bill Hosket of OSU with 210, Jim Dawson of Illinois with 192, Jim Burns of Iowa with 179, Craig Dill of Michigan with 174, and Dave Scholz of Illinois with 164. Indiana now led the Big Ten by themselves, and they added to that with a 96–81 win over Illinois, while Michigan State lost at Columbus, 80–64. Bill Hosket had 20 and Jeff Miller 14 in the OSU upset; MSU was led by Lafayette with 20. In the Indiana win, Payne led five Hoosiers in double figures with 22 and Russell had 19. Jim Dawson led all scorers with 27 and was aided by Dave Scholz with 23 for the Illini.[41]

The next night, the Northwestern tumble continued, this time with a loss to Wisconsin, 110–94. Iowa was also upset, losing at Minnesota, 88–86. Kondla had 37 for the Gophers, while Gerry Jones had 32 to lead the Hawks. In the former game, 11,346 Badger fans saw Jim Johnson score 31 and Chuck Nagle 29 to lead Wisconsin. Jim Burns had 26 for the Wildcats, who might have lost the game at the free-throw line, hitting 16–24, compared to Wisconsin's 26–32.[42] The Hoosiers now had a game and a half edge on their closest pursuers, the Spartans of MSU. The full standings were IU, 7–2; MSU, 5–3: Wisconsin, Iowa, and Northwestern, all 5–4; Ohio State, 5–5; Illinois and Purdue, each 4–5; Minnesota, 3–7; Michigan, 2–7.

Iowa tightened the race a bit by beating Indiana, 75–74, in overtime in Bloomington. Free throws were again the key to the win as the Hawks made 23–35 as a result of 27 Indiana fouls. Indiana was 8–11 from the line, as Iowa was whistled for just 12 fouls. Houston Breedlove had his career high for Iowa with 18, followed by Williams with 16. Joyner and Payne led Indiana with 19 and 15, respectively.[43]

Northwestern finally broke their losing streak, defeating Ohio State, 95–82, in Columbus. Walt Tiberi led Northwestern with 22 and Mike Weaver had 21. Bill Hosket was high for the game with 29. Michigan State failed to take advantage of the Hoosier loss as they too lost, in Madison, 68–64, to Wisconsin. Chuck Nagle led a balanced attack with 18, while Aitch had 23 for game honors for MSU.[44]

The Illinois slush fund scandal re-emerged on February 27 when the High School Coaches of Illinois voted to support (without detailing a rationale) the retention of the three Illinois coaches who had been suspended by Illinois, which was then ordered by the Big Ten to dismiss them or face serious consequences from the conference. The three, football coach Pete Elliott, basketball coach Harry Combes, and top assistant basketball coach Howard Braun, were seen as complicit in the scandal, and Illinois was to dismiss them by March 15 or face possible expulsion from the Big Ten or an extended period of probation. The coaches' association sent a message to Illinois President David Henry, and other backers included Governor Otto Kerner, the University of Illinois football team, U of I alumni, and the board of the Illinois Athletic Association. This situation continued to vie with the Big Ten basketball race for attention in the state's newspapers.[45]

The *Daily Illini*, in a February 24 editorial, said the university had no other choice but to dismiss the three coaches. Their supporters, it was noted, relied on personal loyalty or the rationale that "everyone else is doing the same thing," and the *Daily Illini* felt that this simply was not enough to support the retention of the coaches. It was, it was noted, a matter of principle.[46]

Four days later, a series of letters to the *Daily Illini* were printed that disagreed with the editorial of February 24. One in particular referred to other "scandals," such as the firing of the Michigan State University Alumni Club, but not Biggie Munn, the athletic director; OSU's finding that Woody Hayes was paying players, though he was not replaced; and issues with football head coach Dickerson at Indiana that resulted in no penalties to coaches or suspensions of players.[47]

March saw the slush fund scandal and the conference race continuing to share headlines. Northwestern stayed alive in the title race with a win over Wisconsin, 91–82, before a large crowd (for McGaw) of 6,318. Tiberi had 23 and Kozlicki 20 for the Wildcats, who had five players in double figures, as did the Badgers. Illinois was set to appeal its punishment for its players and coaches. The University stated unequivocally that it would not pull out of the Big Ten.[48]

The Associated Press announced its All-American team, and the weakness of the Big Ten was seen again: only two Big Ten players even received mention, namely Jim Burns on the third team and Sam Williams as Honorable Mention. The first team was impressive: Lew Alcindor, Elvin Hayes, Jimmy Walker, Wes Unseld and Clem Haskins.[49]

The next day there was great anticipation as the Illinois appeal was to be heard. Fourteen players on football and basketball teams had been implicated and two-year suspensions had been recommended for each of them. The father of one of the players, Steve Kuberski, said that his son was authorized by the coaches (Braun and Combes) to take the money, having been told that it came from a Moline sponsor (John Deere) in return for Kuberski's working in their Moline plant on semester and holiday breaks. He said that Kuberski didn't get paid at the plant, but in monthly installments (ranging from $15 to $35) on campus. Interestingly, the NCAA allowed for $15 per month payment to athletes for incidentals, but the Big Ten rules prohibited such extra payments. One of the players implicated, Steve Spanich, from Rock Island, had already transferred to Quincy College in Quincy, Illinois.[50]

The appeal was rejected (which was reported as front-page news in the *Chicago Tribune*) by a vote of 9–0 by the faculty representatives of each Big Ten university, with Illinois abstaining. The three coaches, they said, must be fired, or notified that they were being fired, by March 17, 1967. It was acknowledged that former Athletic Director Doug Mills had also been involved, and his assistant athletic director, Mel Brewer, had administered the off-campus fund. He had exposed the fund to the president of the university, David Henry, after it was announced that Brewer had not been selected as the new athletic director. The fund had operated for five years and upward of 30 athletes were involved, but only 14 still had eligibility.[51]

The next day, details emerged on the punishment for the players. Seven of the 14 were declared ineligible, but seven were reinstated. The latter, other than Randy Crews, a basketball player, were not identified. The seven ineligible athletes included Cyril Pinder, an All-Big Ten halfback, who would go on to star for the Philadelphia Eagles, and had accepted over $3000 for a number of trips home to Florida during the prior two years. He was permanently suspended. The rest of the players all received two-year suspensions and would be ineligible at all Big Ten schools during that time. Spanich had already transferred, but the basketball players named—Rich Jones, Ron Dunlap and Steve Kuberski—would all leave the school. Kuberski, who had periodic assistance of $35 per month, transferred to Bradley University in Peoria, where he sat out a year as a transfer, then played for two years and averaged 23 points per game for Bradley. He was drafted by the Boston Celtics and played in the NBA for nine years. Rich Jones, who also received $35 per month, transferred to Memphis State (now the University of Memphis), where he played one year before being drafted by the Phoenix Suns in 1969. He played professionally in Europe for a year, then five years in the ABA and two more with the New York Nets, after the ABA/NBA merger. Ron Dunlap, who received $15 per month, a total of $410, was married and had a daughter at the time. Interestingly, he stayed at Illinois, maintained his scholarship, and graduated. The Chicago Bulls drafted him in 1968, despite his not playing intercollegiate basketball for nearly two years. Dunlap played in the Continental Basketball Association for four years, as well as in Israel, for Maccabi for two years. After he finished his career, he became a teacher and eventually a school principal in Appleton, Wisconsin.[52]

There was also game news in the conference race that day, after Indiana lost to Illinois, 80–70, in Champaign. The first-half shooting was not impressive as Illinois shot 38 percent and the Hoosiers just 23 percent on 9–40, including two of their first 22 shots. What was impressive was the input of Dave Scholz, who had 31 points and 20 rebounds. Jim Dawson followed with 24. Butch Joyner led Indiana with 18 points. Joyner recalled that Rich Jones entered the auditorium doing warmups and headed for a seat behind the Illinois bench.[53] The crowd gave him a standing ovation and the Illini seemed to get motivation from this.[54]

Michigan State took advantage of the Hoosier loss and picked up a full game with a 75–71 win over Purdue, the Spartans' 20th win in a row at home. Matthew Aitch had 31, while Herm Gilliam led Purdue with 19. Northwestern fell further back, losing at home to Minnesota, 86–84. Tom Kondla, former Riverside-Brookfield High (Illinois) star, celebrated his homecoming with 34 points for Minnesota. Jim Burns had 26 to lead the Wildcats. Iowa and Wisconsin both stayed within hailing distance of the top by winning. Iowa defeated OSU in Iowa City, 90–56. Sam William (20) and Gerry Jones (19) topped Iowa and Bill Hosket (19) led Ohio State. The Badgers edged Michigan, 80–79, in a game played in Detroit as part of the 150th anniversary of Michigan statehood. Only 3,125 fans came out for the "festivities," which included 37 points by Chuck Nagle of the Badgers. Craig Dill had 23 for the Wolverines.[55]

The final AP and UPI polls of the regular season were in agreement on the top five teams, although they switched the schools ranked third and fourth. UCLA was the unanimous #1, followed by Louisville, Kansas (AP), UNC (UPI) and Princeton. No Big Ten teams were in the top 20. The *Chicago Tribune* noted that Illinois would continue the fight to retain their coaches by having a "show cause" hearing before the Big Ten. Indiana was listed in the AP rankings, among "others."

Both Indiana and Michigan State won to keep tied for the Big Ten lead at 9–4 with one game left. MSU defeated Minnesota, 67–59, in Minneapolis. Tom Kondla scored 27 points to set a new Minnesota scoring record with 595 points for the season (24.8 average). Indiana defeated Michigan, 96–90, in Bloomington, but only 6,982 attended the game. Joyner had 27, Payne 23, for the Hoosiers.[56] The Big Ten standings were Indiana and Michigan State, 9–4; Wisconsin and Iowa, 7–5; Northwestern and Purdue, 7–6; Illinois, 6–7; Ohio State, 6–8; Minnesota, 5–9; Michigan, 2–11.

More details emerged on the "slush fund" when President Henry released the case histories of the students implicated. Kuberski had received a total of $490 for less than a week of work, although it was noted that it was okay to work and be paid. Jones had totaled $720 and transportation home (to Memphis), but this was paid by a local businessman, not the fund. Dunlap had received $410 at the rate of $15/month, also from a local businessman, for what were clearly real family needs.[57]

Iowa eliminated Wisconsin and kept their own title hopes alive by defeating the Badgers in Madison, 90–87. Gerry Jones with 29, and Sam Williams with 22, propelled the Hawks. Jim Johnson had 22 for Wisconsin.[58]

The Big Ten presidents issued a statement that they did not want to get involved with the Illinois appeal, at the same time that the University of Illinois trustees issued a statement backing President Henry's stand on the appeal. Woody Hayes disagreed with the Big Ten decision and said that the coaches should not be fired. Hayes speculated that the Big Ten was using this case as a warning for others. Governor Otto Kerner said that he would not interfere with the appeal.[59]

On the last day of the season (and the same day that the first round of the NCAA Tournament began), both Indiana and Michigan State won, creating a tie for the title. It was quite a turnaround for Lou Watson's Hoosiers, who had finished tied for last in the conference the year before. Because Michigan State had more recently gone to the NCAA tourney (1959), the Hoosiers would represent the Big Ten. In their final victory, Michigan State dumped Northwestern in East Lansing, 79–66, with Aitch scoring 21 in his last collegiate contest and Jim Burns leading Northwestern with 22 in his last game for the Wildcats. For Indiana, the 95–82 victory over in-state rival Purdue was doubly sweet. Joyner had 22, Bill Russell 18. Herm Gilliam led the Boilermakers with 19 as 9,554 fans cheered in Bloomington. The Hoosiers would play the winner of Toledo and Virginia Tech in the second round of the NCAA tournament in Northwestern's McGaw Hall on March 17.[60]

### Final Standings and MVPs, 1966–67

| | | |
|---|---|---|
| Indiana | 10–4 | Butch Joyner |
| Michigan State | 10–4 | Matthew Aitch |
| Iowa | 9–5 | Gerry Jones |
| Wisconsin | 8–6 | Joe Franklin |
| Purdue | 7–7 | Herman Gilliam |
| Northwestern | 7–7 | Jim Burns |
| Ohio State | 6–8 | Bill Hosket |
| Illinois | 6–8 | Jim Dawson (Big Ten MVP) |
| Minnesota | 5–9 | Tom Kondla |
| Michigan | 2–12 | Craig Dill |

Unlike the previous year, when all of the league MVPs were seniors, this group included four juniors and a sophomore. No player dominated the league and led his team to league dominance. Dawson's selection might be viewed as a tribute to his and the Illinois squad's response to adversity.

Before the Hoosiers went to battle on the 18th, more on the Illinois situation made the news. Congressman Tom Railsback (R-IL) said that he wanted the Big Ten's athletic aid policies and practices investigated. Railsback, who represented Illinois's 19th District, which included Moline and Rock Island (where Kuberski and Spanich lived, respectively), said that the players believed what they were told: that these payments were legal. Not so, he said, with the coaches. "They hardly could have helped but know that this violated the rules of the Big Ten."[61] The next day former Illinois athletic director Doug Mills, under whom the fund was administered, denied saying that President Henry knew of the fund, explaining that he (Mills) had been "misinterpreted" in a recently published story. The trustees of the university urged Illinois to keep fighting (they did not make any corny references to the Fighting Illini), approving Henry's efforts at appeal.[62]

In NCAA action, Indiana would face Virginia Tech, who had toppled Toledo, 82–76, in the first round of the tournament. The other contest played in Evanston would pit Tennessee, who had edged Kentucky for the SEC title, against Dayton.

In a startling turn of events, both of the favored teams from the power conferences were upset. Dayton, led by Don May, defeated Tennessee, 53–52, and Indiana was dumped by Virginia Tech, 79–70. Vern Payne led the Hoosiers with 18 points and Johnson had 15, but the game was lost at the free-throw line. Tech made 25 of 33 free throws, while Indiana could convert on just 14 of 29. Indiana did manage to win the 3rd place game in the Mideast regional, 51–44 over Tennessee the next night, before Dayton took the regional title, 71–66, in overtime.[63] It was a disappointment to Joyner and his teammates, but their goal had always been to win the Big Ten, and they had done that. The NCAA tournament was not that big a deal at that time, the games not being telecast until the final rounds.[64]

In other regionals, North Carolina defeated Boston College, 96–80 for the east; Houston topped SMU (who had upset Louisville), 83–75; and UCLA breezed through the west, beating Pacific, 80–64. North Carolina and UCLA were favored to meet in the championship.

The University of Illinois made its final appeal to the Big Ten presidents on March 18 at a "show cause" hearing to present its case why the Big Ten should not force Illinois to fire its coaches and/or be suspended from the conference. The decision was to uphold the decision by the athletic directors that had been sustained by the faculty representatives and deny Illinois's appeal. All three coaches would have to be fired by March 21 or Illinois would face suspension from the Big Ten. The three coaches quit the next day. Professor Leslie Bryan, who had been acting athletic director since November 23, agreed to serve until the newly hired athletic director, Gene Vance (a former "Whiz Kid" from the 1940s, who had played professionally in the BAA and NBA for five seasons), began work on April 1, 10 days later.[65]

The contretemps had not ended yet. On March 22, a group headed by a Champaign businessman who had apportioned part of the slush fund announced that they were attempting to raise $30,000 in order to provide $10,000 gifts to each of the ex-coaches. The next day the ex-coaches announced that they would not accept such gifts, but would attend a dinner that was being held in their honor. The day after that, Representative Henry Hyde (R–Chicago) announced that he wanted Congress to investigate the Big Ten in the Illinois case. In that story, Mike Ditka, Chicago Bears star, who attended the University of Pittsburgh, talked of his recruitment by Indiana, where he and other recruits were told that they would all receive $50 a month. He also noted that he was offered even more by some Ivy League schools.

Five days later, the University of Illinois announced that Jim Valek, South Carolina assistant coach (and an assistant coach at Illinois in 1959–60), had been hired as the new football coach, and Harve Schmidt, a 31-year-old Illinois alum, and assistant coach at New Mexico, would be the new basketball coach. On the same day, the Illinois legislature announced that they would probe the Big Ten and Illinois, regarding recruiting and rules violations.[66] In summarizing his view of this series of events, ex-Big Ten Commissioner Tug Wilson concluded: "The Big Ten had weathered its most critical storm of modern times. The University of Illinois had preserved its integrity in reporting violations it had, itself, uncovered. The Conference had backed up its most important regulation despite the possible loss of one of its most honored members. The wounds, in healing, would find the Big Ten morally stronger than ever before."[67]

Still, there was basketball, a Final Four, in fact, even if the Big Ten had no involvement. In the first contest, Dayton surprised UNC with a 76–62 win, led by Don May's 34 points. In the second, UCLA rolled over Elvin Hayes and Houston, 73–50. Alcindor was held to 19, but Lynn Shackleford had 22 and Lucius Allen had 17. Hayes led the game in scoring with 25. The game was played before 18,889 in Louisville's Freedom Hall, but had no television coverage.

In the championship contest, UCLA completed an undefeated season with a 79–64 win over Dayton, after Houston had trounced North Carolina, 84–62 in the 3rd-place game. Ken Spain led Houston with 24, Hayes had 23 in that contest. In the title game, Alcindor led UCLA with 20, Allen had 19 and Mike Warren had 17 for the Bruins, while Don May had 21 for game-scoring honors. Again, there was no national television package, although in the Chicago market, WGN provided a tape delay of the game at 10:30 p.m. that Saturday night.

The UCLA season, sparked by the dominance of Alcindor, was instrumental in a ruling announced three days after the NCAA final by the National Basketball Committee of the U.S. and Canada. The committee, composed of representatives from the NCAA, the National Federation of State High School Associations, the National Junior College Association, Canadian Collegiate Athletic Association, the Canadian Amateur Basketball Association, and the YMCA, declared that dunking would no longer be allowed in high school or college basketball in the U.S. or Canada. The rationale the committee offered was that "dunking doesn't give the defense an opportunity to block the shot." They also claimed that the dunk caused "a large portion of the player injuries and damage to the goals." The committee also reduced the time that a player could hold or dribble a ball while being continuously guarded before the "held ball" rule was invoked, from 30 seconds to ten. These changes would go into effect immediately, i.e., with the 1967–68 season, which caused some coaches to be critical of the timing. John Wooden, UCLA mentor, thought that there should be a year or two of experimentation, but the committee chose to not follow this course of action.[68]

In what seemed a kind of coda for the Illinois situation, the athletic director of the University of Pennsylvania claimed that he was fired from Penn for challenging the use of a slush fund at that school.[69]

After such an excruciating year, all parties were probably relieved to have some time off to regroup and not have to address the ugly issues that had been raised in the 1966–67 season. Nevertheless, there was a new season to look forward to, and it was clear that a number of teams would have to be considered for the Big Ten title in 1967–68, including Indiana, Iowa, Purdue, Ohio State and Wisconsin, all of whom had top underclassmen returning. As for Illinois, the university was put on two years' probation and would be ineligible for both the Rose Bowl in football and the NCAA basketball tournament for the next two years, were the Illini to somehow overcome the losses and the stigma of 1966–67.

# XI

## *InsurMOUNTable?*

Heading into the 1967–68 season, Indiana was the initial choice for the Big Ten title, with Purdue also seen as a possibility, based largely on their upcoming sophomore, Rick Mount. Before even playing a varsity game, he was pictured on the cover of *Sports Illustrated*. He was not the only soph seen as having an impact in the conference; Northwestern had Don Adams and Dale Kelley, Michigan welcomed Rudy Tomjanovich, Minnesota liked Larry Overskei, and Iowa had similar feelings about Chad Calabria and Glen Vidnovic. After the weak performance by the league in the previous year, the Big Ten title seemed truly up for grabs in 1967–68. *Sports Illustrated*, now only ranking league finishes, not national ones, liked Purdue to win the title, then saw Illinois as the closest competitor for the Boilermakers, with Northwestern as a dark horse. Iowa and Michigan State would be good, but Iowa lacked height and Michigan State seemed to have no help among its rising sophomores.[1]

Nationally, UCLA was a unanimous choice for #1 in all polls and magazines. *Basketball* picked Louisville as #2, followed by Houston, Princeton, North Carolina and Boston College. Purdue was picked as #17 in the country, the only Big Ten team mentioned. The publication had a first team All-America squad of Lew Alcindor, Elvin Hayes, Don May, Butch Beard and Wes Unseld. The only other Big Ten player noted was Bill Hosket, selected for the fourth team. The Big Ten was clearly not impressing people with its prospects for the upcoming season. The five players chosen in the magazine's "Midwest All-Sectional Team" were all from the Big Ten, however. Two seniors—Tom Kondla of Minnesota and Verne Payne of Indiana; two juniors—Dave Scholz of Illinois and Chuck Nagle of Wisconsin; plus Rick Mount, a sophomore, comprised the team.[2] *Basketball Yearbook, 1968*, edited by Zander Hollander, had Louisville as #2, followed by Houston, Kansas and Princeton. Indiana was selected as #8. In the Midwest section, Indiana was picked to take the Big Ten, followed by Iowa, Purdue, Wisconsin and Michigan State.[3]

In early December a number of Big Ten teams played games against ranked opponents. Michigan was one of the most daring, with games against Kentucky, Davidson and Duke, all of which they lost, but they were games in which their young players, particularly Tomjanovich, learned quite a bit.

In the Kentucky contest, Rudy T. had 17, but was outscored by the Wildcat duo of Dwayne Casey (28) and Dan Issel (18) in the 96–79 contest. Tomjanovich said that "they were just so good" and rugged. He strained both plantar fascia in the game and could barely walk afterwards. He got a cortisone shot for the next game (against Detroit) and "learned that he didn't have to jump so high" to score or rebound. He had 28 in the 104–99 Wolverine win.

The Duke game, played on December 7, was another story. Mike Lewis, recalled Rudy, just "wore me out" as he scored 32 points against sophomore Tomjanovich, who was, he confessed, just learning to play the post. Michigan lost, 93–72. The Wolverines followed that with a 91–70 loss to Davidson and Mike Maloy (18 points), two nights later.[4]

The first UPI poll in mid–December had defending champion UCLA as #1, followed by Houston, Vanderbilt, Louisville, Boston College, Kentucky, Princeton, North Carolina, Davidson and Tennessee. The second ten had Indiana (the defending Big Ten champion) as #12 and Purdue as #15. On that same day, Vietnam was again the big headliner as President Johnson increased the troop number from the 101st Airborne Division by 10,000, pushing the troop total committed to the war in Vietnam past the 1952 peak in Korea of 472,800.[5]

For Big Ten teams, the non-conference season failed to clearly identify contenders for the Big Ten title. Illinois defeated Brigham Young, but lost to Tennessee and Army. Defending champion Indiana had an early unbeaten stretch in which they defeated North Carolina State and Notre Dame (unbeaten at the time), among others, and were ranked at #3 in the late December AP poll. Purdue lost to NCAA champion UCLA, 73 to 71, and seemed poised to make a run at the Big Ten, but lost to New Mexico State two weeks later. Michigan State was up and down. Northwestern started with a loss to Ohio University, then ran off five in a row before a loss at Colorado. Minnesota was uneven, and Tom Kondla, defending Big Ten scoring champion, seemed less engaged. Ohio State won five in a row in December and headed to the Rainbow Classic in Hawaii undefeated. This was despite the loss of junior guard Jeff Miller, who had averaged 14.7 points per game the prior season, now out for the year with a knee injury. Purdue was just as devastated by the loss of top rebounder Roger Blaylock on December 21, after he broke his leg.

As the holiday tournament season began, the world was thrilled by the successful heart transplant surgery performed by Dr. Christian Barnard of South Africa on December 3, 1967. Suddenly, a defective or weakened heart was no longer a death sentence. Today about 3,500 successful heart transplants are performed each year worldwide.

Holiday scores were inconclusive. In Arizona, Michigan defeated Oregon State, 80–61, then were edged by Arizona State, 92–91. Sophomore Rudy Tomjanovich had 22 in the former game. In Philadelphia, at the Quaker City Classic, Wisconsin was edged by Temple, 82–80, then lost again to Duquesne, 76–66. Ohio State topped Bradley, 85–63 in Hawaii, then lost in an upset to host Hawaii, 80–76. Northwestern also lost to Hawaii. In Los Angeles, Iowa defeated Tennessee, handing them their first loss, then dropped a game to Wyoming, 94–87. Undefeated Indiana was upset in Dallas, losing 110–91 to Western Kentucky, then 94–87 to previously winless Southern Methodist.

George Langford, *Chicago Tribune* sportswriter, tried to get a handle on the holiday performances. Five Big Ten teams lost in tournament consolation rounds and the best finish was a 3rd place at the L.A. Classic, where Iowa came back to defeat St. Louis, 76–66. The prospects for the league seemed a bit bleak.[6]

Things got no better. Indiana lost, 99–93, at Detroit, despite five Hoosiers in double figures. Michigan was slaughtered by #2 Houston and Elvin Hayes, who had 31 points. Tomjanovich had 20, however, and continued to improve. His comments on Houston were, "They were so good. They were just dominating [in their play]."[7]

Finally, the Big Ten season began, with the hope that at least one team would assert itself and make the conference proud. Illinois and Northwestern both made moves in that direction, defeating Michigan State and Iowa, respectively. Illinois was led by Dave Scholz with 21 points in the 66–56 win, which was really won on the boards, where Illinois outrebounded the Spartans, 42–29. Northwestern was encouraged by the fact that sophs Don Adams and Dale Kelley led the Wildcats in scoring with 21 and 17, respectively, in the 76–67 victory in Evanston. Sam Williams had 30 for the Hawks. Defending co-champion Indiana topped Minnesota in Bloomington, 74–59, with center Bill Deheer leading with 17, and front courtmates Joyner and Schneider chipping in with 16 each. Wisconsin beat Michigan, 77–75, before 8,959 in Madison, and Joe Franklin had 34 for the Badgers. In Columbus, Purdue was crushed by the Buckeyes, 108–80, before a capacity crowd of 13,497. Rick Mount was held to 19 and Bill Hosket of the Bucks took scoring honors with 35 (and 17 rebounds) on 15–23 shooting. Steve Howell had 24 to back Hosket.[8]

Two days later, Iowa turned things around, but in a non-conference game, topping Loyola in Iowa City, 71–65. Sam Williams had 28 and Ron Norman 21, for most of the Iowa scoring. In conference contests, Indiana knocked off the Illini in overtime in Champaign, 61–60, and Rick Mount scored 40 to lead Purdue to a 99–79 romp over Wisconsin before 13,481 in West Lafayette.[9] The latest UPI poll had no Big Ten team in the top 20.

The next weekend, the mixed-up results continued, as Northwestern defeated Indiana, 86–81, in Bloomington; Illinois edged Minnesota, 61–60, in Minneapolis; Michigan State beat Michigan in Ann Arbor, 86–81; and Iowa beat Ohio State, 74–72, the only winning team to hold home court advantage. Ron Norman hit a 25-footer with five seconds left in overtime to provide the Iowa victory margin. He had 14 points, second to Sam Williams's 32. Bill Hosket had 26 for OSU. Northwestern was down 62–46 with 14:16 to go, before coming back to beat Indiana by five. Dale Kelley had 32 for the Wildcats and Vern Payne had 24 to lead Indiana, but the game was really a free-throw shooting contest. Northwestern went 30–40, while Indiana was just 18–28. Dave Scholz scored with six seconds left for the Illinois win. Scholz had 26, Randy Crews 14; Leroy Gardner had 15 and Tom Kondla 12 for the Gophers.[10]

Later in the week, Purdue continued Indiana's stumble with an 89–60 romp in West Lafayette. Northwestern won against Minnesota, 77–71, to become the early Big Ten leader. Terry Gamber had 24 and Dale Kelley 18 for NU. Al Nuness had 30 to top the Gophers. Northwestern was 29–37 at the line, while Minnesota was just 11–19, the difference in the contest. Purdue was led by Mount's 33, while Indiana had no one in double figures. Free throws were key here, also, as the Boilermakers went 33–42 on 27 IU fouls, while Indiana was 8–18 from 16 Purdue fouls. A Purdue crowd of 14,123 saw their team have their largest victory margin over Indiana since 1934.[11]

The next weekend, Big Ten basketball (and every other game) played second fiddle to the UCLA-Houston contest in the Astrodome before 52,693. Both were undefeated and UCLA was riding a 47-game win streak over parts of three seasons. Earlier in the week, Lew Alcindor had one of his corneas scratched and his vision was blurry. He wore goggles for the game (and would from then on) and professed that his vision was fine, but it clearly was not, as he went four of 18 from the floor and Houston edged the Bruins, 71–69, to take over the #1 spot in the national rankings.[12]

Northwestern lost at defending co-champion Michigan State, 75–62, who were still trying to find their rhythm, but hummed against the Wildcats, winning their 25th in a row at home. Lee Lafayette had 17 and sixth man Heywood Edwards had 16. Kelley had 17 for the 'Cats. Iowa cruised pat Minnesota, 82–70 and Ohio State entertained 13, 025 fans in Columbus with a 103–70 win over Michigan. Steve Howell had 29 to top the scoring.[13]

On Tuesday, the latest AP poll did have Houston #1 and UCLA #2, and they would remain in those positions for the remainder of the regular season. Ohio State was among others listed, the only Big Ten team. The Bucks went to 9–3 with a non-conference win over Georgia Tech in which OSU shot 56 percent from the floor, which would become a trademark of this OSU team.[14]

The next night, Iowa snapped the MSU home winning streak by upending the Spartans, 76–71. Sam Williams had 33 points and 12 rebounds and Ron Norman had 16.[15]

Ohio State and Northwestern won big games that next weekend, the Buckeyes edging Michigan in Ann Arbor, 95–92, and the Wildcats beating Purdue, 82–74, in Evanston, despite 27 points from Mount. Northwestern, in a rare sellout of 8,851 tickets, was led by Terry Gamber's 20 and Mike Weaver's 16 points. Ohio State relied on Bill Hosket for 26 and Steve Howell with 14 to edge the Wolverines, who got Dennis Stewart's biggest game ever, 32 points. Bob Sullivan backed him with 23. Tomjanovich recalled that he was "sandwiched on a rebound in that game by Hosket and Howell and it was the hardest that he had ever been hit."[16]

The next week Purdue turned the tables on Northwestern, beating them 98–89 in West Lafayette, with Mount getting 30. Herm Gilliam had 23 and Northwestern was led by Dale Kelley with 20. Purdue made the most of their free-throw attempts, going 24–27 (89 percent), while Northwestern made just 21 of 35 (60 percent). Ohio State continued winning, defeating Wisconsin easily, 86–64, before 13,497 Buckeye fans. Dave Sorenson had 23 and Hosket 17 in the victory. Illinois surprised Iowa with a 66–63 victory in Champaign. Scholz and Crews each had 15 for Illinois, but Williams topped game scoring with 25.[17]

The standings at the beginning of February had OSU at 4–1; Illinois at 3–1; Northwestern, 4–2; Iowa, Purdue, and Wisconsin, all at 3–2, MSU, 3–3; Indiana, 2–3; Minnesota, 1–5; and Michigan, winless in five contests.

On Tuesday, February 5, the Buckeyes were nearly upset in Bloomington, saved only by a last-second shot by Dan Andrews to give them a 78–77 victory. Ohio State was deadly from the field, hitting 57.9 percent, to Indiana's 44 percent. Hosket and Howell each had 18, while Joyner had 22 and Payne 18 for the Hoosiers.[18]

The Vietnam War was still the dominant story for the U.S. and the world. When North Vietnamese troops stormed the camp at Lang Vei, former Vice-President Richard Nixon used that as his jumping-off point to call for winning the war in Vietnam. He said he had a plan to limit the ground war and use greater air and sea power against targets in North Vietnam. As if that wasn't enough, the USS *Pueblo*, an American intelligence ship was boarded and captured in January by North Korean forces, who claimed it was spying in North Korean waters. All U.S. personnel aboard were taken to North Korean prisons and the U.S. immediately responded by sending more troops to South Korea.[19]

All this was going on amidst the Winter Olympics in Grenoble, so the Big Ten race was certainly less of a concern to many Midwesterners, but certainly not to the players and coaches involved. Iowa held off Purdue in Iowa City for a 94–87 victory, while Northwestern beat Illinois, 78–71, in Evanston before 8,349 in McGaw Hall, another capacity crowd. Iowa was buoyed by more than the victory, because sophomore Glenn Vidnovic, newly eligible, scored 17 points, backing Williams with 24 and Norman with 20. Mount had 31 for Purdue. Ohio State increased its Big Ten lead with a 90–62 win over Michigan State before 13,497 in Columbus. Purdue came back from the Iowa loss to pound Minnesota, 89–62, before 14,123 in West Lafayette. Iowa, led by Williams with 26 and Calabria with 23, toppled Michigan, 98–86, in Ann Arbor, despite the pleas of 10,470 Wolverine rooters.[20]

The Michigan loss was not the big news on campus, however; two student journalists from the *Michigan Daily* had investigated allegations that Michigan athletes were getting discounts on merchandise and free meals from local restaurants in Ann Arbor, without the approval of their coaches. The story was picked up by the *Chicago Tribune*, sensitive to such charges after the University of Illinois slush fund scandal just concluded. The president of the university announced that he would cooperate in the investigation of the charges.[21]

Two days later, similar charges were leveled at Michigan State athletes, again from the *Michigan Daily*. These included long-distance phone calls, extra meal allowances, excessive comp tickets for football games, and other perks not legal under Big Ten rules. Duffy Daugherty, the Michigan State football coach, immediately denied that such actions were transpiring with Michigan State athletes. He said in denying the charges, "Kooks get coverage," referring to the Michigan student journalists.[22] One might have thought that the Big Ten, like the *Chicago Tribune*, would be quite sensitive to these charges under the circumstances, but there was no immediate comment from the Big Ten office.

That same day there seemed to be some hope for an end to the war in Vietnam, when the U.S. announced that American troops would be withdrawn in six months if South Vietnam would be assured of self-determination in its government. While this seemed quite generous, it was also antithetical to the fact that the North Vietnamese were fighting to consolidate Vietnam, not ensure its division, which had been created by the French colonialists.[23] The war continued.

And the Big Ten war also continued, made more competitive by Ohio State's second conference loss on February 12, at Wisconsin, 86–78. The Badgers were now 5–3, just a game behind the 6–2 Buckeyes. Wisconsin shot an unbelievable 57 percent for the game (33–58), offsetting the usual reliable OSU shooting, which was still 48 percent (31–64). Wisconsin outrebounded the Bucks, 36–25. Joe Franklin (23) and Chuck Nagle (19) topped the Badger scoring, matched by Bill Hosket (23) and Dave Sorenson (19).

Northwestern dropped to 5–3 with a loss at Minnesota, 85–80. Free throws were the difference here as the Gophers were 31–48 and the Wildcats 22–36, in a game with 53 fouls. Tom Kondla had 29 to lead the Gopher scoring; Dale Kelley had 27 for Northwestern.[24]

The race became even tighter on February 17 as OSU was upset by Minnesota, Iowa beat Wisconsin, and Northwestern topped Michigan State. Purdue also reinserted itself into consideration with a big win at Illinois, 75–68, before 11,941, the biggest crowd in Champaign in years. Mount had 28 in the win, but Dave Scholz almost matched him with 26. Purdue outrebounded Illinois, 47–31. Tom Kondla was the key to the Gopher win with 32 points, backed by Gardner's 19. Hosket (25) and Sorenson (24) were the Buckeye one-two punch.[25] OSU reserve Craig Barclay noted, "The team wasn't playing well. Fred [Coach Taylor] tried various combinations and none of them worked."[26] Northwestern's 69–61 victory in McGaw was keyed by Kelley's 24 and Gamber's 15, but rebounds were the big difference as the Wildcats snared 56 to MSU's 31.[27]

The standings now had Iowa on top at 6–2, Northwestern and Ohio State at 6–3, Purdue at 5–3, and Wisconsin 5–4, the only teams above .500. Big Ten scoring had Mount on top with 236 points (29.5 ppg), Kondla with 220 (22.0), Franklin with 219 (24.3), Williams with 212 (26.5) and Hosket with 202 (22.4). The AP poll had no Big Ten teams in the top ten, but Iowa was listed among "others." In scarier news, President Johnson, in response to an attack on the Saigon airport, authorized more troops, if needed, above the previous authorized level of 525,000.[28]

The Ohio State-Northwestern game in Columbus would possibly determine a new conference leader, were Iowa to lose. And the Hawkeyes did lose, to Purdue, and Rick Mount's 38 points in West Lafayette. Iowa could only counter with Chad Calabria's 19 and Sam Williams's 18 in the 86–73 contest. OSU destroyed the Wildcats, 87–67, shooting 55 percent from the floor and having all five starters in double figures. Hosket and Sorensen led the attack with 23 and 22, respectively. The Wildcats hit only 30 percent, and their leading scorers, Terry Gamber and Mike Weaver, each had just 12 points. OSU was now on top of the league at 7–3 with both Purdue and Iowa half a game back at 6–3.[29]

The next day (February 21) there was finally some response to the *Michigan Daily* assertions, when it was noted that Big Ten Commissioner Bill Reed had returned from the Olympics in Grenoble and would join the investigation. Further comments would be forthcoming.[30]

The Big Ten standings reshuffled once again, as Purdue, before 14,123 Boiler fans, dropped Ohio State, 93–72. Purdue "made 12 fast break goals caused by Ohio State's poor offensive execution."[31] Mount had 34 and Gilliam 26, nearly the OSU total. The Bucks got 18 from Sorenson and 16 from Howell. Iowa tied Purdue for the conference lead with a 78–70 victory in Bloomington over Indiana. Chad Calabria went 10–18 from the floor in scoring 26 points, and Sam Williams was right behind with 25. Schneider led the Hoosiers with 18. The miserable Indiana year (they were now 3–7 in conference) had clearly turned off the Hoosier faithful, since only 7,739 showed up for the game. Illinois's 62–61 victory over Northwestern moved them past the Wildcats, and just a game back of the leaders. The game was dominated by Dave Scholz, who scored 42 of the Illini's 62 points, breaking a record for Assembly Hall set by Dave Schellhase with

41 in 1965. Scholz was 15–26 from the field and 12–14 from the line and the crowd of 13,857 loved every minute of it.[32]

Now every game seemed to be important in the title race. Ohio State entertained the Illini and were very bad hosts, beating their guests 95–75 before 12,591 Buckeye fans. Howell and Sorenson were high scorers with 26 and 21, while Scholz and Mike Price led Illinois with 25 and 23, respectively. The next night Purdue lost to Michigan, 104–94, and Iowa defeated MSU, 76–58, pushing the Hawkeyes back into the conference lead. Michigan got 30 points and 15 rebounds from sophomore Rudy Tomjanovich, and Jim Pitts knocked in 22 to offset Mount's 35 and Keller's 23 for Purdue. The keys were rebounds (Michigan had 61 to Purdue's 45) and free throws (Michigan was 20–31 with 12 fouls, and Purdue was 6–12 with 23 fouls). In the Iowa victory, Calabria had 25 and Williams 22, while MSU was led by Heywood Edwards with just 15.[33]

On the next weekend, Iowa beat Illinois, 61–56; Wisconsin topped Purdue, 104–84; and Ohio State pounded Indiana, 107–93, to keep their title hopes alive. Iowa got 18 from Williams and 14 from Glen "The Stick" Vidnovic (He was 6'6", 165), and Illinois was led by Dave Scholz with 21. Wisconsin got a monster game from Joe Franklin, who had 31 points and 27 rebounds, backed by Chuck Nagle, with 30 points. Rick Mount had just 10 points. Gilliam (28) and Keller (23) led the Boilers. Hosket and Howell each had 25 in the OSU win. Iowa now led the conference at 9–3 and OSU was 9–4. If Iowa won their next two games, there was nothing OSU could do to stop a Hawkeye title, their first since 1956.[34]

It was also reported that day that Bill Reed, Big Ten Commissioner, felt that the Michigan charges were not serious and seemed to be no more than a "technical deviation from the rules than a direct violation." The article also noted that Reed was a Michigan alumnus and had also been an editor of the *Michigan Daily* when an undergraduate at Michigan.[35]

Iowa and Ohio State both won on the road on March 4, the Hawks, 91–72, in Minnesota, and the Bucks, 67–60, at Illinois, only the third Ohio State road win of the Big Ten season. Sam Williams had 34 and Chad Calabria had 26 for the Hawkeyes, while Tom Kondla had 29 for the Gophers. Kondla set a Minnesota record for most points in three seasons, which was the only Gopher highlight that night. Howell (25) and Hosket (19) led the Buckeye attack, as usual, while Pace (18) and Scholz (17) were Illini high scorers.[36] There was still jockeying for the third spot in the conference, and Purdue solidified their claim to it with a 93–75 win over Michigan State, before 14,123 in West Lafayette. Mount had 34 and Keller 20 for the Boilers.[37] The weekly AP poll had no Big Ten teams in the top ten, but both Iowa and Ohio State were listed as "others receiving votes." The UPI had Iowa as #17 in their top 20 teams.

In their last regular season game, Iowa was upset by Michigan (a 15-point underdog) in Iowa City, 71–70, before 12,900 crushed Hawkeye rooters. Denny Stewart with 21 and Bob Sullivan with 17 were the leading Wolverine scorers, but got good team support in order to offset the duo of Williams with 30 and Calabria with 14. Iowa and Ohio State would have to meet in a playoff (a change in protocol being implemented for the first time by the conference) for the title. That would be held at Purdue on March 12, three days later. Purdue, led by Mount's 29 points, clinched third with a 68–64 win over Indiana in Bloomington.[38]

The Big Ten playoff coincided with the New Hampshire primary, and the big winner there was Richard Nixon, who overwhelmed Nelson Rockefeller on the way to the Republican nomination for president. Senator Eugene McCarthy received 41 percent of the vote against Lyndon Johnson, indicating the great schism that had formed in the U.S. over the war in Vietnam.[39]

The Big Ten playoff was conducted before just 4,816 fans; the attendance was held down by a snowstorm that swept Central Indiana, but the game was hot enough to melt the snow. Ohio State emerged as the victor, 85–81, despite Iowa's 54–44 advantage on rebounds. The top two scorers for each team were the usual. Hosket (24) and Howell (22) led Ohio State, and Williams (29) and Calabria (17) led Iowa. Williams's shooting was uncharacteristically off as he went just 8–22 from the floor.[40]

Tom Kondla set a Minnesota scoring record in 1967–68 (since broken) and was team MVP in that year and 1968–69 (University of Minnesota Athletics).

Ohio State went from surprise Big Ten champions to immediate preparation for meeting Ohio Valley Conference champion East Tennessee State, who topped Florida State, 79–69. The OSU-ETSU contest was played in Lexington, Kentucky, on the home court of the University of Kentucky. It would be preceded by Marquette-Kentucky. Al McGuire, the coach of Marquette, predicted that his team would win, but all that did was anger Adolph Rupp, the legendary Kentucky coach, who urged his #3-ranked team to a 107–89 victory. Ohio State had a much more difficult time with ETSU, before triumphing 79–72. The Bucks shot 54 percent from the field, while holding ETSU to 36 percent. Howell with 22, and Hosket with 18 (plus 20 rebounds), led the Buckeye attack. The next night OSU would face Kentucky.[41]

Kentucky was heavily favored to beat OSU and head to the Final Four in the Los Angeles Sports Arena, but OSU shocked Kentucky with an 82–81 victory. OSU's shooting was not up to its usual quality, as they were just 36–82 (44 percent), but Kentucky was no better (36–81). Ohio State outrebounded the Wildcats, 44–38, however, and that was important. Sorenson had 24 points on 11–17 shooting and Hosket had 21 with 12 rebounds. Dan Issel had 19 and Dwayne Casey had 16 for the losers.[42]

Unranked Ohio State now had a week to prepare for their NCAA semifinal opponent, North Carolina, #4 in the AP's final poll of the year. Houston and UCLA continued as #1 and #2, respectively, with St. Bonaventure and Bob Lanier at #3. The All-Big Ten team was announced, and the first team consisted of Rick Mount (Purdue), the league's leading scorer and #6 in the country with 28.5 ppg; Sam Williams (IA); Bill Hosket (OSU); Dave Scholz (IL) and Joe Franklin (WI). Teams were also selecting their MVPs.

### Final Standings and MVPs, 1967–68

| Team | Record | MVP |
|---|---|---|
| Ohio State | 10–4 | Bill Hosket |
| Iowa | 10–4 | Sam Williams (Big Ten MVP) |
| Purdue | 9–5 | Herm Gilliam and Bill Keller |
| Northwestern | 8–6 | Mike Weaver |
| Wisconsin | 7–7 | Joe Franklin |
| Illinois | 6–8 | Dave Scholz |
| Michigan | 6–8 | Jim Pitts |
| Michigan State | 6–8 | Lee Lafayette |
| Indiana | 5–9 | Vern Payne |
| Minnesota | 5–9 | Tom Kondla |

The next week, the semifinal pairings were Ohio State against east champion, #4 North Carolina; and #1 Houston, Midwest champion, against #2 UCLA, west champion. UCLA was a team seeking revenge for an embarrassing loss to Houston in January, which the Bruins felt should have been theirs, despite Alcindor's eye impairment. UCLA routed Houston, 101–69, as five Bruins scored double figures, led by three players with 19: Alcindor, Allen and Lynn. Elvin Hayes was held to just 10 points.

Ohio State was no match for North Carolina, which also had five players in double figures, led by Jeff Miller with 20. The Tar Heels shot 46.5 percent from the floor, which was better than most teams did against the Buckeyes. OSU, however, could not find the basket, shooting just 35.4 percent, and the game was a romp for UNC, 80–64. Jody Finney with 16, and Bill Hosket with 14, led the Buckeye scoring.[43]

The next night, before 14,438 in the L.A. Sports Arena, the Buckeyes defeated Houston in the 3rd-place game, 89–85, a game both coaches (Fred Taylor and Guy Lewis) favored eliminating from tournament play. Steve Howell had 26, and Bill Hosket and Dave Sorenson had 19 each. Elvin Hayes had 34 and Theodis Lee had 27 for the losers. The championship game wasn't nearly as close, as UCLA won, 78–55, the largest championship margin to date.[44]

## The 1968–69 Season

Despite Ohio State's loss in the semifinals, it had achieved an unexpectedly high finish, and the Big Ten seemed to recapture some of the respect, nationally, that it had lost in previous years. UCLA seemed superior to every other college team, but the privilege of gaining a slot in the NCAA, and trying to reach that goal of meeting or toppling UCLA, was still very much desired by every Big Ten squad. For the next season, Ohio State would seem a bit weaker, as would Iowa, but both would be seen as strong possibilities to repeat their championship, with Purdue also seen as a strong contender to win the title.

## XI. InsurMOUNTable?

*Sports Illustrated* returned to rating teams nationwide in the College Basketball issue in December of 1968. Besides selecting two-time champion UCLA as the #1 team in the nation, they saw the next five as North Carolina, Kentucky, Davidson and Kansas. Purdue was selected as #18, but in the "Best of the Rest" section of the Midwest, three other teams were noted. First, Ohio State, who had lost Hosket to graduation, but still had Sorenson and Howell back to lead the returnees. Second, Iowa, who had lost Williams, but welcomed junior college transfer John Johnson, and the return from military service of Ben McGilmer, who had started two years before.

Michigan and Rudy Tomjanovich were also seen as possibly breaking into the Top Twenty in the nation.[45] The Wolverines had a new head coach as Dave Strack moved into athletic administration and Johnny Orr, Strack's top assistant and former head coach at University of Massachusetts, took over the head coaching reins. Tomjanovich thought that Strack was a great guy, and felt the same way about Orr, who Rudy said was open and honest.[46] Fife said that Orr's philosophy was "score in transition; take the first good shot." For many Big Ten teams at the time, "defense" was outscoring the other team, making for a lot of running and shooting, recalled Fife.[47]

With shooters like Tomjanovich, Dennis Stewart and Bob Sullivan, Fife knew that his role was to make good passes, but shoot open shots. "Rudy had range to 20–25 feet, but was also strong inside; the best offense was finding him inside, often by the drive and dish. He was not stationary and moved to open spots as guys drove."[48]

One team not seen as "in the hunt" was Minnesota, who had lost top scorer Tom Kondla to graduation, as well as veteran and future Hall of Fame coach John Kundla to retirement. Kundla moved into teaching physical education and avoided the constant coaching pressures he had endured with professional and Big Ten helmsmanship.[49]

*Basketball Yearbook 1969* also picked Top 20 teams, with the same first five teams as *SI*, above, as well as including Purdue as the only Big Ten team mentioned, coming in at #14 nationally. Prediction for the Big Ten standings had Purdue, followed by Northwestern, Ohio State, Illinois, Indiana, and then Iowa at 6th in the league.[50] "With nine of 11 major contributors back from the champions and the league looking stronger, Fred Taylor said, 'I'll go for 10–4 again,'" feeling that would lead to another championship.[51]

Sam Goldaper of *Basketball Special, 1968–69* picked UCLA and Kentucky as #1 and #2, then listed 23 other teams alphabetically. Again, Purdue was the only Big Ten team listed. Of the top 25 players in the country, only Mount made the list from the Big Ten. Other possible players to watch in the Midwest included Lee Lafayette of Michigan State, Chuck Bavis of Purdue, Dave Scholz of Illinois and Chuck Nagle of Wisconsin.[52]

*Complete Sports 9th Basketball* volume also had UCLA and Kentucky as #1 and #2. No Big Ten teams were ranked in their top 20; Rick Mount was picked as first team All-America. The All-Sectional Midwest team included Dave Scholz of Illinois, Dave Sorenson of Ohio State, and Rudy Tomjanovich of Michigan.[53]

As the basketball season began, Iowa got a tremendous boost when Ben McGilmer, a starter on the 1965–66 Hawkeye squad, who had been drafted into the army when he let his academic work lapse, was made eligible by the Big Ten immediately after applying, and the course that troubled him in 1965–66 was "wiped off the board" by the university. The Hawks had returned four starters, only losing Sam Williams, the Big Ten MVP, but now with McGilmer, and junior college transfer John Johnson, the Hawkeyes looked ready for a title-contending season, despite the various pundits' views.[54]

McGilmer played in the Hawkeyes' big contest at Wichita the same day that he was declared eligible and scored nine points, but the Hawks lost to the Shockers, 93–88, despite having five players in double figures, led by Chad Calabria and Luke Jensen, each with 20. It was a foul-prone contest, with Wichita making 27–35 free throws on 27 Iowa fouls, while Iowa made 18–30 on 22 Wichita fouls.[55] And a small aside on that same day was a note from the Southeastern Conference, where both Florida and Georgia had signed "Negros," the former in football, the latter in track; these were the first African American athletes at these two schools.[56]

Michigan State came out of the gate fast with four wins in a row, with the fourth against Butler, 70–60. Junior Jim Gibbons stepped into a starting role and scored 20 points and snared 15 rebounds to lead the Spartans.[57]

It was announced that day that a seeming violation by the Minnesota Gophers resulted in censure by the Big Ten, but no players lost eligibility, nor were any coaches punished in any way. Four freshmen football players had "hitched rides" from the South to Minneapolis on private planes owned by industrial firms, set up by an assistant coach at the university. Big Ten Commissioner Bill Reed said that the violations resulted "from ignorance of the rules" and the university was put on one-year probation, which would result in a larger penalty were it to commit any violations during that period of time. An interesting penalty, in light of Illinois's harsh penalties in 1966–67, as well as the apparent dropping of any pursuit of charges after the initial allegations of Michigan and Michigan State the prior season.[58] The next night the Gophers defeated Loyola, 76–71, led by a familiar name in Minneapolis, Mikan, but it was George's son, Larry, who was the Mikan of note, as he scored 18 points to lead to the victory in a "sparsely attended" double-header in Chicago Stadium.[59]

Purdue started to live up to their pre-season hype with a 100–89 win over Ohio University, in which Mount had 43 points and Gilliam 21. Illinois handed Iowa State its first loss of the young season, 75–48, before 10,051 in Champaign. Dave Scholz had 18 points, backed by Greg Jackson, with 13 and 18 rebounds. Indiana had no trouble with North Carolina State, winning 77–62 with Bill DeHeer topping the scoring with 19 points. Defending Big Ten champion Ohio State dumped Harvard in Columbus, 89–74. Dave Sorenson had 27 and Jody Finney 19 for the Buckeyes.[60] The Bucks had lost earlier in the season to national champion UCLA in Columbus, 84–73, but had acquitted themselves well. UCLA also topped Purdue, 94–82, on that Midwestern road trip.

The December 17 UPI poll had UCLA getting all first-place votes, followed by North Carolina, Davidson, Cincinnati, Kentucky, New Mexico and Villanova. Purdue was rated #12, Illinois #16, while Michigan State and Ohio State were among others mentioned. The AP had the same top teams, with a bit of variation from five to eight. Purdue was #12 and Ohio State #17, with Illinois, Michigan and Wisconsin getting votes. Ohio State barely won that same day, edging Washington State in Pullman, 75–74. Sorenson had 24 and Finney 18 for the Bucks.[61]

Illinois won six contests in a row to remain unbeaten and Northwestern won their fifth in a row after an opening loss. The Illini topped Ohio, 95–82, before 10,031 Illinois rooters, then humbled Tulane, 105–71, in Champaign before another crowd of better than 10,000. Scholz led scoring in each game, 28 against Ohio, and 24 against Tulane. Northwestern also beat Ohio University, 89–80, in Evanston, led by Dan Davis's 22 points.[62]

Big Ten teams fanned out to play in various holiday tournaments. In the Sun Devil Classic, Purdue won its opener, 98–81, over California, as Mount had 35 and Gilliam 23 in the 98–81 win. Michigan lost to Kentucky in a "run and gun" battle at the Kentucky Invitational, 112–103, with Rudy Tomjanovich and Dennis Stewart each scoring 26 points in the loss. Michigan then won a consolation game with Bradley, 95–93. Sophomore Dan Fife and Tomjanovich each had 23 in the win. Bradley's high scorers were L.C. Bowen with 31 and Steve Kuberski, the former Illini, with 26. The game was telecast back to Michigan, and Fife received lots of congratulations from the home state crowd.[63]

A couple of key games not in tournaments were Illinois's victory at Houston, 97–84, and Ohio State's defeat of Washington State, 84–69. In the former game, Scholz and Greg Jackson had 21 points each, while in the latter, Sorenson scored 24 and Cleamons 17 to lead the Buckeyes. In other important news that day, WGN in Chicago announced that they would televise ten Big Ten games, each on Saturday at 1 p.m. (Central).[64]

The last UPI poll of the calendar year had UCLA at #1, followed by North Carolina, Davidson, Kentucky and Villanova. Purdue and Illinois were among "others." This was released on Christmas Day, and holiday tourneys continued after that. Northwestern defeated Florida at the Gator Bowl Classic in Jacksonville, Florida, then defeated Boston College, 77–68, the next night, to take the tourney. Dan Davis had 25 and Dale Kelley 16 in the former victory, and Kelley had 22 in the latter, to top the NU scoring. Illinois topped Creighton at the Hurricane Tournament in Miami, then beat the host squad, 86–76, to take the title. Dave Scholz had 50 points in the two games.[65]

Drake topped Minnesota in Dallas at the All Sports Tournament, then the Gophers defeated Mississippi, 72–58, for the consolation victory in Dallas. Larry Mikan led the team in scoring in both games with 12 and 24, respectively. Wisconsin won at the Milwaukee Classic, 74–68, over Ohio University, then lost in the title game to Marquette, 59–56, with Kenny Johnson scoring 21, adding to his point totals of 38 for the two games. In Hawaii, Purdue opened with a victory over Arizona, 92–72, with Mount (25) and Gilliam (20) as top scorers. They then lost to Columbia, 74–72. The Lions were led by Haywood Dotson (27) and Jim McMillan (23). Mount (30) and Gilliam (14) led Purdue. The Boilermakers came back to take third, defeating the host team, Hawaii, 97–68, with Mount going for 38 and Gilliam 20.[66]

The world marveled at American astronauts Borman, Lovell and Anders, who took their *Apollo 8* spacecraft to the moon, did ten orbits and returned to earth. It would be just a matter of time, it was thought, before a moon landing would happen.[67]

The Big Ten season was finally ready to begin. Undefeated Illinois, Purdue and Northwestern had the best records in nonconference play, but Ohio State and Iowa would certainly be in the mix. Illinois, Northwestern, Ohio State and Purdue all won their conference openers, but Iowa stumbled against Michigan, 99–92, in overtime. Fife and Richard Carter each had 25 for the Wolverines, while Calabria and Vidnovic led the Hawks with 26 and 21, respectively. The game was won on the backboards, as Michigan snared 48 rebounds to just 30 for the Hawks. In Champaign, the Illini had five in double figures, topped by Scholz with 20, as they humbled Minnesota, 80–58, the 10th victory in a row for the undefeated Illini. In Evanston, Kelley (19) and Gamber (17) led Northwestern scoring in the 85–71 victory. Purdue's 86–80 win in Wisconsin had Mount with 33 and Gilliam with 16. Clarence Sherrod scored 20 to lead the Badgers. In Bloomington, the fans were staying away in droves. Just 4,691 showed up to see the 90–82 loss. Sorenson led five Buckeyes in double figures, with 24 points. Joe Cooke had 21 for Indiana. Free throws were a deciding factor, as OSU made 30–35, while Indiana made just 12–19.[68]

The next day, January 6, there were two interesting comments from the NCAA office. The first was related to the conference and to the NCAA, generally, in noting that "the eligibility of freshmen is still vexing the NCAA."[69] A number of leagues had raised the question of first-year eligibility, but the NCAA had not softened its position on the issue. Clearly, it would not go away, but the NCAA moved with glacial speed in finally declaring freshmen eligible for varsity play beginning in 1972. The second issue involved Illinois. After more than two years the university remained on NCAA probation as a result of the slush fund scandal of 1966. The reason that the university was still on probation was that the request to remove them from that status from Commissioner Bill Reed was "not submitted in the proper manner,"[70] certainly a cause for embarrassment, if not derision.

That night, Purdue handed Illinois its first defeat of the season, 98 to 84, in West Lafayette, before a sellout crowd of 14,123. Rick Mount had 37, while Dave Scholz (23) and Mike Price (22) led Illinois. Purdue shot 58 percent from the floor to secure the victory. In Ann Arbor, Michigan edged Indiana in overtime, 89–87, behind a 48-point performance by Rudy Tomjanovich, which tied the Michigan one-game scoring record set by Cazzie Russell in 1966. Dan Fife said that Tomjanovich was "unconscious" and that they fed him the ball every chance that they could. He had range to 20–25 feet and could get his own shot off the dribble.[71] Kenny Johnson had 21 and Eric Branaugh 17 for the Hoosiers. Michigan State defeated Wisconsin, 77–67, in East Lansing. The big difference in the contest was fouls (MSU had 12, Wisconsin, 23) and concomitant free throws (MSU was 29–39, Wisconsin 9–14).[72]

The latest UPI poll had few surprises. UCLA had all the first-place votes, to be a unanimous #1. The Bruins were followed by North Carolina, Santa Clara, Davidson and Illinois. Purdue was #13 and Northwestern was #19.

The second weekend of the conference season was the same weekend as Super Bowl III, which was the first big upset in the short history of that contest. Joe Namath and the Jets shocked the favored Colts of Johnny Unitas to win 16–7, and Namath became an instant folk hero.

Illinois recovered from their loss to Purdue, and the only thing close to a folk hero in the Big Ten, Rick Mount, with an 82–77 win over Northwestern, ending the Wildcats' nine-game win streak. The overtime victory in Evanston was keyed by Jodie Harrison's 20 points and 25 rebounds. Mike Price knocked in 17 and senior Dave Scholz had 16. For the 'Cats, Don Adams had 19 and Jim Sarno 17. This loss would send the Wildcats into a tailspin and result in the early retirement of their coach, Larry Glass, in February. But for now, it just seemed like a "bump in the road."[73]

**Rudy Tomjanovich shooting his fabulous jumper (Bentley Historical Library, University of Michigan).**

In other contests, Ohio State topped Wisconsin, 84–69; Iowa defeated Indiana, 91–72; and Minnesota surprised Michigan, 94–67, in Minneapolis, where the temperature was 30 below zero and the Michigan shooting (29 percent) seemed to reflect that.[74] Dave Sorenson with 21, and Steve Howell with 20, led the Buckeye attack. In Iowa City, returning veteran Ben McGilmer had 27 and Glen Vidnovic 18 for the Hawkeyes, who had five players in double-figure scoring. Larry Mikan had 23 and Al Nuness 20 in the Gopher win.[75]

Indiana added to Northwestern's new woes with an 87–70 win in Bloomington on January 14. Joe Cooke led all scorers with 32 for the Hoosiers, who shot a season-high 49 percent from the floor, and Ken Johnson had 21 points and 16 rebounds. For the Wildcats, Dale Kelley had 22 and Don Adams 18, but Northwestern shot just 36 percent in the loss. In other games, Iowa topped MSU, 77–76, and Wisconsin defeated Minnesota, 68–61. The difference in the narrow Iowa win was that the Hawkeyes went 27–33 from the line, while MSU was a dismal 12–23.[76]

A new week brought no relief to the embattled Wildcats, as MSU handed them their third defeat in a row, 89–75. Ohio State beat Michigan handily, 98–85, in Ann Arbor before 13,451 disappointed Wolverine rooters. Sophomore sensation Jim Cleamons led all scorers with 31, and was supported by center Dave Sorenson's 26. Denny Stewart led the Maize and Blue with 24, but Rudy Tomjanovich was held to 18 (he was averaging 27.4). Coach Johnny Orr of Michigan said of Cleamons, "[He] wasn't just great, he was super great."[77] Iowa romped past Minnesota, 89–68, as Ben McGilmer dropped in 30 points.[78]

Michigan then lost at Northwestern, to end the Wildcats' losing streak, 100–85. Tomjanovich had 27 and Stewart 21, but the Wolverines shot just 44 percent from the floor to Northwestern's 56 percent. Jim Sarno had 26 and Dale Kelley had 18 for the 'Cats.

Purdue finally returned to action on January 25 and tied OSU for first place with an easy 102–79 win over Minnesota. Rick Mount had 34 and Herm Gilliam had 23 to send the 10,387 Gopher fans home disappointed. That same evening, Michigan State double-teamed Rudy Tomjanovich all game and held him to seven points on 3–11 shooting, but Dan Fife (19), Denny Stewart (18) and Bob Sullivan (18) picked up the slack to lead to the Michigan win, 75–70, in East Lansing. Michigan went 15–26 from the line and MSU continued to shoot itself in the foot with its 6–13 performance from the line.[79] Fife recalled, "I think we lost to them once in my three years,"[80] but that loss would come two weeks later in Ann Arbor when MSU topped the Wolverines, 86–82.

In one of the first meaningful clashes of the conference season, Ohio State defeated Illinois, 76–67, in Columbus, before 12,974 Buckeye fans. Dave Sorenson was huge with 30 points, but both teams shot well (50 percent for each). Dave Scholz led the Illini with 20. The difference in the contest was fouls and free throws, as Illinois picked up 20 fouls, leading to OSU's shooting 22–27 from the line, while the Illini hit 11–15 from the stripe, off just 13 Buckeye fouls.[81]

Jim Cleamons was the MVP in the Big Ten in 1971 before going on to a nine-year NBA playing career, after which he coached in the NBA (The Ohio State University Archives).

That set up an even bigger clash three nights later in West Lafayette, where the last two unbeatens in the league met. The game lived up to the hype as Purdue defeated Ohio State in overtime, 95–85, as 14,123 fans screamed for joy. Dave Sorenson took game honors with 30, and Jim Cleamons had 17 for the Bucks. Rick Mount was "held" to 20, but Herm Gilliam had 22 and Bill Keller 21 for the Boilermakers. Illinois tried to stay close to the leaders with an 86–73 win against Wisconsin in Champaign. Sophomore Greg Jackson led the Illini with 36. The following weekend, Purdue stomped Iowa, 99–87, as Mount set a Purdue scoring record with 45 points in the game. Herm Gilliam knocked down 26, so the two accounted for 72 percent of the points. The victory left the Boilermakers as the only undefeated team in the league at 5–0, with OSU 4–1 and Illinois and Iowa at 3–2, the only teams in the league over .500.[82]

OSU then helped Purdue by losing at Wisconsin, 77–73, while Purdue topped Northwestern in Evanston, 97–84. Mount had 31 and Gilliam 20 for the Boilers, who were outrebounded by Northwestern, 56–48. The big factor again was fouls and free throws. Northwestern had 31 fouls, leading to Purdue sinking 41–45 free throws, while Purdue's 22 fouls led to only 20–27 for the Wildcats from the line. In Madison, the Badgers had good balance led by Clarence Sherrod with 18 and Al Henry with 15. Cleamons took game scoring honors with 28. Illinois got some separation from Iowa with a 98–69 win over the Hawks in Champaign. Denny Pace (21) and Greg Jackson (20) led the hot-shooting Illini, who had 45–75 from the floor (60 percent). Iowa had just 19–54 (35 percent), led by John Johnson's 19 points and Glen Vidnovic's 18. A mob of 16,128 fans crammed into Assembly Hall to cheer on their Illini.[83]

The next week's UPI and AP polls agreed on the top three teams in the nation: UCLA, North Carolina and Santa Clara. Both had Purdue at #8, with Illinois at #9 (UPI) and #10 (AP). That would surely be altered when Purdue suffered its first conference loss, to Ohio State, 88–85, in Columbus. Jody Finney had 28 and Dave Sorenson 24 to lead the Buckeye attack. Mount got 35 points, but got little help from anyone else. Purdue was just 7–13 from the line on 12 OSU fouls, while the Bucks sank 26 of 31 off 25 Purdue violations. Purdue coach George King said, "It's just that Ohio State doesn't foul.... They play tough defense and don't foul."[84] Illinois was upset by Michigan, 92–87, in Ann Arbor, to dampen their hopes of advancement. Tomjanovich had 37 and Stewart 17 to pace the Wolverines. Jackson (29) and Scholz (22) were the Illini big guns. Michigan played just five players the entire 40 minutes.[85] There were only 8,113 fans at the game and Dan Fife noted that "there were other important things going on in the world, like the war in Vietnam and athletics were not as important as the rest of the world."[86]

The next weekend, Purdue bounced back with a crushing defeat of Wisconsin, 87–69, in Madison, while Ohio State defeated Minnesota, 58–41, in a slow-down game in Columbus. In the first half, the strategy worked for the Gophers as they sank 11 of 24 from the floor to OSU's 6–21, and Minnesota led 23–16 at the half. Second half was a different story as the Bucks went 14–27 and the Gophers just 10–26. Mikan and Cleamons tied for game scoring honors with 15 each. In Madison, Mount had 35 and Purdue shot 49 percent in the easy victory.[87]

A big surprise that day was the immediate resignation of Northwestern coach Larry Glass, who had announced two weeks earlier that he would resign at the end of the season. His assistant, Brad Snyder, took over and led the Wildcats, who were just 2–6 in the conference, to their third Big Ten win, 91–88 over Indiana.[88]

Three nights later, Purdue extended its lead on Ohio State to two games as the Buckeyes lost at Illinois, 73–57, and the Boilermakers, obviously looking beyond Indiana, managed to edge the Hoosiers in Bloomington, 96–95. For Ohio State, "The game was a team nightmare. Ohio State was outrebounded, 45–29, called for seven more personal fouls, and shot only .438 from the field."[89] The Purdue win was secured by Herm Gilliam's one-and-one made with four seconds left. Purdue had led 68–53 early in the second half, but allowed Indiana to tie the game at 77 with ten minutes to go.

Mount had 32 and Gilliam 21, but it was again free-throw shooting that won for the Boilermakers as they made 32 of 37, while Indiana was just 15–25.[90]

Purdue kept rolling, beating Northwestern, 107–68, with the starters sitting for the last eight minutes, then edging Michigan State in East Lansing, 74–72. Ohio State stayed close with an 88–81 defeat of Iowa, then fell three games back with a 86–83 loss to Northwestern.

The race was becoming a fait accompli for the Boilermakers, but there were some glimmers of excitement in some Big Ten venues. Rudy Tomjanovich set an Assembly Hall record with 19 field goals, breaking Rick Lopossa's mark of 15 set in 1964 for Northwestern. The Wolverines were not sure that Rudy would even play: "He had a bad toothache and his jaw was all swollen,"[91] but he hardly missed as Michigan shot 56 percent as a team in the game. Rudy T. scored 40 points, but the Illini won, 100–92. Greg Jackson had 33 for the Illini.[92]

The Boilermakers were now 10–1 and OSU 7–4, and on March 1, Purdue clinched the championship with a 95–85 victory at Iowa, while OSU lost at Michigan State, 85–72. Mount scored 43 for Purdue in the victory. Illinois managed to tie OSU for second place with a 77–64 win over Indiana. Purdue was now ranked #6 in the nation and Illinois #20. The #1 team, UCLA, had its first loss, falling to USC in another slow-down game, 46–44.[93]

Purdue closed out its conference season with a 120–76 victory over Indiana, just to show the Hoosiers that the close game in Bloomington was a fluke. Mount had 40 and set a new Big Ten season scoring record with 493 (35.2 ppg), breaking Gary Bradds's mark from 1964. He also had 193 field goals, breaking Cazzie Russell's mark of 181, set in 1966.[94] He finished second in the country in scoring (33.3) to Pete Maravich's 44.2.

### Final Standings and MVPs, 1968–69

| | | |
|---|---|---|
| Purdue | 13–1 | Rick Mount (Big Ten MVP) First team All-American |
| Illinois | 9–5 | Dave Scholz |
| Ohio State | 9–5 | Dave Sorenson |
| Michigan | 7–7 | Rudy Tomjanovich |
| Northwestern | 6–8 | Don Adams |
| Minnesota | 6–8 | Al Nuness |
| Michigan State | 6–8 | Lee Lafayette |
| Iowa | 5–9 | John Johnson |
| Wisconsin | 5–9 | Jim Johnson |
| Indiana | 4–10 | Ken Johnson |

Certainly a victory for the Johnsons (not related), but Mount was an obvious winner for the Big Ten award. Purdue and Mount were not finished, however; they had the NCAA tournament, with their first game against Miami of Ohio, who upset Notre Dame, 63–60, in the first round. In a rare occurrence, the game would be telecast in Chicago on independent station, WCIU, Channel 26, a UHF channel with a very small viewing audience.[95]

Purdue won its contest easily, 91–71, with Mount scoring 32 and Keller 19 to lead the way. Now they would face Marquette, who had beaten Kentucky in Lexington, 81–74, led by Dean Meminger and George Thompson, who each scored 22 points. The Marquette-Purdue game went to overtime, but Purdue eked out a victory, 75–73. Mount and Keller were again the scoring leaders with 26 and 17, respectively, while Thompson had 28 and Meminger just 12 for Marquette. The Warriors outrebounded the Boilers, 55–42, but Purdue missed just three free throws (17–20), while Marquette was only 19 of 29.[96]

Purdue was in the Final Four, along with North Carolina, Drake and UCLA. The Boilermakers would play North Carolina in Louisville and the game turned out to be a romp, as Purdue triumphed, 92–65; Mount had 36 and Keller 20. The Boilers would play #1 UCLA, who had struggled to defeat Drake, 85–82. It was the first Big Ten appearance in the title game since Michigan and Cazzie Russell lost in the championship bout in 1966. UCLA had no problem with Purdue, routing the Boilermakers 92–72 in the championship, behind Final Four MOP Lew Alcindor's 37 points and 21 rebounds. Mount had 28, but on 12–36 shooting. Overall, Purdue shot just 27–92 (29 percent), while the Bruins were 32–58 (55 percent). It was the Bruins' third consecutive title, but it had been a grand season for Purdue. With Mount and Keller back for another year, hopes were high for another great year in 1969–70.[97]

**Rick Mount, Big Ten MVP and scoring leader for Purdue in 1969, was best known for his great jump shot, but he could also drive hard to the basket, as he is doing here (Purdue Athletics Communications).**

# XII

# The "Run and Gun" '70s

College basketball would have a new look for the 1969–70 season, or rather, it would *not* have something it had for the past three years: the looming specter of Lew Alcindor leading the UCLA Bruins to another NCAA title. Alcindor and two other starters had been graduated and the feeling was that UCLA would be an excellent team, but that they would not be the NCAA champions, largely because Alcindor was irreplaceable. The national recruiting done by UCLA coach John Wooden had been groundbreaking, since most state schools still recruited exclusively in-state or in contiguous states. Wooden had snared Walter Hazzard from Philadelphia, who, along with Gail Goodrich, had been the backbone of the 1964 and 1965 NCAA champions. Other state schools slowly began to replicate the process, but the Big Ten largely did not, mainly because the stock of outstanding players within the Midwest was so huge. Nevertheless, Big Ten recruiters now began pursuing players outside the region in earnest during this new decade.

Every campus was rumbling with the dissent of the Vietnam War, with some more than others. Dan Fife noted that the players, like the rest of the students, were acutely aware of Vietnam and the antiwar concerns. Mark Wagar remember that he and roommate Dave Merchant had to slip off campus surreptitiously after the Ohio State campus was shut down following the Kent State shootings in 1970.[1]

The great success of Purdue in the 1968–69 season made them one of the early favorites for the Big Ten title in 1969–70. They welcomed back the Big Ten's MVP, Rick Mount, as well as George Faerber and Larry Weatherford, but they had lost three key starters, Herman Gilliam, Bill Keller and Chuck Bavis. The Boliers would be hard-pressed to repeat, but they surely had the scoring to make a title run possible. Ohio State had Dave Sorenson, Jody Finney and Jim Cleamons returning and looked to be as good as anyone in the league. Illinois had lost Dave Scholz and Jodie Harrison, but returned Mike Price, Rick Howat, Greg Jackson, Fred Miller and Randy Crews. The Illini would also be in the thick of the race. Iowa had five of their top scorers returning, and they would be joined by sophomore Fred Brown. The bench would be short, but the six made Iowa a dangerous opponent and league contender.

The rest of the league was not such a pushover, either. Minnesota had Larry Mikan and Larry Overskei, as well as soph sensation Eric Hill. Michigan had Rudy Tomjanovich, who would become Michigan's leading scorer. Michigan State had sophomore and potential star Ralph Simpson. Wisconsin would be tough with Clarence Sherrod and Al Henry, but they would be weak inside. Northwestern had returning starters Dale

Kelley and Don Adams, who were both top players, but the quality dropped quite a bit after that. Indiana was young, with James "Bubbles" Harris and Joby Wright gaining the experience that would help the Hoosiers in later years.

As the season opened, the Vietnam War was still the leading concern in the United States and worldwide. Richard Nixon had been elected in 1968 with his statement that he had a plan to end the Vietnam War and he defeated Hubert Humphrey, who had come to represent the escalation of the war. Humphrey was also hurt by the candidacy of George Wallace, as an independent, who sucked away potential Democratic votes. Now a year after his election, Nixon announced new GI recalls, although the exact numbers and timing were not revealed.[2]

Big Ten teams began the season topping most of their non-conference opposition, and early pollsters seemed to feel that Ohio State, Purdue and Illinois were the class of the league, as all three appeared in the top twenty AP and UPI rankings in early December. Pre-season magazines had not quite agreed with *Sports Quarterly Basketball* in ranking Purdue and Iowa in the top 30 teams, by not ranking any teams but the top three: South Carolina, Kentucky and UCLA. The magazine's Sam Goldaper selected 30 top college players, and the only Big Ten players were Rick Mount, Dave Sorenson and Rudy Tomjanovich.

*Basketball Yearbook 1970*, edited by Zander Hollander, had South Carolina and UCLA as #1 and #2 with Purdue as #3. Ohio State was selected as #15, with Iowa, Illinois and Michigan State completing the top five in the league. Mount was selected as a first team All-American, the only Big Ten player to gain that recognition.[3]

*Basketball 1969–70* was so enamored of Mount that not only was he picked as an All American, but Purdue was picked as their selection for #1 in the nation, followed by North Carolina and Davidson. UCLA was #6 and South Carolina #7. Ohio State came in as #13 and Illinois as #15. The magazine provided no league predictions, but Rudy Tomjanovich was selected for their 4th team, the only other Big Ten player. The Midwest All-Sectional team included Dave Sorenson, Larry Mikan of Minnesota, and sophomore Ralph Simpson of Michigan State, a very insightful selection.[4]

Larry Fox of *True Magazine Basketball Yearbook* selected South Carolina, Kentucky and Dayton as the top three teams in the nation with Purdue #12 and Illinois #20. He also picked Mount as one of the nation's top players and Simpson as one of the country's top sophomores.[5]

Finally, *Sports Illustrated* was back to pre-season ranking of national teams, and selected South Carolina, New Mexico State, UCLA, Purdue and Duquesne as the top five teams in the nation. In the Big Ten, *SI* saw Illinois and Ohio State as Purdue's biggest challengers, but Iowa and Michigan were also strong. Depending on sophomore Ralph Simpson, they considered Michigan State a dark horse.[6]

A number of Big Ten teams started the season strongly. Illinois was undefeated until late December, when they lost to Washington State, 59–58, in the Far West Classic in Portland, Oregon. Greg Jackson was a horse for the Illini with 20 points and 17 rebounds, but he fouled out with 3:22 to go and the Illini could not overcome that. The Illini then lost to USC in Portland, 65–62, to end a forgettable tournament.[7] The Illini had played some good teams in their win streak, including Creighton, DePaul and Wichita, to move to a #12 ranking in the nation. Purdue blasted Butler, 100–64, as

Mount rested with a bruised knee; they also lost to Evansville, 80–78, without Mount playing. Mount returned to score 30 against Manhattan in an 89–79 victory in the Holiday Festival Tournament in New York's Madison Square Garden. Mount followed this with 37 against Penn in an 88–85 Purdue victory, before St. Bonaventure crushed the Boilermakers 91–75, behind 50 points from Bob Lanier in the Holiday Festival championship game. Mount had just 19.[8] Purdue was ranked #18 on December 24.

Ohio State was ranked as high as #11 on December 10, but then lost to state rival Ohio University, 82–80, before beating Fresno State at home by just seven points and topping TCU in Ft. Worth, 89–80. Northwestern was a surprise third-place finisher in the Sun Devil Classic, defeating Arizona State, 101–91, then defeated Rutgers at the Fayetteville Classic, 78–77, before losing in the finals to North Carolina State, 98–75.[9]

The new year of 1970 began with the Nixon administration attempting to find some way to end the war in Vietnam, either through more troop call-ups or de-escalation, although that was not the administration's favored approach. As 1969 ended, Vice-President Spiro T. Agnew went to South Vietnam to confer on the war with South Vietnamese President Nguyen Van Thieu.[10]

The Big Ten's conference season began shortly afterwards, with Illinois and Michigan winning close contests on the road. The Wolverines edged Northwestern, 96–92, behind 24 points from both Richard Carter and Dan Fife. Dale Kelley (35) and Don Adams (23) provided the Northwestern firepower. Michigan shot 55 percent from the floor to snatch the victory from the Wildcats, who shot 45 percent. In Madison, Illinois defeated Wisconsin, 74–69, as Fred Miller and Mike Price each had 19 for Illinois. Clarence Sherrod led Wisconsin with 23. Illinois sealed their victory from the free-throw line, going 28–36, while Wisconsin was just 15–19.[11]

In Iowa City, Rick Mount scored 53 points, but Iowa topped Purdue, 94–88. John Johnson had 28 and Fred Brown 26 for the Hawks. Ohio State defeated Min-

Ron Behagan played in the NBA for seven seasons, but may be best known for his part in the brawl with Ohio State on January 25, 1972 (University of Minnesota Athletics).

nesota in Columbus, 78–71. Jody Finney picked up 24 and Jim Cleamons 20 for the Bucks, while Larry Mikan scored 22 and Eric Hill 18 for the Gophers, who played the whole game without any substitutions. In Bloomington, Michigan State upset the Hoosiers, 85–84, as Ralph Simpson debuted for the Spartans with 34 points. Joe Cooke had 26 for IU, who were just 8–15 from the foul line. MSU was 25–31.[12]

Three nights later, Illinois filled its new Assembly Hall with 15,392 to see the Illini crush Indiana, 94–74. Six Illini were in double figures, led by Price's 19. Joe Cooke had 19 for the Hoosiers. Purdue bounced back from the Iowa loss to beat Wisconsin in West Lafayette, 90–74, as Mount went for 36. Iowa surprised Michigan, defeating them in Ann Arbor, 107–99. The Hawkeyes got 34 from Johnson, 24 from Chad Calabria and 23 from Brown to more than offset Rudy Tomjanovich's 37. Fife said, "They were a great team; everyone could score and they were fast on the break."[13] That week's AP and UPI polls had no Big Ten teams in the top 20 in the nation; the polls were topped by UCLA, Kentucky and South Carolina.

Illinois affirmed its power against Ohio State the next week, beating them soundly, 77–59, as the Bucks had 23 turnovers. Rebounds were hardly a factor in the game with only 53 in total, as the teams combined to shoot 57 percent from the floor. Illinois was led by Fred Miller and Bill Howat, each with 20, as 16,128 roared the Illini home.

Iowa had an easy time with Wisconsin in Madison, beating them 92–74. Johnson (31), Calabria (22) and Brown (22) again led the Hawkeye scoring. Purdue won at Michigan, 103–96, with Mount going for 39 and Tomjanovich for 30. Fife said that with his range, Mount had to be picked up at half-court and he might have scored 40 or 50 a game with the 3-point shot in effect. Early on, it looked like Illinois, Iowa and Purdue would be the powers in the league.[14]

The pattern continued, as Illinois went to 5–0 in conference with an easy win over Northwestern in Evanston, 101–80, and a struggle to victory in Ann Arbor, 75–73. After the Northwestern game, Coach Brad Snyder picked Illinois to win the conference title. Greg Jackson led the scoring in both wins, with 24 against the Wildcats and 26 against the Wolverines.[15]

After the week off for fall semester exams, the conference roared back to life on January 24 with three games, two of which were upsets: Minnesota over Ohio State, 77–76, in Minneapolis; and Northwestern over Purdue, 66–65, in Evanston. In the latter game Northwestern resorted to "slow down basketball and roughhouse rebounding," according to the *Chicago Tribune*'s Big Ten reporter, Richard Dozer. The Wildcats outrebounded the Boilermakers, 53–37, and both teams shot just 34.3 percent each. Mount led the scoring with 27, while Kelley had 23 for Northwestern, despite fouling out with 15:27 to go.[16] The AP poll now had Illinois as #10 and Iowa as #20, while UCLA, Kentucky and St. Bonaventure held the top three spots.

Purdue came back to life, beating Michigan 116–103, as Mount, celebrating his new fatherhood, scored 53, and Tomjanovich 36 (plus 21 rebounds). Fife noted that Mount was beating single-man coverage. "We played man-to-man; everyone did. If your man beat you, there was little helping on defense. It wasn't until [Bob] Knight came into the league (in 1971–72, as coach of Indiana) and emphasized tough *team* defense with constant help on open players and double teams low on the ball. He changed the league, being the first to emphasize defensive strategies."[17]

Iowa had their way with Indiana, 100–93, then defeated Minnesota, 90–77, behind 33 by Johnson and 19 from Calabria. This latter win moved the Hawks ahead of Illinois, as the Illini were shocked at home by the Badgers, losing 66–65; Sherrod scored 21 and Henry 15. The Illini lost the game at the line, going 15–31. Wisconsin had far fewer throws, but made them count as they went 14–17. Purdue stayed in the race with a 105–86 win over Michigan State. Mount had 41 for the winners and Simpson had 35 for the Spartans.[18]

Big Ten standings were now Iowa, 5–0; Illinois, 5–1; OSU and Purdue, 4–2; Minnesota, 4–3; Wisconsin, 2–3; MSU, 2–4; Michigan, 2–5; Indiana, 1–4; Northwestern, 1–6. The top three seemed to be holding their positions, but the top spot was still uncertain. Iowa extended its winning streak against Indiana, 104–89, with Johnson getting 33 and Brown 23. Joby Wright had 29 to lead the Hoosiers. Illinois fell back another game by losing in Minneapolis, 82–73. Ollie Shannon had 34 to lead the upset, "hitting from all angles and driving, even with four fouls," according to the *Tribune* report. Illinois lost at the line, going 11–19 to Minnesota's 20–35. Jackson had 21 for the Illini. Purdue tied the Illini for second with an 88–85 victory in Columbus over Ohio State. Mount had 34 for the Boilers and Weatherford 20. Cleamons (28) and Sorenson (24) led the Buckeye scoring, as they played only five men. The latest poll that week had Iowa the only ranked Big Ten team, at #14.[19]

Iowa stayed undefeated in the conference, topping Wisconsin, 119–100, for their 9th win in a row. Johnson and Calabria each had 29 in the rout. Sherrod had 35 and Henry 22 for the Badgers. Purdue crushed Indiana, 98–80, as Mount, with his 41 points, set a new Purdue career scoring record with 2,093 points, topping Dave Schellhase.[20]

Two nights later, Purdue pushed Illinois further back in the standings by routing them, 83–49, behind 28 points from Mount. Iowa continued to win, defeating Michigan State, 103–77, despite 34 points from Spartan sophomore sensation Ralph Simpson. For the Hawks, Johnson had a game-high 36 and Brown 25. The Buckeyes sought to reinsert themselves into the race with a 100–83 victory over Indiana in Bloomington. Finney had 27 and Sorenson 25 for the Bucks, while Ken Johnson had 28 and Jim Harris 22 for the Hoosiers. The standings now had Iowa at 8–0, Purdue at 7–2, and Minnesota and Ohio State tied at 6–3. Illinois was at 5–3.[21]

Another national story that continued to unfold in the Midwest was the ongoing trial of the Chicago Seven (formerly Eight until Judge Julius Hoffman severed Bobby Seale from the others). Their crimes arose from the demonstrations against the Vietnam War that were done at the 1968 Democratic Convention in Chicago. Judge Hoffman was now sentencing the guilty: John Froines, Lee Weiner, Jerry Rubin, David Dellinger, Rennie Davis, Abbie Hoffman, Tom Hayden, as well as their lawyers, Leonard Weinglass and William Kuntsler. The verdicts and sentences would be appealed.[22]

And in the Big Ten, Iowa continued to win, going to 9–0, at the difficult venue of Assembly Hall in Champaign, before 16,128. The score was 83–81 with Brown (22), Johnson (17) and Calabria (17) leading five Hawks in double figures. Rick Howat led the Illini and all scorers with 32.[23]

That same day a new NBA 3-year television contract was announced with ABC, which increased the number of games broadcast per season from 18 to 28, and the amount per year from $1.5 million to $5.6 million. And yet, the NCAA could still not get their tournament broadcast on national television. That time would come eventually.

Iowa faced another difficult opponent on their home floor four days later in Columbus, but the Hawks remained undefeated in the conference, topping Ohio State, 97–89. Johnson had 38, Vidnovic 20 for the Hawks, while Cleamons went for 31 and Sorenson 23 for the Bucks. Dan Andreas guarded Johnson for OSU and said, "He had 38 and I thought I did a good job. He could score from anywhere."[24] Purdue, still clinging to hope for another title, defeated Illinois in Champaign, 88–81, as Mount got 40. For Michigan State, in the midst of a dismal season, there was some joy in Ralph Simpson's setting a new season scoring record, breaking that of Julius McCoy, set in 1965–66. The biggest national basketball news, however, was the defeat of UCLA at Oregon, 78–65, breaking the 25-game winning streak of the Bruins.[25] The latest AP poll dropped UCLA to #2, behind Kentucky, with St. Bonaventure #3 and South Carolina #4. The UPI poll kept UCLA at #1, followed by Kentucky, South Carolina and St. Bonaventure. AP had Iowa at #9; UPI had them at #8.

Both Iowa and Purdue continued to win. The Hawks beat Northwestern in a high-scoring contest, 116–97, before 13, 515 in Iowa City. Johnson had 49 and 15 rebounds for the Hawkeyes. Northwestern was topped by Kelley's 28. In Minneapolis, Mount had 42 to lead the Boilers to a 108–94 victory. Larry Mikan had 25 for the Gophers.[26] That same day, one of the most momentous dates in NCAA tournament history occurred, although it was little realized at the time. Al McGuire, the coach of Marquette, rejected the invitation from the NCAA to be one of 25 teams in the national tournament because his team would be assigned to the Midwest, rather than the Mideast, and would have to play in Ft. Worth for its opening game. He felt that they deserved to be in the Mideast and play in Dayton or Columbus, rather than travel so far. He and his team would accept a bid to play in Madison Square Garden in the NIT tourney, which they subsequently won. The NCAA was furious, and over the summer passed legislation that said that no team could refuse a bid to the NCAA and choose to play elsewhere.[27]

On the last day of February, Iowa clinched the Big Ten title with a 108–107 win over Purdue in West Lafayette. Rick Mount scored 61 points on 27–47 shooting, but the Hawkeyes countered with four players who got more than 20 points, led by John Johnson's 26 and Chad Calabria's 25. The game had controversy when the referees called a technical foul on the Purdue crowd for throwing objects on the floor after a previous warning.[28] The Hawks made both free throws, then scored a basket for a kind of four-point play, turning a 70–67 deficit into a 71–70 lead. Both teams shot tremendously: Purdue, 46–88 (52 percent) and Iowa, 38–73 (52 percent), but the big difference was at the line, where Purdue was 15–22 on 16 Iowa fouls, while Iowa was 32–40 on 31 Purdue fouls.[29]

Two days later, the All-Big Ten teams were named with few surprises. The first team was Rick Mount, John Johnson, Rudy Tomjanovich (eighth in the country in scoring at 30.1 ppg), Dave Sorenson and Ralph Simpson. Second team was Freddie Brown (IA), Clarence Sherrod (WI), Jim Cleamons (OSU), Eric Hill (MN) and Glen Vidnovic (IA). Playing out the season, Iowa won its last two contests, 113–92 over OSU and 115–101 over Northwestern. Purdue also kept winning and Mount kept pouring in the points, getting 37 against Michigan State in a 101–98 win, and 22 more against Minnesota in a 48–44 win, as the Gophers held the ball up to two minutes per possession to slow down the Boilermakers. Mount set a Big Ten career scoring record of 1,461 in 42 games, breaking the mark of Don Schlundt set in 60 games. Mount's 552 points and 39.4 ppg average were also Big Ten records.[30] He was also third in the country with 35.4 ppg, exceeded only by Maravich's 44.5 for LSU and Austin Carr of Notre Dame at 38.1.

### Final Standings and MVPS, 1969–70

| | | |
|---|---|---|
| Iowa | 14–0 | John Johnson |
| Purdue | 11–3 | Rick Mount (Big Ten MVP) First team All-American |
| Ohio State | 8–6 | Dave Sorenson |
| Illinois | 8–6 | Mike Price |
| Minnesota | 7–7 | Larry Mikan |
| Wisconsin | 5–9 | Al Henry |
| Michigan State | 5–9 | Ralph Simpson |
| Michigan | 5–9 | Rudy Tomjanovich |
| Northwestern | 4–10 | Dale Kelley and Don Adams |
| Indiana | 3–11 | Jim Harris |

The Hawkeyes would open their NCAA run on March 2 against the winner of Jacksonville and Western Kentucky, which turned out to be Jacksonville, by a score of 109–96. The Dolphins were in their first NCAA tournament, and their record had been built on the shooting of Rex Morgan and the inside play of 7'3" Artis Gilmore. They had not played a lot of traditional power programs, so it was difficult to assess how strong they really were. The Hawkeyes, on the other hand, had gone undefeated in one of the best conferences in the country, the first squad to do so since the Ohio State Buckeyes of 1960–61, who had gone on to lose in the NCAA championship game. Hopes were high that Iowa could replicate such a run. There were concerns, however. George King, the coach of Purdue, expressed them in noting that both the bench and the lack of a tough center would be issues for Iowa in the tournament. His insight proved to be correct.

The contest against Jacksonville was tight from start to finish, but the Dolphins scored with three seconds left on a tip-in by Pembroke Burrows III, who had the game of his life with 23 points, to win 104–103. Artis Gilmore led Jacksonville with 30 points and Rex Morgan had 23, like Burrows. The Dolphins shot 43–76 from the field, 57 percent. Iowa was led by Brown with 27, Vidnovic with 24 and Calabria with 21. They shot 42–83, 51 percent. What hurt the Hawks, said Coach Ralph Miller, was their free-throw shooting, which was just 19–31 (61 percent), their worst performance from the line since December, he noted. It was a sad, swift and unexpected ending for the Hawks.[31]

Iowa raced past Notre Dame in the 3rd-place game in the Mideast region, 121–106. Johnson and Calabria each had 31 and Vidnovic 24 to overpower the Irish, whose Austin Carr took game honors with 45 points.[32] The regular Big Ten beat reporter for the *Chicago Tribune*, Roy Damer, noted that the Hawkeyes had gotten a unlucky break in their loss, when a 25-foot shot dropped short, rather than a normal long rebound, but the Hawks were incredibly impressive in their rout of Notre Dame, shooting 65 percent from the floor. Ralph Miller said that his club had the potential "to beat anyone in the nation on any given night."[33] Jacksonville went on to defeat top-ranked Kentucky, 106–100, and go on to the championship bout against UCLA, where they lost 80–69 to UCLA, the winners of their fourth NCAA championship in a row.

## The 1970–71 Season

The 1970–71 season would be almost as surprising as the prior year, when Iowa, a dark horse at the start of the season, went undefeated and won the league going away. The early polls seemed to favor Indiana, an interesting choice since they had been last in the league in 1970. Iowa had lost most of their firepower in Johnson, Vidnovic and Calabria, as well as their coach, Ralph Miller, who moved to Oregon State. Purdue had lost Mount. Illinois looked strong with the return of Greg Jackson, Rick Howat, Fred Miller and Mike Price. Ohio State had a great sophomore class coming to join Jim Cleamons, while Minnesota had Shannon and Hill back, along with sophomore sensation Jim Brewer. Michigan State lost Ralph Simpson to the American Basketball Association after just one year of Big Ten basketball. In early December, the UPI ranked the top teams nationally as UCLA, South Carolina, Kentucky, Jacksonville and Marquette, with Indiana the only Big Ten team ranked (#11). The poll of the Big Ten coaches had Illinois favored, followed by Purdue, Indiana, Minnesota, Ohio State, Michigan, Wisconsin, Iowa, Michigan State and Northwestern.[34]

*Basketball Yearbook, 1971*, edited by Zander Hollander, selected South Carolina as their #1, followed by UCLA, Marquette, Kentucky and Notre Dame. Indiana was selected as #16. Ray Marquette of the *Indianapolis Star*, wiring in that same magazine, had Indiana as the Big Ten leader, followed by Purdue, Illinois, Michigan and Ohio State. He also noted, "One of the best sophomore crops in league history should keep the title chase wild and wooly, with Purdue right back knocking, as Larry Weatherford tries his hand at throwing in the long one-handers in place of Mount."[35]

Sam Goldaper, writing in *Basketball Extra, 1970–71*, also saw the Big Ten as a real toss-up among Indiana, Michigan, Minnesota, Iowa, Ohio State and Illinois. He waxed euphoric about Gopher sophomore Jim Brewer, as well as Indiana sophs George McGinnis and Steve Downing, neither of whom had played on the freshman team because of failing to meet the required Big Ten 1.7 entrance exam standards. Instead, they "played with local amateur teams where they averaged more than 40 points a game." Both had played in high school at state champion Indianapolis Washington, and McGinnis broke all of Oscar Robertson's Indianapolis scoring records. Thus, the high ranking of a team that had finished last in the league the year before seemed almost justified. Other top sophs mentioned were Henry Wilmore and Ken Brady with Michigan, Nick Weatherspoon of Illinois and, at Ohio State, Alan Hornyak and Luke Witte.[36] Dave Merchant, part of that OSU sophomore group, said, "We were just a bunch of naïve kids trying to fit it. We had no idea what to expect[37] [from Big Ten and nationally ranked teams]?"[38]

Early season non-conference games yielded no clear favorite. Illinois beat some good programs: Vanderbilt and Iowa State, as well as weaker ones like Northern Michigan. Indiana played well and, in an early season test, barely lost to #3-ranked Kentucky, 95–93 in overtime. Their lineup had been greatly enhanced by the addition of super sophomore George McGinnis, who scored 38 (with 20 rebounds) against the Wildcats, then 29 in a victory over Notre Dame, 106–103.[39]

Purdue made the biggest splash by upsetting Kentucky, 89–83, in Lexington, snapping the Wildcats' 26-game home-court winning streak. Larry Weatherford had 27 and Rob Ford 21 to lead the Boilermakers to the Kentucky Invitational title.[40]

Michigan won against some weaker opponents like Eastern Michigan and Detroit, and were beaten by Notre Dame, Kentucky and Duke, so gauging how good they were was unclear until they won their own cage tournament, handily romping over Harvard and Wyoming. After the Duke loss, the players had had a team meeting, called by Fife as captain. He said that they could have a great season, but this had to be a team effort. Their resolution was summed up by Fife: "Don't miss curfew. Play together."[41] And they did. Henry Wilmore was leading them in scoring, and rebounding strongly, considering his 6'3½" stature. Still, the Wolverines were just 4–3 as the conference season began. The Big Ten coaches had this predicted order of finish: Illinois, Purdue, Indiana, Minnesota, Ohio State, Michigan, Wisconsin, Iowa, Michigan State, and Northwestern.[42]

On December 27, every Big Ten team had a non-losing record, with Northwestern and Iowa at 4–4 and the rest above .500. Indiana and Michigan State were 6–2, Illinois and Minnesota 5–2, Purdue was 7–3, Wisconsin and Ohio State 4–3, and Michigan 4–3. Of course, the quality of the pre-season competition varied, so little was truly known at this point about which squads would actually be that strong.

In the Far West Classic the next day, Ohio State lost to Stanford, 78–74, but came back to beat Harvard the next day, 103–87. The leading scorers seemed to always be senior Jim Cleamons or sophomores Luke Witte and Alan Hornyak. No matter who was the top scorer, the key to the team's success was Cleamons, noted Dave Merchant, a Buckeye regular from 1971 to 1973. "Cleamons was amazing and the only guy who could really control Al [Hornyak] and make him stay within the team concept. He [Cleamons] was strong and could really run things on and off the court. We all wanted to be like Cleamons."[43] Hornyak "was quick to catch on to things; you'd show him a play once and he'd see where everything was going (and he'd be there at the end to shoot)."[44]

Indiana defeated San Jose State in that same tourney, 86–76, with George McGinnis (41) and Joby Wright (23) the leading scorers as they had been for most games in the pre-conference season. That week the Hoosiers were the highest rated Big Ten squad at #14, with Purdue slipping into the top 20 at #20.[45]

The early season success prompted a headline of "9 Big Ten Winners to open Tomorrow" in the *Chicago Tribune* on January 8. The teams had a combined record of 55–35, with top scorers being McGinnis, Jim Brewer of Minnesota, Nick Weatherspoon of Illinois, Henry Wilmore of Michigan, Bill Kilgore of Michigan State, and Alan Hornyak and Luke Witte of Ohio State, all sophomores.[46]

The winners on Saturday were no surprise, for the most part. Indiana defeated Northwestern, 101–90, in Evanston, as McGinnis debuted in the conference with 38 points and 23 rebounds. The Wildcats had five players in double figures, led by Ron Shoger's 31, but it was not enough to derail the Hoosiers. Illinois crushed Michigan State, 89–61, with Rick Howat (21) and Greg Jackson (17) leading the attack. Michigan edged Wisconsin, 90–89, in Madison as Henry Wilmore scored 44 points in his first league contest. Clarence Sherrod had 31 for the Badgers. Purdue surprised Minnesota with a victory, 83–76, over the Gophers in Minneapolis. Larry Weatherford had 25 for the winners, while sophomore Jim Brewer led the Gophers with 30. Ohio State had an easy time in Iowa City, winning 97–76. Hornyak had 30 and senior Jim Cleamons had 23. Fred Brown had 35 for the Hawks in what was the worst home loss for Iowa since 1954.[47] "Fred Brown," whom he had to guard, "was very, very good," noted Dave Merchant. "Nothing flashy, he just did everything well."[48] Mark Wagar remembered that he shot from "anywhere" and scored from anywhere, also.[49]

Three nights later, Purdue, Illinois and Indiana continued winning, defeating Northwestern, Wisconsin and Minnesota respectively. The latter victory, 99–73, was decisive, as McGinnis scored 31 and Joby Wright 18 in the win.[50] The victory surely helped Indiana's national stature, as they were rated #11 in the AP poll. UCLA, Marquette, Southern Cal, Penn and Western Kentucky were rated the top five.

Ohio State won the next night, January 13, in Morgantown, West Virginia, 83–74, and were already seen as favorites by at least one writer, Roy Damer of the *Chicago Tribune*, who noted that the schedule seemed to favor them because they were playing some top-league teams only at home. OSU was led by senior All-American Jim Cleamons and the great sophomore class that included Witte, Hornyak, Mark Wagar, Mink Minor, Dave Merchant and Bob Siekmann. The coaches, Damer noted, still saw six teams as legitimate contenders for the title, every team but Northwestern, Wisconsin, Michigan State and Iowa.[51]

Fred Brown in action for the University of Iowa, where he starred from 1969 to 1971, earning the nickname "Downtown" for his deep jump shots, while playing in the NBA (Hawkeye Yearbook Collection, University Archives, The University of Iowa Libraries).

The next weekend brought an early season surprise as Michigan upended Indiana, 92–81. Wilmore had 35 and Ken Brady 18 to offset the 37 and 25 by McGinnis and Wright, respectively. McGinnis had "a fully mature body, well muscled and broad. It was hard to believe that he was a sophomore. He was strong, could jump and shoot."[52] This victory "put them on the map and was the turning point of the season," said Dan Fife, indicating that they were a team to contend with.[53] Ohio State had little trouble against Wisconsin, 83–69, but Illinois struggled against Michigan State in East Lansing, 69–67. Purdue also was pushed by Minnesota before winning in overtime, 97–92. Rob Ford had 36 and Larry Weatherford 24 for the Boilermakers, while Ollie Shannon (28) and Jim Brewer (24) led the Gophers.[54]

An unusual aside: UCLA was to play Loyola on Friday, January 22, in Chicago Stadium, then go on to Notre Dame the next night. The Chicago sportswriters had set up a conference call as a press conference with John Wooden. In the course of that interview, one writer asked if Wooden thought that Loyola might try a slowdown to keep the score close and maybe steal a win against the Bruins. Wooden replied that he didn't think George Ireland, Loyola coach, would do that, but he had no idea. He then went on to say, "I haven't scouted them, and, in fact, don't do much scouting." This from a six-time (as of 1970) national championship coach.[55]

The Big Ten was on virtual hiatus with fall semester exams, but returned to action on January 23 with two meaningful games. The first was a win by Michigan over Northwestern, 97–87, with Henry Wilmore and Dan Fife each getting 20 for the Wolverines. Fife recalled that the Northwestern game was rough, and that was certainly indicated by the 87 free throws that the two teams combined to take (Michigan was 33 of 50, while Northwestern was 29 of 37).[56]

The second game was a narrow victory by Ohio State at Minnesota, 68–66. The latter game, in Williams Arena, was an emotional turning point for the Buckeyes, according to Mark Wagar. They had been down by eight at the half, by 14 with nine minutes to go, and whittled away the lead to win on a tip-in by Witte with five seconds left. This seemed to get the team to think that they really could win the Big Ten. The Bucks rallied behind sophs Witte (22) and Hornyak (18) to down the stubborn Gophers, who got 27 from Ollie Shannon and 18 from Jim Brewer.[57] For Minnesota and their fans, this game would not be soon forgotten.

The game that got most of the attention, however, was in South Bend, where the Irish ended UCLA's undefeated season with an 89–82 victory.[58] The next poll reflected the UCLA loss and dropped them to second behind Marquette, with USC, Penn and Kansas completing the top five. Illinois at 8–2 was now ranked #18, the highest for a Big Ten team at that point of the season.

Illinois seemed to justify that ranking the next Saturday in Chicago Stadium with a victory over Notre Dame, 69–66, in overtime, behind 30 points from Rick Howat. Either team could have won in regulation with better free-throw shooting: Illinois was 9–19; Notre Dame, 10–17. Ohio State lost to Michigan State in Columbus, 82–70, scrambling the early Big Ten standings. Michigan State had a strong team effort as Kilgore had 21, while Benjamin and Gutkowski had 19 each. Witte had 19 and Cleamons 16 for the Bucks, who seemed to be playing an intrasquad game because Michigan State's uniforms had been stolen earlier in the day from the visiting locker room. They wore OSU's road jerseys for the contest.[59] Despite the "humor" in this, the OSU players were clearly affected by it, often hesitating on passes and sometimes having unexpected turnovers. The game was a real letdown for the Ohio State players after the big win at Minnesota; they were not well prepared, and it showed.[60]

A week later, the Bucks reversed the results in East Lansing, winning 87–76, with Hornyak scoring 25 and Witte 21. Wagar recalled that he was booed by the Spartan fans because he set a pick on Gus Ganakas on a fast break. Ganakas hit his head on Wagar's hip and was knocked cold.[61] The victory made the Buckeyes 4–1 in conference, but Michigan was undefeated, having topped Minnesota 97–79, Purdue 85–69, and Northwestern 82–81, in the week to go to 6–0 in Big Ten play.

Wilmore, the 6'3" sophomore forward for Michigan, continued to lead in scoring with 31, 23 and 22 in the three games. He also was leading the team in rebounds.[62]

Both Indiana and Illinois stumbled as they tried to keep pace. Illinois lost to Iowa on February 2, 92–84, then defeated Minnesota, 93–78, as five Illini scored in double figures, led by Nick Weatherspoon with 27. Indiana lost to Purdue, 85–81, in Bloomington, despite well-distributed team scoring led by McGinnis with 21 and Wright with 20.[63] The UPI poll of February 8 had UCLA back on top and Marquette #2, despite the fact that the Warriors were undefeated. The next three teams were USC, Penn and Kansas with Michigan at #12 and Illinois at #15, tied with two other teams.

Over the next week, Michigan, Ohio State and Indiana kept winning, but Illinois was crushed in Columbus by the Buckeyes, 92–72. Witte and Cleamons did the most damage with 27 and 23, respectively. In an earlier win at Purdue, 69–67, Hornyak led with 27 and Witte dropped in 17 (plus 16 rebounds), while Ford had 22 for Purdue. Indiana topped Michigan State in East Lansing, 71–70, behind 24 from McGinnis and 16 from Wright, then defeated Iowa, 86–84, in Iowa City. McGinnis had 34 points and 15 rebounds for the Hoosiers. Michigan remained undefeated (7–0) in conference with a win at Purdue, 81–74, as Dan Fife and Wayne Grabiec each scored 19.[64]

And the war in Vietnam dragged on, despite the "plan" that Richard Nixon claimed he had for ending the war, as part of his campaign in 1968. The South Vietnamese Army, abetted and led by their American advisers and allies, invaded Laos in an effort to cut of the flow of arms to North Vietnam. Just as the invasion of Cambodia had provoked hundreds of protests in the United States and in Europe, so, too, did this latest invasion of a neutral country, though one through which the Ho Chi Minh Trail ran. The *Chicago Tribune* noted that a "new storm of protest gathered force in Congress."[65] The next week an American general claimed that the invasion had been a success in cutting off some of the flow of arms, ultimately helping to shorten the war and save American lives. His claim was greeted with skepticism by many.[66]

Ohio State and Michigan were beginning to distance themselves from the rest of the league, and that was reflected in their AP rankings the week of February 16, with Michigan at #16 and Ohio State at #20. Indiana stayed close, but Illinois had now fallen back. The standings, as of mid–February, had Michigan at 7–0; Ohio State, 7–1; Indiana, 5–2; Purdue, 5–3; Illinois, 4–3; Iowa, 3–4; MSU and Minnesota, 2–6; Wisconsin, 1–5; Northwestern, 1–6. Ohio State was pressing, but Michigan refused to lose.

On February 20, Michigan and Ohio State won again, the Wolverines at home, 108–90, against Minnesota, and the Buckeyes at home against Northwestern, 84–72.

Wilmore (33) and Grabiec (24) led the Wolverines, while Brewer and Shannon each had 28 for the Gophers. In Columbus, Hornyak had 24, but the second-leading scorer was super-sub, Bob Siekmann, with 20. Purdue and Indiana also won, with the Hoosier victory, 88–86, at Illinois, the death knell of Illini hopes for the season.[67]

And then it happened: Michigan lost. In Bloomington, before 9,230 fans, the Hoosiers ambushed the Wolverines, 88–79, as McGinnis scored 33 and snared 15 rebounds, and high school teammate Steve Downing had 28 points and 17 rebounds. Indiana outrebounded Michigan, 68–43. Wilmore led the Wolverines with 26 points and 10 rebounds. "They just beat us," said Dan Fife.[68]

Ohio State won, 80–71, against Iowa, to tie for the lead, but there was gloom in the locker room, because earlier in the day team doctors had said that Cleamons had what was preliminarily described as a fractured wrist, an injury that would end his season. Hornyak (23) and Witte (22) had led the scoring, while game honors went to Iowa center Kevin Kunnert with 26 and Fred Brown with 24.[69]

In what was the biggest game of the season, so it seemed, Ohio State went to Ann Arbor and defeated the Wolverines, 91–85, as Hornyak scored 37 and Witte 24 along with 18 rebounds. Fife, among others, guarded Hornyak, and he noted, "I was never screened so much in my life"[70] as Hornyak got open jumpers. Henry Wilmore took game honors with 42 (and 13 rebounds) for Michigan. Wilmore could "jump out of the gym, [he was] a 6'3" scorer and rebounder," remembered Fife.[71] The Bucks were doubly buoyed by the return of Cleamons, who had a severe sprain, rather than a fracture. He scored two points in limited action, as Dave Merchant started in his place. OSU was now 10–1 and both Indiana and Michigan, 8–2. The Buckeyes could win out and have another championship.[72]

Ohio State and Michigan both won on March 2, the Bucks over Minnesota, 84–70, and the Wolverines over Illinois, 75–74, in Champaign. Witte and Hornyak were the leading scorers for OSU with 26 and 22, respectively. After leading 71–65 with five minutes to go, Indiana lost at Wisconsin in double overtime, 94–87, despite 36 points from McGinnis. Glen Richgels led Wisconsin with 27. That same day, the NCAA announced first-round pairings for March 13: the Mideast would pair Marquette against Miami of Ohio, with the winner playing the Big Ten champion on March 18. Ohio State needed one more win to clinch a title tie.[73]

That win came four nights later at the expense of Northwestern, in Evanston, 68–67. "The Bucks led 64–52, but a Wildcat rush made Merchant's free throw, with 11 seconds left, the game winner."[74] Hornyak had 22 and Witte 15, but, more importantly, Cleamons had 14, played most of the game and showed no ill effects from the wrist sprain. "We were just awful," said Merchant, but they held on to win.[75] Michigan stayed alive with a win at home over rival MSU, 88–63, as Wilmore led with 26. Indiana, too, kept pace, with a 104–88 drubbing of Iowa. McGinnis went for 28, and Downing and James Harris each had 23. Brown (26) and Kunnert (22) led the Hawkeye attack.[76]

A most surprising announcement came from the Big Ten offices on March 8, i.e., that Big Ten basketball teams could play in the National Invitational Tournament later that month and in subsequent years. Big Ten coaches had made a similar request the previous season that had been denied by the Big Ten Athletic Council, then had reiterated that request in December of 1970. Now, the vote had gone the coaches' way. The

**George McGinnis, Indiana MVP in 1970–71, goes to the basket to score against Kentucky in a December 1970 game (University Archives, Indiana University).**

agreement was that "the N.I.T. will first select the league runner-up and, then, any others it wants."[77] One caveat to this was that earlier that season the NCAA had decreed that any team invited to the NCAA must accept it or be prohibited from participating in any post-season tournament, referred to by many as "the Al McGuire rule," which came about from his spurning the NCAA for the NIT tournament in 1970.

That night, the league race ended, as Ohio State pounded Indiana, 91–75, in Columbus. Cleamons had 30 and Hornyak 24 for the Bucks, who outrebounded the Hoosiers, 53–35. "It was the most exciting game of my life," said Dave Merchant.[78] McGinnis (25) and Wright (22) topped the Indiana scoring. The Buckeyes pressed the Hoosiers, and that led to a number of turnovers by the Indiana guards. "McGinnis grew so frustrated that he waved the guards away and brought the ball up himself; he did everything in that game," recalled Mark Wagar.[79] Jim Cleamons, in retrospect, said the Bucks won because of Fred Taylor. "There was not a better coached team in the Big Ten. Fred outcoached people."[80]

Immediately after the game, Indiana Coach Lou Watson resigned, effective immediately, after the complaints of several Indiana players about favoritism and lack of team discipline. Watson had already been considering retiring because of his health and family issues, but these complaints simply accelerated his decision. His assistant, Jerry Oliver, would coach the final game.[81] Watson held a tenured position as an associate professor of physical education and would continue at Indiana, but he had had enough of complaints from his players. This would certainly seem to affect the NIT's interest in Indiana, as well as the university's interest in the NIT.[82]

The latest UPI poll had UCLA (24–1), Marquette (27–0), USC (24–1), Penn (26–0) and Kansas (23–1) as the top teams with OSU, (18–5) #11. There was still a scramble for second in the Big Ten and a place in the NIT. Michigan defeated Iowa, 86–82, in Iowa City with Wilmore scoring 35, matched by Iowa's Fred Brown. Purdue won easily at Wisconsin, 81–77.[83] The winners would be top candidates for the NIT, along with Indiana. The NIT acted swiftly, on March 10, to invite the Wolverines to their party in Madison Square Garden.

First-round NCAA games began on March 13 with Notre Dame topping TCU, as Austin Carr scored 52; Marquette defeating Miami (OH), 62–47; and Wake Forest surprising Jacksonville, the 1970 NCAA runner-up, 74–72. In addition, UCLA defeated #3 USC, 73–62, to earn the Pacific 8 bid to the tournament. Curtis Rowe had 15, as five players from the Bruins scored in double figures.[84]

The Big Ten season ended the same day with Purdue smashing Iowa, 110–84, and Michigan routing Wisconsin, 93–73. A demoralized Indiana squad lost to Illinois in Bloomington, 103–84.

### Final Standings and MVPs, 1970–71

| Team | Record | MVP |
|---|---|---|
| Ohio State | 13–1 | Jim Cleamons (Big Ten MVP) |
| Michigan | 12–2 | Dan Fife and Henry Wilmore |
| Purdue | 10–3 | Larry Weatherford |
| Indiana | 9–5 | George McGinnis |
| Illinois | 5–9 | Rick Howat |
| Minnesota | 5–9 | Jim Brewer |
| Iowa | 4–10 | Fred Brown |
| Michigan State | 4–10 | Bill Kilgore |
| Wisconsin | 4–10 | Glen Richgels |
| Northwestern | 3–11 | Rick Sund |

The AP All-Big Ten team had a number of those same players.

FIRST TEAM

George McGinnis, Indiana; Henry Wilmore, Michigan; Fred Brown, Iowa; Jim Cleamons, Ohio State; Alan Hornyak, Ohio State (three sophs and one junior and a senior)

SECOND TEAM

Luke Witte, OSU; Clarence Sherrod, Wisconsin; Rob Ford, Purdue; Jim Brewer, Minnesota; Rick Howat, Illinois (2 sophs, 2 juniors, 1 senior)

McGinnis led the league in scoring with 29.9 (fourth nationally with 30.0), followed by Brown (28.9), Wilmore (27.9 and 10th nationally at 27.6), Sherrod (24.6) and Hornyak (23.5). McGinnis also led in rebounding with 14.9 per game, followed by Kilgore of MSU, 13.6.

The Buckeyes opened their NCAA tourney by meeting #2 Marquette, in Athens, Georgia. Marquette was undefeated, but Ohio State handed them their first defeat, 60–59; Hornyak hit two free throws with six seconds left to give the Bucks a 60–57 lead and the last bucket by Marquette was uncontested. Wagar called it a "veritable chess match between Al McGuire, the Marquette coach, and Fred Taylor of the Buckeyes.

They had a kind of 'wheel offense' and we worked a lot on defending that in preparation for the game. When they altered their offense, we altered our defense."[85] Cleamons had 21, Witte 13 and Hornyak 11. The Bucks would face Western Kentucky, who had crushed favored Kentucky, 107–83.[86]

Two nights later, the Buckeye season ended with an 81–78 overtime loss to Western Kentucky. Jim McDaniels, a big man who could shoot outside, had 31 for the Hilltoppers, while Hornyak (26) and Witte (23) led the Bucks in scoring. Fouls and key missed shots sent the game into overtime after the Bucks had led most of the way; they were outscored 12–9 in the extra period. Ohio State's season was done; they ended up #10 in the final AP and UPI polls. The Big Ten, however, was not finished.[87]

The NIT had selected both Michigan and Purdue for the 16-team field and they both played in New York on March 21. Michigan defeated Syracuse, 82–76, and Purdue lost to St. Bonaventure, 94–79. Wilmore (22) and Grabiec (21) were the top Wolverine scorers, while Ford and Weatherford each had 21 in the Purdue loss. Three days later, Michigan ("We didn't shoot well and we didn't play together"[88]) lost to Georgia Tech, led by All-American center, Rich Yunkus, 78–70. Yunkus had 27 for game honors; Brady (20) and Wilmore (18) led Michigan. Tech lost to North Carolina in the NIT championship, 84–66.[89]

In the NCAA tourney, Western Kentucky was bounced by Villanova (whose wins were subsequently vacated because star Howard Porter had signed a pro contract), 92–89, and Villanova lost to UCLA in the championship game, 68–62, for the fifth consecutive NCAA championship for UCLA. On the date of the championship game, Indiana announced that it had hired a new coach, Bobby Knight, the 31-year-old coach at Army and a former Ohio State player. His impact on the league would be felt, but not immediately. Minnesota also hired a new coach after George Hanson resigned after one season, saying that his record (11–13, 5–9 conference) was unsatisfactory. In his place, the Gophers selected Bill Musselman from Ashland College. His impact would be felt the next year in a manner that few coaches would envy.[90]

The 1971–72 season looked extremely bright for the Big Ten, what with the great success of the league's sophomores. The new policy allowing Big Ten teams to play in the NIT added to the prestige and recruiting potential for the conference. Shortly after the season ended, George McGinnis followed the lead of Ralph Simpson, who had left Michigan State after his sophomore season to sign a contract with the American Basketball Association's Denver Nuggets. McGinnis signed with his hometown Indiana Pacers, despite the fact that Simpson had professed great disillusionment with his own signing, noting that most of his big pay was deferred until his 40s, 50s and 60s. The loss of McGinnis and the addition of Knight would significantly alter Indiana basketball the next year, but it was not clear precisely how.

## The 1972 Season

The 1971–72 season looked to be another year with UCLA in the national title mix, but many observers did not see them winning another title; after all, they would be dependent on an unproven sophomore, Bill Walton, in the center position, as well as two other sophomores, Greg Lee and Keith Wilkes, to provide vital scoring and minutes. Instead, some pundits, like *Sports Illustrated*'s staff writers, selected Marquette as the #1 team in the nation, after their top performance the prior year, and the return of players like Bob Lackey, Jim Chones and Marcus Washington. *SI* selected North Carolina in the #2 slot, followed by Long Beach State, UCLA and Maryland. Ohio State was tabbed at #6, with Minnesota, even with a new coach and a number of junior college transfers, at #20. The other teams that they saw contending for the Big Ten title were Purdue, Illinois and Michigan.[91]

*Street & Smith's*, the famous baseball magazine publisher, had ventured into basketball, and their picks for national stature in 1971–72 were the following: 1. USC, 2. North Carolina, 3. Ohio State, 4. Long Beach State, 5. Jacksonville, 6. UCLA, 7. Marquette, and down at 18, Michigan. In the Big Ten, Bob Pille of the *Chicago Sun-Times* saw Indiana, Purdue and Minnesota trailing the Bucks and the Wolverines. Pille's closing comment on Minnesota would prove to be prescient: "How far the Gophers rise above last season's 11–13 could be determined by 6–7 junior college star Clyde Turner and some JC imports."[92]

The various pundits seemed spot-on, initially, as Ohio State started off well. In December contests, the Buckeyes were upset by Ohio University, but won the rest of their contests until December 30, when they were crushed by the defending national champions, UCLA, 79–53, in the Bruin Classic in Los Angeles. All the UCLA starters were in double figures, while OSU had Witte with 19, Gerhardt with 12 and Hornyak with 10. Bill Walton, just a sophomore, was dominant, causing Dave Merchant to gush that "he was the best player I have ever seen."[93] OSU came back to beat Creighton the next week and maintained their top-ten ranking headed into the Big Ten season.[94]

Minnesota also started well with key wins against Butler and TCU, but key losses to Temple in Hawaii and to Marquette in Milwaukee, 55–40. Marquette was topping everyone, including Big Ten rivals Michigan and Wisconsin. It was still hard to tell how good the Big Ten was and who would take the title, since all Big Ten teams had won every home game that they had played by December 16, and the overall league won-lost record was 34–12. Some victories were quite notable, such as Indiana's rout of Notre Dame, 94–29, on December 18, or Indiana and Michigan State's defeats of Kentucky, in Louisville, 90–89, and in Lexington, 91–85, respectively.[95]

It was not all good news, however. In late December, it appeared that Michigan star Henry Wilmore might be lost for the entire season. Coach Johnny Orr said that he had fallen making a layup against Ohio University and the initial prognosis was very pessimistic. Center Ken Brady was already gone, having had knee surgery in October, but the hope was that he'd return in January. In Columbus, Allan Hornyak was coming back from a heel injury that was limiting his minutes, causing him to play as a reserve in the mid–December OSU games.[96]

Christmas brought better news for many, of course. For labor leader Jimmy Hoffa, it meant he would be freed from prison, as President Nixon commuted his sentence for jury tampering and mail fraud, after he had served nearly five years in Lewisburg Federal Penitentiary. For Johnny Orr, it was the revelation that Henry Wilmore would be ready for the Big Ten opener on January 8, and that Ken Brady would be able to play in the Far West Classic in Portland right after Christmas.[97]

The first day of the Big Ten season brought few surprises as Illinois topped Northwestern, 67–63; Ohio State defeated Purdue, 78–70; Michigan edged Michigan State, 83–75; Wisconsin topped Iowa, 81–80; and Minnesota slowed down Indiana (who were outscored, 6–0, in the final minutes), 52–50, in the Barn, before 19,121, a total that would never be reached again because fans were sitting in the aisles, arousing the ire of the fire marshal. For OSU, Hornyak had 28, picking up where he left off the prior season. In Ann Arbor, Wilmore had 21 and was helped greatly by Ernie Johnson with 24. In Minneapolis, junior college transfers Clyde Turner and Ron Behagan had 14 each, to lead the Gophers.[98]

The next week began with another Michigan victory as they defeated Illinois, 75–70, with five players in double figures, led by Johnson's 19. The latest UPI poll had UCLA as #1, followed by Marquette, UNC, South Carolina and Penn with Ohio State at #8, Illinois at #14 and Indiana at #20.[99]

Dave Winfield, more famous as a Hall of Fame outfielder for six major league baseball teams, was a starter on the 1972 Big Ten champions, the Minnesota Golden Gophers (University of Minnesota Athletics).

The end of the week found the first of a number of coach-player differences that would emerge in the Big Ten this season as Coach Brad Snyder of Northwestern suspended leading returning scorer, Barry Moran, for what he called "loafing." Moran said that they had long had a personality conflict. Moran would not be invited to return to the basketball team for the remainder of the season. In game action, Purdue topped Illinois, 85–74; Wisconsin nipped Indiana in overtime, 66–64; Ohio State had a decisive win over Michigan, 84–73, with Hornyak scoring 25 and Luke Witte 20. Wilmore had 26 for Michigan. Wisconsin's win was crafted without two starters, Leon Howard and Gary Watson, and a key reserve, Lamont Weaver, all suspended by Coach John Powless because of curfew violations.[100]

Even the return of the suspended players could not keep Wisconsin from losing to Minnesota in Madison, 65–59. Keith Young had 27 and Ron Behagan 17 for the Gophers. Frasor had 16 and Lee Oler 14 for the Badgers.[101]

Secret peace talks on Vietnam were being held, but they were abruptly halted when the North Vietnamese said that President Nixon broke a pledge not to disclose those talks. His doing so, it was speculated, had to do with his upcoming trip to China and his re-election campaign.[102]

On the weekend of January 21–22, Iowa played in Chicago Stadium and upset South Carolina, the #4-ranked team in the nation, 91–85. Iowa was not a strong Big Ten team, so it was difficult to discern if South Carolina was just off for this game, or whether the Big Ten was that good in 1971–72. Rick Williams, a 6'3" guard, dropped 40 and Kevin Kunnert, the 7' center, had 20 points and 14 rebounds to lead the Hawkeyes. Kevin Joyce and Tom Riker, the two potential All-Americans for the Gamecocks, had 20 and 18, respectively. In conference play, Michigan, Minnesota and Ohio State all won. Michigan had a surprisingly tough time with Northwestern before winning, 83–79. Minnesota had an easier time in East Lansing, winning 67–57, behind 31 by Clyde Turner and 23 from Ron Behagan. Mike Robinson, the sensational Spartan sophomore, was held to 15. Ohio State won a decisive game with Indiana, 80–74, in Columbus. Hornyak had 36 and Witte 21. John Ritter led Indiana with 27.[103]

The weekend games left Ohio State and Minnesota as the only two unbeaten squads in the Big Ten, and #6 and #16 rankings in the country, making the clash in Minneapolis two nights later, on January 25, a real key to the season of both teams. Under new coach Bill Musselman, the Gophers had been winning and drawing great crowds. Musselman had started a type of Globetrotter warm-up at Ashland College with his players dribbling and handling the ball in entertaining manners, to the tune of "Sweet Georgia Brown." The fans went a bit wild and it carried over into their cheering in the game. Musselman adapted the same routine at Minnesota, even bringing his manager with him to Minnesota on a scholarship, to lead the warm-up, juggling four balls and doing various dribbling routines. The Minnesota crowds loved it, even if the other teams did not. The Big Ten opener had drawn 19,121, but the fire marshal, as noted earlier, would not allow that to occur again. The seating capacity of 17,800 would be strictly enforced. The game had been a sellout for a couple weeks. Coincidentally, the game was on the same night as the National Hockey League's All-Star game, which was being played in the Minnesota North Stars' Met Center Arena, not far away in Bloomington.[104]

Luke Witte was an All-Big Ten center, most famously known as the victim of the Minnesota–Ohio State brawl in January of 1972. He played briefly in the NBA before becoming a minister (The Ohio State University Archives).

The game was rugged and deliberate. The fans were quite raucous, both because of the warm-up and because of memories of the narrow loss that OSU had inflicted upon the Gophers at home the previous season. The first half ended with a foul by Witte in which he hit a Minnesota player (Bob Nix) in the head on a drive. That seemed innocuous enough until the events that occurred later.

With 36 seconds left in the game, and OSU leading 50–44, Witte was fouled hard by Turner on a put-back and went down. Corky Taylor leaned down, apparently to help him up, but instead, kneed him hard to the groin. Taylor said afterward that Witte had spat on him (but later changed that allegation, and days later went back to it). Then, the tension exploded into malevolent action as players came off both benches, but it was the Minnesota players who seemed intent on real mayhem. While Witte writhed on the floor, Ron Behagan, who had fouled out with 13:34 to go in the game, ran to Witte and stomped on his head. Fans came out of the stands to join in the melee. When order was restored, Taylor was hit with an automatic ejection for a "flagrant personal foul." That action was moot, since the commissioner of the Big Ten, Wayne Duke, was in the audience. After consulting with the referees, Duke declared the contest over, with Ohio State the 50–44 winner. Wardell Jackson had led the Bucks with 16 and Witte had 14, while Turner was the leading Gopher with 13. Three OSU players were taken to the hospital—Witte, Mark Minor and Mark Wager.[105]

The ramifications from the fight would take center stage in the Big Ten basketball race, drawing attention from the actual games. The next day, it was announced that Big Ten Commissioner Duke would begin a probe in coordination with the Universities of Minnesota and Ohio State. Corky Taylor, the instigator of the fight, was quoted as saying, "As I tried to pick Witte up, he spat on me," and he then reacted with a knee to Witte's groin. Max Nichols, sports editor of the *Minneapolis Star*, who was at the game, said that there was no excuse for the action. Dave Merchant, standing right behind Witte, said that the spitting story was just that, a story. He was frightened when the fans stormed out of the stands to escalate the fight, because, with the raised floor in "the Barn," there was nowhere to run. He ran to a corner of the court and saw Wager and Minor being beaten by Dave Winfield as Minnesota fans held the OSU players.[106] The game was rough, but not unusual, and the allegation of spitting (later withdrawn) certainly was not enough to warrant such a reaction. Nichols totally supported the suspensions, but only regretted that Winfield was also not punished, since he was pounding Mark Minor directly in front of Nichols, but it was apparently not caught on any films from the game.[107] Nichols was not the only one to notice Winfield's actions. *Minneapolis Star* reporter Dick Gordon, in his account of the game, reported, "Dave Winfield singled out Minor and got in some real punches."[108]

Coach Fred Taylor thought that the game's atmosphere and resultant frenzy that brought fans out of the stands to join in the melee and the battering of Buckeyes was a result, at least indirectly, of the Minnesota warm-ups that incited the fans. Taylor was quoted as saying that he was going to ask Commissioner Duke "to order the Gophers to cease their pregame warmups."[109] He also said that he did not find the suspensions of Taylor and Behagan "tough enough." Johnny Orr, Michigan coach, thought that Musselman should be punished, too.[110]

Five days after the melee, Ohio State, playing without Witte or Wagar, who were both out with concussions, faced Michigan in Ann Arbor. The Wolverines won, 88–

78, with Wilmore scoring 26 and Johnson 19. Hornyak had 24 and Jackson 14 for OSU. In what seemed to be an effort to call every possible foul, the referees assessed OSU with 32 fouls and Michigan with 18. Five Buckeyes fouled out and three Wolverines. OSU had one more bucket, 29 to Michigan's 28, but the home team was 32–50 from the line, compared to 20–25 by the Buckeyes. That same evening the Gophers played in Iowa City in a much more deliberate game (the *Minneapolis Star* referred to the Gophers as "gracious" in the contest),[111] which saw the Gophers triumph, 61–50, to move into a tie for the Big Ten lead. Indiana blew a chance to keep pace by losing at Michigan State, 83–73, as Mike Robinson went for 34 for the Spartans.[112]

One week after the events in Minneapolis, Witte was cleared to play against Iowa. Roy Damer of the *Chicago Tribune*, reporting on his return, described the violent game's events as "revolting beatings carried out by Gopher players and fans" and "an exhibition of crazed animal behavior." The game was close, but Witte seemed to be relatively unaffected by the concussion, as he scored 17 points and took 14 rebounds in the 82–77 Ohio State victory. Despite the appearance, Merchant said that Witte, who had been getting better and better, never really recovered and did not show that level of improvement ever again.[113] Alan Hornyak scored 37 points to lead all scorers, while Rick Williams (24) and Kevin Kunnert (23) led Iowa. This was the only Big Ten game that night, but there was plenty of other news as the Big Ten athletic directors approved "red-shirting" beginning the next season, something most other major schools and conferences had already approved. There were also efforts made at reconciling grants-in-aid and grade requirements between the NCAA and the stricter Big Ten rules. In addition, the athletic directors ratified Commissioner Duke's and the University of Minnesota's suspensions of Taylor and Behagan for the rest of the season (and they would not be allowed to practice with the team), although, as it turned out, Minnesota may only have supported a three-game suspension for the two.[114]

The Minnesota suspensions would be news for the remainder of the season as appeals continued, but so did the Big Ten season. Michigan's chances were hurt by a loss at Purdue, 84–74. Rob Ford (29) and Bill Franklin (28) were the biggest contributors, while Wilmore (26) and Johnson (15) led the Wolverines. OSU stayed winning against Wisconsin, 79–69 with Gerhard (19) and Jackson (18) the unusual leading scorers. Minnesota defeated Iowa, 53–52, without any incidents.[115]

Continuing an unwelcome trend for this Big Ten season, Coach Harv Schmidt suspended center Bill Morris "for an attitude detrimental to the club," just before the Northwestern game, but the Illini still topped the Wildcats, 68–57, with Conner and Weatherspoon leading the attack with 16 and 15, respectively. Mark Sibley had 16 for Northwestern. Morris did not help himself two days later when he missed the Illinois flight to Michigan State for the game in East Lansing. He had been reinstated to the team the day before. It was too bad for all parties concerned, because the Illini could have used him, as they lost to MSU, 89–79. Mike Robinson, the small (5'9") but incredibly quick shooter, had 29 for the Spartans. Weatherspoon led the Illini with 22.[116]

During this period, the sports pages of newspapers, nationwide and internationally, were led by the outcomes of events at the 1972 Winter Olympic Games in Sapporo, Japan. Of the most interest to *Chicago Tribune* readers were the speed skating events in which skaters from Northbrook, Illinois, a northern suburb of Chicago, were dominant. Diane Holum and Anne Henning took all four of the American medals in the speed skating events, with each taking a gold, Holum a silver, and Henning a bronze.

Back in the Big Ten race, both Ohio State and Minnesota lost on February 8, the Buckeyes in Iowa City, 80–67, and the Gophers in a slowdown at Indiana, 61–42. Joby Wright had 23 and Steve Downing 19 in a game totally dominated by the Hoosiers, who led 37–18 at the half. Jim Brewer had 10 for Minnesota. The deliberate, defense-dominating Indiana game was a foreshadowing of Indiana and the Big Ten's shift over the next decade. In Iowa, Rick Williams had 23 and Gary Lusk 22 for the Hawks. Hornyak matched Williams with 23 for OSU.[117]

In an announcement that same day, the NCAA changed the basketball semifinals and finals for the next season from Thursday-Saturday to Saturday-Monday. The NCAA gave three reasons for the shift: (1) for television (*Monday Night Football* had opened up this night to major sporting events; (2) players would miss less class time; (3) players would get more rest. Roy Damer, the *Tribune*'s Big Ten basketball writer, countered that both of the latter two were not so, thus the only reason to shift was for television. Not surprisingly, there would be a new contract in 1973.[118] The latest UPI poll had UCLA, Marquette, UNC, Louisville and Penn as the top five teams. Ohio State was #7, the only Big Ten team ranked in the top 20.

The criticism for creating the atmosphere that led to the Minnesota attacks on OSU on January 25 was pointed, by many, at Coach Bill Musselman. Reporters went to Ashland College for comments on his coaching patterns there and got quite an earful. The feelings toward Musselman were really a dichotomized love/hate situation. These comments started with his semi-Globetrotters pre-game routine and continued through the actions and attitudes of his players during games. There were two prior fight incidents, both the fault of the Ashland players, during Musselman's tenure, and many quoted Musselman himself, who preached the mantra, "Defeat is worse than death." Interestingly, one of Musselman's critics and sharpest observers was Luke Witte's father, who was a professor of philosophy at Ashland.[119]

Taylor and Behagan retained attorneys, who sued in U.S. District Court to end the players' suspension. These proceedings would continue to hang over the Big Ten season, especially since the Gophers kept winning and Minnesota might represent the Big Ten in the NCAA tourney. Ohio State, meanwhile, had Witte and Wagar back, but lost Gerhard to mononucleosis. Both teams won on February 12 and they were tied for first, with Michigan close behind. No other team in the league was over .500.[120]

The restraining order requested by the attorney for Behagan and Taylor was denied, but a hearing was set for later in the month on a requested injunction against the Big Ten. On February 19, the Illini defeated Ohio State in the regionally televised Big Ten Game of the Week, 64–62, in Champaign. Weatherspoon had 20 and Jim Krelle 14 for Illinois, while Hornyak had 23 and Gerhard (apparently recovered from what had to be a misdiagnosis of mono), 13. The game was lost at the foul line, where the Bucks were just 12–28 and the Illini 34–46. Four Bucks and one Illini fouled out. Minnesota snatched first place with a 76–73 victory over Wisconsin. Clyde Turner had 29 to lead all scorers, while Bob Frasor and Gary Anderson each had 14 for Wisconsin.[121] The latest AP poll had no changes at the top, but OSU had fallen to #15 and both Minnesota and Michigan were now listed as "others receiving votes."

The judicial hearing for Behagan and Taylor was set for February 24. The U.S. District Judge had ruled that the two should get a hearing before the Big Ten Athletic Directors in order to satisfy the issue of due process. The judge also noted that the Big Ten had no constitution and was governed by "precedents and formal resolutions."

That same day Angela Davis was released on bail, accused of supplying guns in the shooting at the Marin County Courthouse in August of 1970, where four were killed, including Superior Court Judge Harold Haley. She was found not guilty in her trial later in 1972. Internationally, President Richard Nixon was in China, following the visits of Henry Kissinger that had led to the opening of diplomatic relations between the U.S. and China.[122]

The Big Ten Athletic Directors, by an 8–0 vote (Minnesota and OSU abstaining), upheld the suspensions, and the effect on Minnesota was immediate, as the Gophers lost to Michigan, 64–52, in Ann Arbor. Wilmore had 20 to lead the Wolverines and Brady tossed in 17. Winfield and Turner each had 15 for Minnesota. The victory moved Michigan into the Big Ten lead. The game was won in the second half, when Michigan went 16–24 (67 percent) from the floor and Minnesota went 7–38 (18 percent). For the game, the Gophers shot 22–70 (31 percent) and the Wolverines 26–51 (51 percent).[123]

In less "meaningful" action, Illinois, behind 26 from Nick Weatherspoon, and two-platoon basketball, topped Michigan State, 91–86, and Purdue edged Indiana, 70–69, in West Lafayette, after the Hoosiers blew a nine-point lead with 13:11 remaining. The Boilermakers were led by Rob Ford with 24, but were shaken by the loss of leading scorer Bill Franklin, who had hired an agent the day before, and was immediately ineligible.[124]

On the last day of February, the Big Ten race flipped over again. Ohio State and Minnesota won, while Michigan lost, putting the Gophers and Buckeyes back into the conference lead. OSU had romped past Illinois, 103–70, behind Hornyak's 27 and Jackson's 23. Minnesota, playing just five men, had ground out a 48–43 win over Purdue. Michigan was upset by Indiana, 79–75, before 13,908 Hoosier fans, as Wright scored 26 and Downing 19. Wilmore (27) and Grabiec (24) were high for the Wolverines.[125]

Four days later, Minnesota claimed the Big Ten lead after defeating Illinois, 91–62. A sloppy 31 Illinois turnovers made the Gopher win that much easier. The game drew 14,666 and helped Minnesota set an all-time home attendance record with 157,209 for the year. Ohio State, playing in Indiana before 16,492, lost 65–57, despite a game-high 25 by Hornyak. Downing (21) and Wright (19) led the Hoosiers, as usual. Michigan State hurt Michigan's chances with a 96–92 win in East Lansing. Mike Robinson was unstoppable, with 37 points for the Spartans. Wilmore (22) and Lockard (21) led Michigan's scoring. The Big Ten standings had Minnesota at 10–3, Ohio State 9–4, Michigan 8–4, and Indiana 7–5. The AP poll continued to have undefeated UCLA at #1, with Penn, UNC, Louisville and Long Beach State following. Minnesota was #16 (16–6) and Indiana #20 (15–7).[126]

The race ended three days later when Minnesota won at Purdue, 49–48. Again playing just five players, the Gophers were led by Turner and Brewer, each with 12. Ford had 24 for Purdue. Indiana and Ohio State kept pace, but it was too late for them; Indiana won over Northwestern, 72–67, and Ohio State beat Michigan State, 92–73, despite Mike Robinson's 30 points for the Spartans.[127]

The next day, the Faculty Athletic Representatives also voted 8–0 to uphold the suspensions of Behagan and Taylor, meaning that the two would not be eligible for the NCAA tournament. In reporting this, Roy Damer of the *Chicago Tribune* noted that Ohio State was "not the same team after January 25, when they led the league with a 4–0 record." Dave Merchant echoed that, saying that both Witte and Coach Taylor spent too much time feeling sorry about what had happened."[128] Mark Wagar said that "the team simply lost focus, especially with the constant questions about the melee. Plus the continual legal wrangling by the lawyers for the Minnesota players kept the focus on that and it did spill over to the OSU players."[129] In that same meeting, the athletic reps also gave final approval to freshman competition in varsity football and basketball. It would be a new day for Big Ten football and basketball starting in the fall of 1972.[130]

The NIT came calling at that point and Indiana answered the call, while Ohio State did not. According to Ohio State athletic administrators, "The boys feel now that they want to turn to the exams and rest." The "boys" didn't see it quite that way. Merchant said that there was a real split between those who had made Spring Break plans or were just ready to end the season, and those who wanted to go to Madison Square Garden and play. The former faction won out and had been supported by Coach Taylor, who had really changed after the melee in Minnesota and looked back a lot, rather than forward, according to Merchant.[131] Wagar said that many of the players were just disillusioned by the season, questioning, "What's it really all about? Who needs it?"[132]

The season was not quite over, and another player issue arose just before the last game when Illinois captain Jim Krelle quit the team. No explanation was given and the Illini lost their final game the next day, 97–84, to Wisconsin. Lee Oler led the Badgers with 21, while Weatherspoon (28) and Morris (19) were leading scorers for Illinois. Iowa topped Michigan, obviously down from their elimination from the Big Ten title, 95–69, in Iowa City. Ricky Williams led the winners with 23, while Wilmore had 27 in his last game for the Wolverines.[133]

### Final Standings and MVPs, 1971–72

| | | |
|---|---|---|
| Minnesota | 11–3 | Jim Brewer (Big Ten MVP) |
| Ohio State | 10–4 | Mark Minor |
| Indiana | 9–5 | Joby Wright |
| Michigan | 9–5 | Henry Wilmore |
| Purdue | 6–8 | Rob Ford |
| Wisconsin | 6–8 | Leon Howard |
| Michigan State | 6–8 | Bill Kilgore |
| Illinois | 5–9 | Nick Weatherspoon |
| Iowa | 5–9 | Kevin Kunnert and Ricky Williams |
| Northwestern | 3–11 | Paul Douglass |

The All-Big Ten teams were as follows:

FIRST TEAM

Hornyak (OSU), Wilmore (MI), Wright (IU), Robinson (MSU), Ford (Purdue), Turner (MN).

SECOND TEAM

Williams (IA), Howard (WI), Kunnert (IA), Witte (OSU), Downing (IU).

The UPI All-American team had Hornyak on the second team, Wilmore on the third and Witte, Honorable Mention.

The NCAA tourney started on March 11 and, in the Mideast, Marquette defeated Ohio University, 73–49, and would meet Kentucky in Dayton. Minnesota was to meet Florida State, a winner over Eastern Kentucky, 83–81. But then, Marquette was ruled ineligible because Bob Lackey would not sign a statement affirming that he had no agent and had not signed a pro contract; this was done on advice of Coach Al McGuire. The Warriors had already lost first team All-American Jim Chones, who had signed a contract with an agent with five games to go in the season and was immediately ineligible. The NCAA's president, Earl Ramer, the faculty representative of the University of Tennessee, stated, "The NCAA intends to let the American people know that we stand for honesty and integrity."[134] If Marquette were to be declared ineligible, then Ohio University would take their place in the next round of the tournament, but the next day, Marquette was reinstated when Lackey signed the required document. The crisis was over and basketball, not legal issues, would take center stage, at least for a while.[135]

On March 16, both Marquette and Minnesota lost, Marquette to Kentucky, 85–69, and Minnesota to Florida State, 70–56, before 13,458, in Dayton. The two teams played, two nights later, for third place in the Mideast regional, and Minnesota won 77–72 behind 25 by Turner, 18 by Young and 22 rebounds by Brewer. The Gophers shot 47 percent from the floor to 36 percent by Marquette. Both teams had lost key players during the year and "what might have been" had to be in the minds of all concerned.[136]

The Final Four would be Florida State, Louisville, North Carolina and UCLA, but the Big Ten season wasn't over until Indiana lost to Princeton, 68–60, on March 19, in the NIT. Joby Wright had 21 and Steve Downing 14 as the Hoosiers went out in the first round, but finished the season ranked #20 by the AP.[137]

UCLA would go on to win their eighth consecutive title, defeating Florida State, 81–76, on March 25. What was new about this tourney was the new television coverage of the NCAA semifinals, live from Los Angeles, on NBC, although it was only for one of the games, Florida State versus North Carolina, at 6 p.m. (PST). The championship game on Saturday, March 25, 1972, was also shown live on NBC, starting at noon PST from the Los Angeles Sports Arena. The NIT championship was also telecast that afternoon, on CBS, starting at 2 p.m. in the east, from Madison Square Garden.[138]

The Big Ten season had been tumultuous, and it marked the end of an era because of all the changes that would go into effect in 1973. Half of the Big Ten MVPs were underclassmen and seven of the eleven Big Ten First and Second teamers would be returning in 1972–73. Freshmen would be eligible to play varsity the next year and red-shirting would be possible. It promised to be a different and better season for the conference.

# *Afterword*

From its inception, the Western Conference was recognized as the football power conference of the west, rivaling and then surpassing its eastern "equivalent," the Ivy League. Most of the eastern schools remained as independents for a long time. In the west, conferences formed more quickly. As for the Western Conference, the Big Ten, it soon grew into a basketball powerhouse, as basketball became more prominent on college campuses and in the national media.

In the 1930s, the Big Ten may have been the best conference in the nation, but there was little intersectional play and no national tournament that could cement such a claim. The creation of a "national" tournament at the end of the 1937–38 season was an effort to correct this uncertainty, but there were only six teams, with three from the East, one from the Rockies, one from the Great Plains and one from the Midwest. None were from the Big Ten and little was really proven when Temple University captured the tournament.

The 1939 National Association of Basketball Coaches tournament, which was co-sponsored by the NCAA, was a better effort at a true national tournament, with an eastern and western set of teams. Ohio State represented the Big Ten as one of the selected teams, finishing second to Oregon in a game played at a Big Ten venue, Patten Gym on the Northwestern University campus. This was an eight-team tournament, but it expanded, first to 16 teams in 1951, then to 22 in 1953, and 25 by 1974, all the time limiting a conference to one team.

Over the period from 1939 to 1972, a Big Ten team appeared in the championship contest ten times, second to the Pacific 8's 13 (with eight of those appearances being UCLA). More impressive, however, was the number of Final Four appearances by Big Ten teams during that period (21) with the Pacific Coast (or Pac 8) second with 19. Of those 19, nine were by one school, however, with five different Pacific schools represented. Of the 21 Final Four appearances by Big Ten teams, eight different schools were represented, showing both power and balance in the conference. Third was the Missouri Valley with 10 Final Four appearances during that time. The Southeastern Conference had six Final Fours, all by Kentucky. The Atlantic Coast Conference, not created until 1953–54, had eight Final Four appearances from that period until 1972. Two schools that were later part of the new conference were in the Final Four before the creation of the league, North Carolina in 1946 and N.C. State in 1950.

The Big Ten was, at times, a mirror as to the social or global situations of the nation. Regarding the latter, World War II had a significant effect upon the conference, and rules regarding eligibility reflected that. Freshmen were eligible during and directly after the war, since there were so many athletes who had enlisted or were drafted into the service during this period of time. Eligibility was extended for older, returning servicemen after the war.

It was also during the war that the league became integrated in basketball with the appearance of Dick Culberson for Iowa in 1944. Culberson was part of a naval unit stationed in Virginia, and he had played at Virginia Union, before he was transferred to Iowa and played for the Hawkeyes, while part of the naval unit on campus. Culberson's time in a Hawkeye uniform would have made the further integration of the conference by Bill Garrett playing for Indiana in 1948 a bit easier. By 1954, at the time of the *Brown v. Board of Education of Topeka* ruling, the conference would have six schools that had African American basketball players. As the Civil Rights Movement began to accelerate, the other four schools integrated their teams, with Minnesota and Wisconsin the last to do so in 1963.[1]

The Vietnam War was a national issue from the early 1960s, but became *the* national issue from the period 1965 to 1974, and much of the dissent against the war played out on college campuses. Players and coaches were not immune to such demonstrations, which sometimes created rifts among teammates or between coaches and teammates. Still, there were not the same kind of concessions to the war that occurred during World War II, mostly because freshmen had become eligible as of July of 1972, and would have four years of eligibility, negating a need for another "special" legislation.

Television, obviously, became more and more important to college basketball in the 1970s, and the Big Ten seemed to be a leader in that arena also. As early as the 1950s, the Big Ten had a loosely organized series of stations that carried some Big Ten games. By the early 1960s this had become a network of sorts, put together by a compiler, with regular Saturday afternoon telecasts to each of the Big Ten viewing areas. Sadly, neither the Big Ten, nor affected television stations, nor the Big Ten institutions themselves, have archival records of these agreements. Only television schedules and oral recall brings this to life. Quite a contrast to what would become today's Big Ten Network.

The eligibility of freshmen for four years of intercollegiate play would change all of the major conferences, including the Big Ten, and would also directly impact recruitment. The creation of the American Basketball Association, which signed players before their eligibility was completed, also had an impact on recruitment. In the Big Ten, the signing of Ralph Simpson and George McGinnis would open the door to more signings and alter the way coaches would plan for their teams' long-range possibilities. Compounding that would be the signing of Moses Malone out of high school by the ABA, and his reneging on an agreement to go to the University of Maryland.

The signing of Bob Knight as the new head coach at Indiana for the 1971–72 season was not initially seen as an act that would have enormous ramifications for the manner in which Big Ten basketball was played. Knight's emphasis on defense would change the way the entire conference played, especially when that emphasis led to such unqualified success.

Thus, it seems most appropriate to end this volume as the Big Ten embarked on a new era with younger rosters, a new direction on manner of play, and the movement to begin the "winding down" of the war in Vietnam. The Big Ten had a bright future, one that was matched by a glorious past.

# Appendix 1: The First African American Players at Each Big Ten University

1944–45—Dick Culberson, Iowa (one year as transfer from Virginia Union)
1948–49—Bill Garrett, Indiana
1951–52—Don Eaddy, John Codwell, Michigan
1951—Ernest Hall (dropped from team in February 1952), Purdue
1952–53—Deacon Davis, Iowa; Rickey Ayala, Michigan State
1953–54—Cleo Vaughn, Ohio State; Wally Choice, Indiana
1954–55—Lamar Lundy, Purdue
1957–58—Govonor Vaughn, Mannie Jackson, Illinois
1958–59—Willie Jones, Northwestern
1959–60—Ralph Wells, Northwestern
1963–64—Archie Clark, Lou Hudson, Don Yates, Minnesota
1963–64—Ken Barnes, Wisconsin

# Appendix 2: Big Ten Coaches, 1947–1972

Illinois: Harry Combes (1947–67), Harve Schmidt (1967–74)

Indiana: Branch McCracken (1938–43, 46–65), Lou Watson (1966–72)

Iowa: Pops Harrison (1942–50), Rollie Williams (1950–51), Bucky O'Connor (1951–58), Sharm Scheuerman (1959–64), Ralph Miller (1964–1970), Dick Schultz (1970-74)

Michigan: Ozzie Cowles (1946–48), Ernie McCoy (1948–52), Bill Perigo (1952–60), Dave Strack (1960–68), Johnny Orr (1968–80)

Michigan State: Ben Van Alstyne (1926–49), Alton Kircher (1949–50), Pete Newell (1950–54), Fordy Anderson (1954–65), John Bennington (1965–69), Gus Ganakas (1969–76)

Minnesota: Dave McMillan (1927–42, 1945–48), Ozzie Cowles (1948–59), John Kundla (1959–68), Bill Fitch (1968–70), George Hanson (1970–71), Bill Musselman (1971–75)

Northwestern: Arthur Lonborg (1927–50), Harold Olsen (1950–52), Waldo Fisher (1952–57), Bill Rohr (1957–63), Larry Glass (1963–69), Brad Snyder (1969–73)

Ohio State: Harold Olsen (1923–46), Tippy Dye (1946–51), Floyd Stahl (1951–58), Fred Taylor (1958–76)

Purdue: Mel Taube (1946–51), Ray Eddy (1951–65), George King (1965–72)

Wisconsin: Harold "Bud" Foster (1934–59), John Erickson (1959–68), John Powless (1968–76)

# Appendix 3:
# Big Ten Champions, 1943–1972

| Team | Coach |
|---|---|
| 1943 Illinois (12–0) | Doug Mills |
| 1944 Ohio State (10–2) | Harold Olsen |
| 1945 Iowa (11–1) | "Pops" Harrison |
| 1946 Ohio State | Harold Olsen |
| 1947 Wisconsin | Harold "Bud" Foster |
| 1948 Michigan (10–2) | Ozzie Cowles |
| 1949 Illinois (10–2) | Harry Combes |
| 1950 Ohio State (11–1) | Tippy Dye |
| 1951 Illinois (13–1) | Harry Combes |
| 1952 Illinois (12–2) | Harry Combes |
| 1953 Indiana (17–1) | Branch McCracken |
| 1954 Indiana (12–2) | Branch McCracken |
| 1955 Iowa (11–3) | Bucky O'Connor |
| 1956 Iowa (13–1) | Bucky O'Connor |
| 1957 Indiana (10–4) tie | Branch McCracken |
| 1957 Michigan State (10–4) tie | Fordy Anderson |
| 1958 Indiana (10–4) | Branch McCracken |
| 1959 Michigan State (12–2) | Fordy Anderson |
| 1960 Ohio State (13–1) | Fred Taylor |
| 1961 Ohio State (14–0) | Fred Taylor |
| 1962 Ohio State (13–1) | Fred Taylor |
| 1963 Ohio State (11–3) tie | Fred Taylor |
| 1963 Illinois (11–3) tie | Harry Combes |
| 1964 Michigan (11–3) | Dave Strack |
| 1964 Ohio State (11–3) | Fred Taylor |
| 1965 Michigan (13–1) | Dave Strack |
| 1966 Michigan (11–3) | Dave Strack |
| 1967 Indiana (10–4) tie | Lou Watson |
| 1967 Michigan State (10–4) tie | John Bennington |
| 1968 Ohio State (10–4) tie | Fred Taylor |
| 1968 Iowa (10–4) tie | Ralph Miller |

1969 Purdue (13–1)          George King
1970 Iowa (14–0)            Ralph Miller
1971 Ohio State (13–1)      Fred Taylor
1972 Minnesota (11–3)       Bill Musselman

# Chapter Notes

## Chapter 1

1. Kenneth L. (Tug) Wilson's *The Big Ten*, written with Jerry Brondfield, provides the best official history of the conference. Wilson served as the second Big Ten Commissioner from 1945 to 1961.
2. Dale Raterman, *The Big Ten: A Century of Excellence* (Champaign, IL: Sagamore Publishing, 1996).
3. *Spalding's Official Basketball Guide, 1927–28* (New York: American Sports Publishing, 1927), p. 121.
4. See Murry Nelson, *The National Basketball League: A History, 1935–1949* (Jefferson, NC: McFarland, 2009) for details on the league and Wooden's performance in it.
5. John Behee, *Hail to the Victors!* (Ann Arbor: Ulrich Books, 1974), p. 39.
6. Oswald Tower, ed., *Spalding's Official Basketball Guide, 1939–40* (New York: American Sports Publishing, 1939), p. 9.
7. This was old Patten Gym, which has since been razed. There is a new Patten Gym on the campus on Sheridan Road.
8. Peter C. Bjarkman, *Big Ten Basketball* (Indianapolis: Masters Press, 1995), p. 100.
9. Bob Hunter, *Buckeye Basketball: Ohio State University* (Huntsville, AL: Strode Publishers, 1981), p. 118.
10. See Jeff Eisenberg, "How the NCAA Bought Its Basketball Tournament in 1940 for Less than the Price of a Used Car Today." http://sports.yahoo.com/blogs/ncaab-the-dagger/ncaa-bought-rights-men-basketball-tournament-shocking-bargain-130045967—ncaab.html.
11. *Lafayette Courier and Journal*, Editor, *Most Memorable Moments in Purdue Basketball History* (Champaign, IL: Sagamore Publishing, 1998), p. 223.
12. http://www.crimsonquarry.com/2012/6/11/3075685/great-expectations-the-1949-50-indiana-hoosiers.
13. Wilson and Brondfield, p. 242.
14. Again, see my NBL book, noted earlier.
15. Bjarkman, p. 198.
16. The most informative source for this is Seymour Smith, Jack Rimer and Dick Triptow's loving work, *A Tribute to Armed Forces Basketball, 1941–1969*.
17. Why would a guy named "Ed" be nicknamed "Jack"? It was all because of the aviation comic strip that originated in the *Chicago Tribune* in 1933, ultimately titled *Smilin' Jack*, with its hero-protagonist, "Smilin' Jack" Martin, which ran until 1973.
18. Wilson and Brondfield, p. 253.
19. "N.U. Beats Great Lakes; 1st Victory," *Chicago Tribune*, January 3, 1943, Pt. 2, p. 1.
20. "Illinois Whips Stanford, N.C.A.A. Champion, 38–26," *Chicago Tribune*, January 3, 1943, Pt. 2, p. 1.
21. "Illinois Wins: Wisconsin Beats N.U. 67 to 65," *Chicago Tribune*, January 10, 1943, Pt. 2, p. 1.
22. "Illinois Beats Wisconsin, 52–40; N.U. Beats Michigan," *Chicago Tribune*, January 12, 1943, Pt. 3, p. 1.
23. "Illinois Defeats N.U., 68–51, for 5th Straight," *Chicago Tribune*, February 2, 1943, p. 15.
24. "Indiana Loses; Illini Win, 67–43, Take Lead," *Chicago Tribune*, February 16, 1943, p. 21.
25. Edward Prell, "Big Ten Waives Freshman Rule for All Sports," *Chicago Tribune*, February 22, 1943, p. 21.
26. "Illini Beats Badgers as Phillip Breaks Record; Indiana Wins," *Chicago Tribune*, February 21, 1943, Pt. 2, p. 1.
27. "Illini Beats Badgers as Phillip Breaks Record; Indiana Wins," *Chicago Tribune*, February 21, 1943, Pt. 2, p. 1; "Illinois Five Wins Title; Breaks 11 Records," *Chicago Tribune*, March 2, 1943, p. 17; "Purdue Deals Indiana Second Setback, 41–38," *Chicago Tribune*, March 2, 1943, p. 17.
28. Wilson and Brondfield, p. 256; "Illini Dominate Big Ten First Team," *Chicago Tribune*, March 4, 1943, p. 21.
29. The poll taken at that time had them as #1 with Wyoming as #2.
30. Wilson and Brondfield, p. 256.
31. Bjarkman, p. 8.
32. Bjarkman, p. 200.
33. Raterman, p. 188.
34. "Depaul to Play in NCAA Meet," *Chicago Tribune*, March 9, 1943, p. 23; "Menke, Smiley, Mathisen Get Calls to Duty," *Chicago Tribune*, March 14, 1943, Pt. 2, p. 1.
35. Wilson and Brondfield, p. 262.
36. "Wildcats Beat Purdue, 63–54: Sailors Win," *Chicago Tribune*, February 2, 1946, p. 15.
37. "N.U. Deals Notre Dame 1st Defeat, 56–55," *Chicago Tribune*, February 3, 1946, Pt. 2, p. 1.
38. "Northwestern Beats Minnesota, 72 to 49," *Chicago Tribune*, February 9, 1946, p. 19.
39. "Iowa Wins; N.U. Beats Illinois, 48 to 43," *Chicago Tribune*, February 17, 1946, Pt. 2, p. 1.
40. "Illini Beat Iowa; Ohio Wins, Leads Big 10," *Chicago Tribune*, February 24, 1946, Pt. 2, p. 1. It might be asked how the Stadium could keep "Expanding" and

getting larger crowds. The answer was complete disregard for any fire laws regarding sitting in the aisles, which was routinely done, or standing throughout the mezzanines, also done as a matter of course. This continued at least through the 1960s, as the author experienced aisle sitting many times at Chicago Blackhawk games.

41. "Indiana Beats Iowa, 49–46, Title to Ohio State," *Chicago Tribune*, February 26, 1946, p. 21; "N.U. Names Max Morris Most Valuable," *Chicago Tribune*, March 1, 1946, p. 29; "Max Morris Leads Big Ten Basket Team," *Chicago Tribune*, March 6, 1946, p. 26. Morris signed almost immediately with the Chicago Rockets of the All American Football Conference and played pro football for three years. He also played pro basketball for four years in the NBL and NBA. He is the last Northwestern athlete to be named first team All-American in both sports.

42. "Musial Discharged, Hitches to Donora to See Folks," *Chicago Tribune*, March 2, 1946, p. 18.

43. Bill Butterfield telephone interview, August 28, 2015.

44. "21 to Ballot on Big Ten's Most Valuable," *Chicago Tribune*, March 7, 1946, p. 32; "Morris Named Big Ten's Most Valuable Player," *Chicago Tribune*, March 17, 1946, Pt. 2, p. 1.

45. "Ohio State Five Beats Harvard," *Chicago Tribune*, March 22, 1946, p. 23; "Oklahoma A&M Wins Western NCAA Crown," *Chicago Tribune*, March 24, 1946, Pt. 2, p. 2.

46. Wilfrid Smith, "Buckeyes Lose Overtime Game," *Chicago Tribune*, March 24, 1946, Pt. 2, p. 1; "Oklahoma A&M Wins College Crown," *Chicago Tribune*, March 28, 1946, p. 25.

47. Mike Douchant, *Encyclopedia of College Basketball* (New York: Gale Research, 1995), p. 45.

## Chapter 2

1. "Illinois Whips Northwestern, 55 to 40," *Chicago Tribune*, January 12, 1947, Pt. 2, p. 1.

2. "Indiana Beats Iowa, 50 to 48; Michigan Wins," *Chicago Tribune*, January 19, 1947, Pt. 2, p. 1; "Purdue Scores 52 to 46 Upset Over Iowa," *Chicago Tribune*, January 21, 1947, Pt. 2, p. 1.

3. Bill Butterfield telephone interview, August 28, 2015.

4. "Illinois Wins; Gophers Beat N.U., 63–61(Ot)," *Chicago Tribune*, February 2, 1947, Pt. 2, p. 1.

5. "Wisconsin Wins in Last 2 Seconds, 52–51," *Chicago Tribune*, February 11, 1947, p. 29; "Badgers Near Title; Defeat N.U., 54–42," *Chicago Tribune*, February 16, 1947, Pt. 2, p. 1.

6. "Illinois Whips Indiana, 59–50; Gains 2d Place," *Chicago Tribune*, February 16, 1947, Pt. 2, p. 1.

7. "Hawkeyes Win," *Chicago Tribune*, February 16, 1947, Pt. 2, p. 1.

8. "Wisconsin Loses; Illinois Beats N.U., 52–51," *Chicago Tribune*, February 23, 1947, Pt., , p. 1.

9. Wilfrid Smith, "Depaul Upsets Notre Dame; N.U. Loses, 62–42," *Chicago Tribune*, March 1, 1947, p. 17.

10. Butterfield interview.

11. "Wisconsin, Illinois Lose; Await Play-Off," *Chicago Tribune*, March 2, 1947, Pt. 2, p. 1.

12. The game had been scheduled for West Lafayette, but with the collapse of the stands, Butler Fieldhouse became the new venue, noted Hiner and Hutchins in their *Indiana University Basketball Encyclopedia*, p. 247.

13. "Indiana Beats Purdue, Retains Title Hope," *Chicago Tribune*, March 4, 1947, p. 21; "Station WGN to Carry Purdue-Wisconsin Game," *Chicago Tribune*, March 5, 1947, p. 30.

14. Butterfield interview.

15. "Selbo Named Big Nine's Most Valuable," *Chicago Tribune*, March 18, 1947, p. 21.

16. "Badgers Beat Illini, 52–47; Northwestern Loses," *Chicago Tribune*, January 3, 1948, Pt. 2, p. 1; "Illini Beat Wildcats; Badgers Win," *Chicago Tribune*, January 6, 1948, p. 25; "Iowa Wins; Wisconsin Beats Indiana, 58–54," *Chicago Tribune*, January 11, 1948, Pt. 2, p. 1.

17. "Wisconsin Beats Iowa, 60–51; N.U. Wins," *Chicago Tribune*, January 13, 1948, p. 25; "Michigan Beats Badgers, 43–39; Illini Lose," *Chicago Tribune*, January 18, 1948, Pt. 2, p. 1; "Wisconsin Wins, Iowa Bows, 72–56," *Chicago Tribune*, January 20, 1948, p. 23.

18. "Michigan Tops N.U., 53–37 to Take 1st Place," *Chicago Tribune*, February 1, 1948, Pt. 2, p. 1; "Michigan Beaten by Ohio," *Chicago Tribune*, February 3, 1948, p. 25; "Michigan Beats Illinois, 66–57; Badgers Win," *Chicago Tribune*, February 8, 1948, Pt. 2, p. 1.

19. "New Code Will Be Studied by Big 9 Chiefs," *Chicago Tribune*, February 1, 1948, Pt. 2, p. 1.

20. "Iowa Defeats Illini, 70–61; Purdue Wins," *Chicago Tribune*, February 10, 1948, Pt. 3, p. 1; "Michigan 69, Purdue 56," *Chicago Tribune*, February 15, 1948, Pt. 2, p. 1.

21. "Wolverines Lead Big 9; Badgers Lose," *Chicago Tribune*, February 17, 1948, Pt. 3, p. 1; "Wolverines Win; Badgers Lose to Iowa," *Chicago Tribune*, February 22, 1948, Pt. 2, p. 1.

22. "Wolverines Win 46–35, Over Purdue," *Chicago Tribune*, February 24, 1948, Pt. 3, p. 1.

23. "Michigan Clinches Title Share; Iowa Wins," *Chicago Tribune*, February 29, 1948, Pt. 2, p. 1.

24. "Michigan Wins Title; Beats Iowa, 51 to 35," *Chicago Tribune*, March 2, 1948, Pt. 3, p. 1.

25. "Coaches Name Weir, Eddleman, Elliott to Big 9 Star Five," *Chicago Tribune*, March 3, 1948, Pt. 2, p. 2.

26. Mike Douchant, p. 47.

27. Finding a box score from this game was quite challenging. The *Chicago Tribune* only had the score, as did the *Los Angeles Times* and *Philadelphia Inquirer*. The *New York Times* carried the two box scores.

28. Smith, Wilfrid, "7 Teams to Join Big 10 Race Tonight," *Chicago Tribune*, January 8, 1949, Pt. 2, p. 1.

29. Many sources credit Dick Culberson of Iowa in 1944–45 as the first African American in Big 10 basketball, but because he was a transfer from Virginia Union who only was on the Iowa roster for one year as a reserve, Garrett is usually identified as the first. An excellent biography of Garrett is by Tom Graham and Rachel Graham Cody, *Getting Open: The Unknown Story of Bill Garrett and the Integration of College Basketball* (New York: Simon & Schuster, 2011).

30. Graham and Cody, pp. 146–147.

31. "Arrest Four in East on Basket Fix," *Chicago Tribune*, January 4, 1949, Pt. 3, p. 1.

32. "Gophers Beat Wolverines' Five, 45 to 31," *Chicago Tribune*, January 9, 1949, Pt. 2, p. 3.

33. "Foster Claims Gophers Win, but Lose Faris," *Chicago Tribune*, January 12, 1949, Pt. 3, p. 2.

34. "Illinois Beats Ohio, 64–63; Gophers Win," *Chicago Tribune*, January 11, 1949, Pt. 3, p. 1; "Purdue Beats Michigan Five, 45–36," *Chicago Tribune*, January 11, 1949, Pt. 3, p. 1.
35. "Gophers Beat Purdue; N.U. Loses," *Chicago Tribune*, January 16, 1949, Pt. 2, p. 1; "Wisconsin, Iowa, Score 1st Victories," *Chicago Tribune*, January 16, 1949, Pt. 2, p. 4.
36. "Gophers Defeat Iowa, 61 to 45; Take Lead," *Chicago Tribune*, January 18, 1949, Pt. 2, p. 1.
37. "Unbeaten Gophers Stop Indiana, 35 to 28," *Chicago Tribune*, January 23, 1949, Pt. 2, p. 1.
38. Wilfrid Smith, "Illini Rally to Whip Gophers, 45–44," *Chicago Tribune*, January 30, 1949, Pt. 2, p. 1.
39. "Illini Take Big Ten Lead; Gophers Lose, 48–39," *Chicago Tribune*, February 6, 1949, Pt. 2, p. 1.
40. "Illinois Beats Ohio, 64–49; Gophers Win," *Chicago Tribune*, February 13, 1949, Pt. 2, p. 1.
41. "Illinois Routs Iowa, 80–49; N.U. Loses, 57–46," *Chicago Tribune*, February 22, 1949, Pt. 3, p. 1.
42. "Illinois Beats N.U., 81–64; Minnesota Triumphs," *Chicago Tribune*, February 27, 1949, Pt. 2, p. 1.
43. "Illinois Champions; Badgers Upset Gophers, 45–43," *Chicago Tribune*, March 6, 1949, Pt. 2, p. 1.
44. Wilson and Brondfield, p. 295.
45. "Kentucky Defeats Illini, 76–47," *Chicago Tribune*, March 17, 1949, Pt. 4, p. 1.

# Chapter 3

1. Ab Nicholas telephone interview, March 11, 2015.
2. Nicholas interview.
3. Wilson and Brondfield, p. 305.
4. "Illini Trip in Debut, 59–50, at Wisconsin," *Chicago Tribune*, January 3, 1950, Pt. 4, p. 1. "Bradley Deals Ohio State 2d Defeat, 65–46," *Chicago Tribune*, January 3, 1950, Pt.4, p.2. "Indiana Checks Spartans, 60–50," *Chicago Tribune*, January 3, 1950, Pt. 4, p. 2.
5. Wilfrid Smith, "N.U. Defeats Purdue in Overtime, 60–58," *Chicago Tribune*, January 8, 1950, Pt. 2, p. 1; "Illini Beaten; Iowa Loses to Michigan," *Chicago Tribune*, January 8, 1950, Pt. 2, p. 1; "Indiana Defeats Wisconsin, 61–59," *Chicago Tribune*, January 8, 1950, Pt. 2, p. 1.
6. Hiner with Hutchens, p. 255.
7. "Illinois Hands Ohio First Defeat, 66–50," *Chicago Tribune*, January 22, 1950, Pt. 2, p. 1; "Gophers Win, 60 to 52, Over Michigan," *Chicago Tribune*, January 22, 1950, Pt. 2, p. 1.
8. Edward Prell, "Ohio Defeats Gophers, 63–58," *Chicago Tribune*, January 29, 1950, Pt. 2, p. 1; "Ohio Beats Wisconsin, 61–47; Illini Win," *Chicago Tribune*, February 5, 1950, Pt. 2, p. 1.
9. "Ohio Tops Indiana, 56–55; N.U. Loses," *Chicago Tribune*, February 7, 1950, Pt. 3, p. 1.
10. "Iowa Upsets Illinois, 70–65; Badgers Whip N.U.," *Chicago Tribune*, February 12, 1950, Pt. 2, p. 1.
11. Wilfrid Smith, "Rehfeldt's 35 Beat N.U., 66–59," *Chicago Tribune*, February 12, 1950, Pt. 2, p. 1.
12. "Ohio Routs Indiana; Gains Share," *Chicago Tribune*, February 21, 1950, Pt. 3, p. 1.
13. "Big Ten Scoring," *Chicago Tribune*, February 22, 1950, Pt. 3, p. 1.
14. "Badgers Lose; Ohio State Wins Big Ten Title," *Chicago Tribune*, February 26, 1950, Pt. 2, p. 1; "N.U. Routs Wolverines; Loyola Wins," *Chicago Tribune*, February 26, 1950, Pt. 2, p. 1.
15. "Rule Prohibits Post-Season Games," *Chicago Tribune*, February 26, 1950, Pt. 2, p. 4.
16. "Ohio Wins 69 to 58; N.U. Loses," *Chicago Tribune*, February 28, 1950, Pt. 3, p. 1.
17. "Rehfeldt Gets 21, 8 Too Few as Badgers Win," *Chicago Tribune*, March 5, 1950, Pt. 2, p. 1.
18. "Big Ten Approves 14 Game League Slate," *Chicago Tribune*, March 12, 1950, Pt. 2, p. 2.
19. "Ohio Wins Over Depaul, 70–63, in Tourney Tuneup," *Chicago Tribune*, March 19, 1950, Pt. 2, p. 4.
20. Louis Effrat, "City College and N.C. State Quints Gain Eastern Final," *New York Times*, March 24, 1950, p. 31.
21. "City College Whips Ohio State, 56 to 55," *Chicago Tribune*, March 24, 1950, Pt. 6, p. 1. For a fuller discussion of the point-shaving scandals, see Stanley Cohen, *The Game They Played* (New York: Carroll & Graf, 2001), as well as Charley Rosen, *The Scandals of '51: How the Gamblers Almost Killed College Basketball* (New York: Seven Stories Press, 1999).
22. Douchant, p. 54.
23. "Illinois Opens Race Tonight at Wisconsin," *Chicago Tribune*, January 1, 1951, Pt. 6, p. 3; "Illini Defeat Badgers, 71–69," *Chicago Tribune*, January 2, 1951, Pt. 4, p. 1.
24. Charles Bartlett, "Spartans Beat N.U., 67–62," *Chicago Tribune*, January 7, 1951, Pt. 2, p. 1.
25. "Pacific Coast Colleges Ban Football TV," *Chicago Tribune*, January 6, 1951, Pt. 3, p. 1.
26. *Ibid.*
27. "N.U. Beats Michigan; Illini Win," *Chicago Tribune*, January 9, 1951, Pt. 3, p. 1; "Illini Beat Michigan, 68–47; Indiana Wins," *Chicago Tribune*, January 14, 1951, Pt. 2, p. 1; "N.U. Wins, 73–70; Fendley Stars," *Chicago Tribune*, January 14, 1951, Pt. 2, p. 1; "Badgers Whip Ohio; Gophers Win," *Chicago Tribune*, January 14, 1951, Pt. 2, p. 5.
28. "Indiana Whips Illinois, 64–53; N.U. Loses," *Chicago Tribune*, January 16, 1951, Pt. 3, p. 1.
29. "Illini Victory Adds to Iowa Travel Woes," *Chicago Tribune*, January 21, 1951, Pt. 2, p. 1; Robert Cromie, "N.U. Wins Over Ohio State," *Chicago Tribune*, January 21, 1951, Pt. 2, p. 1; "Michigan State Triumphs Over Michigan," *Chicago Tribune*, January 21, 1951, Pt. 2, p. 2.
30. "Indiana Whips Ohio, 69–59; Iowa Triumphs," *Chicago Tribune*, January 23, 1951, Pt. 3, p. 1.
31. "N.U. 97, Purdue,79! Indiana Wins 32 to 26!" *Chicago Tribune*, January 28, 1951, Pt. 2, p. 1.
32. "N.U. Free Throws Beat Ohio State, 78–67," *Chicago Tribune*, January 30, 1951, Pt. 3, p. 1.
33. Nicholas interview.
34. "Badgers Whip Gophers, 47–44," *Chicago Tribune*, February 4, 1951, Pt. 2, p. 1; "Illini Beat Purdue, 85–76; N.U. Loses," *Chicago Tribune*, February 6, 1951, Pt. 3, p. 1.
35. "Indiana Loses; Illini Win, Lead Big Ten," *Chicago Tribune*, February 11, 1951, Pt. 2, p. 1; "Indiana Wins; Illini Defeat Ohio, 79 to 59," *Chicago Tribune*, February 13, 1951, Pt. 3, p. 1; "Purdue Beats Badgers; N.U. Loses," *Chicago Tribune*, February 13, 1951, Pt. 3, p. 1.
36. "Scandal Forces Long Island from Sports," *Chicago Tribune*, February 21, 1951, Pt. 3, p. 1.
37. Hiner with Hutchens, p. 258.

38. Wilfrid Smith, "Illinois Rally Turns Back Indiana, 71–65," *Chicago Tribune*, February 20, 1951, Pt. 3, p. 1.

39. "Illinois Beats Ohio, 89–69: Indiana Wins," *Chicago Tribune*, February 25, 1951, Pt. 2, p. 1; "Iowa Routs Michigan," *Chicago Tribune*, February 25, 1951, Pt. 2, p. 5.

40. "Michigan State Loses, 35 to 29, at Wisconsin," *Chicago Tribune*, February 25, 1951, Pt. 2, p. 5.

41. "Indiana Defeats Iowa; N.U. Wins," *Chicago Tribune*, February 27, 1951, Pt. 3, p. 1.

42. Wilfrid Smith, "Illini Stave Off N.U., 80–76; Clinch Tie," *Chicago Tribune*, March 4, 1951, Pt. 2, p. 1; "Indiana Whips Michigan, 57–42," *Chicago Tribune*, March 4, 1951, Pt. 2, p. 1.

43. Hiner with Hutchens, p. 259.

44. Wilson and Brondfield, p. 312.

45. "Kansas State Romps, 91–72, Over Illinois," *Chicago Tribune*, March 15, 1951, Pt. 6, p. 2.

46. Smith, Wilfrid, "Illini Hand Columbia 1st Defeat, 79–71," *Chicago Tribune*, March 21, 1951, Pt. 3, p.1.

47. "N.C.A.A. Meet Headed Back to Campus-Wilson," *Chicago Tribune*, March 22, 1951, Pt. 4, p. 2.

48. "Kansas State Routs Oklahoma Aggies in Western N.C.A.A.," *New York Times*, March 25, 1951, Sec. 5, p. 4.

49. "Illini Beat N. Carolina State, 84–70; Kentucky Wins, 59–43," *Chicago Tribune*, March 23, 1951, Pt. 3, p. 1; Louis Effrat, "Kentucky Beats St. John's and Gains N.C.A.A. Eastern Final with Illinois," *New York Times*, March 23, 1951, p. 25.

50. Louis Effrat, "Kentucky Quintet Defeats Illinois in Final, 76 to 74," *New York Times*, March 25, 1951, Sec. 5, p. 1; "Kentucky Beats Illini in Final, 76 to 74," *Chicago Tribune*, March 25, 1951, Pt. 2, p. 1.

51. "Doubts Referees in on Gambling," *Chicago Tribune*, March 25, 1951, Pt. 2, p. 1.

52. "Kentucky Beats Kansas State Quint in N.C.A.A. Final," *New York Times*, March 28, 1951, p. 41; "Kentucky Takes N.C.A.A. Title, 68 to 58," *Chicago Tribune*, March 28, 1951, Pt. 3, p. 1.

53. Spivey's play in the ABL is described in Murry Nelson's *Abe Saperstein and the American Basketball League, 1960–63: The Upstarts Who Shot for Three and Lost to the NBA* (2013).

54. Bobby Leonard and Lew Freedman, *Boom Baby: My Beautiful Life in Basketball* (Chicago: Triumph Books, 2013), 46.

55. Leonard and Freedman, 48.

56. In a very sad footnote, Sunderlage played for Chanute Air Force Base in Rantoul, Illinois, after graduating. He spent two years in the NBA and was named to the 1954 All-Star team, but was cut by the Milwaukee Hawks after the 1955 season. In July of 1961, he died in a car accident while returning to Chicago from Lake Geneva, Wisconsin. He was just 31.

57. Bjarkman, 9.

58. "Illini Win 7th in a Row, 68–57," *Chicago Tribune*, January 1, 1952, Pt. 4, p. 1.

59. "Michigan State Whips Notre Dame," *Chicago Tribune*, January 3, 1952, Pt. 4, p. 1.

60. Robert Cromie, "N.U. Wins, 75–70; Illinois Beats Minnesota," *Chicago Tribune*, January 6, 1952, Pt. 2, p. 1. Robert Cromie, the reporter, would later become the book columnist for the *Tribune*. He would also host a show on the local PBS station, *Book Beat*, and another on the local NBC affiliate titled *Critic's Corner*.

61. "Illini Beat Badgers, 53–49; Indiana Loses," *Chicago Tribune*, January 8, 1952, Pt. 3, p. 1. This was the era when there was a movement to spell more phonetically, and the *Tribune* from 1934 to 1975 was filled with what would be seen today as unusual spellings such as "Sofomore" and "Frater" (freighter). "Michigan 9th Victim, 54–46, for Iowans," *Chicago Tribune*, January 8, 1952, Pt. 3, p. 1.

62. Wilfrid Smith, "N.C.A.A. Bans Outside Aid for Athletes," *Chicago Tribune*, January 13, 1952, Pt. 2, p. 1. The sanity or purity code is discussed in great length in Ron Smith's *Pay for Play: A History of Big-Time College Athletic Reform* (Urbana: University of Illinois Press, 2013), pp. 88–99.

63. "Illinois Wins, 67–51; Iowa Beats Indiana, 78–59," *Chicago Tribune*, January 13, 1952, Pt. 2, p. 1.

64. "Illinois Wins, 67–51; Iowa Beats Indiana, 78–59," *Chicago Tribune*, January 13, 1952, Pt. 2, p. 1.

65. "Purdue Drops Basketball Player After Fight," *Chicago Tribune*, January 15, 1952, Pt. 3, p. 1.

66. "Illini Beat Indiana, 78 to 66; N.U. Loses," *Chicago Tribune*, January 15, 1952, Pt. 3, p. 1.

67. Robert Cromie, "N.U. Loses; Iowa Jars Minnesota, 76 to 59," *Chicago Tribune*, January 20, 1952, Pt. 2, p. 1.

68. Dick Culberson, a transfer from Virginia Union, played one season for Iowa in 1944–45 to integrate the Big Ten, although it is unclear if he played in a Big Ten contest.

69. "Indiana Upsets Iowa, 82 to 69; N.U. Wins," *Chicago Tribune*, January 22, 1952, Pt. 3, p. 1.

70. Wilfrid Smith, "Depaul Snaps 11-Game Illini String, 69–65," *Chicago Tribune*, January 27, 1952, Pt. 2, p. 1.

71. "N.U. Wins; Illinois Beats Ohio, 66 to 62," *Chicago Tribune*, February 3, 1952, Pt. 2, p. 1; Robert Cromie, "Wildcats Win in Overtime, 86–76," *Chicago Tribune*, February 3, 1952, Pt. 2, p. 1. Ohio State home games were played at the Ohio Fairgrounds, where the facilities were substandard and the capacity was no more than 10,000. A new, on-campus arena would not open until 1957.

72. "Gophers Whip Ohio, 84 to 56," *Chicago Tribune*, February 5, 1952, Pt. 3, p. 1.

73. This was an option at the time; the rule was changed in the early 1960s to eliminate the choice option, making teams shoot after the seventh foul, no matter what.

74. Wilfrid Smith, "Iowa Jolts Illinois, 73–68: Ties for Lead," *Chicago Tribune*, February 10, 1952, Pt. 2, p. 1; George Strickler, "Michigan Rally Beats N.U., 71–69," *Chicago Tribune*, February 10, 1952, Pt. 2, p. 1; "Gophers Win as Badgers Fade in 3d Period, 54–47," *Chicago Tribune*, February 10, 1952, Pt. 2, p. 1.

75. "Iowa Wins; Illini Rout Spartans, 84–62," *Chicago Tribune*, February 12, 1952, Pt. 3, p. 1.

76. "College Heads Hold Firm on Sports Code," *Chicago Tribune*, February 17, 1952, Pt. 2, p. 1.

77. "Illini Defeat Ohio; Iowa Wins, 90–67," *Chicago Tribune*, February 17, 1952, Pt. 2, p. 1; "Minnesota Tops Michigan, 52–44, for 8th Victory," *Chicago Tribune*, February 17, 1952, Pt. 2, p. 2.

78. "Illinois Whips Indiana, 77–70; Iowa Wins, 75–62," *Chicago Tribune*, February 19, 1952, Pt. 3, p. 1.

79. "Michigan Stall Sends Badgers to Cellar, 56 to 55," *Chicago Tribune*, February 19, 1952, Pt. 3, p. 1; Behee, p. 39.

80. Wilfrid Smith, "Illini Whips Iowa, 78–62; Takes

Lead," *Chicago Tribune*, February 24, 1952, Pt. 2, p. 1; "Ohio Wins as Ebert Hits 40 Points; Gophers Triumph," *Chicago Tribune*, February 24, 1952, Pt. 2, p. 3.

81. "Iowa Beats N.U., 77–68: Illini Win, 82–71," *Chicago Tribune*, March 2, 1952, Pt. 2, p. 1; Wilfrid Smith, "Hawkeyes Stay in Title Chase," *Chicago Tribune*, March 2, 1952, Pt. 2, p. 1.

82. Wilfrid Smith, "Iowa Loses; Illinois Takes Big Ten Title," *Chicago Tribune*, March 4, 1952, Pt. 3, p. 1; "Iowa Upset by Badgers, 78–75," *Chicago Tribune*, March 4, 1952, Pt. 3, p. 1.

83. "Darling Voted to All-America Basket Squad," *Chicago Tribune*, March 6, 1952, Pt. 4, p. 2.

84. "Illini Camps Upset, 58–48 by Wisconsin," *Chicago Tribune*, March 9, 1952, Pt. 2, p. 1; "Kansas Rejects Illinois Bid to Warmup Game," *Chicago Tribune*, March 9, 1952, Pt. 2, p. 2.

85. Douchant, p. 57.

86. "Illinois, Duquesne Gain Regional Final," *Chicago Tribune*, March 22, 1952, Pt. 4, p. 1.

87. Edward Prell, "Illini Whip Duquesne, 74 to 68, for Regional Title," *Chicago Tribune*, March 23, 1952, Pt. 2, p. 1.

88. "Kentucky Upset by St. John's in N.C.A.A., 64–57," *Chicago Tribune*, March 23, 1952, Pt. 2, p. 1.

89. "St. John's Eliminates Illinois, 61 to 59," *Chicago Tribune*, March 26, 1952, Pt. 6, p. 1; "Kansas Beats St. John's , 80–63," *Chicago Tribune*, March 27, 1952, Pt. 4, p. 1.

# Chapter 4

1. "Iowa's Early Attack Conquers Michigan, 85–77," *Chicago Tribune*, December 14, 1952, Pt. 2, p. 1.

2. "Badgers Win; Illini Rout Michigan, 96–66," *Chicago Tribune*, December 16, 1952, Pt. 3, p. 1.

3. "Indiana Wins; Purdue Jars Badgers, 65–59," *Chicago Tribune*, December 21, 1952, Pt. 2, p. 1.

4. "Indiana Wins; Michigan Rips Purdue, 88–73," *Chicago Tribune*, December 23, 1952, Pt. 3, p. 1.

5. "Gophers' Free Throws Beat Illini, 77–73," *Chicago Tribune*, December 24, 1952, Pt. 2, p. 1.

6. "Illinois Routs Ohio, 87 to 62," *Chicago Tribune*, December 28, 1952, Pt. 2, p. 1; George Strickler, "Spartans Halt N.U.'S Rally to Win, 52–47," *Chicago Tribune*, December 28, 1952, pt. 2, p. 1.

7. Phil Judson telephone interview, January 22, 2014.

8. "N.U. Deals Gophers 1st Big Ten Loss, 71–65," *Chicago Tribune*, January 4, 1953, Pt. 2, p. 1; "Indiana Beats Michigan, 91–88," *Chicago Tribune*, January 4, 1953, Pt. 2, p. 1; "Michigan State Wins from Ohio," *Chicago Tribune*, January 4, 1953, Pt. 2, p. 2.

9. "Illini Win; Indiana Beats Spartans, 69–62," *Chicago Tribune*, January 6, 1953, Pt. 3, p. 1; "Gophers Stop Badger Aces, Win, 64 to 53," *Chicago Tribune*, January 6, 1953, Pt. 3, p. 1.

10. "Indiana Whips Gophers, 66–63; Illini Win," *Chicago Tribune*, January 11, 1953, Pt. 2, p. 1.

11. Edward Prell, "N.U. Wins from Michigan, 84–57," *Chicago Tribune*, January 11, 1953, Pt. 2, p. 1.

12. "Illini Whip N.U.; Indiana Routs Ohio, 88–68," *Chicago Tribune*, January 13, 1953, Pt. 3, p. 1.

13. "Indiana Whips Illini in 2d Overtime, 74–70," *Chicago Tribune*, January 18, 1953, Pt. 2, p. 1; "Wisconsin Speed Routs N.U.; Gophers Beat Iowa," *Chicago Tribune*, January 18, 1953, Pt. 2, p. 1; "Spartans Beat Michigan, 66–64, 5 Seconds to Go," *Chicago Tribune*, January 18, 1953, Pt. 2, p. 2.

14. "Indiana Whips Purdue, 88–75; Illini Win," *Chicago Tribune*, January 20, 1953, Pt. 3, p. 1; "Tempers Flare as Iowa Wins Over N.U., 69–68; Badgers Beat Ohio, 64 to 51 for 3d in Row," *Chicago Tribune*, January 20, 1953, Pt. 3, p. 2.

15. "Declare Mistrial in Spivey Perjury Case," *Chicago Tribune*, January 27, 1953, Pt. 3, p. 1. Spivey continued to assert his innocence, and although the charges were dropped, he was blacklisted by the NBA, along with the 31 other players named in indictments, and never played in the league. He died in 1995 at age 66.

16. "Illini Win, 65–61; Indiana Whips N.U., 88–84," *Chicago Tribune*, February 8, 1953, Pt. 2, p. 1; "Gophers Win, 74–50," *Chicago Tribune*, February 8, 1953, Pt. 2, p. 1; "Spartans Move into 3d," *Chicago Tribune*, February 10, 1953, Pt. 3, p. 1.

17. "Indiana Wins, 65–50; Illinois Beats Iowa," *Chicago Tribune*, February 15, 1953, Pt. 2, p. 1.

18. "Indiana 72, Badgers 70; Illini Win," *Chicago Tribune*, February 17, 1953, Pt. 3, p. 1.

19. "Wisconsin Jars Michigan, 74–52; Spartans Win," *Chicago Tribune*, February 22, 1953, Pt. 2, p. 6. The Big Ten was still following its version of the NCAA-rejected sanity code. This would finally come to a head in the conference in 1956–57.

20. "Big Ten Slaps Mich. State for Sport Sins," *Chicago Tribune*, February 23, 1953, Pt. 4, p. 1.

21. "Indiana Wins, 113–78; 4 Marks Fall," *Chicago Tribune*, February 24, 1953, Pt. 3, p. 1.

22. "Illinois Beats Minnesota," *Chicago Tribune*, February 24, 1953, Pt. 3, p. 1; "Michigan State Cracks Badger Zone, 53–45," *Chicago Tribune*, February 24, 1953, Pt. 3, p. 3.

23. "Shah leaves for Iraq-Moslem Insurgents to Rouse Premier," *Chicago Tribune*, March 1, 1953, Pt. 1, p. 1.

24. "Indiana Wins Title; Beats Illinois, 91–79," *Chicago Tribune*, March 1, 1953, Pt. 2, p. 1.

25. Leonard and Freedman, p. 50.

26. Phil Judson telephone interview, January 22, 2014.

27. "Indiana Beats N.U. in Overtime, 90 to 88," *Chicago Tribune*, March 3, 1953, Pt. 3, p. 1; "Illini Clinch Tie for 2d," *Chicago Tribune*, March 3, 1953, Pt. 3, p. 1; "Gophers Lose, 81–79, to Iowa in Overtime," *Chicago Tribune*, March 3, 1953, Pt. 3, p. 1.

28. "Indiana String Snaps; Gophers Win, 65 to 63," *Chicago Tribune*, March 8, 1953, Pt. 2, p. 1.

29. Wilson and Brondfield, p. 336.

30. Leonard and Freedman, p. 60.

31. Wilfrid Smith, "Indiana Beats L.S.U., 80–67 in N.C.A.A. Test," *Chicago Tribune*, March 18, 1953, Pt. 4, p. 1.

32. Bjarkman, p. 22.

33. Wilson and Brondfield, p. 328; Wilfrid Smith, "Indiana Wins N.C.A.A. Title, 69–68," *Chicago Tribune*, March 19, 1953, Pt. 4, p. 1.

34. Telephone interviews with Phil Judson, January 22, 2014, and Bill Ridley, February 5, 2014.

35. Hiner with Hutchens, p. 263.

36. Telephone interview with Bill Ridley, February 5, 2014.

37. "Illini Lose; Indiana Beats Michigan, 62–60," *Chicago Tribune*, January 3, 1954, Pt. 2, p. 1; Phil Judson

telephone interview, January 22, 2014. Ridley himself, in a telephone interview on February 5, 2014, said that he was more of a point guard.

38. Edward Prell, "Illinois Beats N.U., 66–65; Indiana Wins," *Chicago Tribune*, January 5, 1954, Pt. 3, p. 1; "Iowa Wins, 73–63," *Chicago Tribune*, January 5, 1954, Pt. 3, p. 1.

39. "Illini Lose; Indiana Whips Gophers, 71–63," *Chicago Tribune*, January 10, 1954, Pt. 2, p. 1; "Ohio Wins, 91–74; Iowa Defeats Badgers, 71–54; Cain Scores 20," *Chicago Tribune*, January 10, 1954, Pt. 2, p. 2.

40. Phil Judson telephone interview, January 22, 2014; Carl Cain telephone interview, September 9, 2015.

41. "Pro Basket Rookie Banned for Betting," *Chicago Tribune*, January 11, 1954, Pt. 4, p. 1. Charley Rosen examines Molinas's "Career" in depth in *The Wizard of Odds: How Jack Molinas Almost Destroyed the Game of Basketball* (New York: Seven Stories Press, 2002).

42. Telephone interviews with Phil Judson, January 22, 2014, and Bill Ridley, February 5, 2014.

43. "Minnesota Halts Iowa; Indiana Wins," *Chicago Tribune*, January 17, 1954, Pt. 2, p. 1; "Illinois Whips Ohio, 82–78; N.U. Loses, 78–63," *Chicago Tribune*, January 17, 1954, Pt. 2, p. 1.

44. "Indiana Wins, 94–72; Schlundt Sets Mark," *Chicago Tribune*, January 19, 1954, Pt. 4, p. 1; "Iowa Beats Illinois," *Chicago Tribune*, January 19, 1954, Pt. 4, p. 1.

45. "Indiana Beats Stubborn Spartans, 79–74," *Chicago Tribune*, February 7, 1954, Pt. 2, p. 1; "Indiana Routs Minnesota, 90–77," *Chicago Tribune*, February 9, 1954, Pt. 3, p. 1; "Illini, Kerr, Win from Purdue," *Chicago Tribune*, February 9, 1954, Pt. 3, p. 1.

46. "Northwestern Upsets Indiana, 100 to 90," *Chicago Tribune*, February 14, 1954, Pt. 3, p. 1; "Iowa Defeats Gophers, 86–82," *Chicago Tribune*, February 14, 1954, Pt. 2, p. 1; "Purdue Uses 5 Players; Gains 64–50 Triumph," *Chicago Tribune*, February 14, 1954, Pt. 2, p. 2.

47. "N.U. Tops Purdue; Indiana Triumphs, 63–61," *Chicago Tribune*, February 21, 1954, Pt. 2, p. 1.

48. Carl Cain telephone interview.

49. "Indiana Beats Ohio, 84–68; Illini Whips Michigan, 79–61," *Chicago Tribune*, February 28, 1954, Pt. 2, p. 1; "Iowa Rallies to Win, 60–48, Over Spartans," *Chicago Tribune*, February 28, 1954, Pt. 2, p. 1.

50. "Illini Beat N.U., 84–82; Iowa Wins," *Chicago Tribune*, March 2, 1954, Pt. 3, p. 1; "Badgers Win, 79–56; Set Free Throw Record," *Chicago Tribune*, March 2, 1954, Pt. 3, p. 2.

51. Wilson and Brondfield, p. 337.

52. "Indiana Wins, 67–64: Keeps Big 10 Title," *Chicago Tribune*, March 7, 1954, Pt. 2, p. 1.

53. "NBC to Televise Basket Finals Nationally," *Chicago Tribune*, March 9, 1954, Pt. 4, p. 1.

54. Wilson and Brondfield, p. 337.

55. This was a result of the Wildcats' suspension from intercollegiate play as a result of the point-shaving scandals of 1951. The players still voted to go to the tourney, but Rupp declined, overruling them. Hagan, Ramsey and Tsioropoulos had remained in school and played in 1953–54 because SEC rules allowed them to do so. Such a situation now seems almost quaint when one considers the "One and Done" players in major college basketball today. All three went on to pro careers with the Boston Celtics, although Hagan spent most of his career with the St. Louis Hawks. "Kentucky Withdraws from N.C.A.A. Meet," *Chicago Tribune*, March 10, 1954, Pt. 4, p. 1.

56. Leonard and Freedman, p. 69.

57. "Irish Win in N.C.A.A. Opener, 80–70," *Chicago Tribune*, March 10, 1954, Pt. 4, p. 1.

58. Leonard and Freedman, p. 70.

59. "Moose Krause Joins Protest on Bonus Foul," *Chicago Tribune*, January 4, 1955, Pt. 3, p. 2.

60. "Badgers Take 79–64 Victory Over Illinois," *Chicago Tribune*, January 2, 1955, Pt. 2, p. 1.

61. "N.U. Wins; Indiana Beats Michigan, 95–77," *Chicago Tribune*, January 4, 1955, Pt. 3, p. 1.

62. Iowa 86; "Wisconsin 69," *Chicago Tribune*, January 4, 1955, Pt. 3, p. 1; "Ohio Whips Spartans," *Chicago Tribune*, January 4, 1955, Pt. 3, p. 1.

63. "Gophers Beat Iowa," *Chicago Tribune*, January 9, 1955, Pt. 2, p. 1; "Illini Break Record," *Chicago Tribune*, January 9, 1955, Pt. 2, p. 1.

64. "Record Set as Spartans Win, 94–77," *Chicago Tribune*, January 9, 1955, Pt. 2, p. 4.

65. "Illini Tops Purdue, 83–73: Iowa Wins, 94–81," *Chicago Tribune*, January 11, 1955, Pt. 3, p. 1; "Free Throws Decide," *Chicago Tribune*, January 11, 1955, Pt. 3, p. 2.

66. "Gophers Rip Purdue, 102–88; Badgers Win," *Chicago Tribune*, January 16, 1955, Pt. 2, p. 1; "N.U. Wins, 93–88; Iowa Beats Illini, 92–80," *Chicago Tribune*, January 18, 1955, Pt. 3, p. 1.

67. Edward Prell, "Minnesota Lose; N.U. Beats Iowa, 93–73," *Chicago Tribune*, January 23, 1955, Pt. 2, p. 1.

68. "Gophers Batter N.U., 102–82; Share Big Ten Lead with Iowa," *Chicago Tribune*, January 25, 1955, Pt. 3, p. 1.

69. Cain interview.

70. "Gophers Win in 6th Overtime, 59–56," *Chicago Tribune*, January 30, 1955, Pt. 2, p. 1.

71. "Illini Wins; Iowa Ties for Big 10 Led," *Chicago Tribune*, February 6, 1955, Pt. 2., p. 1; "51 Personal Fouls Called as Illini Beat N.U., 104–89," *Chicago Tribune*, February 6, 1955, Pt. 2, p. 1.

72. "Gophers Win, 82–56; Lead Big 10," *Chicago Tribune*, February 8, 1955, Pt. 3, p. 1. Kramer went on to star for the Green Bay Packers and Detroit Lions after graduating in 1957.

73. "Gophers Beat Illini, 78–71: 2 Overtimes," *Chicago Tribune*, February 13, 1955, Pt. 2, p. 1; "Iowa Checks Schlundt and Wins, 90–75," *Chicago Tribune*, February 13, 1955, Pt. 2, p. 1.

74. "Minnesota Beats Indiana, 80–70," *Chicago Tribune*, February 15, 1955, Pt. 3, p. 1; "Iowa Wins No.7," *Chicago Tribune*, February 15, 1955, Pt. 3, p. 1; "Michigan Nips N.U., 72–70," *Chicago Tribune*, February 15, 1955, Pt. 3, p. 1.

75. "Gophers Win; Iowa Beats Illinois," *Chicago Tribune*, February 22, 1955, Pt. 3, p. 1.

76. "Iowa Clinches Tie for Big 10 Title," *Chicago Tribune*, March 1, 1955, Pt. 3, p. 1; "Michigan Loses as Illini Clinch 3d in Big 10," *Chicago Tribune*, March 1, 1955, Pt. 3, p. 2.

77. "Iowa Takes Title; Badgers Beat Gophers," *Chicago Tribune*, March 6, 1955, Pt. 2, p. 1; "Schlundt Ends Record Career with 47 Points," *Chicago Tribune*, March 6, 1955, Pt. 2, p. 6; "Iowa Loses Final, 71–58," *Chicago Tribune*, March 8, 1955, Pt. 3, p. 1.

78. Wilson and Brondfield, p. 346.

79. Wilson and Brondfield, p. 346.

80. William Mokray, *Ronald Encyclopedia of Basketball*, pp. 4–103.
81. "Marquette Jolts Kentucky; Iowa Wins," *Chicago Tribune*, March 12, 1955, Part 3, p. 1.
82. "Iowa Halts Marquette Rally; Wins, 86–81," *Chicago Tribune*, March 13, 1955, Pt. 2, p. 1; Wilfrid Smith, "Lasalle Nips Iowa; San Francisco Wins," *Chicago Tribune*, March 19, 1955, Pt. 3, p. 1.
83. Wilfred Smith, "San Francisco Wins Title; Beats Lasalle, 77–63," *Chicago Tribune*, March 20, 1955, Pt. 2, p. 1.

## Chapter 5

1. Linn, Ed, "Frank Howard, the Man Behind the New Babe Ruth Myth," *Sport*, April 1961, p. 64.
2. Phone interview with Ron Smith, March 9, 2015. Smith was a better baseball player, and when he quit the basketball team early for the opening of baseball practice, he "Made Two Teams Better," in his own words.
3. Phone interview with Phil Judson, January 22, 2014.
4. "Illini Rally Beats Spartans, 73–65," *Chicago Tribune*, January 3, 1956, Pt. 6, p. 1; "Purdue Wins, 78 to 66," *Chicago Tribune*, January 3, 1956, Pt. 6, p. 1; "Indiana Beats N.U.," *Chicago Tribune*, January 3, 1956, Pt. 6, p. 1.
5. "Michigan State Rally Beats Iowa, 65–64," *Chicago Tribune*, January 8, 1956, Pt. 2, p. 1; "Purdue Beats N.U.," *Chicago Tribune*, January 8, 1956, Pt. 2, p. 1; "Michigan Wins," *Chicago Tribune*, January 8, 1956, Pt. 2, p. 1; "Indiana Beats Wisconsin on Rally, 75 to 71," *Chicago Tribune*, January 8, 1956, Pt. 3, p. 1; Hiner and Hutchins, 2013.
6. "Illinois Takes Big 10 Lead," "Iowa Beats Ohio," "Gophers Win, 77–71" "Purdue Halted, 74–67," all *Chicago Tribune*, January 10, 1956, Pt. 4, p. 1.
7. "Illini Beat Indiana, 96–72; Third in Row," "Ohio Wins Marathon," "Iowa Triumphs, 84–62," *Chicago Tribune*, January 15, 1956, Pt. 2, p. 1.
8. "Purdue Triumphs," *Chicago Tribune*, January 15, 1956, Pt. 2, p. 5.
9. "Illini Repulse Purdue Challenge, 92–76," *Chicago Tribune*, January 17, 1956, Pt. 3, p. 1; "Indiana Wins, 79–70," *Chicago Tribune*, January 17, 1956, Pt. 3, p. 1.
10. "Purdue Wins, 70 to 69; Drops Ohio to 5th," *Chicago Tribune*, January 22, 1956, Pt. 2, p. 1; "Iowa Defeats Michigan, 78–67," *Chicago Tribune*, January 22, 1956, Pt. 2, p. 1; "N.U. Loses; Iowa Beats Purdue, 67 to 63," *Chicago Tribune*, January 24, 1956, Pt. 3, p. 1.
11. Telephone interview with Ron Smith, March 9, 2015.
12. "Gophers Win, 83–67, Over Northwestern," "Spartans Win, 94–91," *Chicago Tribune*, January 29, 1956, Pt. 2, p. 1.
13. "Illini Beat Gophers, 95–84; N.U. Loses, 78–68," *Chicago Tribune*, January 31, 1956, Pt. 3, p. 1.
14. "Badgers Whip N.U., 79–55: Purdue Wins, 75–67," *Chicago Tribune*, February 5, 1956, Pt. 2, p. 1; "Ohio Wins 100 to 82," *Chicago Tribune*, February 5, 1956, Pt. 2, p. 1.
15. Ridley telephone interview; Smith telephone interview.
16. "Iowa Wins; Illini Whip Indiana, 92–89," *Chicago Tribune*, February 7, 1956, Pt. 4, p. 1; "Spartans Win, 86–76," *Chicago Tribune*, February 7, 1956, Pt. 4, p. 4.
17. Dick Dozer, "Illinois Wins, 111–64; Iowa Beats N.U.," *Chicago Tribune*, February 12, 1956, Pt. 2, p. 1.
18. "Illini Beat Michigan, 89–66, for No.8," *Chicago Tribune*, February 14, 1956, Pt. 4, p. 1; "Iowa Wins, 88–75," *Chicago Tribune*, February 14, 1956, Pt. 4, p. 1.
19. "Illini Win; Iowa Beats Wisconsin, 80–66," *Chicago Tribune*, February 19, 1956, Pt. 2, p. 1; "Illinois Wins; Iowa Beats Indiana," *Chicago Tribune*, February 21, 1956, Pt. 4, p. 1; "Ohio Whips Badgers," *Chicago Tribune*, February 21, 1956, Pt. 4, p. 1.
20. This was the explanation in the *Chicago Tribune*, but Ridley, nearly 60 years later, disputed that in a telephone interview (February 5, 2014). He said that he did not have a bad back, but that Freeman simply outplayed him and had a fabulous game. Freeman, he noted, was the best shooter he ever played against.
21. "Ohio Upsets Illinois; Iowa Ties for Lead," *Chicago Tribune*, February 26, 1956, Pt. 2, p. 1; "Purdue Wins, 63–56," *Chicago Tribune*, February 26, 1956, Pt. 2, p. 1.
22. Dick Dozer, "Indiana Free Throws Defeat N.U., 84–82," *Chicago Tribune*, February 26, 1956, Pt. 2, p. 2.
23. "Illini Rally Beats Gophers; Iowa Wins, 86–68," *Chicago Tribune*, February 28, 1956, Pt. 3, p. 1.
24. Dick Dozer, "Iowa Rips Illinois for Title Share," *Chicago Tribune*, March 4, 1956, Pt. 2, p. 1.
25. "Freeman's 43 Sparks 96 to 84 Triumph," *Chicago Tribune*, March 4, 1956, Pt. 2, p. 2; "Purdue Wins, 73 to 71," *Chicago Tribune*, March 4, 1956, Pt. 2, p. 2.
26. Dick Dozer, "N.U. Upsets Illini, 83–82; Iowa Champion," *Chicago Tribune*, March 6, 1956, Pt. 4, p. 1; "Gophers Upset Ohio; Freeman Misses Record," *Chicago Tribune*, March 6, 1956, Pt. 4, p. 1.
27. Wilson and Brondfield, p. 352.
28. Mokray, pp. 4–104.
29. Dick Dozer, "Iowa Defeats Morehead State, 97 to 83," *Chicago Tribune*, March 17, 1956, Pt. 3, p. 1; Dick Dozer, "Iowa Reaches N.C.A.A. Finals; Beats Kentucky 89–77," *Chicago Tribune*, March 18, 1956, Pt. 2, p. 1.
30. Dick Dozer, "Iowa, San Francisco Gain N.C.A.A. Final," *Chicago Tribune*, March 23, 1956, Pt. 4, p. 1.
31. Dick Dozer, "Dons Keep N.C.A.A. Title; Whip Iowa, 83–71," *Chicago Tribune*, March 24, 1956, Pt. 3, p. 1.
32. Buck Turnbull, "Chuck Darling, Denison, 1966," *Des Moines Register*, June 25, 2005, http://www.desmoinesregister.com/article/19660403/SPORTS11/50625002/Chuck-Darling-Denison-1966. Accessed January 22, 2014.
33. See Carson Cunningham, *American Hoops: U.S. Men's Olympic Basketball from Berlin to Beijing* (Lincoln: University of Nebraska Press, 2010) for the most in-depth analysis of men's basketball in the Olympic Games.
34. Richard Dozer, "Big Ten Coaches Pick Illinois on Eve of Race," *Chicago Tribune*, January 4, 1957, Pt. 4, p. 2.
35. Nolden Gentry telephone interview, April 9, 2015.
36. Richard Dozer, "N.U. Wins, 75 to 54; Illinois, Iowa Lose," *Chicago Tribune*, January 6, 1957, Pt. 2, p. 1; "Ohio Beats Iowa," *Chicago Tribune*, January 6, 1957, Pt. 2, p. 1; "Boilermakers Win," *Chicago Tribune*, Janu-

ary 6, 1957, Pt. 2, p. 1; "Indiana Wins," *Chicago Tribune*, January 6, 1957, Pt. 2, p. 1.

37. "Illinois Beats Iowa, Ohio, Indiana Win," *Chicago Tribune*, January 8, 1957, Pt. 3, p. 1; "Michigan Wins," *Chicago Tribune*, January 8, 1957, Pt. 3, p. 2.

38. "Michigan Beats N.U., Illini Win," *Chicago Tribune*, January 13, 1957, Pt. 2, p. 1; "Purdue Surge Stops Indiana, 70–64; Iowa Dazzles Gophers," *Chicago Tribune*, January 13, 1957, Pt. 2, p. 1; "Badgers Lose Again," *Chicago Tribune*, Pt. 2, p. 1.

39. "Big 10 Mark Falls as Illini Win, 112–91," *Chicago Tribune*, January 15, 1957, Pt. 3, p. 1; "Ohio Wins, 85–73," *Chicago Tribune*, January 15, 1957, Pt. 3, p. 1; "Michigan Wins," *Chicago Tribune*, January 15, 1957, Pt. 3, p. 1.

40. Richard Dozer, "N.U. Beats Iowa, 70–63; Ohio Wins, 67–64," *Chicago Tribune*, January 22, 1957, Pt. 3, p. 1; "Ohio Beats Michigan State, 70–51; Iowa Wins," *Chicago Tribune*, January 20, 1957, Pt. 2, p. 1.

41. "Ohio State Squelches N.U. Rally to Win, 83–73, for Sixth Triumph in Big Ten," *Chicago Tribune*, January 27, 1957, Pt. 2, p. 1; "Spartans Triumph," *Chicago Tribune*, January 27, 1957, Pt. 2, p. 1.

42. "Michigan State Upsets Ohio, 73 to 64," *Chicago Tribune*, January 29, 1957, Pt. 3, p. 1; "Purdue Halts N.U. Rally," *Chicago Tribune*, January 29, 1957, Pt.3, p.1.

43. "Bonsalle Lost to Illini Team," *Chicago Tribune*, January 29, 1957, Pt. 3, p. 1.

44. "Purdue Beats Illinois, 85–74; N.U. Loses," *Chicago Tribune*, February 3, 1957, Pt. 2, p. 1.

45. Richard Dozer, "Michigan State Wins Third in Row, 77–63," *Chicago Tribune*, February 3, 1957, Pt. 2, p. 1; "Indiana Wins, 82–66," *Chicago Tribune*, February 3, 1957, Pt. 2, p. 1.

46. "Illini Halt Ohio, 96–89; Purdue Loses," *Chicago Tribune*, February 5, 1957, Pt. 3, p. 1.

47. "Upsets Jolt Big 10; Indiana Takes Lead," *Chicago Tribune*, February 10, 1957, Pt. 2, p. 1; "Illini Lose, 70–64," *Chicago Tribune*, February 10, 1957, Pt. 2, p. 2.

48. "Illini Beat N.U., 104 to 97; Indiana Wins," *Chicago Tribune*, February 12, 1957, Pt. 3, p. 1.

49. Virgil M. Hancher to John A. Hannah, February 11, 1957, Series 4/16/1, President E.B. Ford General Correspondence File, 1956–57, Box 274, Folder "Athletic Scholarships," University of Wisconsin Archives. I am indebted to Professor Ron Smith of Penn State for his provision of a copy of this letter.

50. "Indiana Defeats Wisconsin, 85–74; Spartans Triumph," *Chicago Tribune*, February 24, 1957, Pt. 2, p. 1; "Indiana Upset; Spartans Tie for Lead," *Chicago Tribune*, February 26, 1957, Pt. 3, p. 1; "Badgers Fade," *Chicago Tribune*, February 26, 1957, Pt. 3, p. 1.

51. "Illini Conduct Ohio Ceremony," *Chicago Tribune*, February 26, 1957, Pt. 3, p. 1; "Kline Smashes Mark; Gophers Win, 102 to 81," *Chicago Tribune*, February 26, 1957, Pt. 3, p. 4.

52. "Spartans Win; Clinch Title Tie," *Chicago Tribune*, March 3, 1957, Pt. 2, p. 1; "Buckeyes Keep Hopes Alive; Beat N.U., 84–70," *Chicago Tribune*, March 3, 1957, Pt. 3, p. 3.

53. "Spartans Lose; Indiana Ties for Title," *Chicago Tribune*, March 5, 1957, Pt. 3, p. 1; "Gophers Beat Ohio," *Chicago Tribune*, March 5, 1957, Pt. 3, p. 2.

54. Wilson and Brondfield, p. 360.

55. Wilson and Brondfield, pp. 359–360.

56. Mokray, pp. 4–104.

57. Richard Dozer, "Spartans Defeat Irish in N.C.A.A. Tourney, 85–83," *Chicago Tribune*, March 16, 1957, Pt. 2, p. 1; Richard Dozer, "Spartan Rally Whips Kentucky, 80–68," *Chicago Tribune*, March 17, 1957, Pt. 2, p. 1.

58. Richard Dozer, "Spartans Begin N.C.A.A. Title Bid Tonight," *Chicago Tribune*, March 22, 1957, Pt. 4, p. 1.

59. "Hoosiers Pace Spartans," *Chicago Tribune*, March 22, 1957, Pt. 4, p. 5.

60. Bjarkman, p. 63.

61. Richard Dozer, "Spartans Lose in 3d Overtime, 74–70," *Chicago Tribune*, March 23, 1957, Pt. 2, p. 1.

62. Richard Dozer, "No. Carolina Beats Kansas, 54–53, in 3d Overtime," *Chicago Tribune*, March 24, 1957, Pt. 2, p. 1.

63. Editors of *Sport Magazine*, "All–America Basketball Forecast," *Sport* 25, no.1 (January 1958): p. 23.

64. Editors of *Sport*, pp. 22–23.

65. Editors of *Sport*, p. 63. According to Gentry himself, his selection was not based on starring on a freshman team, since his freshman squad played only on-campus squads like the football team. He had been all-state in Illinois as his Rockford West team won the high school championship two years in a row in 1955 and 1956.

66. Nolden Gentry interview, April 9, 2015.

67. "N.C.A.A. Tightens Rules for Its Basketball and Baseball Meets," *Chicago Tribune*, January 5, 1958, Pt. 2, p. 2.

68. "Ohio Upsets Spartans, 70–56; Illini Win, 64–59," *Chicago Tribune*, January 5, 1958, Pt. 2, p. 1. After graduation, Jackson played for the Harlem Globetrotters, and in 1993 was part of an ownership group that purchased the team. He is also the president of the Harlem Globetrotters.

69. Nolden Gentry interview, April 9, 2015.

70. "Indiana Halts N.U. Bid, 68–65," and "Gophers Win 83–76," *Chicago Tribune*, January 5, 1958, Pt. 2, p. 1; "Michigan Beats Iowa," *Chicago Tribune*, January 5, 1958, Pt. 2, p. 2.

71. "Iowa Rally Beats Illinois, 70–68," *Chicago Tribune*, January 7, 1958, Pt. 4 ,p. 1; "Indiana Loses," *Chicago Tribune*, January 7, 1958, Pt. 4, p. 1; "Michigan Wins, 70–49," *Chicago Tribune*, January 7, 1958, Pt. 4, p. 4.

72. Richard Dozer, "N.U. Trounces Michigan; Illini Lose," *Chicago Tribune*, January 12, 1958, Pt. 2, p. 1; "Spartans Win, 84–75," *Chicago Tribune*, January 12, 1958, Pt. 2, p. 4; "Wisconsin Wins," *Chicago Tribune*, January 12, 1958, Pt. 2, p. 4.

73. "Indiana Ties for Lead, N.U. Wins, 82–80," "Badgers Beat Illini, 71–70," "Michigan Wins," all in *Chicago Tribune*, January 14, 1958, Pt. 3, p. 1.

74. Richard Dozer, "Iowa Topples Wisconsin; N.U. Loses," *Chicago Tribune*, January 19, 1958, Pt. 2, p. 1; "Purdue Beats Wisconsin in 2d Half Drive, 62 to 47," *Chicago Tribune*, January 19, 1958, Pt. 2, p. 1.

75. Wilson and Brondfield, p. 365.

76. "Ohio Wins; Badgers Upset Spartans," *Chicago Tribune*, January 21, 1958, Pt. 3, p. 1.

77. "Irish Rout Illini, 81–67, Before 16,212," *Chicago Tribune*, January 26, 1958, Pt. 2, p. 1.

78. "Spartans Rout Wildcats, 74–60," and "Iowa Wins, 73–71," *Chicago Tribune*, January 26, 1958, Pt. 2, p. 1.

79. "Spartans Win, 88–64; Take Big Ten Lead," "Illinois Beats N.U. in Overtime, 102–98," "Iowa Wins, 66–64," "Wolverines Fall," all *Chicago Tribune*, February 2,

1958, Pt. 2, p. 1; "Gophers Win, 69–66," *Chicago Tribune*, February 4, 1958, Pt. 3, p. 1.
80. "Michigan Beats Illinois; Leads Big Ten," "Hoosiers Triumph," *Chicago Tribune*, February 9, 1958, pt. 2, p. 1; "Purdue Takes 2d," *Chicago Tribune*, February 9, 1958, Pt. 2, p. 6.
81. "Spartans, Indiana Win; Tie for Lead," "Illini Beat Purdue," "Wolverines Fail," *Chicago Tribune*, February 11, 1958, Pt. 3, p. 1. Gentry interview.,.
82. "Spartans Defeat Illinois, 69 to 56," "O.S. Beats Michigan," *Chicago Tribune*, February 16, 1958, Pt. 2, p. 1; "Free Throws Help Purdue Top Badgers," *Chicago Tribune*, February 16, 1958, Pt. 2, p. 5; "Spartans Win, 79 to 69: Increase Lead," "Ohio Checks Dees," *Chicago Tribune*, February 18, 1958, Pt. 3, p. 1.
83. "N.U. Trounces Michigan; Spartans Win," "Iowa Keeps Title Hopes Alive," "Purdue Wins, 88–79," *Chicago Tribune*, February 23, 1958, Pt. 2, p. 1; "Purdue Beats Spartans; Tie for Lead," "Wolverines Lose," Spence Sandvig, "Iowa Bolsters Title Bid; Beats N.U., 86–78," *Chicago Tribune*, February 25, 1958, Pt. 3, p. 1.
84. Gentry interview.
85. "Spartans Win; 1 Game from Title," "Boilermakers Lose," Spence Sandvig, "N.U. Defeats Badgers, 82–65," *Chicago Tribune*, March 2, 1958, Pt. 2, p. 1; "Indiana Wins, 96–86; Ties for Big Ten Lead," "Purdue Beats Iowa," *Chicago Tribune*, March 4, 1958, Pt. 3, p. 1.
86. "Champs: Indiana on Court; Illini on Track," *Chicago Tribune*, March 9, 1958, Pt. 2, p. 1.
87. "Big Ten Scoring," *Chicago Tribune*, March 9, 1958, Pt. 3, p. 4.
88. Charles Bartlett, "Big Ten Boosts Aid to Athlete of Low Income," *Chicago Tribune*, March 9, 1958, Pt. 2, p. 5.
89. Cromie, Robert, "Irish Oust Indiana from N.C.A.A Opener, 94–87," *Chicago Tribune*, March 15, 1958, pt. 2, p. 1.

## Chapter 6

1. Dick Schaap, "Basketball's Giant Giveaway: The Recruiting Payoffs," *Sport* 26, no. 6 (December 1958): 82.
2. Editors of *Sport*, "All-America Forecast," *Sport* 27 no. 1 (January 1959): 14.
3. Richard Dozer, "N.U. Wins in Double Overtime, 118–109," *Chicago Tribune*, December 28, 1958, Pt. 2, p. 1.
4. "Purdue Beats Irish; Butler Downs Indiana," *Chicago Tribune*, December 28, 1958, Pt. 3, p. 3.
5. Gentry interview.
6. Gentry interview.
7. Richard Dozer, "Big Ten Opens Basketball Race Today," *Chicago Tribune*, January 3, 1959, Pt. 3, p. 1.
8. Lee Caryer, *The Golden Age of Ohio State Basketball* (Shippensburg, PA: Companion Press, 1991), 13.
9. Richard Dozer, "N.U. Staves Off Iowa Rally; Wins 80–77," "Illini Beat Ohio, 81–80, in Final 16 Seconds," "Hoosiers Fall," *Chicago Tribune*, January 4, 1959, Pt. 2, p. 1; "Purdue Five Is Defeated by Michigan," "Early Gopher Lead Beats Wisconsin," *Chicago Tribune*, January 4, 1959, Pt. 2, p. 2.
10. "N.U. Wins, 83–78; Iowa Beats Spartans," *Chicago Tribune*, January 6, 1959, Pt. 4, p. 1.
11. Richard Dozer, "Illinois, N.U. Lose First Big 10 Games," *Chicago Tribune*, January 11, 1959, Pt. 2, p. 1.
12. "Illini Beat Iowa, 103–97; Indiana Wins," *Chicago Tribune*, January 13, 1959, Pt. 3, p. 1.
13. "Buckeyes Pin 2d Loss on N.U., 88–77," "Hot Hawkeyes (.467) Ruin Hoosier Bid for 1st, 88–78," *Chicago Tribune*, January 18, 1959, Pt. 2, p. 1; "Purdue Rally Fails; Gophers Win, 64–62," *Chicago Tribune*, January 18, Pt. 2, p. 3.
14. "N.U. Loses, 71–67; Four Tied for Lead," "Spartans Rout Ohio, 92 to 77," *Chicago Tribune*, January 20, 1959, Pt. 4, p. 1.
15. Richard Dozer, "Irish Defeat Illini; N.U. Wins," *Chicago Tribune*, January 25, 1959, Pt. 2, p. 1.
16. "Purdue Tags Ohio with 86–69 Loss," *Chicago Tribune*, January 25, 1959, Pt. 2, p. 1.
17. "Illini Bid Fails; Gophers Win, 81–70," "Ohio Beats Iowa," *Chicago Tribune*, January 27, 1959, Pt. 3, p. 1; "3 on Indiana Basket Team Flunk Exams," *Chicago Tribune*, January 27, 1959, Pt. 3, p. 4.
18. "Virginia Loses Integration Case," *Chicago Tribune*, February 1, 1959, Pt. 1, p. 1.
19. "Spartans Beat N.U.; Illini Lose, 102–81," *Chicago Tribune*, February 1, 1959, Pt. 2, p. 1; "Buckeyes Win," *Chicago Tribune*, February 1, 1959, Pt. 2, p. 6.
20. "5 Records Set as Indiana Wins, 122–92," "Michigan Wins," "Spartans Win, 88–57," *Chicago Tribune*, February 3, 1959, Pt. 3, p. 1.
21. Howard Barry, "N.U. Beats Illini; Spartans Lose," "Indiana Wins Battle for Second," *Chicago Tribune*, February 8, 1959, Pt. 2, p. 1.
22. "Illini Halt Indiana; Purdue Upset," *Chicago Tribune*, February 10, 1959, Pt. 3, p. 1.
23. "Spartans Win, Set Record; N.U. Loses," Richard Dozer, "Purdue Wins in Overtime," "Indiana Wins, 62–57," *Chicago Tribune*, February 15, 1959, Pt. 2, p. 1.
24. Richard Dozer, "Spartans Beat N.U., 71 to 68; Purdue Wins," "Michigan Beats Iowa," "Purdue Wins, 94–89," *Chicago Tribune*, February 17, 1959, Pt. 4, p. 1; Gentry interview.
25. Richard Dozer, "N.U. Wins, Spartans Clinch Title Tie," "Illini Win, 100–98," *Chicago Tribune*, February 22, 1959, Pt. 2, p. 1.
26. "Iowa 91, Ohio 79," "Badgers Lose 9th," *Chicago Tribune*, February 22, 1959, Pt. 2, p. 6.
27. "Eliminate 3 Teams from Big Ten Race," "Iowa Checks Purdue Late Rally, 66–62," "Ohio Wins, 92–83," *Chicago Tribune*, February 24, 1959, Pt. 4, p. 1.
28. Richard Dozer, "Spartans Triumph, Clinch Undisputed Big Ten Basketball Title," *Chicago Tribune*, March 1, 1959, Pt. 2, p. 1.
29. "Michigan Beats Illini, 101 to 95," "Ohio Beats Gophers," *Chicago Tribune*, March 3, 1959, Pt. 3, p. 3; Richard Dozer, "Fordy Anderson," *Chicago Tribune*, March 3, 1959, Pt. 3, p. 2.
30. "N.U. Defeats Illinois, 84 to 81, to Tie for 2d," "Spartans Beat Iowa," "Purdue Earns Share," "Foster Quits Badger Post in Basketball," *Chicago Tribune*, March 8, 1959, Pt. 2, p. 1.
31. Wilson and Brondfield, p. 371; Mokray, pp. 4–104.
32. Richard Dozer, "Spartans Win; Kentucky Upset, 76–61," *Chicago Tribune*, March 14, 1959, Pt. 3, p. 1; Richard Dozer, "Louisville Upsets Spartans, 88 to 81," *Chicago Tribune*, March 15, 1959, Pt. 2, p. 1.
33. Editors of *Sport*, All-America Basketball Forecast, January 1960.
34. Caryer, p. 15.
35. Caryer, p. 33.

36. Kundla and the Lakers were part of the roiling professional leagues at the time, winning first in the National Basketball League in 1948, then jumping to the Basketball Association of America and winning the championship in 1949, then winning the championship of the combined leagues, now merged as the National Basketball Association, in 1950, 1952, 1953 and 1954.

37. "Cincinnati Wins, 86–71, Over Bradley," *Chicago Tribune*, December 23, 1959, Pt. 3, p. 1.

38. Gentry interview.

39. "Cincinnati and Iowa Win in Holiday Meet," *Chicago Tribune*, December 27, 1959, Pt. 2, p. 6; "Cincinnati Defeats Iowa, 96–83," *Chicago Tribune*, December 31, 1959, Pt. 3, p. 1. Gentry interview.

40. "Irish, Indiana Win in Hoosier Classic," *Chicago Tribune*, December 23, 1959, Pt. 3, p.1. "Indiana Beats Irish to Take Hoosier Classic," *Chicago Tribune*, December 24, 1959, Pt.3, p. 1.

41. "N.U. Loses; California Beats Illinois," *Chicago Tribune*, December 29, 1959, Pt. 2, p. 6; "Indiana Wins Tourney; Illini Beat N.U.," *Chicago Tribune*, December 30, 1959, Pt. 3, p. 1.

42. "Ohio State Loses," *Chicago Tribune*, December 22, 1959, Pt. 4, p. 1.

43. Richard Dozer, "Three Teams Open Basketball Play in Big 10," *Chicago Tribune*, January 2, 1960, Pt. 3, p. 3.

44. "Spartans Win; Purdue Upsets Indiana," "Gophers Beat Iowa," *Chicago Tribune*, January 3, 1960, Pt. 2, p. 1; Gentry interview.

45. Richard Dozer, "Illini Lose; N.U. Beats Indiana, 61 to 57," "Ohio State Trounces Illinois, 97 to 73," *Chicago Tribune*, January 5, 1960, Pt. 4, p. 1.

46. "N.U. Loses; Ohio Nips Indiana, 96 to 95," "Iowa Wins, 73–59," "Wow! Spartans, 89–58," "Illinois Tops Gophers, 90–82," *Chicago Tribune*, January 10, 1960, Pt. 2, p. 1; "Purdue 99, Badgers 69," *Chicago Tribune*, January 10, 1960, Pt. 2, p. 2.

47. "Illini Defeats Purdue, 81–75; Iowa Wins, 92–79," *Chicago Tribune*, January 12, 1960, Pt. 3, p. 1.

48. Gentry interview.

49. "Iowa Wins; Ohio Defeats N.U., 81–64," "Illinois Heads Off Michigan State, 96–88," *Chicago Tribune*, January 12, 1960, Pt. 2, p. 1; Gentry interview.

50. Richard Dozer. "N.U. Beats Gophers in Last 9 Seconds," "Ohio Satte's Balance Beats Purdue, 85–71," "Spartans Beat Iowa," *Chicago Tribune*, January 24, 1960, Pt. 2, p. 1.

51. "Ohio Routs Michigan State, 111–79," "Gophers Win, 86–72," *Chicago Tribune*, January 31, 1960, Pt. 2, p. 1.

52. "Ohio Wins 6th in Row; N.U. Loses," "Spartans Win," *Chicago Tribune*, February 2, 1960, Pt. 4, p. 1.

53. "Ohio Beats N.U. for 7th in Row, 77–58," *Chicago Tribune*, February 7, 1960, Pt. 2, p. 1; "No.8 for Ohio; Spartans Beat Illini," "Gophers Lose to N.U., 66–64," "Spartans Win," *Chicago Tribune*, February 9, 1960, Pt. 3, p. 1; "Hoosiers Win, 87–74," *Chicago Tribune*, February 9, 1960, Pt. 3, p. 2.

54. "N.U., Illini Win; Ohio State Beats Iowa," *Chicago Tribune*, February 14, 1960, Pt. 2, p. 1; "Illini Win in Overtime," "Hoosiers Win, 91–71," "Gophers Win," *Chicago Tribune*, February 14, 1960, Pt. 2, p. 6; Richard Dozer, "Ohio Whips Illinois, 109–81!" "Badgers End Drouth; Beat Iowa, 63–58," "Gophers Victors," *Chicago Tribune*, February 16, 1960, Pt. 3, p. 1.

55. "Ohio Barely Makes It! Clinches Title Tie," *Chicago Tribune*, February 21, 1960, Pt. 2, p. 1; "Indiana Wins, 79–64," "Gophers Win, 87–61," *Chicago Tribune*, February 21, 1960, Pt. 2, p. 3.

56. Richard Dozer, "N.U. Wins, 71–69; Indiana Beats Illinois," "Badgers Win Again!" *Chicago Tribune*, February 23, 1960, Pt. 3, p. 1.

57. "Ohio Beats Badgers, 93 to 68 for Title," *Chicago Tribune*, February 28, 1960, Pt. 2, p. 1; "N.U. Wins, 68–66," "Indiana Wins," "Tidwell Sets Mark," "Illini Beat Iowa," *Chicago Tribune*, February 28, 1960, Pt. 2, p. 3.

58. Roy Damer, "Indiana Halts Ohio State, 99–83," "N.U. Wins," "Illini Win, 90–61," *Chicago Tribune*, March 1, 1960, Pt. 3, p. 1.

59. Roy Damer, "Illini Hit 51.5 Per Cent to Beat N.U.," "Ohio State Wins," "Hoosiers Win, 86–80," *Chicago Tribune*, March 6, 1960, Pt. 2, p. 1.

60. Wilson and Brondfield, p. 375.

61. Mokray, pp. 4–105.

62. This was a period of disarray over athletic scandals for what had been the Pacific Coast Conference. The conference disbanded in 1959 and five members (Cal, Stanford, Washington, UCLA, USC) formed the Athletic Association of Western Universities. Washington State joined in 1962, making the Pacific Six, and Oregon and Oregon State joined in 1964, forming the Pac 8. Thus Oregon and Cal were not in the same conference in 1960 and were each invited to the NCAA tourney.

63. "Ohio, California Gain N.C.A.A. Finals," *Chicago Tribune*, March 19, 1960, Pt. 3, p. 1.

64. "Ohio State Wins N.C.A.A. Title, 75–55," *Chicago Tribune*, March 20, 1960, Pt. 2, p. 1.

65. Caryer, pp. 10–11.

66. Bjarkman, p. 174; Wilson and Brondfeld, p. 376–378.

67. See Nelson, *Abe Saperstein and the American Basketball League*, pp. 139–145.

68. The best account of this and other USA Basketball Olympic endeavors is Carson Cunningham's *American Hoops: U.S. Men's Olympic Basketball from Berlin to Beijing* (Lincoln: University of Nebraska Press, 2012). Details on the selection process are on pp. 126–127.

69. Caryer, pp. 56–57.

70. "Ohio Wins," *Chicago Tribune*, January 1, 1961, Pt. 2, p. 1.

71. "Ike Warns Reds on Laos," "U.S. Military Ready in Asia," *Chicago Tribune*, January 1, 1961, Pt. 1, p. 1.

72. "Reds Capture Key Plain in Laos," *Chicago Tribune*, January 7, 1961, Pt. 1, p. 1.

73. Richard Dozer, "Big Ten Starts Chasing Ohio Today," *Chicago Tribune*, January 7, 1961, Pt. 2, p. 1.

74. Richard Dozer, "N.U. Loses, 79–64; Ohio Defeats Illini," *Chicago Tribune*, January 8, 1961, Pt. 2, p. 1; "Iowa Triumphs," "Michigan Is Beaten by Indiana," "Badgers Win," *Chicago Tribune*, January 8, 1961, Pt. 2, p. 2.

75. "Indiana Wins, 79–55; Wisconsin Loses," *Chicago Tribune*, January 10, 1961, Pt. 3, p. 1.

76. Roy Damer, "N.U. Loses, 79–45," "Illinois Ends Losses, Beats Michigan, 84–64," "Iowa Beats Spartans," *Chicago Tribune*, January 15, 1961, Pt. 2, p. 1; "Purdue Hands Minnesota 2d Loss in Row," *Chicago Tribune*, January 15, 1961, Pt. 2, p. 2.

77. "Iowa Beats Illinois," "Northwestern Loses, 66–54," *Chicago Tribune*, January 17, 1961, Pt. 4, p. 1; "Spartans Win 81–69 Battle with Michigan," *Chicago Tribune*, January 17, 1961, Pt. 4, p. 2.

78. "Purdue Stops Iowa, Shares Big 10 Lead," "Ohio Wins No. 13," *Chicago Tribune*, January 22, 1961, Pt. 2, p. 1.
79. Richard Dozer, "Wildcats Upset Purdue, 64–62," "Gophers Beat Mich. State," *Chicago Tribune*, January 24, 1961, pt. 3, p. 1.
80. Roy Damer, "Wildcats Lose; Illini Beat Irish," "Ohio State Routs Purdue, 92–62," *Chicago Tribune*, January 29, 1961, Pt. 2, p. 1.
81. "Rocket Chimp Back Alive," *Chicago Tribune*, February 1, 1961, Pt. 1, p. 1; "Ohio Wins; Illini Beat Spartans," "Indiana Loses," *Chicago Tribune*, January 31, 1961, Pt. 3, p. 1.
82. "Ohio Wins Again," *Chicago Tribune*, February 5, 1961, Pt. 2, p. 1; "Ohio Wins Big Showdown," *Chicago Tribune*, February 7, 1961, Pt. 4, p. 1.
83. "Iowa Fires Student," *Chicago Tribune*, February 10, 1961, Pt. 4, p. 1. A total of 14 Iowa athletes were declared ineligible, including the four from the basketball team.
84. "Believe Allen, Harris, Maher Are Ineligible," *Des Moines Register*, February 8, 1961, p. 18.
85. "Ohio Routs N.U.; Iowa, Purdue Win," *Chicago Tribune*, February 14, 1961, Pt. 3, p. 1.
86. "Ohio State Rallies, Beats Iowa, 62–61!" *Chicago Tribune*, February 19, 1961, Pt. 2, p. 1; Caryer, p. 64.
87. "Purdue Wins, 65–64," *Chicago Tribune*, February 19, 1962, Pt. 2, p. 1.
88. "Iowa Wins; Ohio State Beats Indiana," *Chicago Tribune*, February 21, 1961, Pt. 3, p. 1.
89. "Ohio Clinches Tie," "Purdue Wins, 85–74," *Chicago Tribune*, February 26, 1961, Pt. 2, p. 1; "Iowa Wins, 61–43," "Indiana Wins, 93–82," *Chicago Tribune*, February 26, 1961, Pt. 2, p. 4.
90. "Iowa Takes 2d Place, Beats Purdue," *Chicago Tribune*, February 28, 1961, Pt. 4, p. 1; "Ohio State Wins, 91–83," *Chicago Tribune*, March 5, 1961, Pt. 2, p. 1.
91. "Ohio State Finishes Unbeaten," *Chicago Tribune*, March 12, 1961, Pt. 2, p. 1; "Taylor Coach of the Year," *Chicago Tribune*, March 12, Pt. 2, p. 6; "Purdue Ties for 2d; Beats Wisconsin," *Chicago Tribune*, March 12, 1961, Pt. 2, p. 6.
92. "Ohio Beats Louisville in N.C.A.A. Meet, 56–55," Chicago Tribune, March 18, 1961, Pt. 2, p. 1.
93. Crayer, p. 67.
94. "Ohio Moves to N.C.A.A. Finals, 87–74," *Chicago Tribune*, March 19, 1961, Pt. 2, p. 1.
95. "It's Ohio, Cincinnati in Finals Tonight," *Chicago Tribune*, March 25, 1961, Pt. 6, p. 1.
96. Strauss, Ben, "College Games on Television? That Might Work," *New York Times*, April 7, 2013, "Sports Sunday," p. 3.
97. "Cincinnati Beats Ohio in Overtime," *Chicago Tribune*, March 26, 1961, Pt. 2, p. 1; "Cincinnati Upsets Bucks in Overtime," *Los Angeles Times*, March 26, 1961, Sec. H, p. 1.
98. Caryer, p. 71.
99. Caryer, p. 71.

## Chapter 7

1. Bjarkman, p. 166.
2. Frederick J. Augustyn, Jr. "Meanwell, Walter," in David L. Porter, *Basketball: A Biographical Dictionary* (Westport, CT: Greenwood Press, 2005), pp. 320–321.
3. http://www.bigbluehistory.net/bb/helms.html.
4. Augustyn, p. 320.
5. http://www.hoophall.com/hall-of-famers/tag/walter-e-meanwell.
6. http://en.wikipedia.org/wiki/Ralph_Jones.
7. Neil Isaacs, *All the Moves: A History of College Basketball* (New York: Harper and Row, 1975), p. 56.
8. http://www.purduesports.com/sports/m-baskbl/spec-rel/legends-wardlambert.html.
9. Bruce J. Dierenfield, "Lambert, Ward 'Piggy,'" in Porter, p. 270.
10. http://www.hoophall.com/hall-of-famers/tag/ward-l-lambert.
11. See Bob Hunter's *Buckeye Basketball: Ohio State University*, where an entire chapter is devoted to Olsen and his coaching.
12. John L. Evers, "Harold G. Olsen," in Porter, pp. 363–364.
13. http://www.hoophall.com/hall-of-famers/tag/harold-g-olsen.
14. Stan W. Carlson, "Dean, Everett S.," in Porter, p. 109.
15. Isaacs, p. 152.
16. Gregory S. Sojka, "Lonborg, Arthur C. 'Dutch,'" in Porter, p. 287–288.
17. John L. Evers, "Foster, Harold 'Bud,'" in Porter, p. 150.
18. Leonard and Freedman, p. 31.
19. Frederick J. Augustyn, "McCracken, Emmett Branch 'Big Bear' 'Mac,'" in Porter, p. 300.
20. http://bentley.umich.edu/athdept/baskmen/baskmaa/oosterbaa.htm.
21. http://www.hoophall.com/hall-of-famers/tag/harold-g-olsenhttp://news.google.com/newspapers?nid=1873&dat=19500411&id=814pAAAAIBAJ&sjid=NsgEAAAAIBAJ&pg=1579,2561179.
22. Caryer, p. 4.
23. Caryer, p. 6.
24. Bjarkman, p. 167.
25. Dave Merchant, telephone interview, December 29, 2014.
26. Jeff Sanderson and Wayne Patterson, "Taylor, Frederick Rankin 'Fred,'" in Porter, p. 469.
27. Caryer, p. 250–51.
28. Bjarkman, p. 168.
29. http://www.usatoday.com/story/sports/ncaab/2013/12/31/johnny-orr-dies-at-86-iowa-state-michigan/4262817/.

## Chapter 8

1. "Kennedy Reassures Berlin," *Chicago Tribune*, December 26, 1961, Pt. 1, p. 1.
2. Crayer, p. 75.
3. Richard Dozer, "Ohio's Claim to No. 1 Sport Undisturbed," *Chicago Tribune*, January 1, 1962, Pt. 6, p. 3.
4. Hiner with Hutchens, p. 291.
5. "Ohio Opens Title Bid Tonight at N.U.," *Chicago Tribune*, January 3, 1962, Pt. 3, p. 1.
6. Richard Dozer, "Ohio Beats N.U.; Illini, Gophers Win," *Chicago Tribune*, January 7, 1962, Pt. 2, p. 1; "Badgers Win Tho Nelson Sets Record," *Chicago Tribune*, January 7, 1962, Pt. 2, p. 3.
7. "Purdue Defeats Illinois; N.U. Loses," *Chicago*

*Tribune*, January 9, 1962, Pt. 4, p. 1; "Gophers Lose," *Chicago Tribune*, January 9, 1962, Pt. 4, p. 2.

8. "N.C.A.A. Vetoes Irish Rule Review Plan," *Chicago Tribune*, January 14, 1962, Pt. 2, p. 1.

9. "Purdue Sinks Zone Defense of N.U., 90–74," "Ohio Whips Michigan for 12th in Row," *Chicago Tribune*, January 14, 1962, Pt. 2, p. 2; "Gophers Lose, 65–63," *Chicago Tribune*, January 14, 1962, Pt. 2, p. 3; "Illni 66–65 Winners at Mich. State," *Chicago Tribune*, January 14, 1962, Pt. 2, p. 1.

10. "Michigan Upsets Iowa; Purdue Wins," *Chicago Tribune*, January 16, 1962, Pt. 4, P. 1.

11. Richard Dozer, "N.U., Depaul Beaten; Loyola Triumphs," "Buckeyes Win at Minnesota," "Spartans Win 1st," *Chicago Tribune*, January 19, 1962, Pt. 2, p. 1; "Ohio State Routs Purdue, 91 to 65," "Rule Jackson of Wisconsin Is Ineligible," *Chicago Tribune*, January 21, 1962, Pt. 4, p. 1.

12. Hiner with Hutchens, p. 291.

13. "Rayl's 56 Points Set Big 10 Record," "Badgers Triumph," *Chicago Tribune*, January 28, 1962, Pt. 2, p. 1; Richard Dozer, "N.U. Loses; Badgers Beat Illini," "Ohio Wins, 94–73," *Chicago Tribune*, January 30, 1962, Pt. 3, p. 1.

14. "Ohio Crushes N.U., 97–61 for 16th Victory in Row," "Badgers Beat Gophers, 94–88," "Illini Beat Hoosiers," "Purdue Wins, 86–64," *Chicago Tribune*, February 4, 1962, Pt. 2, p. 1.

15. "Michigan Upsets Wisconsin; Illini Win," "Ohio 89 Iowa 63," *Chicago Tribune*, February 6, 1962, Pt. 3, p. 1.

16. "Illinois Beats Iowa; Ohio Ties Record," *Chicago Tribune*, February 11, 1962, Pt. 2, p. 1; "Purdue Wins as Dischinger Sets Record," *Chicago Tribune*, February 11, 1962, Pt. 2, p. 4.

17. "Ohio Wins Record 24th in Row, 72–57," "Wisconsin Wins," *Chicago Tribune*, February 13, 1962, Part 3, p. 1; "Dischinger Gets 38," *Chicago Tribune*, February 13, 1962, Pt. 3, p. 2.

18. "Badgers Lose 2d," "Dischinger, Purdue Beat Illinois, 100 to 88," *Chicago Tribune*, February 18, 1962, Pt. 2, p. 1; "Badgers Stave Off Illini, 103 to 101," *Chicago Tribune*, February 20, 1962, Pt. 3, p. 1.

19. "Badgers Upset! Ohio Wins Big 10 Title," *Chicago Tribune*, February 27, 1962, Pt. 3, p. 1.

20. Caryer, p. 85.

21. "Badgers Upset Ohio," *Chicago Tribune*, March 4, 1962, Pt. 2, p. 1; Caryer, p. 86.

22. "Two Score 60 as Iowa Beats Illinois," "Indiana Wins, 88–71," "Gophers Win, 98–91," *Chicago Tribune*, March 4, 1962, Pt. 2, p. 4.

23. "Gophers Win," "Rayl's 37 Ties Dischinger," *Chicago Tribune*, March 6, 1962, Pt. 4, p. 1.

24. "Lucas, Dischinger Bow Out in Glory," *Chicago Tribune*, March 11, 1962, Pt. 2, p. 1; "Iowa Wins, 81–64," *Chicago Tribune*, March 11, 1962, Pt. 2, p. 5.

25. Wilson and Brondfield, p. 389.

26. Howard Barry, "Ohio and Kentucky Win; Meet Tonight," *Chicago Tribune*, March 17, 1962, Pt. 6, p. 1.

27. Caryer, p. 89.

28. Howard Barry, "Ohio Defeats Kentucky," *Chicago Tribune*, March 18, 1962, Pt. 2, p. 1.

29. Howard Barry, "It's Ohio Vs. Cincinnati Again Tonight," *Chicago Tribune*, March 24, 1962, Pt. 6, p. 1; Caryer, pp. 90–91.

30. Caryer, p. 97.

31. Ed Sainsbury, "College Preview," *Sports Review Basketball* 23, no. 1 (January 1963): p. 48; the editors of *Sport Magazine*, "All-America Basketball Preview," *Sport Magazine* 35, no. 1 (January 1963).

32. "Illini Crush Penn; N.U. Beats Stanford," *Chicago Tribune*, December 27, 1962, Pt. 4, p. 1; "Illini Win 8th in Row, 92–74," *Chicago Tribune*, December 30, 1962, Pt. 2, p. 1.

33. "Gophers Beaten," *Chicago Tribune*, December 28, 1962, Pt. 3, p. 2; "Ohio State Loses," *Chicago Tribune*, December 30, 1962, Pt. 2, p. 1; "Gophers Lose," *Chicago Tribune*, December 30, 1962, Pt. 2, p. 1.

34. "Irish Jolt Indiana," "Boilermakers Win," *Chicago Tribune*, January 3, 1963, Pt. 6, p. 1.

35. "Illini Win; N.U. Loses in Big 10 Openers," "Indiana Beats Spartans; Ohio Victor," *Chicago Tribune*, January 6, 1963, Pt. 2, p. 1; "Wisconsin's Rally Wins at Purdue," *Chicago Tribune*, January 6, 1963, Pt. 2, p. 4.

36. Richard Dozer, "Indiana Wins; Illini Whip Ohio," *Chicago Tribune*, January 8, 1963, Pt. 3, p. 1.

37. "Purdue Loses, 85–71; Wolverines Triumph," *Chicago Tribune*, January 8, 1963, Pt. 3, p. 1.

38. "Ohio Beats Michigan; Illinois Leads Big Ten," "Badgers Lose," *Chicago Tribune*, January 13, 1963, Sec. 2, p. 1; "Gophers 83 Iowa 58," *Chicago Tribune*, January 13, 1963, Sec. 2, p. 3.

39. Richard Dozer, "Illini Jar N.U. on 55-Foot Shot, 78 to 76," "Iowa Rallies to Beat Wisconsin," "Michigan Loses," *Chicago Tribune*, January 15, 1963, Pt. 3, p. 1.

40. "Iowa Upsets Ohio; N.U. Loses, 80 to 68," *Chicago Tribune*, January 20, 1963, Pt. 2, p. 1; Caryer, p. 107.

41. "Gophers Beat Purdue for 3d Big 10 Victory," *Chicago Tribune*, January 20, 1963, Pt. 2, p. 3.

42. Richard Dozer, "20,687 See Loyola, Cincinnati Win," *Chicago Tribune*, January 27, 1963, Pt. 2, p. 1; Richard Dozer, "N.U. Beats Purdue for 1st Victory in Big Ten," *Chicago Tribune*, January 27, 1963, Pt. 2, p. 1; "Minnesota Is 61–59 Victim of Spartans," *Chicago Tribune*, January 27, 1963, Pt. 2, p. 3.

43. "Ohio Defeats N.U., 72–70; Indiana Wins," *Chicago Tribune*, January 29, 1963, Pt. 2, p. 1; "N.U. Upsets Indiana," *Chicago Tribune*, February 3, 1963, Pt. 2, p. 1; "Purdue Loses, 97–96," *Chicago Tribune*, February 3, 1963, Pt. 2, p. 1.

44. "Gophers Win, 69–68," "Michigan Wins, 72–71," *Chicago Tribune*, February 3, 1963, Pt. 2, p. 7.

45. Richard Dozer, "Illinois Hurls Back Indiana, 104–101," "Purdue Hits 55.9%, Beats Mich. State," *Chicago Tribune*, February 5, 1963, Pt. 3, p. 1; "Badgers Win, 81–78," *Chicago Tribune*, February 5, 1963, Pt. 3, p. 2.

46. "Deny Red Build Up in Cuba," *Chicago Tribune*, February 7, 1963, Pt. 1, p. 1.

47. Richard Dozer, "Iowa Beats N.U. in 2d Overtime, 66–65," *Chicago Tribune*, February 10, 1963, pt. 2, p. 1.

48. "Ohio State, 94–70!" *Chicago Tribune*, February 10, 1963, Pt. 2, p. 4; "Buntin Scores 36," "Gophers Halt Late Rally," "Illini Score 6th Big Ten Victory," *Chicago Tribune*, February 10, 1963, Pt. 2, p. 1.

49. "Badgers Deal Illini First Big Ten Loss," "Indiana Takes Gophers Down a Peg, 89 To77," *Chicago Tribune*, February 12, 1963, Pt. 3, p. 1.

50. "Cincinnati, Loyola Upset! Illini Lose," *Chicago Tribune*, February 17, 1963, Pt. 2, p. 1.

51. "Badgers Defeat N.U., 78–65," "Michigan Is Ohio Victim on Rally," "Iowa 73 Purdue 64," "Gophers Win, 75–70," *Chicago Tribune*, February 17, 1963, Pt. 2, p. 4.

52. Richard Dozer, "Michigan Misfires in Last 2 Seconds, Wildcats Win," *Chicago Tribune*, February 19, 1963, Pt. 3, p. 1.
53. "The Winners: Loyola, Illinois and Ohio," *Chicago Tribune*, February 19, 1963, Pt. 3, p. 1; Iowa Drops 72–71 Game to Indiana," *Chicago Tribune*, February 19, 1963, Pt. 3, p. 1.
54. "Illini Win; Jim Rayl Scores Record 56," *Chicago Tribune*, February 24, 1963, Pt. 2, p. 1.
55. "Buckeyes Keep Pace," Chicago Tribune, February 24, 1963, Pt. 2, p. 1; Roy Damer, "Ohio State Beats N.U., 50–45; Illini Win," *Chicago Tribune*, February 26, 1963, Pt. 3, p. 1.
56. "Michigan Is Victor Over Purdue," *Chicago Tribune*, February 24, 1963, Pt. 2, p. 2; "Michigan Wins," *Chicago Tribune*, February 26, 1963, Pt. 3, p. 1.
57. Caryer, p. 110.
58. "Loyola Loses; Ohio Leads Big 10," *Chicago Tribune*, March 3, 1963, Pt. 2, p. 1.
59. "Ohio Clinches Tie for Title; Illini Win," "Badgers Win, 75–69," "Indiana Wins Battle for 4th Place," *Chicago Tribune*, March 5, 1963, Pt. 3, p. 1.
60. "Garland Goal Gives Purdue 94–93 Victory," *Chicago Tribune*, March 5, 1963, Pt. 3, p. 3.
61. "Illini Tie for Big 10 Title; Ohio Loses," *Chicago Tribune*, March 10, 1963, Pt. 2, p. 1; Caryer, pp. 114–115.
62. Wilson and Brondfield, p. 395.
63. "Loyola, Illini Win; Meet Tonight!" *Chicago Tribune*, March 16, 1963, Pt. 3, p. 1.
64. "Loyola Routs Illinois in N.C.A.A. Meet," *Chicago Tribune*, March 17, 1963, Pt. 2, p. 1.
65. *Dell Sports* 1, no. 36 (January 1964). Hudson, Clark and Tony Yates were the first African Americans to have basketball scholarships at Minnesota.
66. Dave Schellhase telephone interviews, May 10 and May 13, 2015.
67. Caryer, p. 117.
68. Caryer, pp. 120–121.
69. Schellhase interview, May 13, 2015.
70. "Big Ten Season Opens!" *Chicago Tribune*, January 4, 1964, Pt. 3, p. 1.
71. "Michigan Defeats N.U.; Illinois Wins," *Chicago Tribune*, January 5, 1964, Pt. 2, p. 1.
72. "Iowa 72, Indiana 71," "32 by Bradds Leads Ohio Rout of Badgers," "Gophers 97, Purdue 93," *Chicago Tribune*, January 5, 1964, Pt. 2, p. 1.
73. Schellhase interview.
74. Larry Glass telephone interview, November 5, 2014.
75. Richard Dozer, "N.U. Halts Indiana 'Double Play,' 79–65," *Chicago Tribune*, January 7, 1964, Pt. 3, p. 1; "Spartans Win," *Chicago Tribune*, January 7, 1964, Pt. 3, p. 2.
76. Richard Dozer, "N.U. Beats Badgers; Illini Win," *Chicago Tribune*, January 12, 1964, Pt. 2, p. 1; "Spartans Win," *Chicago Tribune*, January 12, 1964, Pt. 2, p. 4.
77. "Ohio Triumphs," *Chicago Tribune*, January 12, 1964, Pt. 2, p. 4; "Michigan Wins," *Chicago Tribune*, January 12, 1964, Pt. 2, p. 1.
78. "Gophers Beat Spartans in 103–82 Rout," *Chicago Tribune*, January 15, 1964, Pt. 3, p. 1.
79. "Michigan Routs Ohio, 82–64; N.U. Loses," *Chicago Tribune*, January 19, 1964, Pt. 2, p. 1.
80. "Michigan Rolls On; Purdue Triumphs," *Chicago Tribune*, January 22, 1964, Pt. 3, p. 1; Roy Damer, "Michigan Triumphs Again; N.U. Wins," "Ohio State Wins," *Chicago Tribune*, January 26, 1964, Pt. 2, p. 1.
81. Schellhase interview.
82. "Bradds Gets 48, but Ohio Falls to Spartans, 102–99," *Chicago Tribune*, January 28, 1964, Pt. 3, p. 1.
83. "Illini Ambushed; Ohio Stuns Michigan," *Chicago Tribune*, February 4, 1964, Pt. 3, p. 1; "Purdue Wins, 101–98," *Chicago Tribune*, February 4, 1964, Pt. 3, p. 3.
84. Richard Dozer, "N.U. Wins; Michigan Shrugs Off Illinois," *Chicago Tribune*, February 9, 1964, Pt. 2, p. 1; "Badgers Stop Purdue," "Gophers Win, 76–71," "Ohio Takes 2d," *Chicago Tribune*, February 9, 1964, Pt. 2, p. 4.
85. "Bradds Gets 49 Pts.; Ohio Beats Illini," *Chicago Tribune*, February 11, 1964, Pt. 3, p.1; "N.U. Beats Badgers, 72–64; Ties for 3d," *Chicago Tribune*, February 12, 1964, Pt. 3, p. 1; "Stadium Bookies Seized," *Chicago Tribune*, February 13, 1964, Pt. 1, p. 1.
86. "Michigan, Ohio State Win; Illini Lose," *Chicago Tribune*, February 16, 1964, Pt. 2, p. 1; "Schellhase, Purdue Whip N.U.," *Chicago Tribune*, February 16, 1964, Pt. 2, p. 4.
87. Caryer, p. 127.
88. "Ohio Wins, 99–82; Illini Lose," "NCAA At-Large Bids," *Chicago Tribune*, February 18, 1964, Pt. 3, p. 1.
89. "Voting Rights of Civil Rights Bill Explained," *Chicago Tribune*, February 19, 1964, pt. 1, p. 1.
90. "Michigan Loses; Two-Way Tie for Lead," *Chicago Tribune*, February 19, 1964, Pt. 3, p. 1.
91. Richard Dozer, "Ohio State and Michigan Keep Pace," *Chicago Tribune*, February 23, 1964, Pt. 2, p. 1; "Illini Jolt Gophers," *Chicago Tribune*, February 23, 1964, Pt. 2, p. 1.
92. Richard Dozer, "Falk Tallies 49 as N.U. Triumphs," *Chicago Tribune*, February 25, 1964, Pt. 3, p. 1.
93. "Michigan Defeats Illinois; Ohio Wins," *Chicago Tribune*, March 1, 1964, Pt. 2, p. 1.
94. Schellhase interview.
95. Roy Damer, "Buckeyes Rip Illinois, 86–74; Lead Big 10," *Chicago Tribune*, March 3, 1964, Pt. 3, p. 1; "Ohio Upset; Michigan Wins, Takes Lead," *Chicago Tribune*, March 8, 1964, Pt. 2, p. 1; "Michigan Upset; Yields Share of Title," *Chicago Tribune*, March 10, 1964, Pt. 3, p. 1.
96. Caryer, p. 129.
97. Wilson and Brondfield, p. 400.
98. Cazzie L. Russell, Jr., *Me, Cazzie Russell*, p. 86.
99. "Michigan Ends Loyola's Reign," *Chicago Tribune*, March 14, 1964, Pt. 3, p. 1.
100. "Michigan Wins Regional Title," *Chicago Tribune*, March 15, 1964, Pt. 2, p. 1.
101. "Michigan Loses; Duke, UCLA in Final," *Chicago Tribune*, March 21, 1964, Pt. 2, p. 1.
102. "Michigan Tops Kansas State," *Chicago Tribune*, March 22, 1964, Pt. 2, p. 1.

# Chapter 9

1. *Basketball Yearbook, 1965*, 1964.
2. *Complete Sports 5th Annual Basketball, 1964–65* 1, no. 5 (1964).
3. "College Basketball, 1965," *Sports Illustrated* 21, no. 23 (December 7, 1964).

4. After Joyner's injury, Coach Branch McCracken visited him in the hospital to express his concern and disappointment, telling Joyner that he (Butch) was seen, after camp, as their #1 forward, ahead of both Tom and Dick Van Arsdale. This was quite a compliment, since they went on to long and respected NBA careers (Joyner interview, January 7, 2015).

5. Robert Young, "U.S. Will Cut New Canal," *Chicago Tribune*, December 19, 1964, Pt. 1, p. 1. The newly expanded Panama Canal, designed to accommodate larger ships, opened to traffic in June 2016. Another is planned for Nicaragua with significant funding from China and completion by 2020.

6. "'Hot' Shooting Illinois Wins, 104–86," *Chicago Tribune*, December 19, 1964, Pt. 2, p. 1; "Illinois Wins Kentucky Meet, 91–86," *Chicago Tribune*, December 20, 1964, Pt. 2, p. 1.

7. "Buckeyes Fall," Richard Dozer, "N.U. Off in First Half, Falls to Creighton, 82–70," *Chicago Tribune*, December 20, 1964, Pt. 2, p. 1.

8. Estes was electrocuted on February 8, 1965, after scoring 48 points against the University of Denver in Logan. After the game, he and friends stopped at the scene of a car accident near campus and, while crossing the street, he brushed a downed power line and was instantly killed.

9. "Minnesota Bowls Over Utah State," "Butler Beats Spartans," "Badgers Get 62 to 61 Jolt by Marquette," *Chicago Tribune*, December 20, 1964, Pt. 2, p. 4; "Unbeaten Indiana Routs Irish, 107–81," *Chicago Tribune*, December 22, 1964, Pt. 3, p. 1.

10. Dave Schellhase interview, May 13, 2015.

11. "Unbeaten Gophers Rout Loyola, 89–75," *Chicago Tribune*, December 23, 1964, Pt. 3, P. 1; "N.U. Loses; Michigan and Depaul Win," *Chicago Tribune*, December 24, 1964, Pt. 3, p. 1.

12. "Illini Lose; Indiana Crushes St. Louis," *Chicago Tribune*, December 29, 1964, Pt. 3, p. 1; "Hoosiers Win Meet, 91–68," *Chicago Tribune*, December 30, 1964, Pt. 3, p. 1.

13. "Wolverines Win in E.C.A.C. First Round," *Chicago Tribune*, December 29, 1964, Pt. 3, p. 1; "St. John's Upsets Michigan, 75 to 74," *Chicago Tribune*, January 3, 1965, Pt. 3, p. 1.

14. "Gophers Lose 1st to UCLA," *Chicago Tribune*, December 30, 1964, Pt. 3, p. 1; "Gophers Snap Back; Defeat Titans, 80–66," *Chicago Tribune*, January 3, 1965, Pt. 2, p. 2.

15. Richard Dozer, "Illini Deal Indiana 1st Defeat, 86–81," *Chicago Tribune*, January 5, 1965, Pt. 3, p. 1.

16. Richard Dozer, "Michigan Stops Illini; N.U. Defeated," "Iowa Wins 2d in Big Ten, 85–78," *Chicago Tribune*, January 10, 1965, Pt. 2, p. 1.

17. "Indiana Stops Iowa; Wisconsin Wins," *Chicago Tribune*, January 12, 1965, Pt. 3, p. 1.

18. Richard Dozer, "Michigan Alone on Top; Illinois Wins," *Chicago Tribune*, January 17, 1965, Pt. 2, p. 1; "Twins Star as Hoosiers Defeat Ohio," *Chicago Tribune*, January 17, 1965, Pt. 2, p. 3.

19. "Iowa Beats Indiana in 2d Place Duel," *Chicago Tribune*, January 19, 1965, Pt. 3, p. 1.

20. "Michigan Routs Purdue; N.U. Wins," "Gophers Beat Ohio," *Chicago Tribune*, January 24, 1965, Pt. 2, p. 1; "Gophers Win on Second Half Burst," *Chicago Tribune*, January 26, 1965, Pt. 3, p. 1.

21. "Michigan Wins in Overtime!" *Chicago Tribune*, January 27, 1965, Pt. 3, p. 1; "Michigan Beats Purdue, 98–81," *Chicago Tribune*, January 31, 1965, Pt. 2, p. 1.

22. "Gophers Nip N.U., 70–66," *Chicago Tribune*, February 3, 1965, Pt. 3, p. 1.

23. Schellhase interview.

24. "Reds Kill 8 Gis, Wound 62," *Chicago Tribune*, February 7, 1965, Pt. 1, p. 1; "Illini Set Scoring Mark; Win, 121–93," *Chicago Tribune*, February 7, 1965, Pt. 2, p. 1.

25. "Iowa 78, N.U. 72," *Chicago Tribune*, February 7, 1965, Pt. 2, p. 1; "Gophers Win to Remain in Big Ten Race," *Chicago Tribune*, February 7, 1965, Pt. 2, p. 4.

26. "Michigan Rolls On; Beats Iowa, 81–66," "Illini Beat Ohio State; Tie for 2d," "Hoosiers Rout Spartans," *Chicago Tribune*, February 9, 1965, Pt. 3, p. 1.

27. "Crush Reds at Viet Base," "Negroes Pray for Selma Foe," *Chicago Tribune*, February 13, 1965, Pt. 1, p. 1.

28. "Michigan Victor; Illini Fall," "Gophers 105; Illini 90," "6 Secs Left: Iowa Beats Ohio," *Chicago Tribune*, February 14, 1965, Pt. 2, p. 1; Richard Dozer, "Indiana Defeats N.U., 86–76," *Chicago Tribune*, February 14, 1965, Pt. 2, p. 1.

29. "Michigan Wins in 2d Overtime, 96–95," *Chicago Tribune*, February 16, 1965, Pt. 3, p. 1.

30. "Michigan Captures 9th in Row, 100–61," "Illini Break Mark, 113–94," Robert Markus, "N.U. Felled by Gophers and Flu Bug," *Chicago Tribune*, February 21, 1965, Pt. 2, p. 1.

31. "Purdue Upsets Indiana for Big 10 '1st,'" *Chicago Tribune*, February 23, 1965, Pt. 3, p. 1.

32. "Michigan Wins Showdown Duel, 91–78," "Illinois Routs Iowa, 97 to 80," *Chicago Tribune*, February 24, 1965, Pt. 3, p. 1.

33. "Illini Fail to Stop Michigan," "Minnesota Keeps Hopes Alive, 100–88," "Purdue Pulls Second Upset; Stuns Iowa," *Chicago Tribune*, February 28, 1965, Pt. 2, p. 1.

34. "Michigan Earns Share of Bi10 Title," "Gophers Win, 78–70," *Chicago Tribune*, March 3, 1965, Pt. 3, p. 1; "McCracken Will Retire," *Chicago Tribune*, March 3, 1965, Pt. 3, p. 2. McCracken was succeed by Assistant Coach Lou Watson, who had been a top player while at Indiana, but never seemed to have the same insight as a coach, according to Butch Joyner. He would resign after eight seasons because of lots of player griping.

35. Roy Damer, "N.U. Learns Lessons from Illini, 93–70," *Chicago Tribune*, March 3, 1965, Pt. 3, p. 3; "Pervall Gets 38 as Iowa Beat Illini," "Indiana Beats Purdue," *Chicago Tribune*, March 7, 1965, Pt. 2, p. 4; "Wisconsin Falls to Hoosiers," *Chicago Tribune*, March 9, 1965, Pt. 3, p. 1; "Illini Match School Mark; Win 121–89," *Chicago Tribune*, March 10, 1965, Pt. 3, p. 2.

36. "Michigan Ends Basketball Race by Beating Gophers," *Chicago Tribune*, March 7, 1965, Pt. 2, p. 1; "Cazzie Out, Michigan Beaten, 93–85," *Chicago Tribune*, March 9, 1965, Pt. 3, p. 1; "Gophers Win, 85–84," *Chicago Tribune*, March 10, 1965, Pt. 3, p. 2.

37. "3500 Marines to S. Viet," *Chicago Tribune*, March 7, 1965, Pt. 1, p. 1; "Bars U.S. Troops in Selma," *Chicago Tribune*, March 13, 1965, Pt. 1, p. 1.

38. Buntin was a territorial pick (a 1st round equivalent) of the Pistons in the 1965 NBA draft, but played only one season, scoring 7.7 points and grabbing 6.0 rebounds a game in 42 games. In May of 1968, he suffered a fatal heart attack while playing in a pick-up game in a Detroit neighborhood center.

39. Stallworth used up his eligibility after first semester. Despite that, he made All-American and Wichita made it to the Final Four without him.
40. On February 8, Estes was electrocuted at the scene of a traffic accident in Logan, Utah. He had left his car to see if he could help and walked into a downed power wire that was too high to hit most folks, but low enough to catch him in the forehead, killing him instantly. He was the AP's first posthumous All-American.
41. "Michigan Rolls; Depaul Falls, 83–78," *Chicago Tribune*, March 13, 1965, Pt. 2, p. 1.
42. "Cazzie Pulls Michigan Thru, 87–85," *Chicago Tribune*, March 14, 1965, Pt. 2, p. 1.
43. "Michigan Overwhelms Princeton," *Chicago Tribune*, March 20, 1965, Pt. 2, p. 1.
44. "Goodrich Has 42 Points in Easy Victory," *Chicago Tribune*, March 21, 1965, Pt. 2, p. 1.
45. *Basketball Yearbook, 1966*.
46. *Complete Sports 6th Annual Basketball 1965–66* 1, no. 6 (December 1965).
47. *Dell Sports* 1, no. 48 (January 1966).
48. *Inside Basketball, 1966*, 1965.
49. "Top Twenty 1966," *Sports Illustrated* 23, no. 23 (December 6, 1965).
50. William Anderson, "Expect 200,000 Yanks in Viet," *Chicago Tribune*, December 1, 1965, Pt. 1, p. 5.
51. Richard Dozer, "Duke Beats Michigan; N.U. Wins," *Chicago Tribune*, December 22, 1965, Pt. 3, p. 1; "Iowa 69 Drake 51," "Minnesota 89 Creighton 77," *Chicago Tribune*, December 19, 1965, pt. 2, p. 4. "Hudson of Gophers Out with Injury," *Chicago Tribune*, December 20, 1965, Pt. 3, p. 2.
52. "Butler Upsets Michigan, 79 to 64!" *Chicago Tribune*, December 23, 1965, Pt. 3, p. 1; Richard Dozer, "N.U. Beaten in Last 10 Seconds," "Gophers Routed, 97–72," *Chicago Tribune*, December 24, 1965, Pt. 3, p. 1.
53. "Michigan Upset," *Chicago Tribune*, December 28, 1965, Pt. 3, p. 1.
54. "Gophers Win, 84–82," "Illini Win 96–94," *Chicago Tribune*, December 28, 1965, Pt. 3, p. 4.
55. "Minnesota Crushed by St. Joseph's," "Iowa Wins, 77–75," *Chicago Tribune*, December 30, 1965, Pt. 3, p. 1; "Michigan Wins, 83–74," *Chicago Tribune*, December 28, 1965, Pt. 3, p. 2.
56. "Weary Gophers Play Loyola Tonight," "Illini Fall, 78–69," *Chicago Tribune*, December 31, 1965, Pt. 3, p. 1; "Michigan Is Victory Over Wash. State," "Iowa Upset," *Chicago Tribune*, December 3, 1965, Pt. 3, p. 2.
57. Technically, the conference season started in mid-December when Illinois defeated Wisconsin, a game played then because of various scheduling conflicts.
58. Schellhase interview, May 13, 2015.
59. Joyner interview.
60. Richard Dozer, "N.U. and Illini Triumph; Iowa Upset," *Chicago Tribune*, January 9, 1966, Pt. 2, p. 1.
61. "Michigan Wins," *Chicago Tribune*, January 9, 1966, Pt. 2, p. 2; "Spartans Boost Title Stock; Rout Gophers," *Chicago Tribune*, January 9, 1966, Pt. 2, p. 3.
62. "Indiana Set Down by Michigan," "Spartans Beat Purdue," "N.U. Beaten," *Chicago Tribune*, January 11, 1966, Pt. 3, p. 1.
63. Joyner interview.
64. Richard Dozer, "Illinois Streak Ended; N.U. Beaten," "Spartans Tie for First by Felling Buckeyes," "Minnesota Turns Back Indiana by 9," *Chicago Tribune*, January 16, 1966, Pt. 2, p. 1.
65. Joyner interview.
66. "Indiana Deals Iowa 2d Jolt, 73 to 61," *Chicago Tribune*, January 18, 1966, Pt. 3, p. 1.
67. "Michigan Alone on Top in Big 10 Race," "Iowa Deals Spartans 1st Loss, 90–76," *Chicago Tribune*, January 23, 1966, Pt. 2, p. 1.
68. "Purdue Left in Cold by Spartans, 92 to 74," *Chicago Tribune*, January 25, 1966, Pt. 3, p. 1; "Iowa 98, OSU 89," *Chicago Tribune*, January 25, 1966, Pt. 3, p. 2.
69. "Late Rally Holds Off Badgers," *Chicago Tribune*, January 30, 1966, Pt. 3, p. 1.
70. "Illinois Upsets Michigan, 99 to 93," "Minnesota Triumphs," *Chicago Tribune*, February 2, 1966, Pt. 3, p. 1.
71. "15,191 See Minnesota Win, 66–61," *Chicago Tribune*, February 6, 1966, Pt. 2, p. 2.
72. "Northwestern Upsets Illinois, 80–77," *Chicago Tribune*, February 8, 1966, Pt. 3, p. 1.
73. "Ohio State Falls, 81–61, to Hoosiers," "Badgers Get Negro Coach," *Chicago Tribune*, February 15, 1966, Pt. 3, p. 1.
74. "3 Total 75 as Iowa Jolts Hopes of Gophers, 96–87," *Chicago Tribune*, February 16, 1966, Pt. 3, p. 1.
75. Philip Dodd, "Rusk's Dare: Vote on War," *Chicago Tribune*, February 19, 1966, Pt. 1, p. 1.
76. "Paterno Appointed," *Chicago Tribune*, February 20, 1966, Pt. 2, p. 1.
77. "Michigan Romps," "Badgers Win, 78–77," "Illini Drop Gophers Out of Running," *Chicago Tribune*, February 20, 1966, Pt. 2, p. 1.
78. "Wolverines Upset by Iowa, 91 to 82," *Chicago Tribune*, February 22, 1966, Pt. 3, p. 1.
79. "Spartans Beat Illini in 2d Place Duel," *Chicago Tribune*, February 23, 1966, Pt. 3, p. 1; "Illini Fall, 94–92," "Michigan Defeats Purdue; N.U. Wins," *Chicago Tribune*, February 27, 1966, Pt. 2, p. 1.
80. "Michigan Overpowers Iowa, 103 to 88," "Spartans Win, 98–79," "Illinois Wins," *Chicago Tribune*, March 1, 1966, Pt. 3, p. 1.
81. "Gophers Win, 96–90," "Johnny Orr Quits Post at U. of Mass.," *Chicago Tribune*, March 1, 1966, Pt. 3, p. 3.
82. Joyner interview.
83. "Michigan Wins, Wraps Up Basketball Title; Spartans Bow Out," *Chicago Tribune*, March 6, 1966, Pt. 2, p. 1; "Gophers Beaten," "Illini Defeat Iowa on Day for Freeman," *Chicago Tribune*, March 6, 1966, Pt. 2, p. 4; Robert Markus, "N.U. Enters 1st Division," "Schellhase Wins National Scoring Title," *Chicago Tribune*, March 8, 1966, Pt. 3, p. 1.
84. "Wolverines Upset," *Chicago Tribune*, March 8, 1966, Pt. 3, p. 1.
85. Roy Damer, "Michigan Beats Western Kentucky," *Chicago Tribune*, March 12, 1966, Pt. 3, p. 1.
86. "Governors Back Viet War," *Chicago Tribune*, March 13, 1966, Pt. 1, p. 1.
87. Roy Damer, "Kentucky Defeats Michigan, 84 To77," *Chicago Tribune*, March 13, 1966, Pt. 2, p. 1.
88. By far the best account of the game is Frank Fitzpatrick's *And the Walls Came Tumblin' Down: Kentucky, Texas Western and the Game That Changed American Sports* (New York: Simon & Schuster, 1999).

## Chapter 10

1. *Sports Illustrated* 25, no. 33 (December 5, 1966): p. 58.
2. Zander Hollander, ed., *Basketball Yearbook, 1967*, 1966.
3. These polls were from December 20, 1966.
4. "Kansas State Turns Back Indiana, 82–69," "Michigan Wins," *Chicago Tribune*, December 13, 1966, Pt. 3, p. 1; "Wisconsin Wins First Game, 80–73," *Chicago Tribune*, December 14, 1966, Pt. 3, p. 1; "Purdue Is Victor Over St. Joseph's," *Chicago Tribune*, December 16, 1966, Pt. 3, p. 3.
5. "Big Ten Probes Illinois Slush Fund," *Chicago Tribune*, December 17, 1966, Pt. 2, p. 1.
6. Dan Balz and Larry Miller, "Big Ten to Examine UI; Henry Requests Action," *Daily Illini*, December 17, 1966, p. 1.
7. Balz and Miller.
8. "Iowa Rally Too Much for Drake," "Minnesota Wins, 71–67 Over OU," *Chicago Tribune*, December 18, 1966, Pt. 2, p. 4.
9. "Illini Beat Badgers in Big 10 Opener," "N.U. Victor Over Tulane," *Chicago Tribune*, December 20, 1966, Pt. 3, p. 1.
10. Joyner interview.
11. "Hoosiers Top Irish," *Chicago Tribune*, December 21, 1966, Pt. 3, p. 1; "Mich. State Defeated in New Orleans," *Chicago Tribune*, December 21, 1966, Pt. 3, p. 2.
12. "Illinois Hikes Record to 4–1," "M.S.U. Beats Tulane, 76–66," *Chicago Tribune*, December 22, 1966, Pt. 3, p. 1.
13. A good friend from high school, who was a freshman at Illinois at the time (and prefers anonymity), recalls that he first heard of the investigation of the Illini athletes while in a men's clothing store in downtown Champaign, where he saw a football player being fitted for an expensive suit and was told that athletes could charge clothing to the accounts of alumni. He thought that he probably needed a nice suit, so who cares? He didn't know what defense the athletes had for this action, but he never thought that the athletes saw it as "legal" (electronic interview, June 18, 2015).
14. "Combes, Shocked, Offers to Resign," "Stanford Loses, 77–74, to Hawkeyes," *Chicago Tribune*, December 24, 1966, Pt. 2, p. 1.
15. "Name Fifth Suspended U. of I. Player," *Chicago Tribune*, December 25, 1966, Pt. 2, p. 1.
16. Bob Strohm, *Daily Illini*, January 4, 1967, p. 7.
17. Richard Dozer, "N.U. Travels to New York Tournament," *Chicago Tribune*, December 25, 1966, Pt. 2, p. 3.
18. "Illini Beat Arizona in Los Angeles," *Chicago Tribune*, December 28, 1966, Pt. 3, p. 1; "Spartans Upset by Villanova," "Indiana Nips Oregon in Far West," *Chicago Tribune*, December 28, 1966, Pt. 3, p. 3.
19. "N.U. Defeated by Providence," "Georgetown Routs Purdue," "Spartans Upset," *Chicago Tribune*, December 29, 1966, Pt. 3, p. 1; "U.C.L.A. Routs Wisconsin; Mich. Upset," "Gophers Beaten," *Chicago Tribune*, December 29, 1966, Pt. 3, p. 2; "5th Triumph in Row for Iowa, 94 to 76," *Chicago Tribune*, December 29, 1966, Pt. 3, p. 3.
20. "Illini Lose; Wolverines and UCLA Win," "Purdue Sets Mark," "Duke Scares Ohio State in 83 to 82 Loss," *Chicago Tribune*, December 30, 1966, pt. 2, p. 2.
21. "Iowa and Loyola Triumph in Stadium," *Chicago Tribune*, December 31, 1966, Pt. 2, p. 1; "Rhode Island Rallies, Beats N.U., 91 to 87," "Illini, Badgers and Michigan Triumph in L.A.," "Hoosiers Take 3d," *Chicago Tribune*, December 31, 1966, Pt. 2, p. 3.
22. Caryer, pp. 149–150.
23. "N.U. Wins, 93–73; Spartans Beat Illini," *Chicago Tribune*, January 8, 1967, Pt. 2, p. 1; "Hawkeyes Trip Hoosiers with Flurry," *Chicago Tribune*, January 8, 1967, Pt. 2, p. 3.
24. "Hoosiers Beat Gophers," *Chicago Tribune*, January 10, 1967, Pt. 3, p. 2.
25. Richard Dozer, "N.U. Beats Illini, 104–96," *Chicago Tribune*, January 11, 1967, Pt. 3, p. 1; "Wisconsin Turns Back Wolverines," *Chicago Tribune*, January 11, 1967, Pt. 3, p. 3.
26. "Mao's Edict: Purge Away," *Chicago Tribune*, January 13, 1967, Pt. 1, p. 1.
27. "3 Score 75 as Illini Jolt Michigan, 99–93," "Spartans Beat Iowa, 79 to 70," "Buckeyes Upset," *Chicago Tribune*, January 15, 1967, Pt. 2, p. 1.
28. Joyner interview.
29. "Southern Illinois Keeps Lead in AP Poll," *Chicago Tribune*, January 20, 1967, Pt. 3, p. 6.
30. Richard Dozer, "N.U. Wins Thriller Over Iowa, 90–88," Chicago Tribune, January 22, 1967, Pt. 2, p. 1; "Spartans Dealt 1st Loss by Michigan," *Chicago Tribune*, January 22, 1967, Pt. 2, p. 3.
31. "Iowa Clamps Wolverines' Rally to Win," "Ohio St. Beats Purdue," *Chicago Tribune*, January 24, 1967, Pt. 3, p. 1.
32. Richard Dozer, "N.U. Rolls On; Defeats Ohio, 100–77," *Chicago Tribune*, January 31, 1967, Pt. 3, p. 1.
33. "No Hanoi Peace Bid-LBJ," *Chicago Tribune*, February 2, 1967, Pt. 1, p. 1.
34. Richard Dozer, "Illinois Upsets Northwestern, 93–83," "U.C.L.A. Wins, 40 to 35," *Chicago Tribune*, February 5, 1967, Pt. 2, p. 1.
35. "Hoosiers Triumph; Share Big 10 Lead," *Chicago Tribune*, February 7, 1967, Pt. 3, p. 1.
36. Richard Dozer, "Northwestern Trounces Wolverines," "Hosiers Capture Fifth in Row, 93 to 81," *Chicago Tribune*, February 12, 1967, Pt. 2, p. 1; "Minnesota Romps Past Illinois, 93–81," "Iowa Triumphs," *Chicago Tribune*, February 11, 1967, Pt. 2, p. 4.
37. "Michigan State Beats Indiana, 86–77," *Chicago Tribune*, February 14, 1967, Pt. 3, p. 1.
38. "N.U. Loses; 4-Way Tie for Big Ten Lead," *Chicago Tribune*, February 15, 1967, Pt. 3, p. 1.
39. Joyner interview (the NU coach was actually Larry Glass at that time).
40. Roy Damer, "Wildcats Beaten, 81–79; Big Ten Hopes Dim," "Iowa Upset in Triple Overtime," *Chicago Tribune*, February 19, 1967, Pt. 2, p. 1; "Spartans Win; Goal Disputed by Minnesota," *Chicago Tribune*, February 19, 1967, Pt. 2, p. 4.
41. "Indiana Beats Illini; Spartans Fall," *Chicago Tribune*, February 21, 1967, Pt. 3, p. 1.
42. "Badgers Whip N.U., 110–94," *Chicago Tribune*, February 22, 1967, Pt. 3, p. 1; "Gophers and Kondla Beat Iowa, 88–86," *Chicago Tribune*, February 22, 1967, Pt. 3, p. 2.
43. Butch Joyner remembered this game well and said that one referee, a man named Donald Wedge, made particularly egregious calls against the Hoosiers. Joyner's brother, a med student at the time, attended the game and followed Wedge out of the arena after

the game with malice aforethought, but then thought better of doing anything untoward (Joyner interview.)

44. "Hawkeyes Beat Indiana in Overtime," "N.U. Whips Ohio, 95 to 82; Ends Losing Streak," "Badgers 68, MSU, 64," *Chicago Tribune*, February 26, 1967, Pt. 2, p. 1.

45. "State's Prep Coach Group Backs Illini," *Chicago Tribune*, February 28, 1967, Pt. 3, p. 1. Kerner was sent to prison in 1973 for mail fraud, perjury and related charges.

46. "No Other Choice," Editorial, *Daily Illini*, February 24, 1967, p. 12.

47. "Letters," *Daily Illini* February 28, 1967, p. 9. The latter assertion refers to Phil Dickens, I assume and he was penalized, as was Indiana, in 1960 for recruiting violations of the Big Ten. See http://indiana.247sports.com/Article/Phil-Dickens-actions-led-to-an-unprecedented-penalty-for-IU-82059, accessed July 14, 2015.

48. Roy Damer, "Wildcats Keep Hops Alive, Beat Badgers," *Chicago Tribune*, March 1, 1967, Pt. 3, p. 1; "Illinois Set to Make Its Appeal on Big Ten Action," *Chicago Tribune*, March 1, 1967, Pt. 3, p. 2.

49. "Alcindor Tops Honor Squad in A.P.'S Vote," *Chicago Tribune*, March 1, 1967, Pt. 3, p. 2.

50. "Await Decision Today on Illini Plea," *Chicago Tribune*, March 3, 1967, Pt. 3, p. 3.

51. "Illini Appeal Rejected," *Chicago Tribune*, March 4, 1967, Pt. 1, p. 1.

52. "7 Ineligible, but 7 Cleared," *Chicago Tribune*, March 5, 1967, Pt. 2, p. 1. Jane Dwyre Garton, "When His Hoop Dreams Failed, Building a New Life Became a Matter of Principal," *Chicago Tribune*, May 31, 1999. http://articles.chicagotribune.com/1999-05-31/features/9905310098_1_basketball-court-farragut-high-school-playing.

53. Joyner interview.

54. My high school friend and former Illini undergrad reflected what seemed to be the student sentiment demonstrated at the game. He felt the punishments unfair because the enforcement was selective and that Illinois was a ripe target because "the practices were open, obvious and notorious" (electronic interview, June 18, 2015).

55. "Indiana Ambushed by Illinois," "Spartans Win, 75–71," Roy Damer, "N.U. Loses; 34 by Kondla," *Chicago Tribune*, March 5, 1967, Pt. 2, p. 1; "Iowa Spurt 2d Half Jars Ohio, 90 to 56," "Badgers Win, 80–79," *Chicago Tribune*, March 5, 1967, Pt. 2, p. 5.

56. "Spartans, Indiana Triumph," *Chicago Tribune*, March 7, 1967, Pt. 3, p. 1.

57. "Henry Opens 8 Case Histories of Illini," *Chicago Tribune*, March 7, 1967, Pt. 3, p. 2.

58. "Iowa Beats Badgers, Clings to Title Hopes," *Chicago Tribune*, March 8, 1967, Pt. 3, p. 1.

59. "Illinois Trustees Back Henry's Stand," *Chicago Tribune*, March 10, 1967, Pt. 3, p. 1; "Kerner Won't Interfere," *Chicago Tribune*, March 10, 1967, Pt. 3, p. 6.

60. "Indiana, Spartans Win; Tie for Title," *Chicago Tribune*, March 12, 1967, Pt. 2, p. 1.

61. Aldo Beckman, "Probe Sought of Big Ten's Athletic Aid," *Chicago Tribune*, March 13, 1967, Pt. 3, p. 3.

62. "Mills Denies Saying Henry Knew of Fund," *Chicago Tribune*, March 14, 1967, Pt. 3, p. 1; "Urge Illini to Keep Fighting," *Chicago Tribune*, March 15, 1967, Pt. 3, p. 1; "Mills Denies Statement About UI 'Slush Fund,'" *Daily Illini*, March 14, 1967, p. 1.

63. Roy Damer, "Hoosiers, Vols Upset in Regional," *Chicago Tribune*, March 18, 1967, Pt. 2, p. 1.

64. Joyner interview (actually Larry Glass was the NU coach, then).

65. "Illini Make Final Plea to Big 10 Today," *Chicago Tribune*, March 18, 1967, Pt. 2, p. 1; Roy Damer, "Big 10 Denies Illini Appeal," *Chicago Tribune*, March 19, 1967, Pt. 1, p. 1; "Three Illini Coaches Quit," *Chicago Tribune*, March 20, 1967, Pt. 1, p. 1.

66. "Plan $10,000 Gifts for 3 Ex-Illini Coaches," *Chicago Tribune*, March 23, 1967, Pt. 3, p. 1; "Illini Coaches Refuse $10,000 Gifts," *Chicago Tribune*, March 24, 1967, Pt. 3, p. 1; "Wants Congress to Probe Big 10 in Illinois Case," *Chicago Tribune*, March 25, 1967, Pt. 2, p. 1; "Legislature Starts Probe," *Chicago Tribune*, March 29, 1967, Pt. 3, p. 1.

67. Wilson and Brondfield, p. 414.

68. "Dunk Shot Outlawed for Colleges, High Schools," *Chicago Tribune*, March 29, 1967, Pt. 3, p. 3.

69. "Fired Penn A.D. Hurls 'Slush Charge,'" *Chicago Tribune*, March 30, 1967, Pt. 3, p. 1.

## Chapter 11

1. *Sports Illustrated* 27, no. 23 (December 4, 1967).
2. *Basketball 1967–68* 1, no. 8.
3. *Basketball Yearbook 1968*, 1967.
4. Rudy Tomjanovich, telephone interview, April 7, 2015.
5. "Fly 10,000 Yanks to Viet," *Chicago Tribune*, December 13, 1967, Pt. 1, p. 1.
6. George Langford, "Bad Showing for Big 10," *Chicago Tribune*, January 1, 1968, Pt. 3, p. 3.
7. "Rodwan and Detroit Beat Indiana, 99–93," "Houston Rips Michigan," *Chicago Tribune*, January 3, 1968, Pt. 3, p. 1. Tomjanovich also recalled "some middle-aged man saying how great that Houston was after the game." Rudy really dissed him, later finding out that the middle-aged man was Red Auerbach (Tomjanovich phone interview, April 7, 2015).
8. Richard Dozer, "Illinois and N.U. Win Big Ten Openers," "Indiana Wins," *Chicago Tribune*, January 7, 1968, Pt. 2, p. 1; "Carlin Steals 77–75 Victory for Badgers," "Buckeyes Rip Purdue," *Chicago Tribune*, January 7, 1968, Pt. 2, p. 5.
9. Richard Dozer, "Purdue Wins; Illini Fall in Overtime," *Chicago Tribune*, January 10, 1968, Pt. 3, p. 1.
10. Richard Dozer, "N.U. Jolts Indiana, 86–81; Illini Win," "MSU, Iowa Get First Big Ten Victories," "Iowa 74, OSU 72," *Chicago Tribune*, January 14, 1968, Pt. 2, p. 1.
11. Roy Damer, "Purdue Rips Indiana; N.U. Wins Third," *Chicago Tribune*, January 17, 1968, Pt. 3, p. 1.
12. "U.C.L.A. Stunned by Houston, 71–69," *Chicago Tribune*, January 21, 1968, Pt. 2, p. 1.
13. "Spartans Defeat N.U., 75–62," *Chicago Tribune*, January 21, 1968, Pt. 2, p. 1; "Ohio Crushes Michigan; 3 Total 70 Pts.," *Chicago Tribune*, January 21, 1968, Pt. 2, p. 7.
14. "Ohio State Shoots 56 Per Cent, Controls Boards to Defeat Georgia Tech, 66 to 55," *Chicago Tribune*, January 23, 1968, Pt. 3, p. 2.
15. "Iowa Snaps Long Spartan Home Streak," *Chicago Tribune*, January 24, 1967, Pt. 3, p. 1.
16. Richard Dozer, "Northwestern Stuns Purdue, 82 to 74," *Chicago Tribune*, January 28, 1968, Pt. 2, p. 1;

"Michigan Is Beaten, 95–92, by Ohio State," *Chicago Tribune*, January 28, 1968, Pt. 2, p. 4; Tomjanovich interview, April 7, 2015.

17. "N.U. Fall; Illinois and Ohio Triumph," *Chicago Tribune*, February 4, 1968, Pt. 2, p. 1.

18. "Ohio State Wins on Shot by Andrews," *Chicago Tribune*, February 6, 1968, Pt. 3, p. 1.

19. "More Forces in Korea," *Chicago Tribune*, January 28, Pt. 1, p. 1; "Viet Reds Storm U.S. Camp," Chesly Manly, "Nixon Calls for Winning Viet Conflict," *Chicago Tribune*, February 7, 1968, Pt. 1, p. 1.

20. "Iowa Holds Off Purdue Rally, 94–87," *Chicago Tribune*, February 8, 1968, Pt. 3, p. 2; Roy Damer, "Northwestern Beats Illinois, 78 to 71," *Chicago Tribune*, February 11, 1968, Pt. 2, p. 1; "Ohio State Whips Spartans to Increase Big Ten Lead," "Purdue Wins, 89–62," *Chicago Tribune*, February 11, 1968, Pt. 2, p. 2.

21. David Condon, "Michigan President Will Cooperate in Investigation," "2 Michigan Students Learn Journalistic Facts of Life Quickly," *Chicago Tribune*, February 11, 1968, Pt. 2, p. 1.

22. "Angry Duffy Denies Illegal Aid Charge," "Two Groups Sift Charges of Handouts at Michigan," *Chicago Tribune*, February 13, 1968, Pt. 3, p. 1.

23. "U.S. Renews Peace Offer," *Chicago Tribune*, February 13, 1968, Pt. 1, p. 1.

24. "Ohio Drops 2d Big Ten Duel, 86–78," *Chicago Tribune*, February 13, 1968, Pt. 3, p. 2; "Gophers Beat N.U., 85–80," *Chicago Tribune*, February 14, 1968, Pt. 3, p. 1.

25. "Minnesota Surprises Ohio, 83–79," *Chicago Tribune*, February 18, 1968, Pt. 2, p. 1; "Mount and Purdue Top Illinois," *Chicago Tribune*, February 18, 1968, Pt. 2, p. 2.

26. Caryer, p. 169.

27. Roy Damer, "Wildcats' 2d Half Rally Beats Spartans, 69–61," *Chicago Tribune*, February 18, 1968, Pt. 2, p. 1.

28. "Blast Airport in Saigon," *Chicago Tribune*, February 19, 1968, Pt. 1, p. 1.

29. "Ohio Beats N.U.; Iowa Falls," *Chicago Tribune*, February 21, 1968, Pt. 3, p. 1.

30. David Condon, "Big Ten Chief Home; Enters Investigation," *Chicago Tribune*, February 22, 1968, Pt. 3, p. 2.

31. Caryer, p. 170.

32. Donald Pierson, "Purdue, Iowa Win; Tie for Big 10 Lead," "Scholz' [Sic] 42 Sets Record," *Chicago Tribune*, February 23, 1968, Pt. 2, p. 1.

33. "Ohio State Defeats Illinois, 95 to 75," *Chicago Tribune*, February 27, 1968, Pt. 3, p. 1; "Purdue Loses; Iowa Wins, Leads Big Ten," *Chicago Tribune*, February 28, 1968, Pt. 3, p. 1.

34. "Iowa Beats Illinois; Ohio Keeps Hopes Alive," *Chicago Tribune*, March 3, 1968, Pt. 2, p. 1.

35. "Reed Sees 'No Urgency' in Michigan Sports Probe," *Chicago Tribune*, March 3, 1968, Pt. 2, p. 2.

36. "Iowa Clinches Title Tie; Ohio Wins," *Chicago Tribune*, March 5, 1968, Pt. 2, p. 1.

37. "Purdue Wins, 93–75," *Chicago Tribune*, March 6, 1968, Pt. 3, p. 5.

38. Roy Damer, "Michigan Upsets Iowa; Faces Playoff," *Chicago Tribune*, March 10, 1968, Pt. 2, p. 1; "Indiana," *Chicago Tribune*, March 10, 1968, Pt. 2, p. 1.

39. "Nixon Wins by Big Margin," *Chicago Tribune*, March 13, 1968, Pt. 1, p. 1.

40. "Ohio State Gets Right to Play in NCAA," *Chicago Tribune*, March 13, 1968, Pt. 3, p. 1.

41. Roy Damer, "Ohio State Wins; Marquette Beaten," *Chicago Tribune*, March 18, 1968, Pt. 2, p. 1.

42. Roy Damer, "Ohio State Shocks Kentucky, 82 to 81," *Chicago Tribune*, March 17, 1968, Pt. 2, p. 1.

43. Richard Dozer, "It's U.C.L.A., 101–69; Ohio Falls," *Chicago Tribune*, March 23, 1968, pt. 2, p. 1.

44. "Taylor and Lewis Favor Ending 3rd-Place Game," Richard Dozer, "Ohio Beats Houston for Third Place," *Chicago Tribune*, March 24, 1968, Pt. 2, p. 1; "U.C.L.A. Wins Title," *Chicago Tribune*, March 24, 1968, Pt. 2, p. 1.

45. *Sports Illustrated* 27, no. 23 (December 5, 1968).

46. Tomjanovich telephone interview.

47. Fife telephone interview.

48. Fife interview.

49. Louie Lazar, "Almost 100, 'Forgotten Legend of Basketball' Still Marvels at the Game," *New York Times*, June 2, 2016. http://www.nytimes.com/2016/06/03/sports/basketball/john-kundla-almost-100-lakers-original-coach-still-marvels-at-the-game.html?ref=basketball, accessed June 4, 2016.

50. Zander Hollander, ed., *Basketball Yearbook 1969*, no volume, no number, 1968.

51. Caryer, p. 179.

52. Sam Goldaper, "College Forecast of Top Teams and Players," in Clyde Hirt, ed., *Basketball Special, 1968–69* (New York: Counterpoint, 1968).

53. *9th Annual Basketball* 1, no. 9, 1968.

54. Edward Prell, "Big 10 Rules Iowa's McGilmer Eligible," *Chicago Tribune*, December 13, 1968, Pt. 3, p. 1.

55. "Wichita State Wins," *Chicago Tribune*, December 13, 1968, Pt. 3, p. 2.

56. "Both Florida and Georgia Sign Negros," *Chicago Tribune*, December 13, 1968, Pt. 3, p. 5.

57. "Unbeaten MSU Rolls to 4th in Row, 70–60," *Chicago Tribune*, December 14, 1968, Pt. 3, p. 2.

58. "Gophers Censured by Big Ten for Illegal Plane Recruiting," *Chicago Tribune*, December 14, 1969, Pt. 3, p. 3.

59. Richard Dozer, "Gophers Beat Loyola, 76–71; Mikan Stars," *Chicago Tribune*, December 15, 1968, Pt. 2, p. 1.

60. "Purdue Beats Ohio U. W/43 by Mount," "Illinois Deals Iowa State 1st Loss, 75–48," "Indiana Rolls, 77–62," "Buckeyes Romp," *Chicago Tribune*, December 15, 1969, Pt. 2, p. 7.

61. "Ohio State Slips Past WSU, 75–74," *Chicago Tribune*, December 17, 1968, Pt. 3, p. 4.

62. "Illini Beat Ohio for 5th in Row, 95–82," *Chicago Tribune*, December 18, 1968, Pt. 3, p. 1; "Illinois Takes Sixth in Row; N.U. Wins," *Chicago Tribune*, December 20, 1968, Pt. 3, p. 1.

63. "UCLA Dumps Gophers," *Chicago Tribune*, December 21, 1968, Pt. 2, p. 1; "Bradley, Michigan Lose in Kentucky," *Chicago Tribune*, December 21, 1968, Pt. 2, p. 2; "Wolverines Win," *Chicago Tribune*, December 22, 1968, Pt. 2, p. 2; Dan Fife telephone interview, March 31, 2015.

64. "Undefeated Illinois Beats Houston, 97–84," *Chicago Tribune*, December 22, 1968, Pt. 2, p. 1; "Buckeyes Win," *Chicago Tribune*, December 22, 1968, Pt. 2, p. 2; "WGN Station to Televise 10 Big 10 Games," *Chicago Tribune*, December 22, 1968, Pt. 2, p. 2.

65. "Davis Stars as Wildcats Win, 76 to 72," *Chicago Tribune*, December 27, 1968, Pt. 3, p. 1; "Illini Overtake

Creighton; Wildcats Win," *Chicago Tribune*, December 28, 1968, Pt. 2, p. 1; "Illini Defeat Miami, 86–76, to Take Title," *Chicago Tribune*, December 29, 1968, Pt. 2, p. 2.

66. "Drake Beats Gophers," "Badgers Win, 74–68," "Purdue Wins 92 to 72, in Rainbow Meet," *Chicago Tribune*, December 28, 1968, Pt. 2, p. 2; "Marquette Crowned," *Chicago Tribune*, December 29, 1968, Pt. 2, p. 5; "Gophers Beat Ole Miss for Consolation," *Chicago Tribune*, December 29, 1968, Pt. 2, p. 6; "Purdue Loses in Hawaii," *Chicago Tribune*, December 30, 1968, Pt. 3, p. 5; "Purdue Wins, 97–68," *Chicago Tribune*, December 31, 1968, Pt. 2, p. 2.

67. "World Acclaims Apollo Triumph," *Chicago Tribune*, December 28, 1968, Pt. 1, p. 1.

68. Richard Dozer, "Illini, Wildcats Win Big 10 Openers," "Purdue Wins," "Iowa Loses, Buckeyes Win," *Chicago Tribune*, January 5, 1969, Pt. 2, p. 1.

69. *Chicago Tribune*, January 6, 1969, Pt. 3, p. 2.

70. Ibid.

71. Dan Fife interview.

72. Richard Dozer, "Purdue Deals Illini 1st Loss, 98 to 84," "Wolverines Beat Indiana in Overtime," "Spartans Win, 77–67," *Chicago Tribune*, January 7, 1969, Pt. 3, p. 1.

73. Richard Dozer, "Illini Defeat N.U. in Overtime, 82–77," *Chicago Tribune*, January 12, 1969, Pt. 2, p. 1.

74. Fife interview.

75. "Buckeyes Use Free Throws to Win, 84–69," "Iowa Wins, 91–72," "Wolverines Upset by Gophers, 94–6," *Chicago Tribune*, January 12, 1969, Pt. 2, p. 2.

76. "Indiana Deals N.U. 2d Defeat in Row," "Iowa Beats M.S.U.," *Chicago Tribune*, January 15, 1969, Pt. 3, p. 1; "Badgers 68, Gophers 61," *Chicago Tribune*, January 15, 1969, Pt. 3, p. 2.

77. Caryer, p. 187.

78. Richard Dozer, "Spartans Deal N.U. 3d Defeat in Row," "Ohio State Whips Michigan, 98 to 85; Iowa Beats Minnesota," *Chicago Tribune*, January 19, 1969, Pt. 2, p. 1.

79. "Sarno Gets 26 as N.U. Defeats Michigan, 100–85," *Chicago Tribune*, January 22, 1969, pt. 3, p. 1; "Purdue Ties for First," *Chicago Tribune*, January 26, 1969, Pt. 2, p. 1; "Tomjanovich Held to 7, but Michigan Wins," *Chicago Tribune*, January 26, 1969, Pt. 2, p. 2.

80. Fife interview.

81. "Ohio State Defeats Illinois, 76–67," *Chicago Tribune*, January 29, 1969, Pt. 3, p. 1.

82. "Purdue Beats Ohio in Overtime, 95–85," *Chicago Tribune*, February 1, 1969, Pt. 2, p. 1; "Soph Gets 36 for Illinois in 86–73 Triumph," *Chicago Tribune*, February 1, 1969, Pt. 2, p. 2; "Mount Scores 45; Purdue Beats Iowa, 99–87," *Chicago Tribune*, February 5, 1969, Pt. 3, p. 1.

83. Richard Dozer, "Ohio Loses; Purdue Strengthens Lead," *Chicago Tribune*, February 9, 1969, Pt. 2, p. 1; "Buckeyes Get Bad Surprise from Badgers," *Chicago Tribune*, February 9, 1969, Pt. 2, p. 2; "Hawkeyes Are Stunned by Illini, 98–69," *Chicago Tribune*, February 9, 1969, Pt. 2, p. 4.

84. Caryer, p. 188.

85. "Ohio Deals Purdue 1st Big 10 Defeat," *Chicago Tribune*, February 12, 1969, Pt. 3, p. 1; "Illinois Is Upset by Michigan, 92–87," *Chicago Tribune*, February 12, 1969, Pt. 3, p. 5.

86. Fife interview.

87. "Purdue Rolls, 87–69; Ohio Triumphs," *Chicago Tribune*, February 6, 1969, Pt. 2, p. 2.

88. Roy Damer, "N.U. Defeats Indiana; 1st for Snyder," *Chicago Tribune*, February 16, 1969, Pt. 2, p. 1.

89. Caryer, p. 188.

90. "Purdue Wins, 96–95: Illini Beat Ohio," *Chicago Tribune*, February 19, 1969, Pt. 3, p. 1.

91. Fife interview.

92. "Purdue Beats Northwestern, 107–68," *Chicago Tribune*, February 23, 1969, Pt. 2, p. 1; "Tomjanovich Sets Record," "Ohio Stays in Big 10 Race on 88–81 Triumph," *Chicago Tribune*, February 23, 1969, Pt. 2, p. 2; "Purdue Tops Spartans on Mount's Shot," *Chicago Tribune*, February 26, 1969, Pt. 3, p. 1.

93. "Purdue Captures Big Ten Basketball Championship," "Spartans Kill Final Ohio Hopes, 85 to 72," *Chicago Tribune*, March 2, 1969, Pt. 2, p. 1; "Illinois Wins; Moves to Tie for 2d Place," *Chicago Tribune*, March 2, 1969, Pt. 2, p. 5.

94. "Purdue and Mount Set Records," *Chicago Tribune*, March 9, 1969, Pt. 2, p. 1.

95. "Purdue on TV," *Chicago Tribune*, March 13, 1969, Pt. 3, p. 2.

96. "Marquette, Purdue Win NCAA Tests," *Chicago Tribune*, March 14, 1969, Pt. 3, p. 1; "Purdue Mideast Victor in Overtime," *Chicago Tribune*, March 16, 1969, Pt. 2, p. 1.

97. "UCLA Gets Scare; Purdue Romps," *Chicago Tribune*, March 21, 1969, Pt. 3, p. 1; "U.C.L.A. Routs Purdue, 92–72, for 3rd Title in Row," *Chicago Tribune*, March 23, 1969, Pt. 2, p. 1.

## Chapter 12

1. Dan Fife telephone interview, March 31, 2015. Mark Wagar telephone interview, September 9, 2015. Wagar said that they got to Merchant's girlfriend's house, borrowed her car and drove to Marion, Ohio (where Merchant was from). Wagar then called his parents in Avon, Ohio, to say he was okay.

2. "Nixon: New GI Recall Soon," *Chicago Tribune*, December 9, 1969, Pt. 1, p. 1.

3. *Basketball Yearbook, 1970*, 1969.

4. *Complete Sports 10th Annual Basketball* 10, no. 1 (1969).

5. *1970 True Magazine's Basketball Yearbook*, 1969.

6. *Sports Illustrated* 31, no. 23 (December 1, 1968).

7. "Wash. State Stops Illini in Far West," *Chicago Tribune*, December 28, 1969, Pt. 2, p. 2; "Illini, Spartans Lose in Far West," *Chicago Tribune*, December 31, 1969, Pt. 2, p. 5.

8. "Butler Can't Do It; Purdue Wins as Mount Rests," *Chicago Tribune*, December 10, 1969, Pt. 3, p. 1; "Purdue Upset, 80–78," *Chicago Tribune*, December 21, 1969, Pt. 2, p. 3; "Purdue Wins, 89–79; Mount Gets 30," *Chicago Tribune*, December 28, 1969, Pt. 2, p. 3; "Purdue Wins in Holiday Meet, 88–85," *Chicago Tribune*, December 30, 1969, Pt. 3, p. 2; "Bonnie Feats of 50 Points Rips Purdue," *Chicago Tribune*, December 31, 1969, Pt. 2, p. 1.

9. "Ohio State Loses," *Chicago Tribune*, December 14, 1969, Pt. 2, p. 2; "Ohio State Vs. Fresno St.," *Chicago Tribune*, December 28, 1969, Pt. 2, p. 3; "Northwestern Logs 101 to 91 Triumph Over Arizona State," *Chicago Tribune*, December 21, 1969, Pt. 2, p. 3; "Northwestern Gets by Rutgers, 78 to 77," *Chicago Tribune*, December 27, 1969, pt. 2, p. 2; "N.C. State Defeats N.U. 98–75, to

Win Tourney," *Chicago Tribune*, December 28, 1969, Pt. 2, p. 3.

10. "Agnew Makes Viet Visit," *Chicago Tribune*, January 1, 1970, Pt. 1, p. 1.

11. Don Pierson, "Michigan, Illini Win Big Ten Openers," *Chicago Tribune*, January 4, 1970, Pt. 2, p. 1.

12. "Mount Gets 53, but Iowa Upsets Purdue, 94–88," "Buckeyes Win," "Spartans V. Hoosiers," *Chicago Tribune*, January 4, 1970, Pt. 2, p. 3.

13. "15,392 Watch Illinois Beat Indiana by 20," "Iowa Tops Michigan, 107–99," *Chicago Tribune*, January 7, 1970, Pt. 3, p. 1; Dan Fife interview.

14. "Illini Defeat Ohio, 77–59," *Chicago Tribune*, January 11, 1970, Pt. 2, p. 1; "Badgers Become 3rd Iowa Victims, 92–74," "Purdue V. Michigan," *Chicago Tribune*, January 11, 1970, Pt. 2, p. 2; Fife interview.

15. Richard Dozer, "Illinois Rips Northwestern, 101–80," *Chicago Tribune*, January 14, 1970, Pt. 3, p. 1; "Illinois Wins; Hikes Big 10 Mark to 5–0," *Chicago Tribune*, January 18, 1970, Pt. 2, p. 3.

16. Richard Dozer, "Northwestern Upsets Purdue, 66–65," *Chicago Tribune*, January 25, 1970, Pt. 2, p. 1.

17. Fife interview.

18. "Mount(Ain) of Points Beats Michigan," *Chicago Tribune*, February 1, 1970, Pt. 2, p. 1; "Iowa 100 Indiana 93," *Chicago Tribune*, February 1, 1970, Pt. 2, p. 2; "Iowa Passes Illinois in Big Ten Race," "N.U. Fades in Stretch; Purdue Whips Spartans," *Chicago Tribune*, February 4, 1970, Pt. 3, p. 1.

19. "Iowa Wins; Gophers Upset Illinois," *Chicago Tribune*, February 8, 1970, Pt. 2, p. 1; "Purdue Beats Ohio, 88–85," *Chicago Tribune*, February 8, 1970, Pt. 2, p. 2.

20. "Iowa Stays Undefeated; Purdue Wins," *Chicago Tribune*, February 11, 1970, Pt. 3, p. 1.

21. Richard Dozer, "Purdue Whacks Illinois; Iowa Wins," *Chicago Tribune*, February 13, 1970, Pt.2, p. 1; "OSU Beats Indiana," *Chicago Tribune*, February 13, 1970, Pt. 2, p. 2.

22. "4 Years for Riot 7 Lawyer," *Chicago Tribune*, February 16, 1970, Pt. 1, p. 1.

23. "Unbeaten Iowa Wins at Illinois, 83–81," *Chicago Tribune*, February 18, 1970, Pt. 3, p. 1.

24. Caryer, p. 196.

25. "Iowa Hawking Title, Beats OSU," "Purdue Beats Illinois," *Chicago Tribune*, February 22, 1970, Pt. 2, p. 1; "Simpson Sets Record; MSU Tops Indiana," "UCLA Falls," *Chicago Tribune*, February 22, 1970, Pt. 2, p. 2.

26. "Race Still Alive: Purdue, Iowa Win," *Chicago Tribune*, February 25, 1970, Pt. 3, p. 1.

27. Roy Damer, "Marquette Rejects N.C.A.A.," *Chicago Tribune*, February 25, 1970, Pt. 3, p. 1.

28. This certainly reinforces Dan Fife's observation that the Purdue fans were rabid.

29. Roy Damer, "Iowa Wins Big Ten Basketball Title," *Chicago Tribune*, March 1, 1970, Pt. 2, p.1.

30. "Mount All-Big Ten Third Time," "Mount Scores 37," *Chicago Tribune*, March 3, 1970, Pt. 3, p. 2; Neil Milbert, "Iowa Hustles to Defeat N.U. for 14–0 Mark," *Chicago Tribune*, March 8, 1970, Pt. 2, p. 1; "Mount Hits 22 to Set Big 10 Career Mark," *Chicago Tribune*, March 8, 1970, Pt. 2, p. 4.

31. "Kentucky Conquers Irish; Iowa Loses," *Chicago Tribune*, March 13, 1970, Pt. 3, p. 1.

32. "Jacksonville Ousts No.1 Kentucky," *Chicago Tribune*, March 15, 1970, Pt. 2, p. 1.

33. Roy Damer, "Iowa Loses Regional Test, but Not Cage Reputation," *Chicago Tribune*, March 16, 1970, Pt. 3, p. 4.

34. "Snyder Likes Purdue's Chances," *Chicago Tribune*, December 18, 1970, Pt. 3, p. 5.

35. Ray Marquette, "Midwest," in *Basketball Yearbook, 1971*, 1970.

36. Sam Goldaper, "Top 50 Teams in the Nation," *Basketball Extra, 1970–71*, 1970.

37. Dave Merchant telephone interview with the author, December 29, 2014.

38. The OSU sophs were just part of an outstanding class from the state of Ohio. These included Nick Witherspoon of Canton, who went to Illinois; Bo Lamar of Columbus, who became at All-American at Southwest Louisiana State; Ed Ratleff, who was All-American at Cal-State, Long Beach, under Jerry Tarkanian; and James "Bubbles" Harris of Lorain, who was all-Big Ten at Indiana. My thanks to Andy Stephenson for alerting me to this cache of talent.

39. "Kentucky Trips Hoosiers in Overtime," *Chicago Tribune*, December 13, Pt. 2, p. 1; "Carr Gets 54, but Irish Lose, 106–103," *Chicago Tribune*, December 16, 1970, Pt. 3, p. 1.

40. "Purdue Stuns Kentucky to Win Tourney," *Chicago Tribune*, December 20, 1970, Pt. 2, p. 3.

41. Fife interview.

42. "Snyder Likes Purdue's Chances," *Chicago Tribune*, December 18, 1970, Pt. 3, p. 5.

43. Merchant interview.

44. Merchant interview.

45. "Rose Bowl Preview? Bucks Lose," *Chicago Tribune*, December 29, 1970, Pt. 3, p. 2; "Hoosiers, Ohio Win in West," *Chicago Tribune*, December 30, 1970, Pt. 3, p. 3.

46. "9 Big Ten Winners to Open Tomorrow," *Chicago Tribune*, January 8, 1971, Pt. 3, p. 2.

47. "Indiana Victor in Big Ten Opener," "Illinois Off to Roaring Big 10 Start," "Badgers Lose Late," *Chicago Tribune*, January 10, 1971, Pt. 2, p. 1; "Purdue Defense Stuns Minnesota, 83 to 76," "Ohio State Wins, 97–76," *Chicago Tribune*, January 10, 1971, Pt. 2, p. 2.

48. Merchant interview.

49. Wagar interview.

50. "Illinois Wins; Nu Falls," "Hoosiers Romp, 99–73," *Chicago Tribune*, January 13, 1971, Pt. 3, p. 1.

51. "Ohio State Wins," Roy Damer, "Road Schedule Favors Ohio State," *Chicago Tribune*, January 14, 1971, Pt. 3, p. 3.

52. Fife interview.

53. Fife interview.

54. "Michigan Shocks Indiana; Illinois Wins," "Wisconsin Loses, 83–69, to Ohio State," "Purdue Wins, 97–92," *Chicago Tribune*, January 17, 1971, Pt. 2, p. 2.

55. Roy Damer, "Wooden Bouquet Goes for Wicks," *Chicago Tribune*, January 19, 1971, Pt. 3, p. 2.

56. Fife interview.

57. Wagar interview.

58. "Wolves, Wilmore Defeat N.U., 97–87," "OSU Rally Wins," *Chicago Tribune*, January 24, 1971, Pt. 2, p. 2; "Irish Stop UCLA Win Streak," *Chicago Tribune*, January 24, 1971, Pt. 2, p. 1.

59. Richard Dozer, "Irish Fall to Illini; Trojans Win," *Chicago Tribune*, January 31, 1971, Pt. 2, p. 1; "Ohio State Loses, 82–70, to Spartans," *Chicago Tribune*, January 31, 1970, Pt. 2, p. 2.

60. Merchant interview.

61. Wagar interview.

62. "Michigan Romps," *Chicago Tribune*, January 31, 1971, Pt. 2, p. 2; Roy Damer, "Michigan Claims Lead in Big Ten," *Chicago Tribune*, February 3, 1971, Pt. 3, p. 1; "Wildcats Lose to Michigan," *Chicago Tribune*, February 7, 1971, Pt. 2, p. 2; "Buckeyes Win, 87–76," *Chicago Tribune*, February 7, 1971, Pt. 2, p. 2.

63. "Iowa Deals Illinois First Big Ten Loss," *Chicago Tribune*, February 3, 1971, Pt. 2, p. 3; "Purdue Creeps Past Indiana, 85–81," "Illini Win," *Chicago Tribune*, February 7, 1971, Pt. 2, p. 2.

64. "Buckeyes Triumph," "Indiana Wins," *Chicago Tribune*, February 10, 1971, Pt. 3, p. 4; "Michigan Tops Purdue, 81–74," "Buckeyes Bury Illini," *Chicago Tribune*, February 14, 1971, Pt. 2, p. 1; "Indiana Free Throws Nip Iowa," *Chicago Tribune*, February 14, 1971, Pt. 2, p. 2.

65. "S. Viets Advance in Laos," *Chicago Tribune*, February 9, 1971, Pt. 1, p. 1.

66. "Ho Trail Reported Slashed," *Chicago Tribune*, February 16, 1971, Pt. 1, p. 1.

67. "Michigan Makes Minnesota 8th Victim," "Purdue Wins," "Ohio State Crushes Nu, Keeps Pace," "Hoosiers Nip Illini," *Chicago Tribune*, February 21, 1971, Pt. 2, p. 2.

68. Fife interview.

69. "Hoosiers Upset Michigan," "Buckeyes Romp, 80–71," *Chicago Tribune*, February 24, 1971, Pt. 3, p. 1.

70. Fife interview.

71. Merchant interview. Fife interview.

72. "Ohio State Defeats Michigan, 91 to 85," *Chicago Tribune*, February 28, 1971, Pt. 2, p. 1.

73. "Buckeyes Win; Michigan in 2d," "Wolves Nip Illini," "Hoosiers Beaten," *Chicago Tribune*, March 3, 1971, Pt. 3, p. 1.

74. Caryer, p. 222.

75. Merchant interview.

76. "Buckeyes Gain Cage Title Tie," *Chicago Tribune*, March 7, 1971, Pt. 2, p. 1; "Wolverines Stay Alive, Rip Spartans, 88 to 63," "Hoosiers Rip Iowa," *Chicago Tribune*, March 7, 1971, Pt. 2, p. 2.

77. "Big Ten Closes Dyche to Bears; Allows N.I.T.," *Chicago Tribune*, March 9, 1971, Pt. 3, p. 1.

78. Merchant interview.

79. Wagar interview.

80. Caryer, p. 222; "Ohio Clinches Big Ten Title," *Chicago Tribune*, March 10, 1971, Pt. 3, p. 1.

81. Hiner with Hutchens, pp. 326–27.

82. "N.I.T. Officials Select Wolverines, Sooners," *Chicago Tribune*, March 11, 1971, Pt. 3, p. 4; "Gripes Cause Watson to Quit as I.U. Coach," *Chicago Tribune*, March 12, 1971, Pt. 3, p. 4.

83. "Purdue Triumphs," "Michigan 86 Iowa 82," *Chicago Tribune*, March 10, 1971, Pt. 3, p. 1.

84. "U.C.L.A. Wins Pac-8 Title, Tourney Bid," *Chicago Tribune*, March 14, 1971, Pt. 2, p. 1.

85. Wagar interview.

86. Roy Damer, "Buckeyes Upset Marquette," *Chicago Tribune*, March 19, 1971, Pt. 3, p. 1.

87. Roy Damer, "Ohio Ko'd by Western Kentucky," *Chicago Tribune*, March 19, 1971, Pt. 3, p. 6.

88. Fife interview.

89. "Michigan Wins in N.I.T.; Purdue Loses, 94–79," *Chicago Tribune*, March 22, 1971, Pt. 3, p. 1; "Bonnies, Georgia Tech Win," *Chicago Tribune*, March 25, 1971, Pt. 3, p. 6.

90. "Indiana Gets Knight as Cage Coach," *Chicago Tribune*, March 28, 1971, Pt. 2, p. 6; Caryer, p. 224.

91. *Sports Illustrated* 35, no. 22 (November 29, 1971).

92. Bob Pille, "Midwest," *Basketball, Street & Smith's College and Pro Official Yearbook* (New York: Conde Nast, 1971).

93. Merchant interview.

94. "UCLA Crushes Ohio State by 26 Points," *Chicago Tribune*, December 3, 1971, Pt. 3, p. 1; "Ohio State Rally Beats Creighton," *Chicago Tribune*, January 4, 1972, Pt. 3, p. 1.

95. Roy Damer, "No Place Like Home," *Chicago Tribune*, December 16, 1971, Pt. 3, p. 2; "Spartans Hot After Half, Beat Kentucky 91–85," *Chicago Tribune*, December 14, 1971, Pt. 3, p. 1; "Unbeaten Hoosiers Nip Kentucky, 90–89," *Chicago Tribune*, December 12, 1971, Pt. 2, p. 2; "Ouch! Irish Lose by 65," *Chicago Tribune*, December 19, 1971, Pt. 3, p. 2.

96. "Orr Fears Michigan Star Wilmore Out for Season," *Chicago Tribune*, December 22, 1971, Pt. 3, p. 5; "Ohio State Tops Wisconsin-Milwaukee," *Chicago Tribune*, December 24, 1971, Pt. 3, p. 2.

97. "Nixon Frees Hoffa," *Chicago Tribune*, December 24, 1971, Pt. 1, p. 1. Hoffa vanished, three years later, and is widely believed to have been murdered. "Wilmore Will Be Ready for Big 10 Opener," *Chicago Tribune*, December 25, 1971, Pt. 2, p. 2; "Michigan Loses to Washington," *Chicago Tribune*, December 31, 1971, Pt. 3, p. 4. Brady scored 12 points in his first game back.

98. Roy Damer, "Illini Rally to Down Wildcats, 67–63," *Chicago Tribune*, January 9, 1972, Pt. 2, p. 1; "Ohio State Beats Purdue," "Johnson Sparks Wolverines," "Badgers Stymie Late Iowa Bid," "Gophers' Late Shots Tip Indiana," *Chicago Tribune*, January 9, 1972, Pt. 2, p. 2.

99. "Michigan Dumps Illini; Iowa Tops N.U.," *Chicago Tribune*, January 12, 1972, Pt. 3, p. 1.

100. Roy Damer, "N.U. Coach Snyder Trades Charges with Moran," *Chicago Tribune*, January 13, 1972, Pt. 3, p. 1; "Ford, Franklin Shove Purdue Past Illinois, 85–74," "Ohio State Runs Past Wolverines," "Wisconsin Nips Indiana in Overtime," *Chicago Tribune*, January 16, 1972, Pt. 2, p. 5.

101. "Gophers Conquer Badgers," *Chicago Tribune*, January 19, 1972, Pt. 3, p. 1.

102. "Nixon's Peace Offer Rejected," *Minneapolis Star*, January 26, 1972, Page 1A.

103. Roy Damer, "Iowa Upsets S. Carolina," "Michigan Beats Wildcats, 83–79," *Chicago Tribune*, January 23, 1972, Pt. 2, p. 1; "Buckeyes Clips Hoosiers," "Minnesota Slips Past Spartans," *Chicago Tribune*, January 23, 1972, Pt. 2, p. 2.

104. Roy Damer, "Minnesota Faces Ohio State Tonight," *Chicago Tribune*, January 25, 1972, Pt. 3, p. 1.

105. "Fight Stops Buckeye-Gopher Game," *Chicago Tribune*, January 26, 1972, Pt. 3, p. 1. https://www.bing.com/videos/search?q=1972+minnesota+ohio+state+brawl & FORM=VIRE1-view=detail&mid=7AD417FD3A05A08923587AD417FD3A05A08923585. YouTube video of the brawl is available here.

106. Merchant interview.

107. Max Nichols, "Max Nichols" column, *Minneapolis Star*, January 29, 1972, p. 5D.

108. Dick Gordon, "Big Ten May Slap Gophers for Brawl," *Minneapolis Star*, January 26, 1972, p. 1D. In February Winfield "admitted that he beat up two members of the Buckeyes, but was fortunate be out of camera range," according to a story by Richard Dozer of the *Chicago Tribune*, "Giel Asks Gopher Fans to Be Gracious Hosts," February 6, 1972, Pt. 2, p. 2.

109. "Duke Probes Gopher-OSU Fracas," *Chicago Tribune*, January 27, 1972, Pt. 3, p. 1.
110. "Buckeye Taylor Seeks More Gopher Penalties," *Minneapolis Star*, January 31, 1972, p. 9B.
111. Dan Stoneking, "Gracious Gophers Rip Polite Iowa," *Minneapolis Star*, January 31, 1972, p. 9B.
112. "Michigan Topples Ohio State, 88–78," *Chicago Tribune*, January 30, 1972, Pt. 2, p. 1; "Gophers Triumph, Tie for Big Ten Lead," *Chicago Tribune*, January 30, 1972, Pt. 2, p. 2; "Spartans Keep Hoosiers on Big Ten Skids, 83–73," *Chicago Tribune*, January 30, 1972, Pt. 2, p. 4.
113. Merchant interview.
114. Jim Byrne, "Big Ten Works on Differences in NCAA Rules," *Minneapolis Star*, January 31, 1972, p. 11B.
115. "Ford, Franklin Guide Purdue Past Wolverines," "Buckeyes 79–69 Winners," "Minnesota Beats Iowa by 53–52," *Chicago Tribune*, February 6, 1972, Pt. 2, p. 3.
116. "Illini Suspend Morris, Beat N.U.," *Chicago Tribune*, February 6, 1972, Pt. 2, p. 2; Roy Damer, "Morris Misses Illini Flight to Mich. State; Won't Play Tonight," *Chicago Tribune*, February 8, 1972, Pt. 3, p. 2.
117. "Minnesota and Ohio State Lose," *Chicago Tribune*, February 9, 1972, Pt. 3, p. 2.
118. Roy Damer, "Shift NCAA Finals to Monday in '73," *Chicago Tribune*, February 9, 1972, Pt. 3, p. 2.
119. Don Pierson, "Musselman Stirs Fans in Ashland," *Chicago Tribune*, February 10, 1972, Pt. 3, p. 2. Don Pierson, "'Defeat Worse than Death'—Musselman," *Chicago Tribune*, February 11, 1972, Pt. 2, p. 1.
120. "Gopher Duo Sue to End Suspensions," *Chicago Tribune*, February 12, 1972, Pt. 2, p. 1; Roy Damer, "Gophers Rip N.U.; Tie for First," *Chicago Tribune*, February 13, 1972, Pt. 2, p. 1; "Ohio State Wins," "Michigan Blisters Illinois," *Chicago Tribune*, February 13, Pt. 2, p. 2.
121. "Illini Nip Buckeyes at Line," "Gophers Win; in 1st," *Chicago Tribune*, February 20, 1972, Pt. 3, p. 1.
122. Roy Damer, "Gopher Pair Gets Hearing Tomorrow," *Chicago Tribune*, February 23, 1972, Pt. 3, p. 1; "Angela Davis Out on Bail," *Chicago Tribune*, February 24, Pt. 1, p. 1.
123. "Big Ten Upholds Gopher Suspensions," *Chicago Tribune*, February 26, 1972, Pt. 2, p. 1; Roy Damer, "Michigan Rips Gophers; Takes Big Ten Lead," *Chicago Tribune*, February 27, 1972, Pt. 3, p. 1.
124. "Illni Use 2 Platoons, Win, 91–86," "Ford's Three Points Lead Purdue, 70–69," *Chicago Tribune*, February 27, 1972, Pt. 3, p. 2.
125. "Ohio, Gophers in Tie," "Indiana Upsets Michigan, 79–75," *Chicago Tribune*, March 1, 1972, Pt. 3, p. 1.
126. "Gophers Romp, Lead Big Ten," *Chicago Tribune*, March 5, 1972, Pt. 3, p. 1.
127. Neil Milbert, "Hoosiers 'Garbage' Buries N.U.," "Gophers Win Big 10 Title," "Ohio State Beats Michigan State, 92–73," *Chicago Tribune*, March 8, 1972, Pt. 3, p. 1.
128. Merchant interview.
129. Wagar interview.
130. Roy Damer, "Faculty Reps Uphold Ban on Gophers," *Chicago Tribune*, March 9, 1972, Pt. 3, p. 2.
131. Merchant interview.
132. Wagar interview.
133. "Indiana Tries for First Nit Championship," *Chicago Tribune*, March 9, 1972, Pt. 3, p. 6; "Illinois Captain Krelle Quits," *Chicago Tribune*, March 11, 1972, Pt. 3, p. 3; "Wildcats, Illinois Lose in Windups," *Chicago Tribune*, March 12, 1972, Pt. 3, p. 6.
134. "Marquette Ruled Ineligible by NCAA," *Chicago Tribune*, March 13, 1972, Pt. 3, p. 1.
135. "Marquette Reinstated to NCAA Meet," *Chicago Tribune*, March 14, 1972, Pt. 3, p. 1.
136. "Warriors, Gophers Bow in NCAA," *Chicago Tribune*, March 17, 1972, Pt. 3, p. 1; Box score, *Chicago Tribune*, March 19, 1972, Pt. 3, p. 5.
137. "Big 10 Cage Year Over; Indiana Out," *Chicago Tribune*, March 20, 1972, Pt. 3, p. 2.
138. Most NBC stations picked up one of the two NCAA semifinals, depending on the time zone in which they were located. NBC's Los Angeles outlet picked up both, because it was convenient, with the games being played in Los Angeles. NBC affiliates had the option on showing these games, as well as the finals and third-place games on Saturday afternoon. Almost all showed the championship contest at 5 EST. In Pittsburgh, both the third-place and championship games were televised. In Boston, only the third-place game was shown, since that NBC affiliate also broadcast Red Sox games, and there was a spring training game later that afternoon. The Worcester NBC affiliate picked up the championship game, which some Boston households could get.

# Afterword

1. A list of the first African American players at each of the Big Ten universities appears in Appendix 1.

# Bibliography

## Books

Behee, John. *Hail to the Victors!* Ann Arbor: Ulrich Books, 1974.

Bjarkman, Peter C. *Big Ten Basketball*. Indianapolis: Masters Press, 1995.

Caryer, Lee. *The Golden Age of Ohio State Basketball, 1960–71*. Shippensburg, PA: Companion Press, 1991.

Cohen, Stanley. *The Game They Played*. New York: Carroll & Graf, 2001.

Cunningham, Carson. *American Hoops: U.S. Men's Olympic Basketball from Berlin to Beijing*. Lincoln: University of Nebraska Press, 2010.

Douchant, Mike. *Encyclopedia of College Basketball*. New York: Gale Research, 1995.

Fitzpatrick, Frank. *And the Walls Came Tumblin' Down: Kentucky, Texas Western and the Game that Changed American Sports*. New York: Simon & Schuster, 1999.

Graham, Tom, and Rachel Graham Cody. *Getting Open: The Unknown Story of Bill Garrett and the Integration of College Basketball*. New York: Simon & Schuster, 2011.

Hiner, Jason, with Terry Hutchins. *Indiana University Basketball Encyclopedia*. 2nd ed. New York: Sports Publishing, 2013.

Hunter, Bob. *Buckeye Basketball, Ohio State University*. Huntsville, AL: Strode Publishers, 1981.

Isaacs, Neil. *All the Moves: A History of College Basketball*. New York: Harper and Row, 1975.

*Lafayette Courier and Journal*, Editor. *Most Memorable Moments in Purdue Basketball History*. Champaign, IL: Sagamore Publishing, 1998.

Lamb, Dick, and Bert McGrane. *75 Years with the Fighting Hawkeyes*. Iowa City: University of Iowa Athletic Department, 1964.

Leonard, Bobby, and Lew Freedman. *Boom Baby: My Beautiful Life in Basketball*. Chicago: Triumph Books, 2013.

Marcus, Jeff. *Biographical Dictionary of Professional Basketball Coaches*. Lanham, MD: Scarecrow Press, 2003.

Mokray, William. *Ronald Encyclopedia of Basketball*. New York: Ronald Press, 1963.

Nelson, Murry. *Abe Saperstein and the American Basketball League, 1960–63: The Upstarts Who Shot for Three and Lost to the NBA*. Jefferson, NC: McFarland, 2013.

_____. *The National Basketball League: A History, 1935–1949*. Jefferson, NC: McFarland, 2009.

Porter, David L. *Basketball: A Biographical Dictionary*. Westport, CT: Greenwood Press, 2005.

Raterman, Dale. *The Big Ten: A Century of Excellence*. Champaign, IL: Sagamore Publishing, 1996.

Rosen, Charley. *The Scandals of '51: How the Gamblers Almost Killed College Basketball*. New York: Seven Stories Press, 1999.

_____. *The Wizard of Odds: How Jack Molinas Almost Destroyed the Game of Basketball*. New York: Seven Stories Press, 2002.

Russell, Cazzie L., Jr. *Me, Cazzie Russell*. Westwood, NJ: Fleming H. Revell, 1967.

Smith, Ronald. *Pay for Play: A History of Big-Time College Athletic Reform*. Urbana: University of Illinois Press, 2013.

_____. *Play-by-Play: Radio, Television and Big Time College Sport*. Baltimore: Johns Hopkins University Press, 2001.

Smith, Seymour, Jack Rimer and Dick Triptow. *A Tribute to Armed Forces Basketball, 1941–1969*. 2003.

*Spalding's Official Basketball Guide, 1927–28*. New York: American Publishing, 1927.

Tower, Oswald, ed. *Spalding's Official Basketball Guide, 1939–40*. New York: American Publishing, 1939.

Walker, J. Samuel. *ACC Basketball*. Chapel Hill: University of North Carolina Press, 2011.

Wilson, Kenneth L. (Tug), and Jerry Brondfield. *The Big Ten*. Englewood Cliffs, NJ: Prentice-Hall, 1967.

## Magazine and Journal Articles

Angelopolous, Angelo. "Dischinger the Dedicated." *Sport* 31, no. 3 (March 1961): 24–25, 92–93.

*Basketball 1967–68* 1, no. 8.

*Basketball Yearbook, 1965*, no volume, no number, 1964.

*Basketball Yearbook, 1966*.

*Basketball Yearbook 1968*.

*Basketball Yearbook, 1970*, 1969.

"College Basketball, 1965." *Sports Illustrated* 21, no. 23 (December 7, 1964).

*Complete Sports 5th Annual Basketball, 1964–65* 1, no. 5, 1964.
*Complete Sports 6th Annual Basketball 1965–66* 1, no. 6, 1965.
*Complete Sports 9th Annual Basketball* 1, no. 9, 1968.
*Complete Sports 10th Annual Basketball* 10, no. 1, 1969
*Dell Sports* 1, no. 48 (January 1966).
Editors of *Sport*. "All-America Basketball Forecast." *Sport* 25, no. 1 (January 1958): 23.
———. "All-America Basketball Forecast." *Sport* 27, no. 1 (January 1959): 14–17, 70–71.
———. "All-America Basketball Forecast." *Sport* 29, no. 1 (January 1960): 20–23, 84–85.
———. "All-America Basketball Preview." *Sport* 35, no. 1 (January 1963): 18–21, 64–68.
Eisenberg, Jeff. "How the NCAA Bought Its Basketball Tournament in 1940 for Less Than the Price of a Used Car Today." http://sports.yahoo.com/blogs/ncaab-the-dagger/ncaa-bought-rights-men-basketball-tournament-shocking-bargain-130045967—ncaab.html, Accessed May 2014.
Goldaper, Sam. "College Forecast of Top Teams and Players." In Clyde Hirt, ed., *Basketball Special, 1968–69*, 1968.
———. "Top 50 Teams in the Nation." In *Basketball Extra, 1970–71*, 1970.
Hollander, Zander, ed. *Basketball Yearbook, 1967*, no volume, no number, 1966.
*Inside Basketball, 1966*, 1965.
Linn, Ed. "Frank Howard—The Man Behind the New Babe Ruth Myth." *Sport* 31, no. 4 (April 1961): 61–69.
Marquette, Ray. "Midwest." *Basketball Yearbook, 1971*, 1970.
*1970 True Magazine's Basketball Yearbook*, 1969.
Pille, Bob. "Midwest." *Basketball, Street & Smith's College and Pro Official Yearbook*, 1971.
Sainsbury, Ed. "College Preview." *Sports Review Basketball* 23, no. 1 (January 1963): 48.
Schaap, Dick. "Basketball's Giant Giveaway: The Recruiting Payoffs." *Sport* 26, no. 6 (December 1958): 24–27, 82–84.
"Top Twenty 1966." *Sports Illustrated* 23, no. 23 (December 6, 1965).
"Top Twenty 1967." *Sports Illustrated* 25, no. 33 (December 5, 1966): 58.
"Top Twenty 1968." *Sports Illustrated* 27, no. 23 (December 4, 1967).
"Top Twenty 1969." *Sports Illustrated* 31, no. 23 (December 1, 1968).
"Top Twenty 1972." *Sports Illustrated* 35, no. 22 (November 29, 1971).
Turnbull, Buck. "Chuck Darling, Denison, 1966," *Des Moines Register*, June 25, 2005, http://www.desmoinesregister.com/article/19660403/SPORTS11/50625002/Chuck-Darling-Denison-1966, Accessed January 22, 2014.

## Web Sites

http://articles.chicagotribune.com/1999-05-31/features/9905310098_1_basketball-court-farragut-high-school-playing, Accessed December 2014.
http://bentley.umich.edu/athdept/baskmen/baskmaa/oosterbaa.htm, Accessed November 2014.
http://www.bigbluehistory.net/bb/helms.html, Accessed November 2014.
http://www.crimsonquarry.com/2012/6/11/3075685/great-expectations-the-1949–50-indiana-hoosiers, Accessed May 2014.
http://en.wikipedia.org/wiki/Ralph_Jones Accessed November 2014.
http://www.hoophall.com/hall-of-famers/tag/harold-g-olsen, Accessed November 2014.
http://www.hoophall.com/hall-of-famers/tag/walter-e-meanwell, Accessed November 2014.
http://www.hoophall.com/hall-of-famers/tag/ward-l-lambert, Accessed November 2014.
http://www.purduesports.com/sports/m-baskbl/spec-rel/legends-wardlambert.html, Accessed November 2014.
http://www.usatoday.com/story/sports/ncaab/2013/12/31/johnny-orr-dies-at-86-iowa-state-michigan/4262817/ Accessed November 2014.

## Interviews

Anonymous former Illinois student. Electronic interview, June 27, 2015.
Butterfield, Bill. Telephone interview, August 28, 2015.
Cain, Carl. Telephone interview, September 9, 2015.
Fife, Dan. Telephone interview, March 31, 2015.
Gentry, Nolden. Telephone interview, April 9, 2015.
Glass, Larry. Telephone interview, November 5, 2014.
Joyner, Butch. Telephone interviews, January 7, 2015, and January 14, 2015.
Judson, Phil. Telephone interview, January 22, 2014.
Merchant, Dave. Telephone interview, December 29, 2014.
Nicholas, Ab. Telephone interview, March 11, 2015.
Ridley, Bill. Telephone interview, February 5, 2014.
Schellhase, Dave. Telephone interview, May 10/May 13, 2015.
Smith, Ron. Telephone interview, March 9, 2015.
Tomjanovich, Rudy. Telephone interview, April 7, 2015.
Wagar, Mark. Telephone interview, September 9, 2015.

## Archival data

Virgil M. Hancher to John A. Hannah, 11 February 1957, Series 4/16/1 President E.B. Ford General Correspondence File, 1956–57, Box 274, Folder "Athletic Scholarships," University of Wisconsin Archives.

## Newspapers

*Chicago Tribune*
*Daily Illini*
*Des Moines Register*
*Minneapolis Star*
*New York Times*

# *Index*

Adams, Don 172, 174, 184, 188, 191, 192, 196
Aitch, Matthew 153, 160, 162, 163, 165, 168
Anderegg, Bob 72, 77, 78, 79, 80, 82, 84–90
Anderson, Forrest "Fordy" 7, 71, 75, 89

Bavis, Chuck 181, 190
Behagan, Ron 192, 207–209, 211–213
Bellamy, Walt 84, 85, 87, 88, 89, 90, 92, 94, 95, 99, 104
Bemoras, Irv 36, 38, 41, 42, 43, 46, 47, 48, 49
Benjamin, Rudy 200
Berberian, Bill 19
Big Ten: aid to athletes 80, 130, 159, 169; beginnings 3; compression, wartime, and television 29, 37, 137; payment of officials, redshirting 210; recruiting/maintenance violations 48, 102; sanity code 38, 39, 72, 73; Western Conference expansion 3, 29
Bjarkman, Peter 9, 38, 75, 99
Bolyard, Tom 101, 121, 122, 123, 125, 127, 128, 129
BonSalle, George 57, 63, 64, 65, 66, 67, 70, 71, 72
Bradds, Gary 116, 120–125, 127–135, 137, 139, 140, 188
Brady, Ken 197, 200, 206, 212
Bredar, Jim 38, 40, 41, 42, 43, 46, 48
Brewer, Jim 197, 198, 200, 202, 204, 211, 213, 214
Brody, Tal 122, 123, 128, 132, 133, 139, 140, 141, 144
Brothers, Bruce 57, 65, 67
Brown, Fred 192–196, 198, 199, 202, 204
Bryant, Hallie 67, 72, 73, 74, 112
Buntin, Bill 121–123, 125, 126, 128–135, 137–139, 141, 144, 149, 150
Burmaster, Jack 11, 19
Burns, Jim 139, 143, 152, 153, 156, 159–166, 168

Burton, M.C. 73, 77, 80, 84–90
Burwell, Bill 100, 101, 116, 118, 121, 122, 123, 127, 129, 130
Butterfield, Bill 11, 15

Cacciatore, Bill 95, 101, 117
Cain, Carl 52, 53, 54, 55, 57, 58, 59, 60, 64, 66, 67, 69, 113
Calabria, Chad 172, 176–179, 182, 183, 193–197
Calsbeek, Frank 23, 27, 28, 29, 31, 32, 34, 35
Carter, Richard 183, 192
Chapman, Tom, 161–163
Chicago Stadium 7, 8, 10, 25, 27, 34, 42, 50, 78, 83, 85, 122, 124, 131, 134, 160, 161, 182
Choice, Wally 54, 59, 63, 64, 65, 66, 67, 68
Civil Rights Movement 56, 62, 67, 86, 134, 142, 144, 147, 149, 216
Clark, Archie 130, 133, 139, 141, 143, 147, 152–156
Cleamons, Jim 185–187, 190, 193–195, 198, 200–205
Colangelo, Jerry 100, 101, 116
Combes, Harry 22, 30, 34, 35, 51, 63, 78, 112, 113, 159, 160, 165
Cook, Bob 13, 14, 16, 17, 19
Cooke, Joe 184, 185, 193
Cooke, L.J. 106
Cowles, Ozzie 11, 20, 32, 66
Crews, Randy 174, 175, 190
Cronk, Ray 101, 117, 119
Culberson, Dick 10, 216

Darden, Oliver 130, 131, 139, 142, 148, 150, 152, 153, 157
Darling, Chuck 31, 32, 34, 38, 39, 40, 41, 42, 69, 113
Davis, Dan 163, 183
Davis, McKinley "Deacon" 39, 40, 45, 46, 51, 52, 53, 60
Dawson, Jim 152, 158–165, 167, 168
Dean, Everett 109, 110, 112
Dee, Johnny 10
Dees, Archie 63, 64, 65, 66, 67, 70–76, 78, 79, 80

DeHeer, Bill 182
DeVoe, Don 128, 133, 134
Dill, Craig 161–163, 165, 167, 168
Dischinger, Terry 91, 93, 95, 96, 99–103, 117, 118, 119, 120, 135
Dommeyer, Jed 64, 65, 67, 74
Donham, Bob 26, 27, 29, 30
Downey, Dave 100, 101, 104, 116, 118, 119, 121, 122, 123, 124, 126–130
Downing, Steve 197, 202, 211, 212, 214
Duke, Wayne 209, 210
Dunlap, Ron 160, 167, 168
Dye, Tippy 11, 27, 30

Eaddy, Don 41, 44, 45, 46
Ebert, Paul 38, 40, 41, 42, 45, 46, 50, 54, 55, 118
Eddelman, Dwight "Dike" 18, 19, 20, 22, 23, 25
Eddy, Ray 140, 147
Edwards, Heywood 175, 178
Ehlers, Ed 9, 14
Eison, Jake 79, 80, 84, 85, 86, 87, 88, 90
Elliott, Pete 18, 19, 20, 23, 159, 160, 165
Englund, Gene 6
Erickson, Bill 20, 22, 24, 25, 27
Evanston (IL) High School 10, 11, 16, 31, 38, 40, 46

Falk, Rich 1, 117, 123, 124, 125, 129–133, 135, 136
Ferrari, Al 45, 46, 47, 48, 49, 52, 55, 57, 58, 60
Fife, Dan 2, 181, 183, 184, 186, 187, 190, 192, 193, 198, 200, 202, 204
fight (Minnesota and Ohio State) 209–213
Finney, Jody 180, 182, 187, 190, 193, 194
Flessner, Dion 161, 162
Fletcher, Rod 26, 31, 32, 33, 34, 35, 36, 38, 40, 42, 44
Ford, Rob 197, 200, 201, 204, 205, 210, 212, 213
Foster, Harold "Bud" 20, 48, 89, 107, 111

## Index

Franklin, Joe 161, 168, 174, 176, 177, 180, 210
Freeman, Don 130, 131, 139–142, 144, 152, 154, 155, 156
Freeman, Robin 52, 54, 55, 57, 58, 60, 62–67, 94, 119, 135

Gamber, Terry 174, 175, 177, 184
Ganakas, Gus 201
Garland, Mel 122, 124, 125, 128, 129, 130, 133
Garmaker, Dick 52, 53, 54, 55, 57, 58, 59
Garrett, Bill 20, 21, 26, 27, 28, 30, 31, 32, 33, 34, 35, 37, 70, 76, 216
Gearhardt, Gary 103, 105, 120, 121
Gelle, Bob 38, 40, 45, 46, 48, 49
Gent, Pete 124, 125, 133, 135
Gentry, Nolden 70, 77, 78, 79, 83, 84, 86, 87, 91, 92, 93
Gerhard, Dan 206, 210, 211
Gibbons, Jim 182
Gilliam, Herm 163, 167, 168, 175, 177, 178, 180, 182–184, 186, 187, 190
Glass, Larry 132, 184, 187
Grabiec, Wayne 201, 202, 205, 212
Graham, Otto 7, 8
Grant, Bud 14, 18, 19, 21, 22, 23
Grate, Don 9, 12
Great Lakes Naval Station
Green, Johnny 71–75, 78, 79, 80, 83, 85-90
Groffsky, Paul 45, 50, 51
Gunther, Dave 85, 86, 88, 89
Gutkowski, Ron 200

Hamilton, Ralph 9, 13, 14, 16, 17
Harris, James "Bubbles" 191, 194, 196, 202
Harrison, Bob 17, 18, 19, 21, 23
Havlicek, John 91, 92, 95–98, 100, 103, 104, 114, 117–121, 140
Henry, Al 187, 190, 194, 196
Hill, Eric 190, 193, 195, 197
Hoffman, Paul 14, 16
Hook, Jay 65, 66, 73
Hornyak, Al 197–203-208, 210–214
Hoskett, Bill 153, 154, 161–165, 167, 168, 172, 174–181
Howard, Frank 64, 66, 70–74, 76–80
Howat, Rick 190, 193, 194, 197, 198, 204
Howell, Steve 175, 178–181, 185
Hudson, Lou 130–134, 139, 141, 142, 144–148, 150, 151, 153, 155, 156
Huffman, Marv 5, 6

Inniger, Irv 162–164
integration of the Big Ten 10, 20, 39, 41, 52, 70, 77, 154
Ives, Dick 13

Jackson, Greg 182, 183, 186–188, 190, 193, 194, 197, 198, 210
Jackson, Mannie 77, 78, 85, 86, 87, 88, 90, 93, 95
Jaros, Tony 10
Jensen, Luke 182
Johnson, Ernie 207, 210
Johnson, John "J.J." 181, 182, 187, 188, 192, 194–197
Johnson, Kenny 184, 188, 194
Johnson, Ron 78, 83, 85, 86, 87, 89, 90, 92, 94, 95, 96
Jones, Gerry 140, 152, 153, 160, 161, 163–165, 168
Jones, Ralph 107, 108
Jones, Rich 152, 154, 155, 158, 167, 168
Jorgenson, Noble 13, 14
Joyner, Butch 139, 153, 159, 161, 162, 164, 165, 167–169, 175
Judson, Paul 55, 57, 58, 60, 63, 64, 65, 66, 70
Judson, Phil 49, 51, 52, 62, 70

Kalafat, Ed 38, 39, 41, 42, 45, 49, 52, 54, 55
Keller, Bill 178, 180, 186, 189, 190
Kelley, Dale 172, 174, 175, 177, 183–186, 193, 195, 196
Kerr, Johnny 38, 39, 40, 41, 43, 45–48, 52- 55, 57, 97
Kilgore, Bill 198, 200, 204, 213
King, George 187, 196
Knight, Bob 2, 97, 100, 103–105, 108, 114, 115, 121, 193, 205, 216
Kondla, Tom 152, 164, 165, 167, 168, 172, 173, 177, 178, 180, 181
Kotz, John 6, 7, 8, 9, 15
Kozlicki, Ron 143, 153, 159, 162, 163, 166
Kramer, Ron 58, 59, 60, 62–65, 67, 68, 72- 74
Kuberski, Steve 158, 160, 166–168
Kundla, John 181
Kunnert, Kevin 202, 208, 210, 213, 214
Kunze, Terry 124, 127, 130, 134
Kurland, Bob 12

Lafayette, Lee 159, 162, 164, 165, 175, 180, 181, 188
Lambert, Ward "Piggy" 3, 5, 11, 108, 109
Lee, Herb 85–87, 92, 94
Leonard, Bob 37, 38, 39, 41, 42, 45, 46, 47, 48, 49, 50, 51, 52, 55, 56, 112
Logan, Bill 52, 53, 54, 57, 58, 59, 60, 65, 67, 113
Lonborg, Arthur "Dutch" 110, 111
Lopossa, Rick 1, 123, 124, 125, 128, 132, 133, 135, 188
Lucas, Jerry 82, 91–102, 104, 105, 114, 116–122, 140

Lundy, Lamar 39, 62, 64, 66, 67, 70, 71, 72, 74

Madison Square Garden 12, 17, 36, 91, 122, 131, 141, 160, 161, 192, 195, 204, 213
Magdanz, Eric 118, 119, 121, 122, 124, 125, 129
Mantis, Nick 71, 83, 85
Mast, Dick 57, 58, 63, 66, 67
Mathisen, Art 7, 8, 9
McCoy, Julius 52, 54, 57, 58, 63, 65, 67, 68, 195
McCracken, Branch 5, 48, 51, 110, 111, 112, 117, 147
McGaw Hall 30, 46, 47, 49, 52, 60, 67, 69, 71, 80, 90, 127, 135, 164
McGilmer, Ben 151, 153, 154, 155, 181, 182, 185, 186
McGinnis, George 197–205, 216
McGlocklin, Jon 112, 121, 130, 131, 134, 139, 141, 142, 146, 147
McIntosh, Don 17, 18, 19, 20, 26
McIntyre, Jim 14, 16, 17, 19, 20, 21, 22, 23
McNulty, Carl 32, 34, 35, 39, 40, 42, 67
Meanwell, Walter 3, 106, 107, 109, 111
Mencel, Chuck 40, 41, 45, 46, 48, 49, 53, 57, 58, 59, 60
Menke, Ken 5, 7, 8, 9, 13, 14
Merchant, Dave 190, 197–199, 202, 203, 206, 209, 213
Merriweather, Willie 84, 86, 87, 88, 89
Mikan, George 8, 10
Mikan, Larry 182–184, 187, 191, 193, 195, 196
Miller, Fred 190, 192, 193, 197
Miller, Ralph 143, 196, 197
Mills, Doug 166, 169
Minor, Mark 199, 209, 213
Molinas, Jack 35, 52
Morris, Max 10, 11, 12
Morrow, Paul 55
Mount, Rick 172, 174, 177, 178, 181, 183, 184, 186, 188–197
Municipal Auditorium (Kansas City) 12, 36
Musial, Stan 11
Musselman, Bill 205, 208, 209, 211
Myers, Jim 151, 153, 155

Nagle, Chuck 159, 164, 165, 167, 172, 176, 178, 181
National Association of Basketball Coaches (NABC) Tournament 4, 5, 109, 215
National Collegiate Athletic Association (NCAA) Tournament 29, 43, 60, 68, 69, 74, 75, 80, 89, 90, 96, 97, 104, 105, 120, 121, 127, 129, 134, 135, 137, 138, 146–150, 157,

168–170, 179, 180, 188, 189, 195, 196, 203, 204, 205, 214; determining eligibility 36, 46, 55, 166, 214; practice games 29, 35, 42; sanity code 18, 38, 39
National Invitational Tournament (NIT) 4, 28, 195, 202–205, 213, 214
Nelson, Don 91, 92, 96, 100–104, 116, 117, 118, 119, 120
Newell, Pete 30, 38, 90, 99
Nicholas, Ab 25, 27, 28, 30, 31, 32, 33, 34, 38, 39, 42
Norman, Ron 174–176
Northway, Mel 121–124, 130, 133, 139, 143
Nowell, Mel 91, 92, 93, 96, 97, 100, 102, 103, 105, 114, 118–121, 140
Nuness, Al 174, 188

O'Connor, Frank "Bucky" 68, 84, 113
Ohl, Don 62, 70, 71, 72, 73, 77, 78, 80
Olsen, Harold 11, 12, 109
Oosterbaan, Bennie 11, 113
Orr, Johnny 115, 156, 181, 186, 206, 209
Osterkorn, Walter 22, 23, 24, 25, 27, 28, 29
Overskei, Larry 172, 190

Pace, Denny 187
Patten Gym, Northwestern University 4, 5, 6
Payne, Vern 153, 159, 161, 162, 164, 165, 168, 169, 172, 174, 175, 180
Pearson, Preston 162
Peeples, George 140, 142, 147, 151, 154
Pervall, Chris 140–143, 147, 150–154
Petrancek, Frank 39, 40, 42, 46, 47
Phillip, Andy 8, 13, 14, 15
Pitts, Jim (Michigan) 178, 180
Pitts, Jim (Northwestern) 122, 131, 144, 148, 154, 156, 163
Price, Mike 178, 184, 190, 192, 196, 197
Purkheiser, Bob 135, 140

Quiggle, Jack 71, 73–76

Ragelis, Ray 26, 27, 28, 29, 30–32, 34, 41
Rayl, Jimmy 100, 112, 116, 117, 119, 120, 122, 123, 125–128, 155
Reasbeck, Dick 120–123, 125, 126, 128
Redmon, Bogie 121, 124, 139, 146
Reed, Bill 10, 177, 182, 184
Rehfeldt, Don 17, 20, 21, 23, 25–30, 111

Ricketts, Dick 131–133, 135, 140, 147
Ridley, Bill 51, 52, 57, 58, 63, 64, 65, 66, 67, 68, 70
Riessen, Marty 126, 127, 132, 133
Risen, Arnie 9, 12
Ritter, Don 17, 19, 22
Roberts, Joe 85, 86, 89, 95, 96, 97, 114
Robinson, Mike 208, 210, 212, 213
Rucklick, Joe 71, 72, 73, 74, 77, 79, 80, 83, 84, 85, 86, 87
Russell, Cazzie 99, 130–135, 137–139, 141, 143, 144, 146, 148–157, 184, 188, 189
Rymal, Steve 164

Sarno, Jim 184, 186
Schaap, Dick 82
Schadler, Bernie 15, 16
Schellhase, Dave 130–135, 137, 139, 140, 142–144, 146, 148, 150–156, 194
Scheuerman, Milt "Sharm" 54, 58, 67, 68, 69, 103
Schlundt, Don 37–42, 45–60, 65, 67, 95, 112, 196
Schmidt, Harve 67, 70, 72–74, 170, 210
Schnittker, Dick 19, 20, 21, 23, 26–30
Scholz, Dave 160–163, 165, 167, 172, 174, 175, 177, 178, 180–184, 186–188, 190
Scott, Burke 52, 53, 56–58
Seaberg, Bill 54, 58, 59, 60, 64–68
Selbo, Glen 15, 16, 17
Sepic, Ron 139, 147, 151, 156
Sexton, Joe 62, 64, 66–68
Shannon, Ollie 194, 197, 200, 202
Sherrod, Clarence 184, 187, 190, 192, 194, 195, 198, 204
Siebel, Ken, 118, 119, 120, 122, 123, 125, 126, 127, 128
Siegfried, Larry 84, 85, 86, 88, 89, 90, 92, 96, 97, 98, 100–105, 114
Siekmann, Bob 199, 202
Simonovich, Bill "Boots" 58, 66
Simpson, Ralph 190, 191, 193–197, 205, 216
Skoog, Myer "Whitey" 20, 21, 22, 27, 28, 29, 31, 33, 34, 35, 49
Smiley, Ed "Jack" 7, 8, 9, 13, 14, 16
Smith, Ron 62, 64, 65
Smith, Wilfrid 12, 15, 35
Snyder, Brad 187, 193, 207
Sorenson, Dave 175–188, 190, 191, 194–196
Stewart, Dennis 175, 178, 181, 185–187
Strack, Dave 115, 150, 156, 181

Stuteville, Jerry 28
Sullivan, Bob 175, 178, 181
Sunderlage, Don 23, 27, 30, 31, 32, 33, 34, 35, 36, 38
Suprunowicz, Mac 13, 14, 16, 17, 18, 20, 21, 22, 23, 27, 29
Szykowny, Matt 102, 103

Taube, Mel 11
Taylor, Corky 209, 211–213
Taylor, Fred 26, 27, 28, 84, 97, 103, 105, 114, 115, 128, 161, 177, 180, 181, 203, 204, 209, 213
Taylor, Roger 70, 72, 78, 85, 86, 87, 88, 89
television and basketball 36, 41, 46, 57, 58, 63, 65, 66, 67, 71, 72, 89, 91, 95, 104, 137, 143, 146, 149, 170, 183, 188, 194, 195, 211, 212, 214, 216
Thoren, Skip 121, 129, 132, 133, 135, 139, 140, 141, 143, 147, 148
Thurlby, Tom 20, 27
Tidwell, John 90, 96, 103, 104
Tomjanovich, Rudy 172–175, 178, 181, 183–188, 190, 191, 193, 195, 196
Tosheff, Bill 26, 32, 33, 34, 35
Tregonning, Larry 131, 139, 144, 150
Turner, Clyde 206–209, 211–214

Underman, Jack 10, 11, 12, 14, 15, 16
University of Illinois "slush fund" scandal 159, 160, 165–170, 176, 182, 184

Van Arsdale, Dick 112, 121, 122, 126, 130–132, 134, 137, 139, 141–144, 146–148
Van Arsdale, Tom 112, 121, 122, 130–132, 134, 137, 139, 140, 141, 143, 144, 146–148
Vance, Gene 7, 8, 9, 13–15, 169
Vanderkuy, Leo 28, 34
Vaughan, Govonor 77, 78, 89, 90, 92, 93, 95, 96
Vidnovic, Glen 172, 176, 178, 185, 187, 195–197
Vietnam War 100, 142, 143, 147, 151, 153, 154, 157, 163, 175, 176, 179, 190–192, 194, 201, 208, 216

Wagar, Mark 190, 199–201, 203, 204, 209, 211, 213
Walker, Horace 84, 85, 87, 90, 93, 94, 95
Watson, Lou 2, 14, 20, 22, 26, 27, 29, 168, 203
Weatherford, Larry 190, 194, 197, 198, 200, 204, 205
Weatherspoon, Nick 197, 201, 210–213

Weaver, Mike 153, 154, 161, 163, 164, 175, 177, 180
Weir, Murray 13, 14, 15, 16, 17, 18, 19
Wells, Ralph 91, 92, 93, 94, 95, 101, 104, 119
"Whiz Kids" (University of Illinois) 7, 13
Wilkinson, Herb 15
Williams, Rick 208, 210, 211, 213, 214
Williams, Sam 159, 161–168, 174–182
Williams Arena ("The Barn," University of Minnesota) 21, 37, 59, 65, 207, 209
Wilmore, Henry 197, 198, 200–202, 204–207, 210, 212–214
Wilson, Kenneth L. "Tug" 7, 9, 15, 26, 36, 49, 64, 78, 90, 99, 129, 170, 171
Winfield, Dave 207, 209, 212
Winter, Tex 164
Witte, Luke 197, 198, 200–202, 205–211, 213, 214
Wooden, John 4, 11, 25, 108, 109, 170, 190, 200
Wordlaw, Clarence 70, 71, 80, 85
Wright, Joby 191, 194, 198–201, 203, 211, 213, 214

Yates, Tony 139, 141, 144

Zagar, Ron 91, 101, 102

www.ingramcontent.com/pod-product-compliance
Lightning Source LLC
Chambersburg PA
CBHW081550300426
44116CB00015B/2820